MACMILLAN MASTER SERIES

MASTERING
MODERN WORLD HISTORY

NORMAN LOWE

MACMILLAN

First edition 1982
Reprinted 1982, 1983, 1984 (twice)

Published by
MACMILLAN EDUCATION LTD
London and Basingstoke
Companies and representatives
throughout the world

ISBN 0 333 31295 3 (hard cover)
ISBN 0 333 30449 7 (paper cover)
ISBN 0 333 31069 1 (export edition)

Printed in Hong Kong

Typeset by
Reproduction Drawings Ltd, Sutton, Surrey

CONTENTS

CONTENTS

MAPS

ACKNOWLEDGEMENTS

The author and publishers wish to thank the following who have kindly given permission for the use of copyright material:

The Associated Examining Board for three questions from past examination papers.
Associated Newspaper Group Limited for cartoons by Illingworth and Trog published in the *Daily Mail.*
London Express News and Features Services for a cartoon by the late Sir David Low reproduced by permission of the Low Trustees and the *Evening Standard.*
Mirror Group Newspapers for a cartoon by Vickey published in the *Daily Mirror*.
The University of London for questions from past examination papers.

The author and publishers also wish to acknowledge the following illustration sources. They have made every effort to trace the copyright holders but where they may have failed they will be pleased to make the necessary arrangement at the first opportunity.

Associated Press
Barnaby's Picture Library
B.B.C. Hulton Picture Library
Bettman Archive
Camera Press/Ron McKay/Curtiss/David Robinson/Hassner
John Hillelson Agency
Imperial War Museum
Keystone Press Agency
Novosti Press Agency
Popper foto
H. Roger-Viollet
Suddeutscher Verlag
Ullstein Bilderdeinst
United Nations Organization
United Press International

PREFACE

This book has evolved from teaching notes compiled over a number of years and makes no claim to any originality of content. Its originality lies in its treatment of events:

(i) Instead of presenting a narrative account of events, as so many textbooks do, the book is geared to specific questions of the type which appear on examination papers; this approach encourages students to think analytically, not just about what happened but about why it happened and why it was important.

(ii) At the same time enough material is provided on each topic to enable students to build up their own answers to other questions; sometimes this can be done from the same chapter; sometimes, by using the cross-references and the detailed index, answers can be assembled from more than one chapter, giving students useful practice in collecting and organising essay material.

(iii) Wherever appropriate, mention is made of the disagreements and controversies among historians about why certain major events (such as the First and Second World Wars) happened, and about how successful certain governments or politicians were.

A wide selection of questions taken from examination papers of the various boards is included at the end of each chapter, including a few stimulus questions of the type used by most boards, in which students are required to respond to a cartoon, an extract or a photograph.

Chapter 8 illustrates all three points:

(i) A summary of Section 8.4 (together with a brief mention of Hitler's successes in foreign policy from Section 14.3) directly answers the question: 'Explain how Hitler was able to stay in power for so long after failing to win an overall majority in the 1933 election.'

(ii) Section 8.4 also provides enough information to answer several other questions, such as: 'Describe the main organisations of the Nazi state in Germany and show how Nazi policy affected the SA, the German army, the churches, racial minorities and the unemployed.'

(iii) Section 8.6 mentions conflicting views about the success of Hitler's domestic policies up to 1939.

Section 4.1(b) directly answers the question: 'What problems faced the Lloyd George coalition (1918–22) and how successful was he in dealing with them?' On the other hand the question: 'What were Lloyd George's successes and failures in politics between 1915 and 1922?' would need extra information from Sections 2.3(b) and 2.4(e). There are numerous maps designed to enable students to answer the map questions regularly included by all the boards.

Although it is intended primarily for those studying for a first examination in modern world history, the book should provide an excellent introduction for higher study, and will also be suitable for general and liberal studies courses. I hope too it will be useful for the general reader who wants a short introduction to world affairs. The books recommended are mainly for the general reader who wishes to investigate a topic further, and most of them are too detailed and too advanced for basic examinations. However, books marked with an asterisk are suitable for students at this level.

Finally I must thank the many people who have helped in the preparation of this book. Glyn Jones, Head of Humanities at Bede College, Billingham, read the entire manuscript, while my colleagues at Nelson and Colne College - Dorothy Harrison, Greta Hill and John Munroe - read large sections of it; they made many helpful suggestions and saved me from innumerable mistakes. Mrs Jenny Lee expertly typed the manuscript, and my long-suffering wife Jane sustained me in all sorts of ways. As they usually say at this point, the remaining imperfections are my own.

Norman Lowe

FOREWORD

I am pleased to write this Forword to Norman Lowe's *Modern World History*, one of the first of a new series of basic texts. It is a valuable addition to the growing list of books which cover this complex century, and to my mind it has a number of advantages. Mr Lowe's approach has been to cover the major topics of world history in a clear and concise style, following a consistent pattern in each chapter. After a general introduction, themes are developed in more detail with headings, key words and phrases underlined. Students will find the system of cross referencing easy to follow, while the problem-solving approach will be of considerable benefit to those taking examinations. Controversial issues are highlighted and discussed with refreshing clarity and fairness, admitting the fallibility of human judgement.

Mr Lowe's style is economical yet avoids the sterility of note form. It is lively and comprehensible, with major terms and concepts carefully explained. The text is supported by relevant maps and by sample examination questions including those involving stimulus material which are fast becoming a feature of the 'new' history. The bibliography will be of particular benefit to those who wish to develop themes in greater depth.

I believe that *Modern World History* will provide an excellent basic text for examinations at 16+ in schools and colleges, and will also be a first-class introduction for higher level study. Students taking General and Liberal Studies and the general reader will find its approach comprehensive and well signposted. Although it is written with the examination candidate in mind it is not narrowly conceived, dealing as it does with some of the topics of world history frequently omitted in other basic texts. One particular merit is its treatment of the post–1945 period to which ten chapters are devoted. Events of the very recent past, including, for instance, developments in Latin America, the crisis in Poland, the Russian occupation of Afghanistan and the policies of the Carter Administration are included.

As a teacher and examiner of modern world history over many years I can recommend this book. It fills a much needed gap in the available literature.

Keith Foreman,
Warden,
The Village College,
Comberton,
Cambridge.   March 1981

CHAPTER 1

THE WORLD IN 1914:

OUTBREAK OF

THE FIRST WORLD WAR

1.1 PROLOGUE

Under cover of darkness late on the night of 5 August 1914, five columns of German assault troops, which had entered Belgium two days earlier, were converging on the town of Liège, expecting little resistance. To their surprise they were halted by determined fire from the town's outlying forts. This was a setback for the Germans: control of Liège was essential before they could proceed with their main operation against the French. They were forced to resort to siege tactics, using heavy howitzers. These fired up shells which plunged from a height of 12,000 feet to shatter the armour-plating of the forts. Strong though they were, these Belgian forts were not equipped to withstand such a battering for long; on 13 August the first one surrendered and three days later Liège was under German control. This was the first major engagement of the First World War, that horrifying conflict of monumental proportions which was to mark the beginning of a new era in European and world history.

1.2 THE WORLD IN 1914

(a) Europe still dominated the rest of the world in 1914 and most of the decisions which moulded the fate of the world were taken in the capitals of Europe. Within Europe Germany was the leading power both militarily and economically. She had overtaken Britain in the production of pig iron and steel, though not quite in coal, while France, Belgium, Italy and Austria-Hungary (the Habsburg empire) were well behind. Russian industry was expanding rapidly, but had been so backward to begin with that she could not seriously challenge Germany and Britain. But it was outside Europe that the most spectacular industrial progress had been made over the previous 40 years. In 1914 the USA produced more coal, pig iron and steel than either Germany or Britain and now ranked as a world power. Japan too had modernised rapidly and was regarded as a power to be reckoned with after her defeat of Russia in 1904-5.

(b) The political systems of these world powers varied widely. The USA, Britain and France had democratic forms of government, which means that they each had a parliament containing elected representatives of the people, which had an important say in running the country. Some systems were not as democratic as they seemed: Germany had an elected lower house of parliament (*Reichstag*) but real power lay with the Chancellor (a sort of prime minister) and the *Kaiser* (emperor); Italy was a monarchy with an elected parliament, but the franchise (right to vote) was limited; Japan had an elected lower house, but here too the franchise was restricted and the emperor and the privy council wielded most of the power. Far removed from the democracy of the west were Russia and Austria–Hungary. The tsar (emperor) of Russia and the emperor of Austria (who was also king of Hungary) were autocratic rulers: this means that although parliaments existed the monarchs could simply ignore them and rule according to their own whims.

(c) The European powers had taken part in a great burst of imperialism, the building up of empires in the years after 1880, rushing to take hold of territory overseas, mainly to satisfy the desire for new markets and raw materials. The Scramble for Africa, as it became known, was accompanied by intervention in the crumbling Chinese empire; the European powers, as well as the USA and Japan, all at different times forced the helpless Chinese to grant trading concessions. Exasperation at the incompetence of their government led the Chinese to overthrow the ancient Manchu dynasty and to set up a republic (1911).

(d) Europe itself had divided into two alliance systems: the Triple Alliance of Germany, Austria–Hungary and Italy, and the Triple Entente of Britain, France and Russia. In addition Japan and Britain had signed an alliance in 1902. The two systems, sometimes referred to as 'the armed camps' had on several occasions since 1908 seemed likely to cause a war. In fact in 1912 and 1913 two short conflicts had occurred in the Balkans resulting from the ambitions and squabbles of the Balkan states – Serbia, Bulgaria, Rumania, Montenegro and Turkey; however, the great powers did not become involved and the Balkan Wars remained localised.

Nevertheless there were many other causes of friction which threatened to upset the peace of Europe: Anglo-German naval rivalry; French resentment at the loss of Alsace and Lorraine to Germany at the end of the Franco-Prussian War (1871); German resentment at Russia and France for allegedly trying to 'encircle' her; Russian hostility at Austrian ambitions in the Balkans which was whipped up to fever pitch by the Austrian annexation of Bosnia from Turkey in 1908. Perhaps most dangerous of all was Serbian nationalism (the desire to free one's nation from the control of people of another nationality). Serbia had ambitions of uniting all Serbs and Croats into a South Slav kingdom (Yugoslavia) by seizing Bosnia and other areas from Austria. This threatened to bring about the disintegration of the ramshackle Habsburg empire with its many different nationalities, all of which would demand their independence too if the Serbs and Croats left the fold. Consequently many Austrians were keen for a 'preventive' war against Serbia, to destroy her before she became strong enough to destroy Austria-Hungary.

Fig 1.1   *the Balkans in 1913 showing changes of territory from the Balkan wars (1912-13)*

4

(e) The outbreak of war followed soon after the assassination of the Austrian Archduke Franz Ferdinand (28 June 1914). The Archduke, nephew and heir of the Emperor Franz Josef, was on an official visit to Sarajevo, the Bosnian capital, when he and his wife were shot dead by a member of a secret Serbian terrorist society, the Black Hand. The Austrians chose to blame the Serbian government and sent a stiff ten-point ultimatum, which the Serbs accepted, apart from the policing of Serbia by Austrian troops. That was enough for the Austrians who, assured of German support, declared war on Serbia (28 July). Russia, prepared to support Serbia, ordered a general mobilisation, whereupon Germany declared war on Russia (1 August), and on France (3 August). When German troops entered Belgium on the way to invade France, Britain (who had been pledged to defend Belgian neutrality since 1839) demanded their withdrawal. When the Germans ignored this, Britain entered the war (4 August).

illus 1.1   *Archduke Franz Ferdinand and his wife, shortly before their assassination in Sarajevo*

The war was to have profound effects on the future of the world. Germany was soon to be displaced, for a time at least, from her mastery of Europe, and Europe never quite regained its dominant position in the world.

1.3 WHAT CAUSED THE WAR AND WHO WAS TO BLAME?

It is difficult to analyse why the assassination at Sarajevo developed into a world war and even now historians cannot agree. Some blame Austria for being the first aggressor by declaring war on Serbia; some blame Russia, the first to order full mobilisation, some Germany for supporting Austria, and others Britain for not making it clear that she would definitely support France, which, it is argued, might have dissuaded Germany from declaring war on France.

(a) The point which is beyond dispute is that **the quarrel between Austria and Serbia**, which had become increasingly more explosive since 1908, sparked off the outbreak of the war when Austria seized on the assassination as the pretext for a preventive war with Serbia. Austria genuinely felt that realisation of Serbian and Slav nationalist ambitions for a Yugoslav state would bring about the collapse of the Habsburg empire; Serbia must be curbed. In fairness, they probably hoped the war would remain localised like the Balkan Wars. The Austro-Serb quarrel explains the outbreak of the war, but not why it became a world war. Reasons suggested for the escalation of the war are:

(b) **The alliance system or 'armed camps' made war inevitable**. This explanation is *not convincing*; there had been many crises since 1904 (Morocco, Bosnia, Agadir, Balkan Wars), none of which had led to a major war. In fact there was nothing binding about these alliances. France had not supported Russia when she protested against the Austrian annexation of Bosnia, Austria took no interest in Germany's unsuccessful attempts (Morocco and Agadir Crises, 1906 and 1911) to prevent France taking over Morocco, and Germany had restrained Austria from attacking Serbia during the Second Balkan War. Italy had agreements with both camps and though still a member of the Triple Alliance in 1914, entered the war against it in 1915. No power actually declared war because of an alliance treaty.

(c) **Colonial rivalry in Africa and the Far East**. *Again not convincing*; although there had certainly been disputes, they had always been sorted out without war. In early July 1914 Anglo-German relations were good, an agreement extremely favourable to Germany having just been reached over a possible partition of Portuguese colonies in Africa. One by-product of colonial rivalry which did cause dangerous friction was:

(d) **The naval race between Britain and Germany**. Starting with the Tirpitz Navy Laws (1898) the growth of the German fleet probably didn't worry Britain too much at first because she had an enormous lead; but with the introduction of the powerful British Dreadnought battleship in 1906, which rendered all other ships obsolete, the Germans could begin building Dreadnoughts on equal terms. The ensuing naval building race was the main bone of contention between the two right up to 1914. According to

Churchill, however, in the spring and summer of 1914 naval rivalry had ceased to be a cause of friction, because 'it was certain that we [Britain] could not be overtaken as far as capital ships were concerned.' (W.S. Churchill, *The World Crisis, 1911-1914*, (London, 1931) pp. 178-9).

(e) Economic rivalry. It has been argued that the desire for economic mastery of the world caused German businessmen and capitalists to want war with Britain, who still owned about half the world's tonnage of merchant ships in 1912. There isn't much evidence to support this theory; Germany was already well on the way to victory in that area; as one leading German industrialist remarked in 1913: 'Give us three or four more years of peace and Germany will be the unchallenged economic master of Europe.'

None of these reasons (b) to (e) gets to the crux of the matter. More plausible are the following:

(f) Russia made war more likely by backing Serbia, probably making her more irresponsibly anti-Austrian than she might have been. Russia was the first to order a general mobilisation, which provoked Germany to mobilise. The Russians were worried about the Balkans situation where both Bulgaria and Turkey were under German influence; this would enable Germany and Austria to control the Dardanelles, the main Russian trade route, thereby strangling the Russian economy (this happened during the war). Thus Russia felt herself threatened, and once Austria declared war on Serbia, saw it as a struggle for survival. Also the Russians must have felt that their prestige as Slav leader would suffer irreparable damage if they failed to support Serbia. Perhaps the government even saw war as a good idea to divert attention away from domestic problems. Perhaps the blame lies more with Austria: though she must have hoped for Russian neutrality, she ought to have realised how difficult this would be for Russia and given possible Russian reaction the most careful consideration.

(g) German backing for Austria was crucially important. It is significant that in 1913 Germany restrained Austria from declaring war on Serbia, but in 1914 egged them on, the *Kaiser* urging them to attack Serbia and promising German help without conditions. The important question is *why German policy towards Austria changed*? The answer is the subject of much controversy:

(i) Some historians including the German, *Fritz Fischer,* claim that Germany deliberately provoked war with Russia, France and Britain in order to achieve world domination. Others argue that:

(ii) Germany wanted war because she felt encircled and threatened by British naval power and by the massive Russian military expansion. The German generals decided that a 'preventive' war, a war for survival, was necessary, and that it must take place before the end of 1914;

illus 1.2 *Hitler celebrates the outbreak of World War I. This fascinating picture shows Hitler in the crowd which heard the declaration of war in Munich on 2 August 1914*

after that Russia would be too strong. Some historians reject both (i) and (ii) and suggest that:

(iii) Germany did not want a major war at all; the *Kaiser* and Chancellor Bethmann-Hollweg believed a strong line in support of Austria would frighten the Russians into remaining neutral – a sad miscalculation if true.

(h) The mobilisation plans of the various powers accelerated the tempo of events and reduced almost to nil the time available for negotiation. *The German Schlieffen Plan*, first approved in 1905 and modified by Moltke (German Commander-in-Chief) in 1911, assumed that France would automatically join Russia, so the bulk of German forces were to be sent through Belgium to knock France out in six weeks, after which they were to be switched across to face Russia, whose mobilisation was expected to be slow. Once Moltke knew that Russia had ordered a general mobilisation, he demanded immediate German mobilisation so that the plan could be put into operation as soon as possible. However, Russian mobilisation did not necessarily mean war – their troops could be halted at the frontiers; unfortunately the Schlieffen Plan, depending as it did on the rapid capture of Liège in Belgium, involved the first aggressive act outside the Balkans when German troops entered Belgium on 4 August. Almost at the last minute the *Kaiser* and Bethmann tried to avoid war and urged Austria to negotiate with Serbia (30 July), which perhaps supports point (iii) above. Wilhelm also suggested a partial mobilisation against Russia only, instead of the full plan, hoping that Britain would stay neutral if Germany refrained from attacking France. But it was too late: Moltke, scared of being caught on the hop by the Russians and French, insisted on the full Schlieffen Plan; there was no time to modify it. It looks as though the generals had taken over control of affairs from the politicians. It also suggests that a British announcement on 31 July of her intention to support France would have made no difference to Germany: it was the Schlieffen Plan or nothing even though Germany at that point had no specific quarrel with France.

The most convincing conclusion to be drawn from all these suggestions is that put forward by L. C. F. Turner. Perhaps the Germans did not deliberately provoke a war; it was caused by 'a tragedy of miscalculation'. Most of the leading rulers and politicians seemed to be incompetent. The Austrians miscalculated by thinking Russia would not support Serbia, Germany did so by promising to support Austria, *with no conditions attached*; therefore the Germans were certainly blameworthy, as were the Austrians, *because they risked a major war*. Politicians in Russia and Germany miscalculated by assuming that mobilisation would not necessarily mean war; generals, especially Moltke, miscalculated by sticking rigidly to their plans in the belief that this would bring a quick and decisive victory. No wonder Bethmann, when asked how it all began, raised his arms to heaven and replied: 'Oh – if I only knew!'

QUESTIONS

1. Describe how Europe drifted towards war between 1907 and 1914.
2. Why did Germany go to war in 1914?
3. 'Germany must shoulder the blame for causing the First World War.' How far do you agree?
4. Who or what was responsible for the outbreak of the First World War?

CHAPTER 2

THE FIRST WORLD WAR AND ITS AFTERMATH

SUMMARY OF EVENTS

The sides in the war were *the Central Powers*: Germany, Austria–Hungary, Turkey (entered November 1914) and Bulgaria (October 1915); and *the Allies*: Russia (left December 1917), France, Britain, Italy (entered May 1915), Rumania (August 1916) and the USA (April 1917).

The war turned out to be quite different from what most people had anticipated. It was widely expected to be a short decisive affair, like other recent European wars; hence Moltke's nervous determination not to be left at the post when it came to mobilisation. However, the Schlieffen Plan failed to achieve the rapid defeat of France. Although the Germans penetrated deeply, Paris did not fall, and stalemate quickly developed on the western front - with all hope of a short war gone. Both sides dug themselves in and spent the next four years attacking and defending lines of trenches which were difficult to capture because the increased fire-power provided by magazine rifles and machineguns made frontal attacks suicidal and rendered cavalry useless.

In eastern Europe there was more movement with Russian successes against the Austrians, who constantly had to be helped out by the Germans, causing friction between the two allies. But by December 1917, the Germans had captured Poland (Russian territory) and forced the defeated Russians out of the war. Britain, suffering heavy losses of merchant ships through submarine attacks, and France, whose armies were paralysed by mutiny, seemed on the verge of defeat. Gradually the tide turned; the Allies, helped by the entry of the USA in April 1917, wore down the Germans, whose last despairing attempt at a decisive breakthrough in France failed in the spring of 1918. The success of the British navy in quietly blockading German ports and defeating the submarine threat by defending merchant convoys, was also telling on the Germans. By the late summer of 1918 they were nearing exhaustion. An armistice was signed on 11 November 1918 although Germany itself had scarcely been invaded; a controversial peace settlement was signed at Versailles the following year.

2.1 **1914**

(a) On the western front the Schlieffen Plan was held up by unexpectedly strong Belgian resistance; it took the Germans over two weeks to capture Brussels, an important delay because it gave the French time to organise and left the Channel ports free so that the British Expeditionary Force was able to land. Instead of sweeping round in a wide arc, capturing the Channel ports and approaching Paris from the west, the Germans found themselves making straight for Paris just east of the city. They penetrated to within twenty miles of Paris and the French government withdrew to Bordeaux; but the nearer they got to Paris, the more the German impetus slowed up; there were problems in keeping the armies supplied with food and ammunition and the troops became exhausted by long marches in the August heat. In September the faltering Germans were attacked by the French under Joffre in *the Battle of the Marne* and driven back to the River Aisne, where they were able to dig trenches. This battle was *vitally important*; some historians even call it one of the most decisive battles of modern history. It ruined the Schlieffen Plan once and for all: France would not be knocked out in six weeks; hopes of a short war were dashed and the Germans would have to face full-scale war on two fronts. The war of movement was over; the trench lines event-

Fig 2.1   *the Western Front*

.... Limit of the German advance in 1914

×××××× The trench line for most of the war

ually stretched from the Alps to the Channel coast, and there was time for the British navy to bring to bear its crippling blockade of German ports. The other important event of 1914 was that though the Germans took Antwerp, the British Expeditionary Force held grimly on to *Ypres,* which probably saved the other Channel ports so that more British troops could be landed and kept supplied.

(b) On the eastern front the Russians, having mobilised more quickly than the Germans expected, made the mistake of invading both Austria and East Prussia at the same time. Though they were successful against Austria, occupying the province of Galicia, the Germans called Hindenburg out of retirement and twice defeated the Russians at *Tannenberg* (August) and *the Masurian Lakes* (September), driving them out of Germany. *These battles were important*: the Russians lost vast amounts of equipment and ammunition which had taken years to amass. Although they had six and a quarter million men mobilised by the end of 1914, a third of them were without rifles. The Russians never recovered from this setback, whereas German self-confidence was boosted. When *Turkey entered the war* the outlook for Russia was bleak, since Turkey could cut her main supply line through the Dardanelles. One bright spot for the Allies was that the Serbs drove out an Austrian invasion in fine style at the end of 1914, and Austrian morale was at rock bottom.

2.2 **1915**

(a) In the west the stalemate continued, though several attempts were made to break the trench line. The British tried at Neuve Chapelle and Loos, the French in Champagne while the Germans attacked again at Ypres. *These, like all attacks on the western front until 1918, failed; always the difficulties were the same*: there was no chance of a surprise attack because a massive artillery bombardment always preceded the infantry attack to clear the barbed wire from no man's land between the two lots of trenches, and generally to soften up the enemy; reconnaisance aircraft and observation balloons could spot troop concentrations on the roads leading up to the trenches. Even when the trench line was breached, advance was difficult because the ground had been churned up by the artillery barrage and there was deadly machinegun fire to contend with. Any ground won was difficult to defend since it usually formed a salient or bulge in the trench line, of which the flanks were vulnerable. At Ypres the Germans used poison gas but when the wind changed direction it was blown back towards their own lines and they suffered more casualties than the Allies, especially when the Allies released some gas of their own.

(b) In the east Russia's fortunes were mixed: they had further successes against Austria, but met defeat whenever they clashed with the Germans, who captured Warsaw and the whole of Poland. The Turkish blockade illus 2.1   *Soldiers blinded by poison gas*

of the Straits was beginning to hamper the Russians, who were already running short of arms and ammunition. It was partly to clear the Dardanelles and open up the vital supply line to Russia via the Black Sea that *the Gallipoli Campaign* was launched. This was an idea strongly pressed by Winston Churchill (First Lord of the Admiralty) to escape the deadlock in the west by eliminating the Turks, thought to be the weakest of the Central Powers because of their unstable government. Success against Turkey would enable help to be sent to Russia and might also bring Bulgaria, Greece and Rumania into the war on the Allied side; it would then be possible to attack Austria from the south. The campaign was a total failure; the first attempt in March, an Anglo-French naval attack through the Straits to capture Constantinople, failed because of mines. This ruined the surprise element, so that when the British attempted landings at the tip of the Gallipoli peninsula, the Turks had strengthened their defences and no advance could be made (April). Further landings by Australian and New Zealand troops (Anzacs) in April and British in August were equally useless and positions could be held only with great difficulty. In December the entire force was withdrawn; *the consequences were serious*: besides being a blow to Allied morale, it turned out to be the last chance of relieving Russia via the Black Sea and probably decided Bulgaria to join the Central Powers. A Franco-British force landed at Salonika in neutral Greece to try and relieve Serbia, but it was too late. When Bulgaria entered the war in October, Serbia was quickly overrun by Bulgarians and Germans. The year 1915 therefore was not a good one for the Allies; even a British army sent to protect

Anglo–Persian oil interests against a possible Turkish attack became bogged down in Mesopotamia as it approached Baghdad and was besieged by Turks at Kut-el-Amara from December 1915 until March 1916, when it was forced to surrender.

(c) **In May Italy** declared war on Austria, hoping to seize Austria's Italian-speaking provinces as well as territory along the eastern shore of the Adriatic. *A secret treaty was signed in London* in which the Allies promised Italy Trentino, the south Tyrol, Istria, Trieste, part of Dalmatia, Adalia, some islands in the Aegean and a protectorate over Albania. The Allies hoped that by keeping thousands of Austrian troops occupied, the Italians would relieve pressure on the Russians. But the Italians made little headway and their efforts made no difference to the eventual Russian defeat.

2.3 1916

(a) **On the western front** 1916 is remembered for two terrible battles, Verdun and the Somme.

(i) *Verdun* was an important French fortress against which the Germans under Falkenhayn launched a massive attack in February; they hoped to draw all the best French troops to its defence, destroy them and then carry out a final offensive to win the war. But the French under Pétain defended stubbornly and the Germans had to abandon the attack in June. The French lost heavily (about 315,000 men) as the Germans intended, but so did the Germans with over 280,000 dead, and nothing to show for it.

(ii) *The Battle of the Somme* was a series of attacks, mainly by the British, beginning on 1 July and lasting through to November. *The aim* was to relieve pressure on the French at Verdun, take over more of the trench line as the French army weakened, and keep the Germans fully committed so that they would be unable to risk sending reinforcements to the eastern front against Russia. At the end of it all the Allies had made only limited advances varying between a few hundred yards and seven miles along a thirty-mile front. *The real importance of the battle* was the blow to German morale as they realised that Britain (where conscription was introduced for the first time in May) was a military power to be reckoned with. Losses on both sides, killed or wounded, were appalling (Germans 650,000; British 418,000; French 194,000) and Haig (British Commander-in-Chief) came under severe criticism for persisting with suicidal frontal attacks. However, they probably helped to wear down the German armies: Hindenburg himself admitted in his Memoirs that they could not have survived many more campaigns like Verdun and the Somme. The Somme also contributed to the fall of the British Prime Minister, Asquith, who resigned in December 1916, after mounting criticism.

(b) David Lloyd George became Prime Minister and *his contribution to the Allied war effort and the defeat of the Central Powers was invaluable.* His methods were dynamic and decisive; already as Minister of Munitions since May 1915 he had improved the supply of shells and machineguns, encouraged the development of new weapons (the Stokes light mortar and the tank) which Kitchener (Minister for War) had turned down, and taken control of mines, factories and railways so that the war effort could be properly centralised. As Prime Minister during 1917 he set up a small war cabinet so that quick decisions could be taken, brought shipping and agriculture under government control and introduced the Ministry of National Service to organise the mobilisation of men into the army. He also played an important part in the adoption of the convoy system (see Section 2.4(e)).

(c) In the east the Russians under *Brusilov* attacked the Austrians in June (in response to a plea from Britain and France for some action to divert German attention away from Verdun), managed to break the front and advanced 100 miles, taking 400,000 prisoners and large amounts of equipment. The Austrians were demoralised, but the strain was exhausting the Russians as well. The Rumanians invaded Austria (August) but the Germans swiftly came to the rescue, occupied the whole of Rumania and seized her wheat and oil supplies – not a happy end to 1916 for the Allies.

2.4 THE WAR AT SEA

The general public in Germany and Britain expected a series of naval battles of the Trafalgar type between the rival Dreadnought fleets. But both sides were cautious and dared not risk any action which might result in the loss of their main fleets. The British Admiral Jellicoe was particularly cautious; as Churchill pointed out, he 'was the only man on either side who could have lost the war in an afternoon.' Nor were the Germans anxious for a confrontation because they had only 16 of the latest Dreadnoughts as against 27 British.

(a) The Allies aimed to blockade the Central Powers, preventing goods entering or leaving, and slowly starving them out. At the same time trade routes must be kept open between Britain, her empire and the rest of the world, so that the Allies themselves would not starve. A third function of the navy was to transport British troops to the continent and keep them supplied via the Channel ports. The British were successful in carrying out these aims: they went into action against German units stationed abroad and at *the Battle of the Falkland Islands* destroyed one of the main German squadrons. By the end of 1914 nearly all German armed surface ships had been destroyed, apart from their main fleet (which did not venture out of the Heligoland Bight) and the squadron blockading the Baltic to cut off supplies to Russia. In 1915 the navy was involved in the Gallipoli Campaign (see Section 2.2(b)).

(b) The Allied blockade caused problems: Britain was trying to prevent the Germans using the neutral Scandinavian and Dutch ports to break the blockade; this involved stopping and searching all neutral ships and confiscating any goods suspected of being intended for enemy hands. The USA objected strongly to this, being anxious to continue trading with both sides.

(c) The Germans retaliated with mines and submarine attacks, which was their only alternative since their surface vessels were either destroyed or blockaded. At first they respected neutral shipping and passenger liners, but it was soon clear that the German U-boat blockade was not effective, partly because of insufficient U-boats and partly because of problems of identification, as the British tried to fool the Germans by flying neutral flags and using passenger liners to transport arms and ammunition. In April 1915 the British liner *Lusitania* was sunk by a torpedo attack. (It has recently been proved that the *Lusitania* was armed and carrying vast quantities of arms and ammunition, as the Germans well knew; hence their claim that the sinking was not just an act of barbarism against defenceless civilians.) *This had important consequences*: out of the thousand dead, 118 were Americans. Wilson therefore found that the USA would have to take sides to protect her trade; whereas the British blockade did not interfere with the safety of passengers and crews, German tactics certainly did. For the time being, however, American protests caused Bethmann to tone down the submarine campaign, rendering it even less effective.

(d) The Battle of Jutland (31 May) was the main event of 1916, the only time the main battle-fleets emerged and engaged each other; the result was indecisive. The German Admiral von Scheer tried to lure part of the British fleet out from its base so that that section could be destroyed by the numerically superior Germans. However, more British ships came out than he had anticipated, and after the two fleets had shelled each other on and off for several hours, the Germans decided to retire to base firing torpedoes as they went. On balance the Germans could claim that they had won the battle since they lost only 11 ships to Britain's 14, but *the real importance of the battle* lay in the fact that the Germans had failed to destroy British sea power; the German High Seas Fleet stayed in Kiel for the rest of the war leaving Britain's control of the surface complete. In desperation at the food shortages caused by the British blockade, they embarked, with fatal results, on:

(e) 'Unrestricted' submarine warfare (January 1917). As they had been concentrating on the production of U-boats since the Battle of Jutland this campaign was extremely effective. They attempted to sink all enemy and neutral merchant ships in the Atlantic and although they knew that this was bound to bring the USA into the war, they hoped that Britain and France would be starved into surrender before the Americans could make any vital contribution. They almost did it: the peak of German success came in April 1917 when 430 ships were lost; Britain was down to about six weeks' corn supply and although the USA came into the war in April, it was bound to be several months before their help became effective. However, the situation was saved by Lloyd George who insisted that the Admiralty adopt the convoy system in which a large number of merchant ships sailed together protected by escorting warships. This drastically reduced losses and the German gamble had failed. *The submarine campaign was extremely important* because it brought the USA into the war. The British navy therefore, helped by the Americans, played a vitally important role in the defeat of the Central Powers, and by the middle of 1918 had achieved its three aims.

2.5 **1917**

(a) In the west 1917 was a year of Allied failure. A massive French attack under Nivelle in Champagne achieved nothing except mutiny in the French army, which was successfully sorted out by Pétain. From June

illus **2.2**   *Troops crossing the sea of mud at Passchendaele, 1917*

to November the British fought *the Third Battle of Ypres*, usually remembered as *Passchendaele*, in appallingly muddy conditions; British casualties were enormous - 324,000 compared with 200,000 Germans for a four-mile advance. *More significant was the Battle of Cambrai* which demonstrated that tanks, properly used, might break the deadlock of trench warfare. 381 massed British tanks made a great breach in the German line, but lack of reserves prevented the success from being followed up. However, the lesson had been observed and Cambrai became the model for the successful attacks of 1918. Meanwhile the Italians were heavily defeated by Germans and Austrians at *Caporetto* (October) and retreated in disorder. This rather unexpectedly proved to be *an important turning point*. Italian morale revived perhaps because they were faced with having to defend their homeland against the hated Austrians. The defeat also led to the setting up of an Allied Supreme War Council. The new French premier Clemenceau, a great war leader in the Lloyd George mould, rallied the wilting French.

(b) On the eastern front disaster struck the Allies when *Russia withdrew from the war*. Continuous defeat by the Germans, lack of arms and supplies and utterly incompetent leadership caused two revolutions (see Section 3.2) and the Bolsheviks, who took over in November, were willing to make peace. Thus in 1918 the entire weight of German forces could be thrown against the west; without the USA the Allies would have been hard pressed. Encouragement was provided by the British capture of Baghdad and Jerusalem from the Turks, giving them control of vast oil supplies.

(c) The entry of the USA (April) *was caused partly by* the German U-boat campaign, and also by the discovery that Germany was trying to persuade Mexico to declare war on the USA, promising her Texas, New Mexico and Arizona in return. The Americans had hesitated about siding with the autocratic Russian government, but the overthrow of the tsar in the March revolution removed this obstacle. *The USA made an important contribution to the Allied victory*: they supplied Britain and France with food, merchant ships and credit; actual military help came slowly. By the end of 1917 only one American division had been in action, but by mid-1918 over a half a million men were fighting. Most important was the psychological boost which the American potential in resources of men and materials gave the Allies and the corresponding blow it gave to German morale.

2.6 1918: THE CENTRAL POWERS DEFEATED

(a) The German spring offensive was launched by Ludendorff in a last desperate attempt to win the war before too many US troops arrived and before discontent in Germany led to revolution. It almost came off: throwing in all the extra troops released from the east, the Germans

Fig 2.2 *the Eastern Front*

▤▤▤ Allied territory (Russia, Serbia, Rumania and Italy)
occupied by forces of the Central Powers
early in 1918

– – – New Russian frontier after the Treaty of
Brest-Litovsk

broke through on the Somme (March) and by the end of May were only 40 miles from Paris; the Allies seemed to be falling apart. However, under the overall command of the French Marshal Foch they managed to hold on as the German advance lost momentum and created an awkward bulge.

(b) An Allied counter-offensive began (8 August) near Amiens with hundreds of tanks attacking in short sharp jabs at many different points instead of on a narrow front, forcing the Germans to withdraw their entire line. Slowly but surely the Germans were forced back until by the end of September the Allies were through the Hindenburg Line. Though Germany itself had not yet been invaded, Ludendorff was convinced that they would be defeated in the spring of 1919. He insisted that the German government ask President Wilson for an armistice (3 October) hoping to get less severe terms based on Wilson's 14 points (see Section 2.7(a)). By asking for peace in 1918 he would save Germany from invasion and preserve the army's reputation. Fighting continued for another five weeks, but eventually an armistice was signed on 11 November.

(c) Why did the Central Powers lose the war? The reasons can be briefly summarised:

(i) Once the Schlieffen Plan had failed, removing all hope of a quick German victory, it was bound to be a strain for them, facing war on two fronts.

(ii) Allied sea power was decisive, enforcing the deadly blockade which caused desperate food shortages, while keeping Allied armies fully supplied.

(iii) The German submarine campaign failed in the face of convoys protected by British, American and Japanese destroyers; the campaign itself was a mistake because it brought the USA into the war.

(iv) The entry of the USA brought vast resources to the Allies.

(v) Allied political leaders at the critical time –Lloyd George and Clemenceau - were probably more competent than those of the Central Powers; the unity of command under Foch in 1918 probably helped, while Haig learned lessons from the 1917 experiences about the effective use of tanks and the avoidance of salients.

(vi) The continuous strain of heavy losses was telling on the Germans - they lost their best troops in the 1918 offensive and the new troops were young and inexperienced; an epidemic of deadly Spanish flu did not help the situation, and morale was low as they retreated.

(vii) Germany was badly let down by her allies and was constantly having to help out the Austrians and Bulgarians. The defeat of Bulgaria by the British (from Salonika) and Serbs (29 September) was the final straw for many German soldiers, who could see no chance of victory now. When Austria was defeated by Italy at Vittorio-Veneto and Turkey surrendered (both in October), the end was near.

The combination of military defeat and dire food shortages produced a great war weariness leading to mutiny in the navy, destruction of morale in the army and revolution at home.

2.7 THE PROBLEMS OF MAKING A PEACE SETTLEMENT

(a) When the war started none of the participants had any specific ideas about what they hoped to achieve, beyond that Germany and Austria wanted to preserve the Habsburg empire and to this end thought it necessary to destroy Serbia. As the war progressed some of the governments involved, perhaps to encourage their troops by presenting them with some clear objectives to fight for, began to list their **war aims**:

(i) *Britain*: Lloyd George mentioned (January 1918) the defence of democracy and the righting of the injustice done to France in 1871, restoration of Belgium and Serbia, an independent Poland, democratic self-government for the nationalities of Austria-Hungary, self-determination for the German colonies and an international organisation to prevent war.

(ii) *USA: Woodrow Wilson's famous 14 points* (January 1918) were: (1) abolition of secret diplomacy; (2) free navigation at sea for all nations in war and peace; (3) removal of economic barriers between states; (4) all-round reduction of armaments; (5) impartial adjustment of colonial claims in the interests of populations concerned; (6) evacuation of Russian territory; (7) restoration of Belgium; (8) liberation of France and restoration of Alsace-Lorraine; (9) readjustment of Italian frontiers along lines of nationality; (10) self-government to the peoples of Austria-Hungary; (11) Rumania, Serbia and Montenegro to be evacuated and Serbia given access to the sea; (12) self-government to the non-Turkish peoples of the Turkish empire and permanent opening of the Dardanelles; (13) an independent Poland with secure access to the sea; (14) a general association of nations to preserve peace. These points achieved publicity when the Germans later claimed that they had expected the peace terms to be based on them, and that since this was not the case, they had been cheated.

(b) When the peace conference met (January 1919), it was soon obvious that **a settlement would be difficult because of the differing Allied views about how to treat the defeated powers**:

(i) *France (represented by Clemenceau)* wanted a harsh peace to ruin Germany economically and militarily so that she could never again threaten French frontiers.

(ii) *Britain (Lloyd George)* was in favour of a less severe settlement enabling Germany to recover quickly so that she could resume her role as a major customer for British goods. However, Lloyd George had just won an election (November 1918) with such slogans as 'hang the Kaiser' and talk of getting from Germany everything 'that you can squeeze out of a lemon and a bit more'; the British public therefore expected a harsh settlement.

(iii) *USA (Woodrow Wilson)* had earlier been in favour of a lenient peace, but Wilson's attitude changed after the Germans ignored his 14 points and imposed the harsh Brest-Litovsk treaty on Russia; he now felt that the Germans needed to be punished, and agreed to the British and French demands for reparations (compensation for damages) and German disarmament. *Wilson was also in favour of self-determination*: nations should be freed from foreign rule and given democratic governments of their own choice.

By June 1919, the conference had come up with the *Treaty of Versailles* for Germany, followed by other treaties dealing with Germany's former allies. The Treaty of Versailles in particular was one of the most controversial settlements ever signed and was criticised even in the Allied countries on the grounds that it was too hard on the Germans who were bound to object so violently that another war was inevitable, sooner or later; in addition many of the terms (reparations and disarmament) proved impossible to carry out.

2.8 THE TREATY OF VERSAILLES WITH GERMANY

(a) The terms were:

(i) *Germany had to lose territory in Europe*: Alsace-Lorraine to France; Eupen, Moresnet and Malmédy to Belgium; North Schleswig to Denmark (after a plebiscite), West Prussia and Posen to Poland, though Danzig, the main port of West Prussia, was to be a free city under League of Nations administration, because its population was wholly German. Memel was given to Lithuania; the Saar was to be administered by the League of Nations for 15 years, when a plebiscite would decide whether it should belong to France or Germany. In the meantime France was to have the use of its coalmines. Germany's African colonies were taken away and became 'mandates' under League supervision. This meant that various member states of the league 'looked after' them. Union between Germany and Austria was forbidden. Estonia, Latvia and Lithuania, handed over to Germany by Russia at Brest-Litovsk, were taken away from Germany and set up as independent states – examples of self-determination in practice.

(ii) *German armaments were strictly limited*: a maximum of 100,000 troops and no conscription (compulsory military service); no tanks, armoured cars, military aircraft or submarines, and only six battleships. The Rhineland was to be permanently demilitarised (German troops were not allowed in the area).

(iii) *The War Guilt clause* fixed the blame for the outbreak of the war solely on Germany and her allies.

(iv) *Germany was to pay reparations* for damage done to the Allies; the actual amount was not decided at Versailles, but announced later (1921) after much argument and haggling as £6,600 million.

(v) *A League of Nations was set up*, its aims and organisation being set out in the *League Covenant*.

The Germans had little choice but to sign the treaty, though they objected strongly. The ceremony took place in the Hall of Mirrors at Versailles, where the German empire had been proclaimed less than 50 years earlier.

(b) Why did the Germans object and how far were their objections justified?

(i) *It was a dictated peace*: the Germans were not allowed into the discussions at Versailles; they were simply presented with the terms and told to sign. Although they were allowed to criticise it in writing, all their protests were ignored except one (see point (iii) below). Some historians feel that the Germans were justified in objecting, that it would have been reasonable to allow them to join in the discussions which might have toned down some of the harsher terms, and would certainly have deprived the Germans of the argument much used by Hitler that because the peace was a *diktat* it should not be morally binding. On the other hand one can argue that the Germans could scarcely have expected any better treatment after the scant consideration they had shown the Russians at Brest-Litovsk, also a *diktat* (see section 3.3b).

(ii) They claimed that they had been promised terms based on Wilson's 14 points, that many of the *provisions were not in accordance with the 14 points* and were therefore a swindle. This is probably not a valid objection: the 14 points had never been accepted as official by any of the states involved, and the Germans themselves had pointedly ignored them in January 1918, when there still seemed a chance of outright German victory. By November, German tactics (Brest-Litovsk, destruction of mines, factories and public buildings during their retreat through France and Belgium) caused the Allied attitude to harden and *Wilson to add two further points*: Germany should pay for damage to civilian population and property and should be reduced to 'virtual impotence'; in other words Germany should be disarmed. The Germans were aware of this when they accepted the armistice and, in fact, most of the terms do comply with the 14 points and the additions. There were also objections on specific points:

(iii) *Loss of territory in Europe* (including Alsace-Lorraine and especially West Prussia to give Poland access to the sea). However, both were mentioned in the 14 points. Originally, Upper Silesia, an industrial region with a mixed population of Poles and Germans, was to be given to Poland, but this was the one concession made to the German written objections: after a plebiscite Germany was allowed to keep about two-thirds of the area. In fact most of the German losses could be justified on grounds of nationality. The Germans probably had more grounds for objection to the *loss of their African colonies* which was hardly an 'impartial adjustment'. The mandate system in which Britain took over German East Africa (Tanganyika) and

Fig 2.3 *European Frontiers after the First World War and the Peace Treaties*

Territory lost by Germany

Former territory of tsarist Russia

Austria–Hungary until 1918

Curzon Line – proposed by Britain (Dec. 1919) as Poland's eastern frontier. Russian territory east of the line was seized by Poland in 1920

Fig 2.4 *Africa and the Peace Treaties*

German colonies taken away as mandates by the
Versailles Treaty, 1919

parts of Togoland and the Cameroons, France most of Togoland
and the Cameroons, and South Africa acquired German South West
Africa (now known as Namibia), was really a device by which the
Allies seized the colonies without actually admitting that they were
being annexed.

(iv) *The disarmament clauses were deeply resented,* the Germans claiming
that 100,000 troops were not enough to keep law and order at a
time of political disturbance. Perhaps the German objection was
justified to some extent, though one can also sympathise with the

French desire for a weak Germany. The Germans became more aggrieved later as it became clear that none of the other powers intended to disarm, even though Point 4 mentioned 'all-round reduction of armaments'; however, disarmament was impossible to enforce fully, since the Germans were determined to exploit every loophole.

(v) *The War Guilt clause*: the Germans objected to being saddled with the entire blame for the outbreak of war. There are some grounds for objection here because although later research seemed to indicate Germany's guilt, it was hardly possible to arrive at that conclusion in the space of six weeks during 1919, which is what the Special Commission on War Responsibility did. However, the Allies wanted the Germans to admit responsibility so that they would be liable to pay reparations.

(vi) *Reparations* were the final humiliation for the Germans, and though there could be little valid objection to the general principle of reparations, it is now agreed that the actual amount decided on was far too high at £6,600 million. Many people thought so, including J. M. Keynes, an economic adviser to the British delegation at the conference, who urged the Allies to take £2,000 million, a more reasonable amount which Germany would be able to afford. The figure of £6,600 million enabled the Germans to protest that it was impossible to pay, and they soon began to default on their instalments. This caused resentment among the Allies who were relying on German cash to pay their own war debts to the USA, and there was international tension when France tried to force the Germans to pay (see 13.2(c)). Eventually the Allies admitted their mistake and reduced the amount to £2,000 million (Young Plan, 1929), but not before reparations had proved to be disastrous economically and politically.

The Germans did have some grounds for complaint, but it is worth pointing out that *the treaty could have been even more harsh*: if Clemenceau had had his way, the Rhineland would have become an independent state and France would have annexed the Saar. However, Germany was still the strongest power in Europe economically, so that the unwise thing about Versailles was that it annoyed the Germans yet did not render them too weak to retaliate.

2.9 THE PEACE TREATIES WITH AUSTRIA-HUNGARY

When Austria was on the verge of defeat in the war, the Habsburg empire disintegrated as the various nationalities declared themselves independent. Austria and Hungary separated and declared themselves republics. Many important decisions therefore had already been taken before the peace conference met; however, the situation was chaotic and the task of the conference was to formalise and recognise what had taken place.

(a) The Treaty of St Germain (1919) dealt with Austria which lost Bohemia and Moravia (wealthy industrial provinces with a population of 10 million) to the new state of Czechoslovakia; Dalmatia, Bosnia and Herzegovina to Serbia which, with Montenegro, now became known as Yugoslavia; Bukovina to Rumania; Galicia to the reconstituted state of Poland; the south Tyrol (as far as the Brenner Pass), Trentino, Istria and Trieste to Italy.

(b) The Treaty of Trianon dealing with Hungary was not signed until 1920 because of political uncertainties in Budapest where the Communists under Bela Kun seized power and were then overthrown. Slovakia and Ruthenia were given to Czechoslovakia; Croatia and Slovenia to Yugoslavia; Transylvania and the Banat of Temesvar to Rumania. Both treaties contained the League of Nations Covenant.

These settlements may seem harsh, but it has to be remembered that much of it had already happened, and on the whole the spirit of self-determination was adhered to. More people were placed under governments of their own nationality than ever before in Europe, though they were not always as democratic as Wilson would have liked (especially in Hungary and Poland). There were some anomalies, such as the three million Germans placed in Czechoslovakia (in the Sudetenland) and a million in Poland (by the Treaty of Versailles), but these were justified on the grounds that the new states needed them to be economically viable. It was unfortunate that both these instances gave Hitler an excuse to begin territorial demands on these countries.

The treaties left both Austria and Hungary with serious economic problems: Austria was a small republic, its population reduced from 22 million to 6.5 million, and its industrial wealth lost to Czechoslovakia and Poland. Vienna, once the capital of the huge Habsburg empire, was left high and dry surrounded by farming land which could hardly support it. Not surprisingly Austria was soon facing a severe economic crisis and was constantly having to be helped out by loans from the League of Nations. *Hungary* was just as badly affected, her population reduced from 21 million to 7.5 million, and some of her richest corn land lost to Rumania. Matters were further complicated when all the new states quickly introduced tariffs which hampered the flow of trade through the whole Danube area and made the industrial recovery of Austria particularly difficult. In fact there was an excellent economic case to support a union between Austria and Germany.

2.10 THE SETTLEMENT WITH TURKEY: TREATY OF SÈVRES (1920) AND BULGARIA: TREATY OF NEUILLY (1919)

Turkey was to lose Eastern Thrace, many Aegean islands and Smyrna to Greece; Adalia and Rhodes to Italy; the Straits were to be permanently open; Syria became a French mandate and Palestine, Iraq and Transjordan British mandates. However, the loss of so much territory

Fig 2.5 *Turkey, Bulgaria and the Peace Treaties*

|||||| Turkish territory lost to Greece by the Treaty of Sèvres (1920)
but returned by the Treaty of Lausanne (1923)

▦ Turkish territory lost to Italy

≡ Bulgarian territory lost to Greece by the Treaty of Neuilly (1919)

▨ Bulgarian territory lost to Yugoslavia

to Greece, especially Smyrna, outraged Turkish national feeling (self-determination was being ignored to some extent here). Led by Mustafa Kemal, they rejected the treaty and chased the Greeks out of Smyrna. The Italians and French withdrew their occupying forces from the Straits area, leaving only British troops at Chanak. Following the Chanak incident (1922) (see Section 4.1(b)(vii)) a compromise was reached and the settlement revised by the Treaty of Lausanne (1923) by which Turkey regained Eastern Thrace including Constantinople, and Smyrna. *Turkey, therefore, was the first state to challenge successfully the Paris settlement.* One legacy of the Treaty of Sèvres which was to cause problems was the situation in the mandates which were peopled largely by Arabs who had been hoping for independence after their brave struggle, led by the English officer, T. E. Lawrence (Lawrence of Arabia), against the Turks. Nor were the Arabs happy about the talk of establishing a Jewish 'national home' in Palestine (see Section 11.5).

Bulgaria lost territory to Greece (depriving her of her Aegean coastline), Yugoslavia and Rumania and could complain, with some justification, that at least a million Bulgars were under foreign governments as a result.

In conclusion it has to be said that *this collection of peace treaties was not a conspicuous success.* It had the unfortunate effect of dividing Europe into the states which wanted to revise the settlement (Germany being the main one), and those which wanted to preserve it. On the whole the latter turned out to be lukewarm in support. USA failed to ratify the settlement (see Section 12.4(b)) and never joined the League of Nations; this in turn left France completely disenchanted with the whole thing because the Anglo-American guarantee of her frontiers could not now apply. Italy felt cheated because she had not received the full territory promised her in 1915, and Russia was ignored. All this tended to sabotage the settlement from the beginning, and it became increasingly difficult to apply the terms fully. But it is easy to criticise after the event; Gilbert White, an American delegate at the conference, put it perfectly when he remarked that given the intricacy of the problems involved, 'it is not surprising that they made a bad peace: what is surprising is that they managed to make peace at all.'

QUESTIONS

1. What was the importance to the Allies of the fighting in *two* of the following areas during the First World War:

the western front, 1916–17; the war at sea, 1916–18; the Middle East, 1915–18?

2. Describe and explain the part played in the First World War by the British army.

3. Describe the main features of naval warfare, 1914–18. What part did the British and Allied navies play in the defeat of Germany?

4. 'For most of the First World War the German army was defending its early gains.' Explain this statement.

5. Explain the importance of *four* of the following in the First World War:

the Marne (1914); Dardanelles (1915); Jutland (1916); Verdun (1916); 'unrestricted' submarine warfare (1917); Caporetto (1917).

6. Explain why Germany lost the First World War.

7. How did the Allies finally defeat Germany during the First World War?

8. What were the terms of the peace treaties with (a) Austria (1919) and (b) Turkey (1920)? What problems were created for *either* Austria *or* Turkey by those treaties?

9. What were the main terms of the Treaty of Versailles? Why were the Germans bitter about the treaty?

10. How far were the ideals of Wilson's 14 points reflected in the peace treaties?

11. Describe and comment on the peace settlements made with Germany and Austria in 1919.

12. What were the aims of the peacemakers at Versailles in 1919? Describe the terms of the treaty and account for German dissatisfaction with them.

13. British war aims outlined by Lloyd George in 1918 included: restoration of Serbia, an independent Poland, self-government to the nationalities in Austria–Hungary, self-determination in the German colonies. Show how the peace settlements dealt with these issues.

CHAPTER 3

RUSSIA: 1905-24

SUMMARY OF EVENTS

In the decade before 1914, Russia was in a troubled state. The Tsar
Nicholas II (1894-1917) insisted on ruling as an autocrat (someone who
rules a country as he sees fit, ignoring such constraints as parliaments) but
had failed to deal adequately with the country's many problems. Unrest
and criticism of the government had reached a climax with the Russian
defeats in the war with Japan (1904-5) and in 1905 had burst out in a
general strike and an attempted revolution, forcing Nicholas to make concessions (the October Manifesto) including the granting of an elected
Parliament (Duma). When it became clear that the *Duma* was ineffective,
unrest increased and culminated, after the disasters of the First World War,
in *two revolutions, both in 1917. The first (March) overthrew the tsar* and
set up a *moderate provisional government*; but when this fared no better
than the tsar, it was itself overthrown by *the Bolshevik revolution
(November)*. The new Bolshevik government was shaky at first and its
opponents' (Whites) attempts to destroy it caused a civil war (1918-20).
Thanks to the leadership of *Lenin* and *Trotsky* the Bolsheviks (now calling
themselves *communists*) survived and Lenin was able to begin the task of
leading Russia to recovery (until his death in 1924).

3.1 AFTER 1905: WERE THE 1917 REVOLUTIONS INEVITABLE?

Nicholas had survived 1905 because his opponents were not united,
because there was no central leadership (the whole thing having flared up
spontaneously) and because he had been willing to compromise at the
critical moment. Tsarism now had a breathing space in which Nicholas had
a chance to make a constitutional monarchy work, and to throw himself in
with the people demanding moderate reforms: improvements in industrial
working conditions and pay, cancellation of redemption payments (annual
payments to the government by peasants in return for their freedom,
following the abolition of serfdom in 1861), which had reduced over half

the rural population to abject poverty, more freedom for the press, and genuine democracy in which the *Duma* would play an important part in running the country. Unfortunately he seems to have had very little intention of keeping to the spirit of the October Manifesto, having agreed to it only because he had no choice. *The First Duma* (1906) was not democratically elected, for although all classes were allowed to vote, the system was rigged so that landowners and middle classes would be in the majority. Even so it put forward far-reaching demands such as confiscation of large estates, a genuinely democratic electoral system and the right to approve the tsar's ministers. This was far too drastic for Nicholas who had the *Duma* dispersed by troops after only ten weeks. *The Second Duma* (1907) suffered the same fate, after which Nicholas changed the franchise, depriving peasants and urban workers of the vote. *The Third and Fourth Dumas* were much more conservative and therefore lasted longer, covering the period 1907 to 1917. Though on occasion they criticised the government, they had no real power, since the tsar controlled the ministers and the secret police. Some foreign observers were surprised at the ease with which Nicholas ignored his promises and dismissed the first two *Dumas* without provoking another general strike. The fact was that the revolutionary impetus had subsided for the time being and many leaders were either in prison or exile.

This together with the improvement in the economy beginning after 1906 has given rise to some *controversy about whether or not the 1917 revolutions were inevitable*:

(a) One theory is that given time plus gradually improving living standards, the chances of revolution would fade, and that if Russia had not become disastrously involved in the First World War, the monarchy might have survived; *evidence to support this view*:

(i)   *Peter Stolypin*, prime minister from 1906 to 1911, made determined efforts to win over the peasants believing that given twenty years of peace, there would be no question of revolution. Redemption payments were abolished and peasants encouraged to buy their own land (about 2 million had done so by 1916 and another 3.5 million had emigrated to Siberia where they had their own farms). As a result there emerged a class of comfortably-off peasants (called *kulaks*) whom, Stolypin hoped, the government could rely on for support against revolution.

(ii)   As more factories came under the control of inspectors, there were signs of improving working conditions, and as industrial profits increased, the first signs of a more prosperous workforce could be detected. In 1912 a workers' sickness and accident insurance scheme was introduced.

(iii)   At the same time the revolutionary parties seemed to have lost heart: they were short of money, torn by disagreements, and their leaders were still in exile.

(b) The other view is that, given the tsar's deliberate flouting of his 1905 promises, there was bound to be a revolution sooner or later and the situation was deteriorating again long before the First World War. The evidence to support this view seems more convincing:

(i) By 1911 it was becoming clear that Stolypin's land reforms would not have the desired result, partly because the peasant population was growing too rapidly (at the rate of 1.5 million a year) for his schemes to cope with, and because farming methods were too inefficient to support the growing population comfortably. The assassination of Stolypin in 1911 removed one of the few really able tsarist ministers and perhaps the only man who could have saved the monarchy.

(ii) There was a wave of industrial strikes set off by the shooting of 270 strikers in the Lena goldfields (April 1912). In all there were over 2,000 separate strikes in that year, 2,400 in 1913, and over 4,000 in the first seven months of 1914 – before war broke out. Whatever improvements had taken place, they were obviously not enough to remove all the pre-1905 grievances.

(iii) Apart from one or two exceptions there was little relaxation of the government's repressive policy as the secret police rooted out revolutionaries among university students and professors and deported masses of Jews, thereby ensuring that both groups were firmly anti-tsarist. Thus the situation was particularly dangerous since peasants, industrial workers and intelligentsia were all alike discontented.

(iv) As 1912 progressed, the fortunes of the various revolutionary parties, especially the Bolsheviks and Mensheviks, revived. Both groups had developed from an earlier movement, the Social Democrat Labour Party, which was Marxist in outlook. (Karl Marx (1818-83) was a German Jew whose political ideas were set out in *The Communist Manifesto* (1848) and *Das Kapital* (1867). He believed that economic factors are the real cause of historical change, and that workers (proletariat) are everywhere exploited by capitalists (middle-class bourgeoisie), which must inevitably lead to revolution and the setting up of 'the dictatorship of the proletariat'.) One of the leaders was *Vladimir Lenin* who helped to edit the revolutionary newspaper *Iskra* (The Spark). It was over an election to the *Iskra* editorial board in 1903 that the party had split into the Lenin supporters, the Bolsheviks (the Russian for 'majority') and the rest, the Mensheviks (minority). Both believed in strikes and revolution, but the Bolsheviks felt it was essential to win the support of peasants as well as industrial workers, whereas the Mensheviks, doubting the value of peasant support, favoured close co-operation with the middle class; Lenin was strongly opposed to this. In 1912 appeared the new Bolshevik newspaper *Pravda* (Truth), which was extremely important as a means of publicising Bolshevik ideas and giving political direction to the already developing strike wave.

(v) The royal family was discredited by a number of scandals. It was widely suspected that Nicholas himself was a party to the murder of Stolypin, who was shot by a member of the secret police in the tsar's presence during a gala performance at the Kiev Opera; nothing was ever proved, but Nicholas and his right-wing supporters were probably not sorry to see the back of Stolypin, who was becoming too liberal for their comfort. More serious was the royal family's association with Rasputin, a self-professed 'holy man', who made himself indispensable to the Empress Alexandra by his ability to help the ailing heir to the throne, Alexei. This unfortunate child had inherited haemophilia from his mother's family, and Rasputin had the power, apparently through hypnosis, to stop the bleeding whenever Alexei suffered a haemorrhage. Eventually Rasputin became a real power behind the throne, but attracted public criticism by his drunkenness and his numerous affairs with court ladies. Alexandra preferred to ignore the scandals and the *Duma*'s request that Rasputin be sent away from the court (1912).

According to Richard Freeborn, there was a 'growing agitation among the workers, which, in July 1914, in St Petersburg, had assumed the proportions of incipient revolution with street demonstrations, shootings and the building of barricades.' However, the government still controlled the army and police and may well have been able to hold on even if a full-scale revolution had developed. What historians are sure about is that *Russian failures in the war made revolution certain* and caused troops and police to mutiny so that there was nobody left to defend autocracy. The war revealed the incompetent and corrupt organisation and the shortage of equipment; it caused tremendous social upheaval with the recruitment of 15 million peasants and ruined the economy, bringing rising prices and chronic food shortages. Nicholas made the mistake of appointing himself supreme commander (August 1915) and thus drew upon himself the blame for all future defeats, and for the high death rate, which destroyed the morale of the troops. Even the murder of Rasputin by a group of aristocrats (December 1916) could not save the monarchy.

3.2 THE TWO REVOLUTIONS: MARCH AND NOVEMBER 1917

The revolutions are still known in Russia as the February and October Revolutions. This was because the Russians were still using the old Julian calendar which was 13 days behind the Gregorian calendar used by the rest of Europe. Russia adopted the Gregorian calendar in 1918.

(a) **The first revolution began spontaneously on 8 March** when bread riots broke out in Petrograd (St Petersburg). The rioters were quickly joined by thousands of strikers from a nearby armaments factory, and when troops were ordered to open fire they refused and joined in the demonstrations. Mobs seized public buildings, released prisoners from jails and took over illus 3.1   *Street fighting in Petrograd, 1917*

police stations and arsenals. Some of his senior generals told Nicholas who was on his way back to Petrograd that he would have to renounce the throne; on 15 March, in the imperial train standing in a siding near Pskov, the tsar abdicated in favour of his brother, the Grand Duke Michael; when he refused the throne the Russian monarchy was at an end. There had been nothing organised about this first revolution; it was simply a spontaneous reaction to the chaotic situation which the imperial government had allowed to develop.

(b) The provisional government. The *Duma*, struggling to take control, set up a mainly liberal *provisional government* with Prince George Lvov as prime minister; in July he was replaced by *Alexander Kerensky*, a moderate socialist. The new government was just as perplexed by the enormous problems facing it as the tsar had been, and in November a second revolution took place which removed the provisional government and installed the Bolsheviks.

Why did the provisional government fall from power so soon?

(i) It took the unpopular decision to continue the war, but the June offensive, Kerensky's idea, was another disastrous failure, causing a complete collapse of army morale and discipline and sending hundreds of thousands of deserting troops streaming home.

(ii) The government had to share power with the Petrograd soviet, an elected committee of workers' and soldiers' representatives which tried to govern the city. Other soviets appeared in Moscow and all the provincial cities and when the Petrograd soviet ordered all soldiers to obey only the soviet, it meant that in the last resort the provisional government could not rely on the support of an army.

(iii) Kerensky delayed the meeting of a Constituent Assembly (parliament) which he had promised and did nothing about land reform. This lost him support on all sides.

(iv) Meanwhile, thanks to the new political amnesty, Lenin was able to return from exile in Switzerland (April). The Germans allowed him to travel through to Petrograd in a special 'sealed' train, in the hope that he would cause further chaos in Russia. After a rapturous welcome he urged that the soviets should cease to support the provisional government.

(v) In the midst of general chaos, Lenin and the Bolsheviks put forward a realistic and attractive policy. *He demanded all power to the soviets*, and promised in return an end to the war, all land to be given to the peasants, and more food. By October the Bolsheviks were in control of both the Petrograd and Moscow soviets, though they were still in a minority over the country as a whole.

(vi) On 20 October, urged on by Lenin, the Petrograd soviet took the crucial decision to attempt to seize power. Leon Trotsky, chairman of the soviet, made most of the plans, which went off without a hitch. During the night of 6-7 November, Bolshevik Red Guards occupied all key points and later arrested the provisional government ministers except Kerensky who managed to escape. It was almost a bloodless coup enabling Lenin to set up a new soviet government with himself in charge. The coup had been successful because Lenin had judged to perfection the moment of maximum hostility towards the Kerensky government, and the Bolsheviks, who knew exactly what they wanted, were well disciplined and organised, whereas all other political groups were in disarray.

3.3 LENIN AND THE BOLSHEVIKS IN POWER 1917-24

The Bolsheviks were in control in Petrograd as a result of their coup, but elsewhere the takeover was not so smooth. Fighting lasted a week in Moscow before the soviet won control and it was the end of November before other cities were brought to heel. Country areas were much more difficult to deal with and at first the peasants were lukewarm towards the illus 3.2   *Lenin addressing a crowd, 1917; the man in the left foreground has been identified as Trotsky*

new government, which very few people expected to last long because of the complexity of the problems facing it. As soon as the other political groups recovered their composure, there was bound to be determined opposition to the Bolsheviks, who had somehow to extricate Russia from the war and then set about repairing the shattered economy while at the same time keeping their promises about land and food for the peasants and workers.

How successful was Lenin in dealing with these problems?

(a) The Bolsheviks had nothing like majority support in the country as a whole; the problem was how to keep themselves in power once the public realised what a Bolshevik government involved. One of Lenin's first decrees therefore nationalised all land so that it could be redistributed among the peasants; this increased support for the Bolsheviks and was a great help in their fight with *the Constituent Assembly*. Lenin knew that he would have to allow elections, having criticised Kerensky so bitterly for postponing them, but he realised that a Bolshevik majority in the Assembly was highly unlikely. Elections were held (the only completely free and democratic elections ever to take place in Russia), but the Bolsheviks won only 168 seats out of about 700 while the right Social Revolutionaries had 380, a clear anti-Bolshevik majority. This would not do for Lenin who was aiming for a *'dictatorship of the proletariat'* by which he meant that he and the Bolshevik party working through the soviets would run the country on behalf of the workers and peasants. There was no room in the scheme for any other party. Accordingly, after some anti-Bolshevik speeches at its first meeting (January 1918), the Assembly was dispersed by Bolshevik Red Guards and never met again. Armed force had triumphed for the time being, but opposition was to lead to civil war later in the year.

(b) The next pressing problem was how to withdraw from the war; an armistice between Russia and the Central Powers had been agreed in December 1917, but long negotiations followed, during which Trotsky tried without success to persuade the Germans to moderate their demands. The Treaty of Brest–Litovsk (March 1918) was cruel, Russia losing Poland, Estonia, Latvia and Lithuania, the Ukraine, Georgia and Finland; this included a third of Russia's farming land, a third of her population, two-thirds of her coalmines and half her heavy industry. A terrible price indeed, but Lenin insisted that it was worth it, pointing out that Russia needed to sacrifice space in order to gain time to recover. He probably expected to get the land back anyway when, as he hoped, the revolution spread to Germany.

(c) By April 1918 armed opposition to the Bolsheviks was breaking out in many areas *leading to civil war. The Whites* were a mixed bag, including Social Revolutionaries, Mensheviks, ex-tsarist officers and any other groups which did not like what they had seen of the Bolsheviks; they were not aiming to restore the tsar, but simply to set up a parliamentary government on western lines. In Siberia *Admiral Kolchak*, former Black Sea Fleet commander, set up a White government; *General Denikin* was in the Caucasus with a large White army; most bizarre of all the *Czechoslovak Legion* of about 40,000 men had seized long stretches of the Trans-Siberian Railway in the region of Omsk. These troops were originally prisoners taken by the Russians from the Austro–Hungarian army, who had later fought against the Germans under the Kerensky government. After Brest–Litovsk the Bolsheviks gave them permission to leave Russia via the Trans-Siberian Railway to Vladivostock, but then decided to disarm them in case they co-operated with the Allies, who were already showing interest in the destruction of the new Bolshevik government. The Czechs resisted with great spirit and their control of the railway was a serious embarrassment to the government.

The situation was complicated by foreign intervention to help the Whites with the excuse that they wanted a government which would continue the war against Germany. When intervention continued even after the defeat of Germany, it became clear that the aim was to destroy the Bolshevik government which was now advocating world revolution. The USA, Japan, France and Britain sent troops, with landings at Archangel, Murmansk and Vladivostock. The situation seemed grim for the Bolsheviks when early in 1919 Kolchak, whom the Allies intended to head the next government, advanced with three armies towards Moscow, illus 3.3   *The Red Army in the Crimea during the civil war, 1918*

the new capital. However Trotsky, now Commissar for War, had done a magnificent job creating the well-disciplined *Red Army*, based on conscription and including thousands of experienced officers from the old tsarist armies. Kolchak was forced back, and later captured and executed by the Reds; the Czech Legion was defeated and Denikin, advancing from the south to within 250 miles of Moscow, was forced to retreat; he later escaped with British help. By the end of 1919 it was clear that the Bolsheviks (now calling themselves communists) would survive, though 1920 saw an invasion of the Ukraine by Polish and French troops which forced the Russians to hand over part of the Ukraine and White Russia (Treaty of Riga 1921). From the communist point of view, however, the important thing was that they had won the civil war. The communist victory was achieved because:

(i)   The Whites were not centrally organised; Kolchak and Denikin failed to link up, and the nearer they drew to Moscow the more they strained their lines of communication. They lost the support of many peasants by their brutal behaviour and because peasants feared a White victory would mean the loss of their newly acquired land.

(ii)   The Red Armies had more troops plus the inspired leadership of Trotsky.

(iii)   Lenin took decisive measures, known as *war communism*, to control the economic resources of the state: all factories of any size were nationalised, all private trade banned, and food and grain seized from peasants to feed town workers and troops. This was successful at first in that it enabled the government to survive the civil war, but it had disastrous results later.

(iv) Lenin was able to present the Bolsheviks as a nationalist government fighting against foreigners; and even though war communism was unpopular with peasants, the Whites became even more unpopular because of their foreign connections.

(d) From early 1921 Lenin had the formidable task of **rebuilding an economy shattered by the First World War and then by civil war.** War communism had been unpopular with the peasants who, seeing no point in working hard to produce food which was taken away from them without compensation, simply produced enough for their own needs. This caused severe food shortages aggravated by droughts in 1920-1. In addition industry was almost at a standstill. In March 1921 a serious naval mutiny occurred at Kronstadt, suppressed only through prompt action by Trotsky, who sent troops across the ice on the Bay of Finland.

This mutiny seems to have convinced Lenin that a new approach was needed to win back the faltering support of the peasants; he put into operation what became known as *the New Economic Policy (NEP)*. Peasants were now allowed to keep surplus produce after payment of a tax representing a certain proportion of the surplus. This, plus the reintro-duction of private trade, revived incentive and food production increased. On the other hand heavy industry was left under state control, though some smaller factories were handed back to private ownership; Lenin also found that often the old managers had to be brought back, as well as such capitalist incentives as bonuses and piece-rates. Lenin saw NEP as a temp-orary compromise – a return to a certain amount of private enterprise until recovery was assured; his long-term aim remained full state control of industry, and of agriculture (through collective farms). Gradually the economy began to recover, though there were recurrent food shortages for many years.

(e) **Political problems** were solved with typical efficiency. Russia was now the world's first communist state, the Union of Soviet Socialist Republics (USSR) with power held by the communist party (no other parties were allowed). In March 1921 Lenin banned groups who criticised his policies within the party, and during the rest of that year about one-third of the party members were 'purged' or expelled with the help of the ruthless secret police (OGPU). Control by Lenin and the party was complete. (For his successes in foreign affairs see Section 13.3(a) and (b)).

In May 1922 Lenin had his first stroke; after this he gradually grew weaker, suffering two more strokes until he died in January 1924 at the early age of 53. A. J. P. Taylor sums up his career well: 'Lenin did more than any other political leader to change the face of the twentieth-century world. The creation of Soviet Russia and its survival were due to him. He was a very great man and even, despite his faults, a very good man.'

QUESTIONS

1. Describe the events after 1904 which led to the fall of the Russian monarchy. Why were there two revolutions in 1917?

2. 'The Russian revolutions of 1917 started in 1904.' How far do you agree that the downfall of the monarchy was inevitable after the events of 1904–5?

3. Describe and comment upon events in Russia between February 1917 and the death of Lenin in 1924.

4. What were Lenin's achievements between his seizure of power in November 1917 and his death in January 1924?

5. What were the problems facing Lenin after the October revolution, and how successfully did he deal with them?

6. Why did the Bolsheviks come to power in Russia in 1917? How do you explain the view commonly held in the period 1917–21 that the Bolshevik government would not last long?

7. Why was there a civil war in Russia from 1918–20 and why did the Bolsheviks eventually win it?

8. How do you explain the fact that the provisional government in Russia fell from power before the end of 1917 whereas Lenin managed to remain in power until his death?

9. Explain the importance of four of the following in the history of the Russian Revolutions and the Civil War:

Kerensky, Kolchak, Trotsky, the Mensheviks, the Constituent Assembly, the Czechoslovak Legion, war communism.

CHAPTER 4

BRITAIN 1918-39

SUMMARY OF EVENTS

Between the two wars Britain was faced with a great array of problems: disturbances in Ireland, declining industries, social unrest, the general strike of 1926, mass unemployment during the world economic crisis of the early 1930s, and threats to peace from the aggressive dictators, Mussolini and Hitler. Politically the most important developments were the blossoming of the Labour Party which formed two short governments; the sharp decline of the Liberals, still suffering from the split between Asquith and Lloyd George factions; and the often unhappy experience of coalition governments. In spite of all the problems progress was made in the field of social welfare, education and housing.

When the armistice was signed on 11 November 1918, Lloyd George was still Prime Minister of the wartime coalition, supported by his own section of the Liberal Party and most of the Conservatives. He decided to hold an immediate election (14 December 1918) which resulted in an overwhelming victory for the coalition. Lloyd George remained Prime Minister until 1922 when his coalition fell apart and the country returned to party governments: Conservative (1922-4), Labour (January to October 1924), Conservative (1924-9), Labour (1929-31). Labour's failure to deal with the economic crisis led to the formation of another coalition, known as the National government (1931-40).

4.1 THE LLOYD GEORGE COALITION 1918-22

(a) The election which returned Lloyd George to power was the first since December 1910, and the first to be fought under *the Representation of the People Act* (August 1918) which gave the vote to all men over 21 and to most women over 30.

The coalition won an easy victory mainly because of Lloyd George's great popularity as the man who had led Britain to victory, and his promises to create a 'fit country for heroes to live in' and to make Germany pay 'the whole cost of the war'. The coalition won 484 seats, made up of 338 Conservatives, 136 Lloyd George Liberals, and 10 Labour and other supporters. The main opposition consisted of 59 Labour members, 26 Asquith Liberals and 48 Conservatives who refused to support the coalition. There were also 73 Sinn Feiners, but they refused to take their seats at Westminster and set up their own parliament in Dublin.

(b) What problems faced Lloyd George and how successful was he in dealing with them?
The situation in the aftermath of the war was chaotic and needed all Lloyd George's brilliance:

(i) Difficulties arose with demobilisation when the government began to release holders of key civilian jobs first, leaving the ordinary rank-and-file troops until last. Some alarming protest demonstrations broke out and the government smartly changed its tactics, adopting a 'first in, first out' policy. This worked well, and by the autumn of 1919 over four million troops had been successfully 'demobbed'. Most of them found jobs, thanks to the post-war boom – an encouraging beginning.

(ii) There was a sudden period of inflation at the end of the war partly caused by the removal of government wartime controls on prices, profits and guaranteed wage levels. Prices and profits rose but wages lagged behind. Trade unions were determined to protect their members, and during 1919 and 1920 there were over 2,000 strikes. It was not simply a matter of higher wages though; *there were other causes of labour unrest*: there was a terrible disillusionment among the working class caused by their experiences in the trenches, and this seemed to emphasise the gulf between workers on the one hand and on the other capitalists and profiteers who had done well out of the war. The Russian revolution (1917) gave tremendous publicity to nationalisation and worker control, and some of the strikes in 1919 threw the government into a panic in case they developed into a revolution. In February and March 1919 a strike of Clydeside engineers and shipbuilders demanding a 40-hour week seemed ominously like the start of a revolution: huge demonstrations, rioting and a red flag hoisted in George Square, Glasgow, caused the government to move in troops and tanks. Order was quickly restored and two of the leaders, Willy Gallacher and Emmanuel Shinwell, were sent to jail. The Miners' Federation threatened a national strike if their demands for a six-hour day, a 30 per cent wage increase and continued government control of mines through nationalisation were not accepted. This time Lloyd George avoided a confrontation and played for time: he offered a seven-hour day, continued government control for the time being, and a Royal Commission (the Sankey Commission) to investigate the problem; the miners accepted his offer.

(iii) A slump which began early in 1921 threw about two million people

A land fit for heroes ?

out of work by the end of the year and the unemployment figure never fell below a million until the Second World War. Already in 1920 the government had extended the 1911 National Insurance Act so that unemployment payments were made, for not more than 15 weeks in any one year, to all workers earning less than £250 a year (except agricultural labourers, domestic servants and civil servants). At that point boom conditions still applied and mass unemployment was not expected. When it came in 1921 the new scheme could not cope: payments to the unemployed far outweighed contributions. However, having once conceded the principle of state benefit for the unemployed, the government could hardly do a U-turn simply because unemployment increased. During 1921 therefore, benefit was extended to two 16-week periods in the year with a gap between. Much of this was financed by straight 'gifts' from the treasury and these became known as the 'dole'. Extra payments were introduced for wives and children. The government aid probably eased the situation and may even have prevented revolution; nevertheless it was criticised by Labour because it only treated the symptoms and did nothing to remove unemployment. Labour MPs claimed that the benefits were too low and were 'mocking the poor', while Conservatives condemned them on the grounds that they would demoralise the workers.

(iv) The trouble in the coal industry over whether it should remain under government control or be returned to private ownership had been simmering since the appointment of the Sankey Commission. Matters came to a head on 1 April 1921 when the entire industry came out on strike. This was because the Sankey Commission had been unable to agree on a solution to the problems. Some members recommended nationalisation and others the return of the mines to private ownership. This bitterly disappointed the miners who wanted nationalisation, and gave Lloyd George the opportunity to avoid permanent nationalisation. The government announced that mines and railways would be handed back to private control on 1 April. Mine-owners informed the men that wages would be reduced because of the slump in exports. For a time the miners' strike threatened to develop into a general strike, but on 15 April the miners' allies in the Triple Alliance, the railwaymen and transport workers, decided to abandon the idea, which the miners regarded as a betrayal. The miners persisted and their strike lasted three months; but without support their position was hopeless and they had to give way on all points. Soon afterwards workers in other trades (engineering, ship-building, building, docks, textiles, printing and railways) had to accept wage reductions.

Lloyd George had solved this problem insofar as the strike had failed and a general strike had been averted, but he was fast losing his popularity with the workers.

(v) There was a reduction in government revenue (money flowing into the Treasury from taxation). This was caused partly by the general falling-off of business during the slump and partly by the enormous expense of unemployment benefits. A committee under Sir Eric Geddes recommended drastic cuts, many of which were carried out by the government, saving £64 million. They became known as *the Geddes Axe* and involved greatly reduced expenditure on the army, navy, education, health services, and council house building. The economy measures were successful, but highly unpopular with the working class who criticised the government for 'making the children pay while the ladies of Mayfair spend extravagantly on dresses'.

(vi) Trouble flared up in Ireland immediately after the election when the 73 Sinn Fein MPs (who wanted Ireland to be independent from Britain) set up their own parliament (*Dail*) in Dublin and proclaimed the Republic of Ireland. The IRA began a campaign of terrorism against the police and the government retaliated by using the Black and Tans. Although Lloyd George found a temporary settlement by partitioning Ireland (see Section 11.2(a)), he had made enemies in doing so: many Liberals resented his use of the Black and Tans, whereas the Conservatives were furious at the way in which the union between Britain and Ireland had been destroyed. This was serious for Lloyd George because the survival of his coalition depended on continued Conservative support.

(vii) Problems in foreign affairs also played a part in ruining Lloyd George's reputation. The intervention in Russia to try and destroy the new Bolshevik government was an expensive failure and lost him support among the working class, who thought he was too much under the thumb of the Conservatives (see Section 13.2); the Genoa Conference (1922) was another failure (see Section 13.1(c)). Most damaging of all was the *Chanak incident (1922)* which occurred when the Turks threatened to break the Versailles settlement by moving troops into a neutral zone, thereby clashing with the British occupying force based at Chanak on the Straits (see Section 2.10). Lloyd George took a strong line and warned the Turks to keep out. Eventually a compromise was reached and the crisis passed; but though it was something of a triumph for Lloyd George, many Conservatives thought he had acted too rashly, and that the problem could have been solved equally well with more tactful handling and consequently less risk of war.

(c) The coalition found time for some improvements in domestic affairs:

(i) The Sex Disqualification Removal Act (1919) allowed women to stand for Parliament.

(ii) The Addison Housing Act (1919), the work of Christopher Addison, the Minister of Health, provided subsidies for local authorities to organise the building of 'homes fit for heroes'; 213,800 council houses were built in England and Wales by the end of 1922. Though this was not enough to solve the housing shortage, and the scheme suffered from the Geddes Axe, the principle had been established that housing was a social service and later on local authorities continued Addison's work:

(iii) The extension of unemployment insurance already mentioned meant that an extra nine million workers had at least some cover against unemployment and though the amounts paid were often inadequate, again an important principle had been accepted: it was the state's responsibility to protect workers from the effects of industrial variations.

(iv) The Rent Act (1920) protected working-class tenants against exorbitant rent increases.

(d) The fall of the Lloyd George coalition (October 1922)

Unfortunately for Lloyd George his achievements were not enough to save the coalition. He had been losing working-class support steadily and it was significant that Labour won 13 by-elections between 1918 and 1922. Much depended on whether the Conservative MPs would continue to support him at the next general election which he intended to hold fairly soon. A meeting of Conservative MPs was held at *the Carlton Club* (29 October) and the vote was 187 to 87 in favour of ending their support of Lloyd George. The main anti-Lloyd George speech which swayed the meeting was made by *Stanley Baldwin*. Lloyd George immediately resigned and Andrew Bonar Law became Prime Minister of a Conservative government. Lloyd George was never again to hold an important political office. The Conservatives decided to abandon him partly because of a combination of their resentment at his solution of the Irish problem, his failure at the Genoa Conference, plus what they considered to be his tactless handling of the Chanak incident, and because they feared that if they supported him much longer, he would split the Conservative party in the same way that he had already split the Liberals (by the way in which he had manoeuvred Asquith into resigning in December 1916). They criticised him because he allowed the sale of knighthoods and other honours to unsuitable candidates. This is why Baldwin in his Carlton Club speech spoke of his desire for a return to 'clean government'.

4.2 CONSERVATIVE INTERLUDE: OCTOBER 1922 TO JANUARY 1924

The Conservatives won a clear victory at the general election held in November 1922 with 347 seats, a majority of 88 over all other parties combined. It was a disaster for the Liberals, who fought the election in two separate groups: Asquith Liberals won 60 seats, Lloyd George Liberals 57. The combined Liberal total of 117 seats was well behind Labour's 142, and it was clear that Labour had emerged as the main opposition party to the Conservatives.

However, the new Conservative government did not last long. After Bonar Law's resignation through ill health in May 1923, Stanley Baldwin became Prime Minister. After only a few months in office he decided that another election was necessary even though the Conservatives still had their overall majority. His reason was that he had decided to reintroduce tariffs (import duties) and since Bonar Law had earlier promised that this was exactly what the Conservatives would not do, Baldwin felt it only fair for the electorate to decide for or against protection. Tariffs would make foreign goods more expensive in Britain and thus give a much-needed boost to British industry; the growing unemployment problems would thus be solved. The two sections of the Liberal party reunited under Asquith's leadership and campaigned for free trade, a traditional Liberal policy. Together with Labour they argued that continued free trade and foreign imports would keep down the cost of living for the workers. The results were: Conservatives 258, Labour 191 and Liberals 158, a clear defeat for protection and a further confirmation that Labour had replaced the Liberals as the alternative party to the Conservatives. The Conservatives could not remain in government, because although they were still the largest single party they had lost their overall majority, and both Liberals and Labour were against their policy of protection. Labour, the second largest party, therefore formed a government, with a promise of Liberal support in the Commons. In January 1924 the first Labour government took office, with James Ramsay MacDonald as Prime Minister.

4.3 WHY DID THE LIBERAL PARTY CONTINUE TO DECLINE?

At the time of the great Liberal victory of 1906 very few people could have foreseen that within less than 20 years the Liberals would be on the way out and Labour would be forming a government. Suggested explanations are:

(a) Even before 1914 there were signs of a split in the party between the left (in favour of state action to bring about social reform) and the right (which viewed such ideas with distaste); the party may well have broken up even if the First World War had not accelerated the process.

(b) Lloyd George split the party by the way in which he manoeuvred Asquith into resigning in 1916. Asquith's supporters never forgave Lloyd George for this 'betrayal' and the party remained divided until the election of November 1923, just as Labour was presenting a strong challenge.

(c) It was always possible as more of the working class got the vote (as they did in 1884, 1918 and 1928) that Labour, projecting itself as the party of the working people, might entice them away from the Liberals. Towards the end of the war, local Labour Party organisations were set up in every constituency, and Sydney Webb of the Fabian Society wrote a new programme – 'Labour and the New Social Order' – which included the nationalisation of coal, land, railways, and electricity, plus a levy on capital. Thus in the elections of 1918 and 1922 Labour seemed better organised than the Liberals; in 1922 for the first time Labour won more seats than both groups of Liberals combined (142 to 117).

(d) Asquith did not provide inspiring leadership and no constructive ideas were put forward on either economic or foreign affairs. Unfortunately for the Liberals he did not retire from the leadership until 1926 when it was too late for the party to recover.

(e) The Liberals were beginning to lose right-wing support, as many wealthy businessmen switched to the Conservatives as the surest way of keeping Labour out. This was serious because it removed much of the Liberals' financial support; three elections between 1918 and 1923 left the party short of funds; Labour was able to rely on trade union cash.

(Polarisation)

(f) Once Labour had formed a government in 1924 without the expected social revolution, Liberal election prospects faded; anti-Conservatives began to vote Labour as the only way to keep the Tories out.

(g) The Liberals were at a disadvantage because of the electoral system. With three parties contesting many seats, a high proportion of MPs were returned on a minority vote; many Liberals came second and their votes were not reflected in the Commons. In 1922 Liberals polled slightly more votes than Labour, yet won only 117 seats to Labour's 142. (Hence the Liberal agitation ever since for some sort of proportional representation.)

(h) The 1929 election is usually regarded as the Liberals' last chance; Lloyd George led a united party with an attractive programme, but they managed only 59 seats to Labour's 288. There was a lack of confidence in Lloyd George and a feeling that Baldwin and MacDonald, though less spectacular, were more solid and reliable.

Perhaps the neatest conclusion is that given the circumstances in the years after the First World War, with the Conservatives firmly established as the party of the propertied classes and the ratepayers, and Labour in alliance with the trade unions as the party of the workers, there was no remaining interest group large enough to keep the Liberals going as a serious contender for power.

4.4 THE FIRST LABOUR GOVERNMENT: JANUARY TO OCTOBER 1924

This Labour government, like the one of 1929-31, was a disappointment to its supporters.

(a) Why were they not more successful?

(i)   Both were minority governments lacking an overall majority, and dependent on Liberal votes to stay in office. They had therefore to pursue moderate policies, and it was out of the question to introduce nationalisation and disarmament even if MacDonald had wanted to. This meant that their policies were very little different from those of Liberal governments.

(ii) Labour had difficulty in projecting itself as a truly national party, since from the beginning it had claimed to be the party of the industrial workers and was closely tied to the trade unions. It was distrusted by people of property who feared nationalisation and the link with militant trade unionism.

(iii) Labour could not break its ties with the trade unions because they provided the majority of its funds. In return the unions expected to be able to control the party which caused serious friction because union leaders were preoccupied with furthering the interests of their members. They gave very little support to the 1924 Labour government and made no allowances for its dependence on Liberal support, criticising it for its 'half-measures'. Almost immediately there was a dockers' strike in support of a demand for an extra two shillings a day. This was organised by Ernest Bevin, general secretary of the Transport and General Workers' Union. Following the success of this strike London Transport workers also came out, and the situation became serious enough for MacDonald to proclaim a state of emergency, enabling the government to use armed lorries for moving essential supplies. In the end this was not necessary because the employers gave way and made an acceptable wage offer, but it was embarrassing for the government and left its relationship with the unions strained.

(iv) It proved impossible to work out a joint plan of action between the parliamentary Labour party and the trade unions. When some Labour intellectuals suggested that the two should co-operate to avoid a repetition of the 1924 fiasco, Bevin dismissed the idea; according to him such theorists did not understand the working class.

(v) Both governments were unfortunate enough to have to deal with serious economic problems: a million unemployed in 1924 and the world economic crisis in 1930–1. Labour had no answer beyond nationalisation, and since that was out of the question they were helpless.

(b) Achievements of the first Labour government

The 1924 government managed a few achievements in spite of the disappointments:

(i) Wheatley's Housing Act provided grants of £9 million a year to local authorities for the building of council houses. By 1933 when the subsidy was abolished, 521,700 houses had been built which did much to relieve the housing shortage.

(ii) Old age pensions and unemployment benefit were increased and the gap between the two 16-week benefit periods was removed.

(iii) The number of free places in grammar schools was increased and state scholarships to universities brought back.

(iv) Sir Henry Hadow was appointed to work out the needs of education. Although his report did not appear until 1926 the Labour Minister of Education, C. P. Trevelyan, must take the credit for the initiative. The Hadow Report was an important milestone in English education, introducing the break between primary and secondary education at 11, and recognising the principle that the whole population was entitled to some secondary education.

(v) There were some notable achievements in foreign affairs where MacDonald turned out to be something of an expert (he was Foreign Secretary as well as Prime Minister): he played an important part in drawing up the Dawes Plan (see Section 13.1(d)), began a policy of friendship towards the USSR (see Section 13.2(a)), and strongly supported the League of Nations.

(c) The fall of the first Labour government (October 1924)

The end of the government came rather suddenly over *the Campbell Case*. J. R. Campbell, editor of the communist *Workers' Weekly* was arrested and charged with incitement to mutiny (he had written an article urging soldiers not to fire on their fellow workers in the event of a strike). However, the Labour Attorney-General withdrew the prosecution, and both Conservatives and Liberals, already alarmed by MacDonald's opening of relations with Russia, accused the government of being sympathetic towards communists. The Liberal demand for an inquiry into the matter was carried by 364 votes to 198; MacDonald took this as a vote of no confidence and resigned. The following election was complicated by the affair of *the Zinoviev Letter*. This appeared in the *Daily Mail* four days before polling and claimed to be from the Russian communist leader Zinoviev to the British Communist Party. It was marked 'very secret' and contained instructions on how to organise a revolution. The fact that the Foreign Office protested to the Russians about this interference in British affairs made the letter appear genuine, though it seems fairly certain that it was a forgery. But it caused a sensation at the time and was taken to show that Labour sympathy towards Russia was encouraging the British communists. Labour dropped to 151 seats, Liberals lost disastrously winning only 42 seats, while the Conservatives emerged triumphant with 419 seats.

Labour blamed their defeat on the Zinoviev Letter, but historians seem to agree that the Conservatives would have won anyway. Although short, the first Labour government was not without significance: it proved that a Labour government could work, and it won respect both at home and abroad for its handling of foreign affairs.

4.5 STANLEY BALDWIN'S CONSERVATIVE GOVERNMENT 1924-9

The split in the party was now fully healed and even Winston Churchill drifted back to become Chancellor of the Exchequer after 20 years as a Liberal. It was a fairly uneventful five years with one startling exception: the 1926 general strike. Baldwin was a moderate Conservative who liked to project himself as the plain and honest man, puffing at his pipe. He was a very able politician and a much better manager of people than Lloyd George. His government introduced a mass of useful legislation; Neville Chamberlain, the Minister of Health, was himself responsible for 21 bills passing the Commons.

Conservative achievements:

(i) The Widows, Orphans and Old Age Contributory Pensions Act (1925) provided a pension of 10s. a week for widows with extra for children, and 10s. a week for insured workers and their wives at 65. Both workers and employers contributed to the scheme which was compulsory (the non-contributory pension at 70 still continued).

(ii) The vote was extended to women at the age of 21. Labour objected strongly because the plural vote (the right enjoyed by owners of business premises to vote in the constituencies where their premises were as well as where they lived) was not abolished.

(iii) The Local Government Act of 1929 was Chamberlain's greatest achievement, providing a complete overhaul of local government organisation, rates and provision for the poor: Poor Law Unions and their boards of guardians who had provided relief for the poor since 1834 were abolished, and their function taken over by county and county borough councils. Agricultural land and farm buildings were to be exempt from payment of rates, and industrial property and railways were to pay only one-quarter of the previous rate. This was designed to encourage farmers and industrialists to expand operations and provide more jobs. Local councils would receive a block grant from the government to cover the costs of services to the poor and of other functions such as public health, slum clearance, roads, and town and country planning. This was a much fairer system because expenses were being shared by the whole body of taxpayers in the country, instead of poor areas with high unemployment having to foot the bill from rates collected locally. However, the Labour party protested bitterly that it was an attack on the independence of local councils, since the government could now cut off grants to councils which did not follow their wishes.

(iv) The Central Electricity Board appointed by the Minister of Transport was made responsible for the distribution of electricity. The National Grid was started with its thousands of pylons connecting the generating stations; it was completed by 1933.

(v) The British Broadcasting Company became a public corporation, to be controlled by governors appointed by the Postmaster-General.

(vi) The Locarno Treaties (October 1925) were taken at the time to be a triumph for Austen Chamberlain, the Foreign Secretary, but later this opinion was revised (see Section 13.1(e)).

(vii) The way was prepared for the Statute of Westminster (eventually signed in 1931) which defined the relationship between Britain and the rest of the commonwealth (see Section 11.1(b)).

4.6 THE GENERAL STRIKE (4–12 MAY 1926)

(a) Causes of the strike:

(i) In the background was the post-war economic depression, with falling exports and mass unemployment.

(ii) On the whole, industrialists failed to promote greater efficiency and more mechanisation which would have enabled them to compete better with other countries. They tended to blame declining profits on higher wages, and their attempts to reduce wages caused strained relations with their workforces.

(iii) The problems of the coal industry were important because it was here that the strike began. Coal sales were probably worse hit than those of any other industry, partly because more gas, electricity and oil were being used, and because there was stiff competition from Germany and Poland which had modern mechanised pits. In 1925 only 20 per cent of British output was by coal-cutting machines, the rest was by hand-picks.

(iv) The government had refused to nationalise the mines, though it was widely believed that only government control could bring about the essential modernisation that would enable the industry to survive. Mine-owners were unwilling to take any initiative.

(v) The return to the gold standard in April 1925 worsened the export position of all British industries, not just coal. According to the economist J. M. Keynes, the Chancellor of the Exchequer, Churchill, had over-valued the pound by 10 per cent, making British exports that much more expensive.

(iv) The situation worsened in June 1925 when there was a sudden drop in coal exports, following a brief revival while the German mines in the Ruhr were closed during the French occupation. The owners announced that they would have to lower wages and increase hours. The miners protested but Baldwin saved the situation for the time being by providing a subsidy for nine months to keep wages at the existing levels, and by appointing a Royal Commission under Sir Herbert Samuel to try and find a solution.

(vii) Meanwhile the TUC made it clear that they would support the miners, because if their wages were reduced it was likely that those of other workers would soon follow. This stiffened the attitude of the miners.

(viii) Everything hinged on whether the *Samuel Report* could find a solution. It appeared in March 1926 and was an eminently sensible document. It recommended that mine-owners should press ahead with reorganisation and modernisation, should not insist on longer hours (which would lead to over-production) and should not reduce wages (which would enable them to avoid reorganisation). The government should not continue the subsidy. For the time being until the crisis passed, miners must accept some wage reductions. Neither the owners nor the miners would accept the report, though the TUC welcomed it and tried to keep negotiations going because they were not prepared for a general strike. The government made no attempt to force its acceptance even though one moderate mine-owner, Sir Alfred Mond, urged Baldwin to do so.

(ix) The mine-owners brought a showdown one step nearer by announcing that wages would be reduced on 30 April to which the miners replied that they would strike on 1 May. The owners got in first and staged a lockout on Friday 30 April. The coal strike had begun. Ernest Bevin announced that a general strike would begin on 3 May if a settlement was not reached.

(x) The TUC was still trying to find a solution but was thwarted by circumstances. Negotiations between cabinet and TUC were hampered all through 2 May because the miners' leaders had gone home, leaving the TUC to handle the talks. Baldwin heard that the *Daily Mail* compositors had refused to print an article which claimed that a general strike would be a revolutionary action. He described this as an 'overt act', a sign that the General Strike had begun, whereas in fact it was an unofficial action. Baldwin called off the negotiations and the general strike followed.

(b) The strike itself was an impressive show of working-class solidarity. In the industries called out (road, rail, docks, printing, gas and electricity, building, iron, steel and chemicals), the response was almost 100 per cent, which seemed to show how alienated the workers had become from employers and government. However, by 11 May there was no sign that the government would give way. Baldwin took the view that the strike was an attack on the constitution and not an ordinary industrial dispute; therefore no negotiations could begin until the strike was called off. He concentrated on operating emergency plans prepared months earlier, and these worked efficiently. Volunteers kept food supplies moving, unloaded ships and drove trains and buses. Food convoys were guarded by armoured car, while the navy manned power stations. When Sir Herbert Samuel offered to act as mediator, the TUC accepted. He produced *the Samuel Memorandum* suggesting a short-term renewal of the subsidy to maintain wage levels, no wage reductions until reorganisation was assured, and a National Wages Board.

On 12 May the TUC called off the General Strike, hoping that the memorandum would be accepted, though it was strictly unofficial and Baldwin had given no guarantees. The strike itself lasted unofficially until 14 May, but the miners refused to go back. Since the mine-owners refused illus 4.1   *A food convoy guarded by armoured cars during the General Strike, 1926*

to compromise, the coal strike dragged on until December, but in the end the miners had to give way and go back to longer hours and lower wages. There was much bitterness about the TUC 'betrayal'. The TUC called off the strike so soon for several reasons: there was no sign of a softening in the government's attitude; in fact the cabinet extremists were talking of 'unconditional surrender'; the TUC, completely unprepared for a general strike anyway, was anxious to end it before provocative government actions caused events to take a more violent turn; there were doubts about the legal position; Sir John Simon (a Liberal lawyer) said in the Commons that the strike was 'an illegal proceeding', not an industrial dispute, and that the leaders were liable to be sued for damages and gaoled. The Labour party's attitude was unhelpful and the strike was proving expensive – the TUC had already used £4 million out of their total strike fund of £12.5 million.

(c) Results of the General Strike:

(i)   There was a good deal of working-class disillusionment with the TUC for its 'betrayal' of the miners. Membership dropped from over eight million to well under five million the following year.

(ii)   The TUC turned against the idea of a general strike, convinced that one could never succeed.

(iii)   There was no solution to the coal industry problems and no modern-

isation; the industry continued in slow decline with exports falling
steadily.

(iv) The government introduced *the Trade Disputes Act* (1927) designed
to make another general strike impossible. Sympathetic strikes and
intimidation were illegal. Trade union members were not required to
contribute to the union's political fund (the political levy paid to the
Labour party) unless they chose to do so and gave written notice of
their intention. This was known as 'contracting-in' which now
replaced 'contracting-out' introduced by the 1913 Trade Union Act.
The new act placed the onus on the member; many did not bother
to contract in, hence a fall of over 25 per cent in the Labour party's
income.

   The act seems to have been largely unnecessary since the TUC had
had enough of general strikes, and it was bitterly resented by the
unions. It was not repealed until 1946.

(v) The working class realised that only by parliamentary action could
their aims be achieved and this, plus bitterness at the Trade Disputes
Act and unemployment standing at over a million, caused an
increase in Labour party support and a Labour victory in the 1929
general election.

4.7 THE SECOND LABOUR GOVERNMENT (1929-31) AND THE GREAT DEPRESSION

The most impressive achievements of this government were in foreign
affairs where Ramsay MacDonald and Arthur Henderson, the new Foreign
Secretary, added to their reputation by playing an important part in drawing up the Young Plan and supporting the League of Nations (see Section
13.1(g)). In home affairs the government achieved little beyond the 1930
Housing Act which renewed the subsidy for council house building and
organised the speeding up of slum clearance, and the Coal Mines Act
(1930) reducing the miners' working day from eight hours to seven and a
half. Labour suffered the same disadvantages as in 1924: it was still a
minority government with 287 seats to the Conservatives' 261; since the
Liberals had 59, Labour needed Liberal support so that again socialist
legislation was out of the question. The government was brought down
prematurely by the world economic crisis ushered in by the Wall Street
Crash of October 1929 (see Section 7.2). By May 1931 Britain was feeling
the full impact of the depression, with unemployment at over 2.5 million.
Payment of unemployment benefit was placing a severe strain on government finances, *and events moved rapidly to cause the government's
resignation* (August 1931). The May Report (the result of Sir George
May's committee of enquiry) appeared at the end of July and forecast
that by April 1932 there would be a government deficit of £120 million. It
proposed a 20 per cent reduction in unemployment benefit to stave off
the crisis. This caused foreign investors to conclude that Britain must be
on the verge of bankruptcy and they rushed to withdraw gold, plunging

the country into a deeper financial crisis. The Bank of England informed the government that immediate economies were needed to restore foreign confidence, while French and American bankers demanded economies before further loans could be made. When MacDonald proposed a 10 per cent reduction in unemployment benefit there was fierce argument within the cabinet, and 10 out of the 21 members would not agree.

MacDonald claimed that there was nothing else for it but to resign; he handed in the government's resignation, but to the amazement of almost the whole of the Labour party he stayed on as Prime Minister of what was called a National government with a cabinet consisting of Conservatives, Liberals and just three other Labour men. The formation of the National government was a highly controversial event. The Labour party blamed MacDonald bitterly for deserting them and branded him a traitor, claiming that he had been planning to ditch them for some time; but David Marquand believes that George V and Baldwin persuaded him to stay on as Prime Minister of a coalition government as the best way of restoring confidence.

4.8 THE NATIONAL GOVERNMENT: FINANCIAL PROBLEMS AND RECOVERY

A number of measures were introduced to try and restore confidence, including raising income tax from 4/6 to 5s. in the pound, reducing salaries of public employees and unemployment benefits by 10 per cent. These did not produce the desired effect and foreigners continued to withdraw funds from Britain. Nor was the situation helped by the *Invergordon Mutiny* (September 1931) when naval crews protested against proposed salary cuts, though this soon petered out when the government assured them that cuts would not exceed 10 per cent. In the end the government went off the gold standard, so that the value of the pound fell by about one-quarter on the foreign exchanges. After a general election in October 1931, in which National government supporters won 521 seats, the country gradually began to recover from the depression. However, it was a very gradual recovery due more to favourable circumstances than to any efforts of the government, though it did attempt to help.

(a) Government action:
Free trade was abandoned by Neville Chamberlain's *Import Duties Act of 1932*, placing a 10 per cent duty on most imports, except those from the empire. This, as well as increasing sales of British goods at home, brought in extra revenue, so that Chamberlain was able to avoid raising the income tax again. Defence expenditure and interest on war loans were reduced. Some attempt was made to reorganise iron and steel, shipbuilding, textiles and coal, and to persuade new industry to move into areas of high unemployment though without much success (see Section 4.9(c)). Remaining off the gold standard made British goods cheaper abroad and led to an increase in exports. Bank rate was reduced from 6 per cent to

2 per cent mainly to reduce debt charges; however many local authorities took advantage of low interest rates to borrow money for house building. This provided extra jobs not only for builders but for all the allied trades, including gas and electricity.

These measures helped to stabilise the financial situation and to increase sales at home and abroad, though it can be argued that foreign manufacturers, deprived of markets in Britain by the new import duties, became competitors in export markets.

(b) Favourable circumstances:
These would probably have occurred whatever action the government had chosen to take:

(i) As prices of all products (both British and imported) fell during the depression, the cost of living also fell and, even with wage reductions, there was an increase in real wages (what one could actually buy with the cash available).

(ii) This enabled people to spend their extra cash on British consumer goods and even on luxuries such as radios and holidays, which stimulated the creation of jobs.

By 1936 it was clear that Britain had recovered from the depression, and probably undeservedly the National government took the credit. For a long time it had been a rather thinly disguised Conservative government, and when Baldwin became Prime Minister in June 1935, on MacDonald's retirement, the Conservatives easily won the election of the following October, though they still kept the 'National' label. Two problems with which they did not deal successfully were the dilemma of whether and by how much to rearm, and the persistent unemployment in certain depressed areas.

4.9 UNEMPLOYMENT IN THE 1930s

Unemployment was not a general phenomenon during the 1930s; it was confined to certain trades and certain areas. The total unemployed in Britain were (in millions):

1927 = 1.1	1931 = 2.7	1935 = 2.0
1928 = 1.3	1932 = 2.8	1936 = 1.7
1929 = 1.2	1933 = 2.5	1937 = 1.4
1930 = 1.9	1934 = 2.1	1938 = 1.9

The main industries affected were shipbuilding (30.6 per cent of workers in that industry were unemployed in 1936), steel, coalmining (25 per cent), shipping (22.3 per cent) and textiles (13.2 per cent). The areas where these industries were situated were greatly depressed; they included the whole of Scotland, the Tyne-Tees area, Cumberland, Lancashire, and also Northern Ireland and South Wales. In some towns the individual figures were illus 4.2 *The Jarrow Crusade – unemployed men marching from Jarrow to London in 1936 in protest against lack of work*

startling: Jarrow had 68 per cent of its total workforce unemployed in 1934; in Merthyr Tydfil the figure was 62 per cent, while in St Albans at the same time it was only 3.9 per cent. The midlands and the south were much better off because they had new industries such as motor cars, aircraft, and chemicals.

(a) Why were the depressed areas so bad?

(i)   They contained the older export industries which had been successful until the 1880s but had then begun to decline. Their decline was accelerated after the First World War because many countries which found alternative sources of supply during the war did not resume buying British after 1918. They suffered fierce competition from more highly mechanised and more efficient foreign industries and cheaper foreign goods, such as Japanese and east European textiles; India, the main British market for textiles before the war, was rapidiy developing her own industry. Coal exports were badly hit by cheap coal from Germany and Poland. Very little attempt was made to modernise these industries to make them more competitive.

(ii) There would have been unemployment therefore even without the world economic crisis, but after 1930 this made the situation worse in the depressed areas and caused temporary unemployment elsewhere.

(iii) It is also argued that Chamberlain's import duties worsened the export position of the old industries (see Section 4.8(a)).

(iv) The depressed areas had concentrated exclusively on the old industries so that there was no alternative employment to be had, and since the majority of unemployed could not afford to move elsewhere, they had to stay put.

(b) Suggested remedies:

(i) J. M. Keynes (the Liberal economist) suggested that the government should spend its way out of the depression by investing in order to stimulate new industries, while at the same time organising the contraction of the declining industries. The government should also give financial aid to enable people to move out of depressed areas.

(ii) 'Peace and Reconstruction', a document produced in 1935 by a group of young Conservative MPs led by *Harold Macmillan* (MP for Stockton-on-Tees) set out detailed schemes such as road-building, electrification, housing and national parks which could be organised by government and local authority expenditure, using cash which would have been spent on unemployment benefit.

(c) Government action:

The government's response was unimaginative and its measures failed to get to the root of the problem.

(i) The Unemployment Act (1934) set up the National Unemployment Assistance Board whose branches in every part of the country would pay out benefit after an unemployed man ran out of the normal period of insurance benefit. The way in which this act was applied caused great bitterness among the unemployed since it was based on the *'means test'* introduced in 1931. This took into account the total family income and savings of an unemployed man when assessing the amount of relief he should receive, and caused demoralisation when it appeared that the careful and thrifty were being penalised.

(ii) The Special Areas Act (1934) appointed two unpaid commissioners and provided them with £2 million to try to revive Scotland, west Cumberland, Tyneside and South Wales. This had little effect because employers could not be compelled to move into the depressed areas. Later the government offered rates, rent and income tax remission to encourage firms to move in, which resulted in the setting up of trading estates such as the ones at Treforest (South Wales), North Hillington and Larkhall (near Glasgow); but these provided only a few thousand jobs, many of them for women.

(iii) The Bank Rate reduction mentioned in the previous section helped the housing boom and encouraged local authorities to embark on road-building. But the government partially defeated its own ends by continually warning local authorities to economise, revealing that it only imperfectly understood the workings of economics.

(iv) An attempt was made to revive the steel industry by imposing a tariff on foreign steel and setting up the British Iron and Steel Federation. Government pressure resulted in the building of two new steel works at Ebbw Vale and Corby, but the federation was bitterly criticised for refusing to allow one to be built at Jarrow. However, the steel industry was showing signs of revival.

(v) Loans were provided to encourage shipbuilding, including the completion of the *Queen Mary*.

(vi) From 1936 onwards the rearmament programme helped in the creation of extra jobs.

Although by the end of 1937 total unemployment had fallen to 1.4 million, there had been little improvement in the depressed areas where most of the 1.4 million were concentrated. In spite of plenty of available advice the government had failed to produce any positive strategy for curing long-term unemployment in these areas, largely because it refused to accept that the problem could be solved.

QUESTIONS

1. What problems faced Lloyd George as Prime Minister after the First World War and how successfully did he tackle them?

2. What were the problems facing Britain between 1918 and 1929?

3. What were the causes of the general strike? How did the government deal with it and what were its effects?

4. Account for the successes and failures of Labour governments in Britain between 1924 and 1931.

5. Why did the Liberal Party decline after 1918?

6. How did successive governments in Britain from 1919 to 1935 tackle the following: decline of basic industries, monetary problems, trade unions, housing, unemployment?

7. How and with what success did the National governments in Britain tackle the economic problems facing them in the 1930s?

8. Describe and explain the difficulties from which the British coal industry suffered in the 1920s and 1930s. Explain the powerlessness in these circumstances of the miners' union and of government.

9. Why did Britain suffer an economic depression in the early 1930s? What were the political results of the depression?

CHAPTER 5

FRANCE IN DECLINE
1918-40

SUMMARY OF EVENTS

The history of France between the wars makes sad reading; though victorious in the First World War, the Third Republic seemed completely exhausted by the effort and drained both by the loss of 15 per cent of her male population either killed or incapacitated and by the enormous financial demands of the war effort. As before 1914, the Republic continued to be politically unstable, with constantly changing coalition governments. The years 1919-24 saw a right-wing coalition (*Bloc National*) in power with *Raymond Poincaré* as Prime Minister for part of the time. After his failure over the French occupation of the Ruhr in 1923 (see Sections 13.2(c)) a left-wing coalition took over (*Cartel des Gauches*) for a short time, only to be replaced after a serious financial crisis by another right coalition (*Union Nationale*) from 1926 to 1932. This was followed by six different left coalitions, all of which failed to solve France's economic crisis and culminated in riots organised by fascists and royalists (6 February 1934). After another right coalition (1934-6) had failed both to restore the economy and to prevent the Italian seizure of Abyssinia (see Section 14.2(b)), the famous *Front Populaire* came to power (1936-8). This was a coalition of mainly socialists and communists with *Leon Blum* as Prime Minister, which managed some long-overdue reforms before it was brought down by yet another financial crisis. From then until the outbreak of war *Edouard Daladier* headed what was known as a Government of National Defence.

As successive governments came and went it became clear that one of the most serious problems, apart from economic and financial difficulties, was the widening division between right and left; at times this became so bitter that France seemed on the verge of civil war. When Hitler came to power in Germany (January 1933) France was in no state to make a decisive anti-Nazi stand, and when war came in 1939 she scarcely managed to present a united front. When the Germans invaded in May 1940 everything went wrong for the French: within six weeks they had been defeated and the Third Republic was at an end.

5.1 WHAT WERE THE PROBLEMS FACING FRENCH GOVERNMENTS AND WITH WHAT SUCCESS DID THEY ATTEMPT TO SOLVE THEM?

(a) The impossibility of one political party ever winning an overall majority was one basic problem left over from before the war. The right-wing or conservative groups included representatives of industry and banking, Roman Catholics, royalists, and later, fascists; slightly left-of-centre were the radical-socialists who were not actually socialists at all, but represented, as Shirer puts it, the 'solid, middle-of-the-road, small-town bourgeoisie and well-off peasantry.' On the left were the socialists and, from 1920, the communists. *All governments were unstable coalitions*, because both right and left depended on support from the radical-socialists, whose policies unfortunately were rather vague. They were against drastic changes, since being the party of small farmers, small factory owners and small shopkeepers, they were quite happy for the economy to stay as it was – backward. According to Cobban, 'they believed in reducing government to a minimum, which was a recipe for failure at a time when political and social problems were urgently demanding positive action.' Yet this party was able to bring down the *Cartel des Gauches* in 1926 by withdrawing support, and then, having switched sides, to set up a right-wing coalition; in 1938 they ruined the *Front Populaire* when they grew tired of co-operating with the communists. Thus with the exception of Poincaré's ministry (1926–9) French governments tended not to be in power long enough to pursue successful policies.

(b) France was still economically backward in a number of ways:

(i) There was the old problem of the population expanding more slowly than in any other state in Europe. By 1939 the total population was still only about what it had been in 1913 (40 million compared with at least 80 million Germans).

(ii) Agriculture remained backward because the smallness of most farms made it impossible to introduce mass production methods. The government's protective tariffs kept agricultural prices high (in 1939 the price of wheat was three times higher than in Britain), which removed the incentive to modernise, and kept the cost of living much higher than it needed to be. Yet no government would interfere because of the risk of losing the farmers' votes.

(iii) Industrial production lagged well behind that of the other industrial states, again because of the smallness of factories and workshops and also because of the damage suffered to industrial areas during the war. But there were some signs of progress in industry: when factories were rebuilt new modern equipment could be installed, and government investment encouraged modernisation in the metallurgical, engineering and chemical industries. The most impressive development was the rapid expansion of the motor car industry in firms such as Renault, Citroën and Peugeot.

(c) **There were constant financial problems which caused the value of the franc to fall and prices to rise** (inflation). The causes were:

  (i) Massive borrowing had taken place to finance the war effort and the reconstruction after the war, and these debts now had to be repaid.
 (ii) The government was relying on German reparations payments to enable some of their debts to be paid off; unfortunately the Germans paid very little, and the French attempt to force them by occupying the Ruhr (1923) failed; nor was the Dawes Plan (1924) helpful to France, saying in effect that Germany need pay only what she could afford until she had recovered.
(iii) The situation was always more unstable when a left-wing government was in power, because big business tried to discredit them by withdrawing capital from the economy and investing it abroad, causing a shortage of capital, and a fall in the value of the franc. Between May 1924 and July 1926 when the *Cartel des Gauches* was in power, the franc fell from 70 to 250 to the pound. When the Bank of France refused to make any further loans to the Treasury, confidence in the government was so shaken that it had to resign. In fact, however, there was no real shortage of money in the country; it was simply that people with money to invest, including small property-owners, chose not to invest it because they were suspicious of what a socialist-dominated government might do with their money. When the right-wing Poincaré took over with special powers to ignore parliament and rule by decree, confidence was immediately restored and the franc began to recover almost before he had taken any action.

(d) **The world economic crisis had unfortunate effects on France.** Although this began in 1929, the worst effects reached France only in 1933. As exports of French luxury goods fell sharply, unemployment rose, standing at 1.3 million by the summer of that year. To make matters worse, although Germany paid no more reparations after 1931, the Americans demanded that France should continue to repay her war debts to the USA. It was unfortunate for the left that they had just won the elections of 1932, for they seemed totally incapable of dealing with the problems. One measure which might have helped was the devaluation of the franc, making French goods cheaper abroad and possibly boosting exports; but there was so much opposition to this from the capitalist classes that it was out of the question. No decisive action was taken beyond reducing civil servants' salaries by 6 per cent in order to cut government expenditure. No fewer than six different left-wing cabinets came and went between May 1932 and February 1934, as the socialists and radicals squabbled over what to do next.

(e) **There was a lack of first-rate politicians.** By the early 1930s all the strong men of French politics such as Clemenceau and Briand were dead;

even Poincaré, the saviour in 1926, had retired in 1929. Herriot and Daladier, the leading men of the 1930s, were shrewd and competent but somehow, as Cobban puts it, 'they lacked a cutting edge', while the socialist leader Blum, perhaps the most able of all, was in power for only just over a year, and being a Jew had to endure the most shameful verbal and physical attacks in the growing atmosphere of anti-Semitism.

(f) As the republic showed itself more and more incapable of decisive action, there was a corresponding **growth of left- and right-wing extremists** who believed that something much more authoritarian than the democratic republic functioning through parliament was needed. *On the left the communists* drew support from workers disillusioned with their lot – long hours, fall in real wages, and lack of any effective bargaining power through trade unions. *The right-wing extremists formed themselves into leagues* such as *Action Française* which wanted to restore the monarchy, *Solidarité Française* (founded by François Coty, the millionaire perfume manufacturer) and *Croix de Feu* which were both in favour of some sort of fascist government like the one in Italy. Often anti-Semitic in character, like the German Nazis, the leagues drew support from business and professional classes, and from property-owners – even quite modest businessmen and shopkeepers – who thought their property was threatened by the communists. These groups combined in an attack on parliament on the evening of 6 February 1934, but were beaten off by police and

illus 5.1   *Street fighting during a demonstration in Paris, 1934*

mounted guards. Historians disagree about whether the leagues actually hoped to seize power (as the communists believed) or whether they were simply trying to topple Daladier's government (which they succeeded in doing), but it was an unpleasant incident, 15 people being killed and over 300 injured. Shortly before the 1936 elections Blum was beaten up and almost killed in the street by *Action Francaise* members. The rift between left and right was widening bitterly.

All the problems and weaknesses which plagued the republic were demonstrated in 1936–8 during the unfortunate *Front Populaire* government. It was hailed as the dawn of a new era, a united front of radicals and socialists, supported for the first time by the communists (acting under orders from Moscow in order to put up a strong anti-fascist front). It began well with Blum persuading employers to make concessions (*the Matignon agreement*); these included wage increases averaging 11 per cent, a 40-hour week, an annual 2-weeks holiday with pay and the right of trade unions to negotiate on behalf of the workers; to stimulate exports, the franc was devalued by 25 per cent. Then things began to go wrong: businessmen, still suspicious of the left, preferred to invest abroad, reserves dwindled, the franc dropped in value and inflation ruined the benefit of the wage increases; unemployment persisted at well over a million and there were massive strikes during 1936 and on into 1937 which the right claimed were communist-inspired. The leagues, supported by most of the daily papers, viciously attacked parliament and Blum in particular because he was Jewish; slogans such as 'better Hitler than Blum' were commonplace. Thus when it came to dealing with the problems of foreign affairs and the deteriorating international situation (see Section 14), France was so bitterly divided that no decisive action could be taken. In April 1938 Blum was brought down when the senate threw out his proposal to halt the continual drift of capital out of the country. Some of the *Front Populaire*'s achievements survived, but most of France's major problems remained unsolved on the eve of the Second World War.

5.2 WHY DID FRANCE COLLAPSE SO RAPIDLY IN 1940?

(a) The weaknesses explained in the previous section meant that **France was economically and psychologically unprepared for war**. Bitterly divided between right and left the French public at least agreed on one thing: they did not want another war. The right was fascist in sympathy and favoured an agreement with Hitler, the destruction of the weak Third Republic and its replacement by a strong semi-fascist regime on the German model. Following the non-aggression pact between Germany and Russia (see Section 14.5(b)), the communists were against the war, and ironically criticised Daladier's government as 'fascist' when it arrested many communist deputies.

(b) French morale was damaged by Hitler's subtle tactics in not invading France until May 1940, seven months after the war began which, according to Bury, 'soon had a disintegrating effect' on the French. He argues that the best thing that could have happened for the French would have been a massive German attack in 1939; only that could have produced the same spirit of national unity which had triumphed in 1914. The long period of inaction allowed time for a peace party to develop on the right, headed by Laval, who argued that there was no point in continuing the war now that Poland, whom they were supposed to be helping, had been defeated. The communists lost no opportunity to undermine the morale of the troops; both extremes urged a deal with Hitler, which made it difficult for Daladier to resist when Hitler put out peace feelers.

(c) **There were serious military weaknesses** which hampered the French from the beginning, even though the initial mobilisation went smoothly:

 (i) She was deprived of the advantage of Germany facing war on two fronts, which had been vitally important in the years 1914-17; but Poland succumbed so swiftly in 1939 that France had to face the full weight of an undivided German offensive in 1940.
 (ii) The French High Command was obsessed with the idea of defence and intended to sit tight behind the *Maginot Line*, a line of defences stretching from the Swiss to the Belgian frontiers. Unfortunately the Maginot Line did not continue along the frontier between France and Belgium, partly because that might have offended the Belgians and because Pétain believed the Ardennes would be a sufficient barrier; but this was exactly where the Germans broke through.
 (iii) Although France had as many tanks and armoured vehicles as Germany, the generals had ignored advice from experts such as Charles de Gaulle that all vehicles should be concentrated in completely mechanised units allowing greater speed, instead of being split up so many to an infantry division which slowed them to the speed of marching infantry. On the other hand the Germans had self-contained armoured divisions supported by combat planes, another area neglected by the French.

(d) **The French generals**, including the Commander-in-Chief, Gamelin, **made fatal mistakes**:

 (i) No attempt was made to help Poland by attacking Germany in the west, though military experts believe that such an attack in early September 1939 would have had an excellent chance of success.
 (ii) They failed to act quickly enough when the Germans broke through at Sedan on the Meuse (13 May 1940). Troops should have been moved from Belgium and from the Maginot Line forts (most of which were completely inactive). But Gamelin did neither, and German motorised divisions moved across France with incredible speed, forming the southern arm of an enormous pincer movement, sweeping up towards the Belgian coast to encircle close on half a million French, Belgian and British troops at Dunkirk (4 June). Although a brilliant evacuation was conducted saving 330,000 Allied troops, vast amounts of equipment were lost; it was a disastrous defeat for France.

(e) Meanwhile, as other German divisions advanced rapidly on Rouen and Paris, **organisational problems contributed to the collapse**; there was poor communication between army and air force, so that air defence to drive German bombers off usually failed to arrive; movement of reinforcements was far too slow; relations with their British ally were far from good, the French being convinced that Britain could have done more to help.

(f) Military defeats gave the fascist defeatist elements which had opposed the war from the beginning **the chance to come out into the open**. Tremendous pressure was brought on the Prime Minister, Paul Reynaud, by Laval and by the socialist and communist pacifists to ask for an armistice. Reynaud was a fighter and was determined to continue the struggle even if it meant withdrawing the government to North Africa. However, when even General Weygand, the new Commander-in-Chief, and the 84-year-old Marshal Pétain, hero of Verdun in 1916, urged peace, Reynaud resigned. Pétain became Prime Minister and on 22 June an armistice was signed, in the same railway coach at Compiègne in which the Germans had signed their armistice in 1918. The right felt that military defeat was a reasonable price to pay for the destruction of the hated Third Republic.

QUESTIONS

1. Describe the main internal problems facing French governments between 1919 and 1939. How do you account for the rapid collapse of France in 1940?
2. How and with what success did French governments attempt to solve France's internal problems between 1919 and 1939?
3. How did the Third Republic come to an end in France in 1940? What reasons may be put forward to explain it?
4. Explain the diminishing popularity of the Third French Republic after 1919.

CHAPTER 6

ITALY 1918-45:
THE FIRST APPEARANCE
OF FASCISM

SUMMARY OF EVENTS

The new state of Italy was far from being a great success in the years before 1914; the strain of the First World War on her precarious economy and the bitter disappointment at her treatment by the Versailles treaties caused growing discontent. Between 1919 and 1922 there were five different governments, all of which were incapable of taking the decisive action that the situation demanded. *In 1919 Benito Mussolini founded the Italian fascist party* which won 35 seats in the 1921 elections. At the same time there seemed to be a real danger of a left-wing seizure of power; in an atmosphere of strikes and riots, *the fascists staged a 'march on Rome'* which culminated in King Victor Emmanuel III *inviting Mussolini to form a government* (October 1922); he remained in effective power until July 1943. Gradually Mussolini took on the powers of a dictator and attempted to control the entire way of life of the Italian people. At first it seemed as though his authoritarian regime might bring lasting benefits to Italy, and he won popularity by his adventurous and successful foreign policy (see Section 14.2). Later, however, he made the fatal mistake of entering the Second World War on the side of Germany (June 1940) even though he knew that Italy could ill-afford involvement in another war. After the Italians had suffered defeats by the British who captured her African possessions and occupied Sicily, they turned against Mussolini. He was deposed and arrested (July 1943) but rescued by the Germans in September, and set up as ruler in northern Italy backed by German troops. In April 1945, as British and American troops advanced northwards through Italy towards Milan, Mussolini tried to escape to Switzerland but was captured and shot dead by his Italian enemies (known as partisans).

6.1 WHY WAS MUSSOLINI ABLE TO COME TO POWER?

(a) There was a general atmosphere of disillusionment and frustration in Italy by the summer of 1919 caused by a combination of:

(i) *Disappointment at her gains from the peace settlement*: when she entered the war the Allies had promised her Trentino, the south Tyrol, Istria, Trieste, part of Dalmatia, Adalia, some Aegean islands, and a protectorate over Albania. Although she received the first four areas, the rest were awarded to other states, mainly Yugoslavia (Albania was to be independent). They felt cheated in view of their valiant efforts during the war and the loss of close on 700,000 men. Particularly irritating was their failure to get Fiume (given to Yugoslavia) even though it had not been promised them. Gabriele D'Annunzio, a famous romantic poet, marched with a few hundred supporters and occupied Fiume before the Yugoslavs had time to take it; he held it for 15 months and was applauded as a national hero until he was chased out by Italian government troops.

(ii) *The disastrous effect of the war on the economy and the standard of living.* The government had borrowed heavily, especially from the USA, and these debts now had to be repaid; as the lira declined in value (from 5 to the dollar in 1914 to 28 to the dollar in 1921) the cost of living increased accordingly by at least 5 times. There was massive unemployment as heavy industry cut back its wartime production levels, and 2.5 million ex-servicemen had difficulty finding jobs.

(iii) *Growing contempt for the liberal parliamentary system.* Manhood suffrage and proportional representation were introduced for the 1919 elections, but this made it difficult for any one party to gain an overall majority and coalition governments were inevitable. As a result of the election of May 1921, for example, the groups represented included the old pre-war liberals, nationalists, socialists, communists, the Catholic popular party and the fascists. No consistent policy was possible as five different cabinets with shaky majorities came and went. The general frustration among all classes led to:

(b) **A wave of strikes in 1919 and 1920** accompanied by violence, looting of shops and occupation of factories by workers. In Turin factory councils reminiscent of the Russian soviets were appearing; in the south socialist leagues of farm workers seized land from proprietors and set up co-operatives. The government's prestige sank even lower because of its failure to protect property, and many property-owners were convinced that the revolution was at hand. In fact the chances of revolution were receding as the strikes and factory occupations fizzled out (although workers in some factories tried to maintain production, claiming union control of the factories, this proved impossible without engineers and managers). But the fear of a communist revolution remained strong.

(c) **Mussolini and the fascist party were attractive to many sections of society** because, as he said himself, *he aimed to rescue Italy from feeble government.* Mussolini (born 1883), the son of a blacksmith in the Romagna, had a varied early career, working for a time as a stonemason's mate and then as a primary school teacher. Politically he was a socialist and began to make a name for himself as a journalist, becoming editor of the socialist newspaper *Avanti*. He fell out with the socialists because they were against Italian intervention in the war, and started his own paper *Il Populo d'Italia*. In 1919 he founded the fascist party with a socialist and republican programme and showed sympathy with the factory occupations of 1919–20. The local party branches were known as *fasci di combattimento* (fighting groups); the word *fasces* meant the bundle of rods with protruding axe which used to symbolise the authority and power of the Roman consuls. As the factory occupations began to fail, Mussolini altered course and came out as the defender of private enterprise and property, thus attracting much-needed financial support from wealthy business interests. Beginning in late 1920 black-shirted squads of fascists regularly attacked and burned down local socialist headquarters and newspaper offices and beat up socialist councillors. By the end of 1921, even though his political programme was vague

illus 6.1 *Mussolini addressing a crowd*

in the extreme, he had gained the support of property-owners in general, because they saw him as a guarantee of law and order (especially after the formation of the communist party in January 1921). Having won over big business Mussolini began to make conciliatory speeches about the Roman Catholic Church so that Pope Pius XI swung the Church into line behind Mussolini, seeing him as an anti-communist weapon. When Mussolini announced that he had dropped his republican ambitions (September 1922) even the king became well-disposed towards him.

(d) The anti-fascist groups failed to co-operate with each other and made no determined effort to keep the fascists out. The communists refused to co-operate with the socialists, and Giolitti (liberal Prime Minister from June 1920 to June 1921) held the elections of May 1921 so that the fascists, still unrepresented in parliament, might win some seats and then support his government. He was willing to overlook their violence in the hope that they would become more responsible once they were in parliament. However they won only 35 seats whereas the socialists had 122, so that there should have been no question of a fascist take-over, though the number of fascist squads throughout the country was increasing rapidly. The socialists must take much of the blame for refusing to work with the government to curb fascist violence, causing Giolitti to resign in despair; instead they tried to further their own ends by calling a general strike in the summer of 1922.

(e) The attempted general strike played right into the hands of the fascists who were able to use it by announcing that if the government failed to quell the strike, they would crush it themselves; when the strike failed Mussolini was able to pose as the saviour of the state from communism, by October 1922 the fascists felt confident enough to stage their march on Rome. As about 50,000 blackshirts converged on the capital while others occupied important towns in the north, the Prime Minister, *Luigi Facta*, was prepared to resist. But *King Victor Emmanuel III* refused to declare a state of emergency and instead invited Mussolini, who had remained nervously in Milan, to come to Rome and form a new government, which he obligingly did, arriving by train. Afterwards the fascists fostered the myth that they had seized power heroically, but it had been achieved legally by the mere threat of force, while the army and the police stood aside. *The role of the king was important*: he made the crucial decision not to use the army to stop the blackshirts, though many historians believe that the regular army would have had little difficulty in dispersing the disorderly and poorly armed squads, many of which arrived by train. The march was an enormous bluff which came off. The reasons why the king decided against armed resistance remain something of a mystery since he was apparently reluctant to discuss them; suggestions include lack of confidence in Facta, doubts about whether the army with its fascist sympathies could be relied on to obey orders, and illus 6.2   *Mussolini and supporters shortly after the March on Rome*

fears of a prolonged civil war if it failed to crush the fascists quickly. There is no doubt that he had a certain amount of sympathy with the fascist aim of providing strong government and was also afraid that some of the generals might force him to abdicate in favour of his cousin, the Duke of Aosta, who openly supported the fascists. Whatever his motives the outcome was clear: Mussolini became the first-ever fascist premier in history.

6.2 WHAT DID THE TERM 'FASCISM' STAND FOR?

It is important to try and define what the term 'fascist' stood for because it was later applied to other regimes and rulers such as Hitler, Franco (Spain), Salazar (Portugal) and Peron (Argentina) which were sometimes quite different from the Italian version of fascism. Nowadays there is a tendency among the left to label as 'fascist' anybody who holds right-wing views. The fact that fascism never produced a great theoretical writer who could explain its philosophies clearly in the way that Marx did for communism makes it difficult to pin down exactly what was involved. Mussolini's constantly changing aims before 1923 suggest that his main concern was to acquire power; after that he seems to have impro-vised his ideas as he went along. However after a few years it became clear that fascism as Mussolini tried to put it into practice did involve *certain basic principles*:

(a) **Extreme nationalism**: an emphasis on building up the greatness and prestige of the state, with the implication that one's own nation is superior to others.

(b) **A totalitarian system of government**, that is a complete way of life in which the government attempted to control and organise with strong discipline as many aspects of people's lives as possible. This was necessary to promote the greatness of the state, which was more important than the interests of the individual.

(c) **A one-party state was essential**; there was no place for democracy. Fascism was particularly *hostile to communism*, which accounts for much of its popularity. The fascist party members were the élite of the nation and great emphasis was placed on the cult of the leader/hero who would win mass support with thrilling speeches and skilful propaganda.

(d) **Economic self-sufficiency** (autarchy) was vitally important in developing the greatness of the state; the government must therefore direct the economic life of the country (though not in the Marxist sense of the government owning factories and land).

(e) **Military strength and violence** were an integral part of the way of life. Mussolini himself remarked, 'Peace is absurd: fascism does not believe in it.' Hence they fostered the myth that they had seized power by revolution, they allowed the violent treatment of opponents and critics, and pursued an aggressive foreign policy.

6.3 MUSSOLINI INTRODUCES THE FASCIST STATE

There was no sudden change in the system of government and state institutions; Mussolini was merely the Prime Minister of a coalition cabinet in which only four out of twelve ministers were fascists and he had to move cautiously. Beginning in the summer of 1924 by a mixture of violence and intimidation and aided by hopeless divisions among his opponents, he gradually developed Italian government and society along fascist lines, and at the same time consolidated his own hold over the country. By 1930:

(a) **All parties except the fascists were suppressed.** Persistent opponents of the regime were either exiled or murdered, the most notorious cases being those of the socialists Giacomo Matteotti and Giovanni Amendola, both of whom were beaten to death by fascist thugs. However, the Italian system was never as brutal as the Nazi regime in Germany, and after 1926 when Mussolini felt more secure, violence was much reduced. Although parliament still met, all important decisions were taken by the fascist Grand Council which always did as Mussolini told it; in effect Mussolini, who adopted the title *Il Duce* (the leader), was the dictator.

(b) In local government elected town councils and mayors were abolished and towns run by officials appointed from Rome. In practice the local fascist party bosses, known as *ras*, often had as much power as the government officials.

(c) A strict press censorship was enforced in which anti-fascist newspaper were either suppressed or their editors replaced by fascist supporters. Radio, films and the theatre were similarly controlled.

(d) Education in schools and universities was closely supervised, teachers had to wear uniforms, and new textbooks were written to glorify the fascist system. Children were encouraged to criticise teachers who seemed to lack enthusiasm for the party. Children and young people were forced to join the government youth organisations which indoctrinated them with the brilliance of the *Duce* and the glories of war.

(e) The government tried to promote **co-operation between employers and workers** and to end class warfare in what was known as the *Corporate State*. Fascist-controlled unions had the sole right to negotiate for the workers and both unions and employers' associations were organised into *corporations* and were expected to co-operate to settle disputes over pay and working conditions. Strikes and lockouts were not allowed. By 1934 there were 22 corporations each dealing with a separate industry, and in this way Mussolini hoped to control the workers and direct production. To compensate for their loss of freedom, workers were assured of such benefits as free Sundays, annual holidays with pay, social security, sports and theatre facilities and cheap tours and holidays.

(f) An understanding was reached with the pope by the Lateran Treaty (1929). The Papacy had been hostile to the Italian government since 1870 and, though sympathetic towards Mussolini in 1922, Pope Pius XI disapproved of the increasing totalitarianism of fascist government (the fascist youth organisations for example clashed with the Catholic scouts). Mussolini, though something of an atheist himself, was well aware of the power of the Roman Catholic Church, and put himself out to win over Pius XI who, as the *Duce* well knew, was obsessed with the fear of communism. The result was the Lateran Treaty by which Italy recognised the Vatican City as a sovereign state, paid the pope a large sum of money as compensation for all his losses, accepted the Catholic faith as the official state religion and made religious instruction compulsory in all schools. In return the Papacy recognised the kingdom of Italy. Some historians see the ending of the long breach between church and state as Mussolini's most lasting and worthwhile achievement.

How totalitarian was Mussolini's system?
It seems clear that in spite of his efforts Mussolini did not succeed in creating a completely totalitarian state in the fascist sense of there being 'no individuals or groups not controlled by the state', nor like the Nazis

did in Germany. He never completely eliminated the influence of the king or the pope, and the latter became highly critical of Mussolini when he began to persecute Jews in the late 1930s. The historian, Benedetto Croce, and other university professors were constant critics of fascism and yet they survived, apparently because Mussolini was afraid of hostile foreign reaction if he had them arrested. Even fascist sympathisers admitted that the corporative system was not a success in controlling production. According to Elizabeth Wiskemann, 'on the whole the big industrialists only made gestures of submission and in fact bought their freedom from the fascist state by generous subscriptions to fascist party funds.' As far as the mass of the population was concerned, it seems that they were prepared to tolerate fascism while it appeared to bring benefits, but soon grew tired of it when its inadequacies were revealed by its failures during the Second World War.

6.4 WHAT BENEFITS DID FASCISM BRING FOR THE ITALIAN PEOPLE?

The acid test of any regime is not whether it was fully totalitarian but whether its policies were effective. Did Mussolini rescue Italy from weak government as he had promised, or was he, as some of his critics alleged at the time, just a windbag whose government was as corrupt and inefficient as previous ones?

(a) A promising beginning
Though cautious at first, he was determined and quite decisive in setting up fascist institutions, even though his efforts were not wholly successful. Policies carried out with the new machinery of state were:

 (i) He encouraged industry with government subsidies where necessary, so that iron and steel production doubled by 1930 and artificial silk production increased tenfold. By 1937 production of hydro-electric power had doubled.
 (ii) The 'Battle of Wheat' encouraged farmers to concentrate on wheat production as part of the drive for self-sufficiency; by 1935 wheat imports had been cut by 75 per cent.
(iii) A programme of land reclamation was launched involving the draining of marshes, irrigation and afforestation of mountains, again as part of the drive to improve and increase agricultural yield. The great show-piece was the reclaimed Pontine Marshes near Rome.
(iv) An impressive public works programme was designed, among other things, to reduce unemployment. It included the building of motor-ways, bridges, blocks of flats, railway stations, sports stadiums, schools and new towns on reclaimed land; a start was made on electrifying main railway lines.
 (v) To promote the image of Italy as a great power a virile foreign policy was carried out (see Section 14.2).

(b) Unsolved problems

Even before Italy became involved in the Second World War it was clear that Mussolini had not solved her problems.

(i) Little had been done to remedy her basic shortages of raw materials – coal and oil – whereas much more effort could have been made to develop hydro-electric power. As an iron and steel producer Italy was not in the same league even as France. Although the 'Battle of Wheat' was a victory, it was achieved only at the expense of dairy and animal farming whose output fell; the climate in the south is much better suited to grazing and orchards than growing wheat and this would have been much more lucrative for the farmers. As a result agriculture remained inefficient and farm labourers the poorest class in the state. The attempt at self-sufficiency was a dismal failure.

(ii) Mussolini revalued the lira far too high at 90 to the pound instead of 150 (1926) in an attempt to show that Italy had a strong currency. Unfortunately this made exports more expensive on the world market and led to reduced orders especially in the cotton industry. Many factories were on a three-day week and workers suffered wage reductions of between 10 and 20 per cent – before the world economic crisis.

(iii) The great depression beginning in 1929 with the Wall Street Crash (see Section 7.2) worsened matters. Exports fell further, unemployment rose to 1.1 million, and yet the *Duce* refused to devalue the lira until 1936. Instead wages and salaries were cut, and although the cost of living was falling because of the depression, wages fell more than prices, so that workers suffered a fall in real wages. Particularly galling for industrial workers was that they had no means of protesting since strikes were illegal and the unions weak.

(iv) Another failing of the regime was in the area of social services, where there was nothing approaching a 'welfare state'. There was no official government health insurance until 1943 and only an inadequate unemployment insurance, which was not improved even during the depression.

(v) The fascist regime was inefficient and corrupt so that many of its policies were not fully carried out. For example, in spite of all the publicity about the land reclamation, only about one-tenth of the programme had been carried out by 1939 and work was at a standstill even before the Second World War began. Immense sums of money disappeared into the pockets of corrupt officials.

The conclusion must be therefore that the average Italian can have felt little benefit from the regime and disenchantment had probably set in by the end of 1937. When Mussolini began to discriminate against Jews in 1938 by sacking them from important jobs, many Italians disapproved because they felt he was being dragged along by Hitler and they resented Italy's becoming a German satellite. The Italian entry into the war was disastrous for Mussolini both because the majority of Italians were against the idea and because defeats soon showed up the superficialities of his entire system and the country's economic weaknesses; there were high prices, food shortages and, after November 1942, bombing raids on major cities. By July 1943 many of the fascist leaders themselves realised the lunacy of trying to continue the war. The king was called on to dismiss Mussolini and nobody lifted a finger to save him. Fascism disappeared and most of its work along with it; the only achievements remaining at the end of the war were the agreement with the Church and the public works, and even they, as Elizabeth Wiskemann suggests, could just as well have been achieved by a democratic government.

QUESTIONS

1. How do you explain the successful outcome of Mussolini's bid for power in 1922? Describe and explain the steps by which he created a fascist state in Italy.

2. Explain the reasons for (a) the rise and (b) the fall of Mussolini.

3. What is meant by the term 'fascism'? What aspects of Mussolini's domestic policies can de described as 'fascist'?

4. How did fascism affect the lives of the Italian people between 1922 and 1940?

5. 'It was the aim of Mussolini to rescue Italy from feeble government.' Illustrate the truth of this statement. In what ways was his government any less feeble than previous ones?

6. 'Had Mussolini died before his attack on Abyssinia (1935), the history books would have mourned the loss of a great statesman and leader.' Give reasons for agreeing or disagreeing with this statement.

7. 'In fact fascist Italy was corrupt and inefficient and Mussolini was a windbag who achieved little except to remain in power for 20 years.' Is this a fair verdict on Mussolini's domestic policies?

CHAPTER 7

THE USA AND THE WORLD ECONOMIC CRISIS

SUMMARY OF EVENTS

The USA has a federal system of government with each state having its own legislature for internal affairs, while the Federal Congress in Washington looks after foreign affairs, defence, and matters of war and peace. Congress consists of the Senate and the House of Representatives; its function is to make the laws. The President is elected for four years. There are two main parties, Republicans and Democrats, both of which contain people of widely differing views. The *Republicans* have mostly been the party of the north, supported by big business, and have tended to be the more conservative of the two; the *Democrats* have been able to rely on support from the south and from immigrants, and have tended to be more progressive in home affairs than the Republicans.

When the First World War ended, *Woodrow Wilson* (Democrat) was still President and remained so until the end of 1920, though after a stroke early in October 1919, he was an invalid. He had worn himself out at the Versailles conference and on an exhausting speaking tour of the USA trying to persuade the American people to accept Versailles and the League of Nations. The ailing President suffered two bitter blows in 1920: in March the Senate rejected the Versailles treaties and the League, and in the November presidential election the Democrat candidate, James M. Cox, was easily defeated by the Republican Warren Harding. Wilson died a disappointed man in February 1924.

Following Wilson came three Republican Presidents: *Harding* (1921-3), who died in office, *Calvin Coolidge* (1923-9) and *Herbert C. Hoover* (1929-33). Until 1929 the country enjoyed a period of great prosperity, though not everybody shared in it; the boom ended suddenly with the *Wall Street Crash* (October 1929), which led to the *great depression* or *world economic crisis* only six months after the unfortunate Hoover's inauguration. The effects on the USA were catastrophic: by 1933 almost 14 million were out of work and Hoover's attempts to end the depression failed. Not surprisingly the Republicans lost the elections of November 1932; the new Democrat President, *Franklin D. Roosevelt*, set about solving the problems energetically. Whereas the Republican Presidents had followed a policy of *laissez-faire* (allowing private individuals to run industry with as little government regulation and direction as possible), Roosevelt took the view that the seriousness of the crisis called for a large measure of government direction to put the country on the road to recovery. His policy was known as *the New Deal*. Though not entirely successful, the New Deal achieved enough, together with the circumstances of the Second World War, to keep Roosevelt in the White House until his death in April 1945. He was the only President to be elected for a fourth term.

7.1 THE GREAT BOOM OF THE 1920s

After a slow start as the country returned to normal after the war, the economy began to expand again: industrial production increased to unprecedented levels, and so did sales, profits and wages. There was a great variety of new things to be bought – radio sets, refrigerators, washing machines, vacuum cleaners, smart new clothes, motorcycles and, above all, motorcars; at the end of the war there were already 7 million cars in the USA, but by 1929 there were close on 24 million; Henry Ford led the field with his Model T. Perhaps the most famous of all the new luxuries was the Hollywood film industry which made huge profits and exported its products all over the world.

(a) What caused the boom?

(i) In a sense it was the climax of the great industrial expansion of the late nineteenth century when the USA had overtaken her two greatest rivals Germany and Britain. The war gave American industry an enormous boost: countries whose industries and imports from Europe had been disrupted bought American goods, and continued to do so when the war was over. The USA was therefore the real economic victor of the war.

(ii) The Republican governments' economic policies contributed to the prosperity in the short term. Their approach was one of *laissez-faire*, but there were two significant actions: the Fordney–McCumber tariff (1922) raised import duties on goods coming into America to the highest level ever, thus protecting American industry and encouraging Americans to buy home-produced goods; a general lowering of income tax rates in 1926 and 1928 left people with more cash to spend on such goods.

(iii) As profits increased so did wages (though by nothing like so much); between 1923 and 1929 the average wage for industrial workers rose by 8 per cent. Though this was not spectacular it was enough to enable some workers to buy, often on credit, the new consumer luxuries, encouraged by the vast development of advertising and radio commercials. Mechanisation, especially the moving assembly line, helped to increase productivity and satisfy demand.

(iv) The motorcar itself stimulated expansion in a number of allied industries – road-building, tyres, batteries, petroleum for petrol, garages and tourism.

(b) Problems behind the prosperity

Perceptive observers realised that although the boom was impressive, there were at the same time some less pleasant features; but in the heady optimism of the 1920s the majority could afford to ignore such tiresome details as these:

(i) Farmers were not sharing in the general prosperity. They had done well during the war, but during the 1920s prices of farm produce gradually fell; farmers' profits dwindled and farm labourers' wages in the middle west and the agricultural south were often less than half those of industrial workers in the north-east. The cause of the trouble was simple – farmers with their new combine harvesters were producing too much food, more than the home market would take; this was at a time when European agriculture was recovering from the war and when there was strong competition from Canada, Russia and Argentina on the world market, so that not enough could be exported. The government with its *laissez-faire* outlook did little to help; even when Congress passed the McNary–Haugen Bill, by which the government would have bought up farmers' surplus crops, Coolidge twice vetoed it (1927 and 1928) on the grounds that it might encourage farmers to increase production and thus worsen the problem.

(ii) *The black population was left out of the prosperity.* In the south where the majority of Negroes lived, white farmers always laid off black labourers first; about three-quarters of a million moved north during the 1920s looking for jobs in industry, but they almost always had to make do with the lowest paid jobs, worst conditions at work and slum housing. They also had to suffer the persecutions of *the Ku Klux Klan*, the notorious white-hooded anti-Negro society which had about five million members in 1924. Assaults, whippings and lynchings were common, and although the Klan gradually declined after 1925, prejudice and discrimination against the Negro and against other coloured and minority groups still remained.

(iii) *There was an increase in gang violence and crime* partly because of *Prohibition* (the banning of the manufacture, import and sale of all alcoholic liquor, introduced in 1919). This was the result of the efforts of a well-meaning pressure group during the First World War which believed that a 'dry' America would mean a more efficient and moral America. But it proved impossible to eliminate bootleggers (manufacturers of illegal liquor), who protected their premises from rivals with hired gangs who shot each other up in gunfights. Gangsters became part of the American scene, especially in Chicago where Al Capone made himself a fortune, much of it from bootlegging. In 1933 the government admitted failure by aband-

oning Prohibition and thereafter the crime rate declined since bootlegging was no longer necessary.

(iv) *Industry became increasingly monopolised by large trusts or super-
corporations*, so much so that by 1929 the wealthiest 5 per cent of
corporations took over 84 per cent of the total corporation income.
Although trusts increased efficiency there is no doubt that they
kept wages lower and prices higher than was necessary; they were
able to keep the trade unions weak by forbidding workers to join.
Again the Republicans, pro-business and *laissez-faire*, did nothing
to limit the growth of the super-corporation because the system
seemed to be working well. Unfortunately prosperity based on those
foundations could not last: 'America the Golden' was about to
suffer a profound shock.

7.2 THE GREAT DEPRESSSION ARRIVES : OCTOBER 1929

In September 1929 the buying of shares at *the Stock Exchange in Wall
Street, New York*, began to slow down, and as rumours spread that the
boom might be over, people rushed to sell their shares before prices
fell too far. By 24 October the rush to sell reached panic proportions
and share prices fell dramatically; thousands who had bought their shares
when prices were high were ruined. This disaster is always remembered
as *the Wall Street Crash*. Its effects spread rapidly; so many people in
financial difficulties rushed to the banks to draw out their savings that
thousands of banks had to close; as demand for goods fell away, factories
had to close and unemployment rose alarmingly. The great boom had
suddenly turned into the great depression which rapidly affected not
only the USA but also foreign countries all over the world, so that it
became known as *the world economic crisis*. However, the Wall Street
Crash did not cause the depression; it was just a symptom of a problem
whose real causes lay much deeper.

(a) What caused the great depression?

(i) American industrialists, encouraged by high profits and aided by
increased mechanisation, were producing too many goods for the
home market to absorb (in the same way as American farmers).
This was not apparent in the early 1920s, but as the 1930s approached
unsold stocks of goods began to build up, and manufacturers produced less; since fewer workers were required, men were laid off;
and as there was no unemployment benefit, these men and their
families bought less. And so the vicious circle continued.

(ii) There was a maldistribution of income which means that the enormous
profits made by industrialists were not being shared evenly enough
among the workers. The average wage for industrial workers rose
by about 8 per cent between 1923 and 1929 but during the same

period industrial profits increased by 72 per cent. An 8 per cent increase in wages meant that there was not enough buying power in the hands of the general public to sustain the boom: they could manage to absorb production for a time with the help of credit but by 1929 they were fast approaching the limit. Unfortunately manufacturers, usually in the form of the super-corporation, were not prepared to reduce prices or to increase wages substantially, and so the glut of consumer goods built up. This refusal by the manufacturers to compromise was shortsighted to say the least; at the beginning of 1929 there were still millions of Americans who had no radio, no electric washer and no car because they could not afford them. If employers had been content with rather less profit there is no reason why the boom could not have continued for several more years while its benefits were more widely shared. Even so, a slump was still not inevitable provided the Americans could export their surplus products. However:

(iii) Exports began to fall away, partly because foreign countries were reluctant to buy American goods when the USA herself put up tariff barriers to protect her industries from foreign imports. Thus it became clear that although the Fordney–McCumber tariff (1922) was helping to keep foreign goods out, at the same time it was preventing foreign states, especially those in Europe, from making much-needed profits from trade with the USA. Without those profits European states would be able neither to buy American goods nor to pay in full their war debts to the USA. To make matters worse many states retaliated by introducing tariffs against American goods. A slump of some sort was clearly on the way.

(iv) The situation was worsened by a great rush of speculation on the stock market which began to gather momentum about 1926. *Speculation* is the buying of shares in companies; people with cash to spare like to do this with two possible aims in mind: to get the dividened (the annual sharing-out of the company's profits, assuming that it has made any) or to make a quick profit by selling the shares again for more than they have paid for them. In the mid-1920s the second aim most attracted investors: as profits of companies increased, more people began to buy shares, thus rapidly forcing up share prices and offering plenty of chances for a quick profit from buying and selling shares. The average value of a share rose from 9 dollars in 1924 to 26 dollars in 1929; share prices of individual companies often rose spectacularly: for example the stock of the Radio Corporation of America stood at 85 dollars a share early in 1928 and had risen to 505 dollars in September 1929, and that was a company which did not pay dividends.

Promise of quick profits encouraged all sorts of rash moves: quite poor people spent their savings or borrowed money to buy a few shares; stockbrokers sold shares on credit; banks speculated in shares using the cash deposited with them. It was all something of a gamble but there was enormous confidence that prosperity would continue indefinitely. This confidence lasted well into 1929, but when the first signs appeared that sales of goods were beginning to slow down, better informed investors decided to sell their shares while prices were still high. This caused suspicion to spread – more people than usual were trying to sell shares – something must be wrong! Confidence in the future began to waver for the first time and more people decided to sell their shares while the going was good. And so a process of what economists call *self-fulfilling expectations* developed. This means that by their own actions investors actually caused the dramatic collapse of share prices which they were afraid of. By October 1929 there was a flood of people rushing to sell shares, but because confidence had been shaken, far fewer people wanted to buy; share prices tumbled and unfortunate investors had to accept whatever they could get; one particularly bad day was 24 October – Black Thursday – when nearly 13 million shares were 'dumped' on the stock market at depressingly low prices. By mid-1930 share prices were down to about 25 per cent of the peak level, and even after that they continued to fall, reaching rock bottom in 1932. By then the whole of the USA was in the grip of depression.

(b) How did the depression affect people?

(i) To begin with, the stock market crash ruined millions of investors who had paid high prices for their shares. If investors had bought shares on credit with borrowed money, as millions had, their creditors lost heavily too, since they had no hope of receiving payment.

(ii) Banks were in a shaky position, having themselves speculated unsuccessfully; when, added to this, millions rushed to withdraw their savings in the belief that the cash would be safer at home, many banks were overwhelmed and had to close down for good. There were over 25,000 banks in the country in 1929, but by 1933 there were fewer than 15,000, which meant that lots of ordinary people who had had nothing to do with the speculation were ruined as their life savings disappeared.

(iii) As demand for goods of all types fell away, men were laid off and factories closed. Industrial production in 1933 was only half the 1929 total, while unemployment stood at around 14 million: about a quarter of the total workforce was without jobs, and one in eight farmers lost all their property. There was drop in living standards, with bread queues, charity soup kitchens, evictions when tenants could not afford the rent, and near starvation for many; the 'great American dream' of prosperity for all had turned into a nightmare. In the words of Donald McCoy, 'the American people were affected as though a war had been fought from coast to coast.' And there were no unemployment and sickness benefits to help out.

(iv) Many states outside the USA, especially Germany, were also affected illus 7.1 *A soup kitchen for down-and-outs*

because their prosperity depended to a large extent on loans from America. As soon as the crash came there were no further loans, and the Americans called in the short-term loans they had already made; by 1931 most of Europe was in a similar economic plight. The depression had political results too, for in many states, including Germany, Austria, Japan and Britain, right-wing governments came to power when the existing regimes failed to cope with the situation.

(c) Who was to blame for the disaster?

At the time it was fashionable to blame the unfortunate President Hoover, but this is unfair: the origins of the trouble obviously go much further back, and the Republican party as a whole must share the blame. There were several measures the government could have taken to control the situation: encouraging big business to lower prices and substantially increase wages; encouraging foreign countries to buy more American goods by lowering American tariffs instead of raising them, and it should have taken decisive action in 1928 and 1929 to limit the amount of credit which the stock market was allowing speculators. But their *laissez-faire* approach would allow no such interference with private affairs.

(d) What did Hoover's government do to ease the depression?

Hoover tried to solve the problem by encouraging employers not to reduce wages and lay off workers, by lending money to banks, industrialists and farmers to save them from bankruptcy, by beginning work schemes to relieve unemployment and in 1931 declaring a one-year moratorium on war debts (foreign governments could miss one instalment of their debts to the USA) to encourage them to import more American goods. This came too late to have much effect – American exports in 1932 were less than a third of the 1929 figure. Altogether Hoover's policies made little impact on the depression. Even in a crisis as serious as this one he was against relief payments to individuals because he believed in self-reliance and 'rugged individualism'. It was no surprise when the Democrat Franklin D. Roosevelt, the governor of New York, easily beat Hoover in the presidential election of November 1932.

7.3 ROOSEVELT AND THE NEW DEAL

The 51-year-old Roosevelt came from a wealthy New York family; educated at Harvard, he entered politics in 1910 and was Assistant Secretary to the Navy during the First World War. It seemed as though his career might be over when at the age of 40 he was stricken with polio (1921), which left his legs completely paralysed. With tremendous determination he overcame his disability, though he was never able to walk unaided; and now he brought the same determination to bear in his attempts to drag America out of the depression. He was dynamic, full of vitality and brimming with new ideas; he was a brilliant communicator – his radio talks (which he called his fireside chats) inspired confidence and won him great popularity. During the election campaign he had said, 'I pledge you, I pledge myself, to a new deal for the American people', and he kept his word. The phrase stuck and his policies have always been remembered as the New Deal.

(a) What were the aims of the New Deal?

Basically Roosevelt had three aims: *relief* (to give direct help to the poverty-stricken millions without food and homes); *recovery* to reduce unemployment, stimulate demand for goods and get the economy moving again); and *reform* (to prevent a repeat of the economic disaster). It was obvious that drastic measures were needed and Roosevelt's methods were a complete change from those of the *laissez-faire* Republicans – he was prepared to interfere as much as possible and to spend government cash to pull the country out of the depression, a step the Republicans were reluctant to take.

illus 7.2   *The winner and the loser. Franklin D. Roosevelt waves acknow-
ledgement to the cheering crowds, while defeated candidate
Herbert Hoover looks downcast during their ride through
Washington in March 1933*

(b) What did the New Deal involve and how successful was it?
The measures that go to make up the New Deal were strung out over
the years 1933 to 1940.

(i) It was important to get *the banking and financial system* working
properly again; this was achieved by the government taking over
the banks temporarily and guaranteeing that depositors would
not lose their cash if there was another financial crisis. This restored
confidence and money began to flow into the banks again. *The
Securities Exchange Commission* (1934) reformed the stock exchange
and, among other things, insisted that buyers of shares on credit must
make a down-payment of at least 50 per cent instead of only 10 per
cent.

(ii) *The Farmers' Relief Act* (1933) tried to help farmers, whose main
problem was that they were still producing too much, thereby
keeping prices and profits low. Under the act the government
paid compensation to farmers who reduced output, thereby raising
prices. This had some success - by 1937 the average income of
farmers had almost doubled.

(iii) *The Civilian Conservation Corps* (CCC) was a popular Roosevelt idea to provide jobs for young men in conservation projects in the countryside. By 1940 about 2.5 million had 'enjoyed' a six-month spell in the CCC, which gave them a small wage (30 dollars a month of which 25 had to be sent home to the family) as well as food, clothing and shelter.

(iv) The most important part of the recovery programme was *the National Industrial Recovery Act* (1933) which tried to get people back to work permanently, so that they would then be able to buy more, thus stimulating industry to function more normally. The act introduced the Public Works Administration (PWA) which organised and provided cash for the building of useful works – dams, bridges, roads, schools, hospitals, airports and government buildings, providing several million extra jobs. Another section of the act set up *the National Recovery Administration* (NRA) which abolished child labour, introduced an eight-hour day and a minimum wage, and thus helped to create more employment. Although these were not compulsory employers were pressured to accept them; those who did were privileged to use an official sticker on their goods showing a blue eagle and the letters NRA, and the public was encouraged to boycott firms which refused to co-operate. The response was tremendous, with well over two million employers accepting the new standards.

(v) Further relief and recovery were provided by: *The Federal Emergency Relief Administration* which provided 500 million dollars for dole money and soup kitchens. *The Works Progress Administration* (WPA), founded in 1935, financed a variety of projects such as roads, schools and hospitals (similar to the PWA but smaller-scale projects) and also the Federal Theatre Project which provided jobs for playwrights, artists, actors, musicians and circus people, as well as increasing public appreciation of the arts. *The Social Security Act* (1935) introduced old age pensions and unemployment insurance schemes, to be jointly financed by federal and state governments, employers and workers. However, this was not a great success at the time, because payments were usually much less than generous; nor was any provision made for sickness insurance. The USA was lagging well behind countries such as Germany and Britain in social welfare.

(vi) Two acts encouraged trade unions and helped improve working conditions: *The Wagner Act* (1935), the work of Senator Robert F. Wagner of New York, gave unions a proper legal foundation and the right to bargain for their members in any dispute with management. It also set up the National Labour Relations Board to which workers could appeal against unfair practices by management. *The Fair Labour Standards Act* (1938) introduced a maximum 45-hour working week as well as a minimum wage in certain low-paid trades, and made most child labour illegal.

(vii) Also included in the New Deal were such measures as the *Tennessee Valley Authority* (TVA) which revitalised a huge area of ruined rural America by building dams to provide cheap electricity and organising conservation, irrigation and afforestation to stop soil erosion. There were loans for householders in danger of losing their homes because they could not afford mortgage repayments; slum clearance and building of new houses and flats; increased taxes on the incomes of the wealthy; trade agreements which at last reduced American tariffs in return for tariff reductions by the other party to the treaty (in the hope of increasing American exports); one of the very first measures was the end of prohibition, for as F.D.R. himself remarked, 'I think this would be a good time for beer.'

It was inevitable that such a far-reaching programme should arouse opposition; businessmen objected strongly to the growth of trade unions, the regulation of hours and wages and increased taxation; there was resentment at the extent to which the federal government was interfering with the rights of the separate states; the Supreme Court claimed that F.D.R. was assuming too much power, and ruled a good many measures (including NRA) as unconstitutional, thus holding up their operation. However, the Supreme Court grew more amenable during the President's second term after he had appointed five more co-operative judges to replace those who had died or resigned. There was also opposition from socialists who felt that the New Deal was not drastic enough and still left too much power in the hands of big business. But Roosevelt was tremendously popular with the millions of ordinary Americans, the 'forgotten men' as he called them, who had benefited from his policies, so that even though the forces of the right gathered themselves to remove him in 1936 and 1940, he won two comfortable victories.

(c) What did the New Deal achieve?

It has to be said that it did not achieve all that F.D.R. had hoped. Some of the measures failed completely or were only partly successful, such as the Farmers' Relief Act which certainly helped farmers but threw many farm labourers out of work. Although unemployment was reduced (it was down to under eight million by 1937), it was still a serious problem. Part of the failure was due to the Supreme Court's opposition; but another reason for it was that though bold in many ways, Roosevelt was too cautious in the amounts of money he was prepared to spend to stimulate industry. In 1938 he reduced government spending, causing a recession (a period when sales of industrial products fall) which sent unemployment up to 10.5 million. The New Deal therefore did not rescue the USA from the depression: it was only the war effort that brought unemployment below the million mark in 1943.

Still, in spite of this, it achieved much: in the early days its chief success was in relief for the destitute and jobless, and in the provision of millions of extra jobs; confidence was restored in the government, and some historians believe it may even have prevented a violent revolution. The public works schemes and the Tennessee Valley Authority provided services of lasting value, and much of the rest initiated long-term developments – welfare benefits, national direction of resources, collective bargaining between workers and management – which are all now accepted as normal. Never before had an American government intervened so directly in the lives of ordinary people; never before had so much attention been focused on an American president. Roosevelt's achievement was to rescue what might be termed the American middle way – democracy and free enterprise – at a time when other crisis-ridden states were going over to fascism and communism.

QUESTIONS

1. Explain the policies of the Republican Presidents of the USA from 1921 to 1933. Why was there an economic boom before October 1929?
2. Describe the economic condition of the USA in the 1920s, and contrast it with that of the 1930s.
3. 'We in America today are nearer to the final triumph over poverty than ever before in the history of any land.' What led President Hoover to make this statement in 1929? Did the events of the following three years justify his optimism?
4. What were the causes of the great American boom of the 1920s and why did it suddenly change to depression in 1929?
5. What were the causes of the great depression and what were its effects in the USA?
6. How did the treatment of the depression by the Republicans differ from that prescribed by the Democrats?
7. What was the New Deal in the USA and how successful was it?
8. What did Roosevelt do between 1933 and 1940 to reduce unemployment, help agriculture and improve the standard of living in the USA?
9. What were the achievements of Franklin D. Roosevelt as US President between 1933 and 1940?

CHAPTER 8

GERMANY 1918-39: THE WEIMAR REPUBLIC AND HITLER

SUMMARY OF EVENTS

As Germany drew towards defeat in 1918 public opinion turned against the government, and in October the *Kaiser*, in a desperate bid to hang on to power, appointed Prince Max of Baden as Chancellor. He was known to be in favour of a more democratic form of government in which parliament had more power. But it was too late: in November revolution broke out, the *Kaiser* escaped to Holland and abdicated, and Prince Max resigned. Friedrich Ebert, leader of the Social Democrat party, became head of the government. In January 1919 a general election was held, the first completely democratic one ever to take place in Germany. The Social Democrats emerged as the largest single party and Ebert became first President of the Republic. They had some Marxist ideas but believed that the way to achieve socialism was through parliamentary democracy.

However, the new government was by no means popular with all Germans: even before the election the communists had attempted to seize power (January 1919) in the Spartacist Rising. In 1920 right-wing enemies of the republic occupied Berlin (the Kapp *Putsch*). The government managed to survive these threats and several later ones, including Hitler's Munich Beer Hall *Putsch* (1923).

By the end of 1919 a new constitution had been agreed by the National Assembly (parliament), meeting at Weimar because Berlin was still torn by political unrest. This Weimar constitution (sometimes called the most perfect democracy of modern times, at least on paper) lasted until 1933 when it was destroyed by Hitler. During its short life it was extremely unstable, except for the period from the end of 1923 to the end of 1929, when Gustav Stresemann was the leading politician. Thanks to the Dawes Plan of 1924 by which the USA provided huge loans, Germany seemed to be recovering from her defeat and was enjoying an industrial boom, but this was short-lived. The world economic crisis, beginning with the Wall Street Crash in October 1929, soon had disastrous effects on Germany, producing six and a half million unemployed. The government was unable to cope with the situation and by the end of 1932 the Weimar Republic seemed on the verge of collapse.

Meanwhile Adolf Hitler and his National Socialists (Nazis) had been carrying out a great propaganda campaign blaming the government for all the ills of Germany and setting out Nazi solutions to the problems. In January 1933 President Hindenburg appointed Hitler as Chancellor, and soon afterwards Hitler saw to it that democracy ceased to exist; the Weimar Republic was at an end, and from then until April 1945, Hitler was the dictator of Germany.

8.1 WHY DID THE WEIMAR REPUBLIC COLLAPSE?

(a) It began with a number of disadvantages which hampered it right from the beginning:

(i) It had accepted the humiliating and unpopular Versailles Treaty (see Section 2.8), with its arms limitations, reparations and war guilt clause, and was thus always associated with defeat and dishonour. German nationalists could never forgive it for that.

(ii) There was a traditional lack of respect for democratic government and a great admiration for the army and the 'officer class' as the rightful leaders of Germany. In 1919 the view was widespread that the army had not been defeated: it had been betrayed – 'stabbed in the back' – by the democrats who had needlessly agreed to the Versailles Treaty. What most Germans did not realise was that it was Ludendorff who had asked for an armistice while the *Kaiser* was still in power (see Section 2.6(b)). However, the 'stab in the back' legend was eagerly fostered by all enemies of the republic.

(iii) The parliamentary system laid down in the new Weimar constitution had weaknesses, the most serious of which was that it was organised on a system of proportional representation so that all political groups would have a fair representation. Unfortunately there were so many different groups that no party could ever win an overall majority. For example in 1928 the *Reichstag* (lower house of parliament) contained at least eight groups of which the largest were the Social Democrats (153), conservatives or nationalists (78), and the Catholic Centre Party (62). The communists had 54 seats, while the smallest groups were the Bavarian People's Party (16) and the National Socialists (12). A succession of coalition governments was inevitable, with the Social Democrats having to rely on co-operation from left-wing liberals and Catholic Centre; no party was able to carry out its programme.

(iv) The political parties had very little experience of how to operate a democratic parliamentary system, because before 1919 the *Reichstag* had not actually controlled policy: the Chancellor had had the final authority. Under the Weimar constitution the Chancellor was responsible to the *Reichstag*, but it usually failed to give a clear lead because the parties refused to compromise. The communists and conservatives/nationalists did not believe in the republic anyway and refused to support the Social Democrats. Disagreements became so bitter that almost every party organised its own private army, increasing the threat of civil war. The combination of these weaknesses led on to:

(b) Outbreaks of violence which the government seemed incapable of preventing and managed to control only with great difficulty.

(i) In January 1919 occurred *the Spartacist Rising* (Spartacus was a Roman who led a revolt of slaves in 71 BC) in which the communists, inspired by the success of the Russian Revolution and led by Karl Liebknecht and Rosa Luxemburg, occupied almost every major city in Germany. In Berlin President Ebert found himself besieged in the Chancellory. The government managed to defeat the communists only because it accepted the help of the *Freikorps* (independent volunteer regiments raised by anti-communist ex-army officers). It was a sign of the government's weakness that it had to depend on forces which it did not itself control. The two communist leaders did not receive a fair trial – they were simply clubbed to death by *Freikorps* members.

(ii) *The Kapp Putsch* (March 1920) was an attempt to seize power by right-wing elements sparked off when the government tried to disband the *Freikorps*. They refused to disband and declared Dr Wolfgang Kapp Chancellor. Berlin was occupied by a *Freikorps* regiment and the cabinet fled to Dresden. The German army (the *Reichswehr*) took no action against the *Putsch* and in the end the workers of Berlin came to the aid of the Social Democrat government by calling a general strike which paralysed the capital. Kapp resigned and the government regained control. However, it was so weak that nobody was punished except Kapp himself who was imprisoned, and it took two months to get the *Freikorps* disbanded. Even then their members remained hostile to the republic and many later joined Hitler's private armies.

(iii) A series of political assassinations took place mainly by ex-Freikorps members. Those murdered included Walter Rathenau (the Jewish Foreign Minister) and Gustav Erzberger (leader of the armistice delegation). When the government sought strong measures against such acts of terrorism, there was great opposition from the right-wing parties, who sympathised with the criminals. Whereas the communist leaders had been brutally murdered, the courts allowed right-wing offenders off lightly and the government was unable to intervene. In fact throughout Germany the legal and teaching professions and the civil service, as well as the *Reichswehr*, tended to be anti-Weimar, which was a crippling handicap for the republic.

(iv) Another threat to the government occurred in November 1923 in Bavaria, at the time when there was much public annoyance at the French occupation of the Ruhr (see Section 13.2(c)) and the disastrous fall in the value of the mark (see below). Hitler, helped by General Ludendorff, aimed to take control of the Bavarian state government in Munich and then lead a national revolution to overthrow the government in Berlin. However, police easily broke up Hitler's march and *the Beer Hall Putsch* (so called because the march set out from the Munich beer hall in which Hitler had announced his 'national revolution' the previous evening) fizzled out. Hitler was sentenced to five years imprisonment but served only nine months (which shows how sympathetic the Bavarian authorities were to his aims).

(v) The violence died down during the period 1924 to 1929, but as unemployment grew in the early 1930s *the private armies expanded* and regular street fights occurred between Nazis and communists; all parties had their political meetings broken up by rival armies. The police seemed powerless to prevent it happening.

Again, therefore, the government was shown to be incapable of keeping law and order, and respect for it dwindled. An increasing number of people began to favour a return to strong, authoritarian government, which would maintain strict public order.

Probably the crucial cause of the collapse of the Weimar Republic was:

(c) It was constantly plagued by economic problems which the government failed to solve permanently:

(i) In 1919 Germany was close to bankruptcy because of the enormous expense of the war which had lasted for longer than most people had expected.

(ii) Her attempts to pay reparations instalments made matters worse. In August 1921 after paying the £50 million due, she requested permission to suspend payments until her economy recovered. France refused and in 1922 Germany could not manage the full annual payment.

(iii) In January 1923 French troops occupied the Ruhr (an important German industrial area) in an attempt to seize goods from factories and mines. The German government ordered the workers to follow a policy of passive resistance, and German industry in the Ruhr was paralysed. The French had failed in their aim, but the effect on the German economy was catastrophic and the mark collapsed. The normal rate of exchange was 4 marks to the dollar, but even before the Ruhr occupation reparations difficulties had caused the mark to fall in value so that by 1922 a dollar would buy 191.8 marks. By July 1923, with the Ruhr at a standstill, a dollar would buy 160,000 marks, and at the end of November 1923 the mark was completely worthless at 4,200,000 million to the dollar. Its value was falling so rapidly that a worker paid in mark notes had to spend them immediately; if he waited until the following day his notes would be valueless.

illus 8.1 *Inflation in Germany. Boys making kites out of worthless banknotes in the early 1920s*

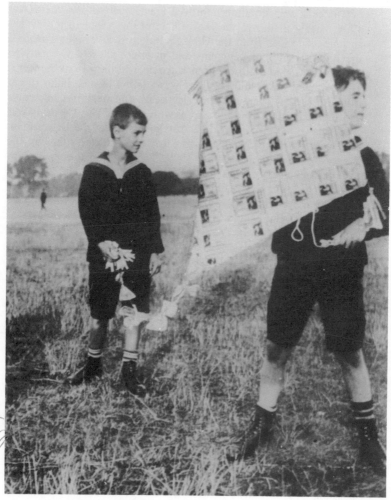

This financial disaster had profound effects on German society: the working classes were badly hit; wages failed to keep pace with inflation and trade union funds were wiped out. The middle classes and small capitalists lost their savings and many began to look towards the Nazis for improvement. On the other hand landowners and industrialists came out of the crisis well, because they still owned their material wealth - rich farming land, mines and factories. This strengthened the control of big business over the German economy. Some historians have even suggested that the inflation was deliberately engineered by wealthy industrialists with this aim in mind. However, this accusation is impossible to prove one way or the other, though the currency and the economy recovered remarkably quickly.

The economic situation improved dramatically in the years after 1924, largely thanks to the Dawes Plan of that year which provided an immediate loan from the USA equivalent to £40 million, relaxed the fixed reparations payments and in effect allowed Germany to pay what she could afford; French troops withdrew from the Ruhr. The currency was stabilised, there was a boom in such industries as iron, steel, coal, chemicals and electricals, and wealthy landowners and industrialists were quite happy with the republic. Germany was even able to pay her reparations instalments under the Dawes Plan. The work of the Dawes Plan was carried on a stage further by the Young Plan agreed in October 1929. This reduced the reparations total from £6,600 million to £2,000 million, to be paid in annual instalments over 59 years. There were other successes for the republic in foreign affairs, thanks to the work of Stresemann (see Section 13.1). But behind this success there was a fatal weakness:

(iv) *The prosperity was much more dependent than most people realised on American loans.* If the USA were to find herself in financial difficulties so that she stopped the loans, or worse still wanted them paid back quickly, the German economy would be shaken again. Unfortunately such a situation developed in 1929:

(v) Following *the Wall Street Crash* (October 1929) *the world economic crisis developed* (see Section 7.2). The USA stopped any further loans and began to call in many of the short-term loans already made to Germany. This shook the currency and caused a run on the banks, many of which had to close. The industrial boom had led to world-wide over-production, and German exports, along with those of other countries, were severely reduced. Factories had to close, and by the middle of 1931 unemployment was approaching four million. Sadly for Germany, Gustav Stresemann, the politician best equipped to deal with the situation, died of a heart attack in October 1929 at the early age of 51.

(vi) *The government of Chancellor Brüning* (Catholic Centre Party) reduced social services, unemployment benefit, and salaries and pensions of government officials, and stopped reparations payments. High tariffs were introduced to keep out foreign foodstuffs and thus help German farmers, while the government bought shares in factories hit by the slump. However, these measures did not produce quick results: unemployment continued to grow and by the spring of 1932 it stood at over six million. The government came under criticism from almost all groups in society, especially industrialists and the working classes who demanded more decisive action. The loss of working-class support because of increasing unemployment and the reduction in unemployment benefit was a serious blow to the republic. Thus by the end of 1932 the Weimar Republic had been brought to the verge of collapse. Even so it might have survived if there had been no other options. As it happened, however:

(d) Hitler and the Nazi party offered what seemed to be an attractive alternative just when the republic was at its most incapable. The fortunes of the Nazi party were linked closely to the economic situation: the more unstable the economy, the more seats the Nazis won in the *Reichstag*:

March	1924 -	32 seats (economy still unstable after 1923 inflation);
December	1924 -	14 seats (economy recovering after Dawes Plan);
	1928 -	12 seats (comparative prosperity);
	1930 -	107 seats (unemployment mounting - Nazis second largest party);
July	1932 -	230 seats (massive unemployment - Nazis largest single party).

There is no doubt that the rise of Hitler and the Nazis, fostered by the economic crisis, was one of the most important factors in the downfall of the republic. (Note that the same factors to some extent explain both the decline of the republic and the rise of Hitler.)

What was it about the Nazis that made them so popular?

(i) They offered national unity, prosperity and full employment by ridding Germany of what they claimed were the real causes of the troubles - Marxists, the 'November criminals' (those who had agreed to the armistice in November 1918 and later the Versailles Treaty), Jesuits, Freemasons and, above all, Jews. Great play was made in Nazi propaganda with the 'stab in the back' myth.

(ii) They promised to overthrow the Versailles settlement, so unpopular with most Germans, and to build Germany into a great power again. This would include bringing all Germans (in Austria, Czechoslovakia and Poland) back into the *Reich*.

(iii) The Nazi private army, the SA (*Sturmabteilung* - Storm Troopers), was attractive to young people out of work; it gave them a small wage and a uniform.

(iv) Wealthy landowners and industrialists encouraged the Nazis because they feared a communist revolution and they approved of the Nazi policy of hostility to communists. There is some controversy among historians, though, about how far this support went. Some German Marxist historians claim that from the early 1920s the Nazis were financed by industrialists as an anti-communist force, that Hitler was in effect 'a tool of the capitalists'. But Joachim Fest believes that the amounts of money involved have been greatly exaggerated, and that though some industrialists were quietly in favour of Hitler becoming Chancellor, it was only *after* he came to power that funds began to flow into the party coffers from big business.

(v) Hitler himself had extraordinary political abilities. He possessed tremendous energy and will power and a remarkable gift for public speaking which enabled him to put forward his ideas with great emotional force. Large numbers of Germans began to look towards him as some sort of Messiah figure. A full version of his views and aims was set out in his book *Mein Kampf* (My Struggle) which he wrote in prison after the Beer Hall *Putsch.*

(vi) The striking contrast between the governments of the Weimar Republic and the Nazi party impressed people: the former were cautious, respectable, dull and unable to maintain order, the latter promised strong, decisive government and the restoration of national pride – an irresistible combination.

(vii) Without the economic crisis though, it is doubtful whether Hitler would have had much chance of attaining power; it was the widespread unemployment and social misery which gained the Nazis mass support, not only among the working classes but also among the lower-middle classes – office workers, shopkeepers, civil servants, teachers and small-scale farmers.

In July 1932 then, the Nazis were the largest single party, but Hitler could not become Chancellor, partly because the Nazis still lacked an overall majority (they had 230 seats out of 608 in the *Reichstag*), and because he was not yet quite 'respectable'. Given these circumstances, *was it inevitable that Hitler would come to full power?* This is still a matter for disagreement among historians. Some feel that nothing could have saved the Weimar Republic and that consequently nothing could have kept Hitler out; others believe that already the first signs of economic improvement could be seen, and that it should have been possible to block Hitler's progress. In fact Brüning's policies seem to have started to pay off, though he himself had been replaced as Chancellor by Franz von Papen (conservative/nationalist) in May 1932. This theory seems to be supported by the election results of November 1932 when the Nazis lost 34 seats and about 2 million votes, a serious setback. Perhaps the republic was weathering the storm and the Nazis would fade. However, at this point a further influence came into play, which killed off the republic by letting Hitler into power legally:

(e) A small clique of right-wing politicians with support from the Reichswehr decided to bring Hitler into a coalition government with the conservatives and nationalists. The main conspirators were Franz von Papen and General Kurt von Schleicher. Their reasons for this momentous decision were:

(i) They were afraid of the Nazis attempting to seize power by a *Putsch.*

(ii) They believed they could control Hitler better inside the government than if he remained outside it.

(iii) The Nazi votes in the *Reichstag* would give them a majority, which might make possible a restoration of the monarchy, and a return to illus 8.2   *Hitler with a crowd of young admirers*

the system which had existed under Bismarck (Chancellor 1870-90), in which the *Reichstag* had much less power. Though this would destroy the Weimar Republic, they were prepared to go ahead because it would give them a better chance of controlling the communists.

There was some complicated manouevring involving Papen and Schleicher who persuaded President Hindenburg, now completely senile, to dismiss Chancellor Brüning and appoint Papen himself as Chancellor. They hoped to bring Hitler in as Vice-Chancellor, but he would settle for nothing less than himself as Chancellor. In January 1933, therefore, they persuaded Hindenburg to invite Hitler to become Chancellor with Papen as Vice-

Chancellor, even though the Nazis had by then lost ground in the elections of November 1932. Papen still believed Hitler could be controlled and remarked to a friend: 'In two months we'll have pushed Hitler into a corner so hard that he'll be squeaking.'

(f) In fact, therefore, Hitler was able to come to power legally because all the other parties including the *Reichswehr* failed to recognise the danger from the Nazis and therefore failed to unite in opposition. It ought to have been possible to keep the Nazis out - they were losing ground and had nowhere near an overall majority. But instead of uniting with other parties to exclude them the conservatives made the fatal mistake of inviting Hitler into power.

In conclusion, according to J. W. Hiden: though there were signs of economic improvement by the late summer of 1932, it was perhaps inevitable that the Weimar Republic would collapse, since the powerful conservative groups and the army were prepared to destroy it. But it was not inevitable that Hitler should take its place: that need not have happened; Papen, Schleicher and Hindenburg must take the blame for inviting him to become Chancellor.

8.2 WHAT DID NATIONAL SOCIALISM STAND FOR?

What it did *not* mean was nationalisation and the redistribution of wealth. The word 'socialism' was only included to attract the support of the German workers, though it has to be admitted that Hitler did promise a better deal for the workers. In fact it bore marked similarities to Mussolini's fascism (see Section 6.2).

The movement's general principles were:

(a) It was more than just one political party among many, it was a way of life. All classes in society must be united to make Germany a great nation again and restore national pride. It followed therefore that communists and other political groups would be eliminated.

(b) Great emphasis was laid on the ruthlessly efficient organisation of all aspects of life under the central government in order to achieve greatness, with violence and terror if necessary. The state, therefore, was supreme; the interests of the individual must be subordinated to the good of the state, that is a totalitarian state.

(c) Since it was likely that greatness could be achieved only by war, the entire state must be organised on a military footing.

(d) The race theory was that mankind could be divided into two groups, Aryans and non-Aryans. The Aryans were the Germans, ideally tall, blond and handsome; they were the master race, destined to rule the world. All the rest, such as Slavs, coloured peoples and particularly Jews were inferior and were destined to become the slave races of the Germans.

All the various facets and details of the Nazi system sprang from these four basic concepts.

8.3 HITLER CONSOLIDATES HIS POWER

Hitler was an Austrian, the son of a customs official in Braunau-am-Inn on the border with Germany. He had hoped to become an artist but failed to gain admittance to the Vienna Academy of Fine Arts, and afterwards spent six down-and-out years living in Vienna dosshouses and developing his hatred of Jews. In Munich he had joined Anton Drexler's tiny German Workers' Party (1919) which Hitler soon took over and transformed into the National Socialist party. Now, in January 1933, he was Chancellor of a coalition government of National Socialists and conservatives/nationalists, but he was not yet satisfied with the amount of power he possessed: Nazis held only three out of eleven cabinet posts. He therefore insisted on a general election in the hope of winning an overall majority for the Nazis.

The election of 5 March 1933

The election campaign was an extremely violent one. The Nazis, now in power, were able to use all the apparatus of state, including press and radio, to try and whip up a majority. Senior police officers were replaced with reliable Nazis, and 50,000 auxiliary policemen were called up, most of them from the SA and the SS (*Schutzstaffel* – Hitler's second private army). They had orders to avoid hostility to the SA and SS but to show no mercy to communists and other 'enemies of the state'. Meetings of all parties except Nazis and nationalists were wrecked and speakers beaten up, while the police looked the other way.

The climax of the election came on the night of 27 February when the *Reichstag* was badly damaged by a fire apparently started by a young half-witted Dutch anarchist called van der Lubbe, who was arrested, tried and executed for his pains. It has been suggested that the SA knew about van der Lubbe's plans, but allowed him to go ahead and even started fires of their own elsewhere in the building with the intention of blaming it on the communists. There is no conclusive evidence for this, but what is certain is that Hitler used the fire to stir up fear of communism and as a pretext for the banning of the party. However, in spite of all their efforts, the Nazis still failed to win an overall majority. With almost 90 per cent of the electorate voting, the Nazis won 288 and the nationalists 52 out of 647 seats, almost 40 short of an overall majority. Hitler was still dependent on the support of Papen and Hugenberg (leader of the nationalists). As it turned out this was the Nazis' best performance in a 'free' election: they never won an overall majority. It is worth remembering that even at the height of their electoral triumph the Nazis were supported by only 44 per cent of the voting electorate.

8.4 HOW WAS HITLER ABLE TO STAY IN POWER FOR THE NEXT 12 YEARS, AFTER FAILING TO WIN AN OVERALL MAJORITY?

(a) The legal basis of his power was **the Enabling Law** which was forced through the *Reichstag* on 23 March 1933. This stated that the government could introduce laws without the approval of the *Reichstag* for the next four years, ignore the constitution and sign agreements with foreign countries. All laws would be drafted by the Chancellor and come into operation the day after they were published.

This meant that Hitler was to be the complete dictator for the next four years, but since his will was now law he would obviously be able to extend the four-year period indefinitely. He no longer needed the support of Papen and Hindenburg: the Weimar constitution had been abandoned. Such a major constitutional change needed approval by a two-thirds majority, yet the Nazis lacked a simple majority.

How was it achieved?

The method was typical of the Nazis. The Kroll Opera House (where the *Reichstag* had been meeting since the fire) was surrounded by black-shirted SS troops, and MPs had to push their way through solid ranks to get into the building. The 81 communist MPs were simply not allowed to pass (many were in jail already). Inside the building rows of brown-shirted SA troops lined the walls. It took courage to vote against the bill in such surroundings with the SS outside chanting 'We want the bill, or fire and murder.' When the Catholic Centre Party decided to vote in favour, the result was a foregone conclusion: it passed by 441 votes to 94 (all Social Democrats).

(b) Hitler followed a policy of **Gleichschaltung (forcible co-ordination)** which turned Germany into a **totalitarian or fascist state**. As many aspects of life as possible were totally controlled by the government using a huge police force and the notorious *Gestapo* (*Geheime Staatspolizei* – Secret Police). It became dangerous to criticise or oppose the government in any way. *The main features of the Nazi totalitarian state were*:

(i)   All political parties except the National Socialists were banned so that Germany became a one-party state (like Italy and USSR).

(ii) The separate state parliaments (*Länder*) still existed but lost all power. Most of their functions were taken over by a Nazi Special Commissioner appointed in each state by the Berlin government, who had complete power over all officials and affairs within his state. There were no more state, provincial or municipal elections.

(iii) The civil service was purged; all Jews and other suspected 'enemies of the state' were removed until it was fully reliable.

(iv) Trade unions, a likely source of resistance, were abolished, their funds confiscated and their leaders arrested. They were replaced by the German Labour Front to which all workers had to belong. The government dealt with all grievances and strikes were not allowed.

(v) The education system was closely controlled so that children could be indoctrinated with Nazi opinions. Schools textbooks were often rewritten to fit in with Nazi theory, the most obvious examples being in history and biology. History was distorted to fit in with Hitler's view that great things could be achieved only by force. Human biology was dominated by the Nazi race theory. Teachers, lecturers and professors were closely watched to make sure they did not express opinions which strayed from the party line, and many lived in fear lest they be reported to the *Gestapo* by children whose parents were convinced Nazis.

The system was supplemented by the Hitler Youth which all boys had to join at 14; girls joined the League of German Maidens. They all learned that 'the *Führer* is always right' and that their first duty was to obey him. They were even encouraged to betray their parents to the *Gestapo*, and many did so.

(vi) All communications were controlled by the Minister of Propaganda, Dr Joseph Goebbels. Radio, newspapers, magazines, books, theatre, films, music and art were all supervised. By the end of 1934 about 4,000 books were on the forbidden list because they were 'un-German'. It was impossible to perform the plays of Bertholt Brecht (a communist) or the music of Felix Mendelssohn and Gustav Mahler (they were Jewish). Writers, artists and scholars were harassed until it became impossible to express any opinion which did not fit in with the Nazi system. By these methods public opinion could be moulded and mass support assured.

(vii) The economic life of the country was closely organised. Although the Nazis, [unlike the Bolsheviks,] had no special economic ideas, *they did have two main aims*: to remove unemployment and to make Germany self-sufficient by boosting exports and reducing imports (known as autarky). Nazi policies involved:
- Telling industrialists what to produce, depending on what the country needed at that moment; closing factories down if their products were not required.
- Moving workers about the country to places where jobs existed.
- Controlling food prices and rents.
- Manipulating foreign exchange rates to avoid inflation.
- Introducing vast schemes of public works (slum clearance, land drainage and *Autobahn* building).
- Forcing foreign countries to buy German goods either by refusing to pay cash for goods bought from those countries so that they had to accept German goods instead (often armaments), or by refusing

permission to foreigners with bank accounts in Germany to withdraw their cash, so that they had to spend it in Germany on German goods.

- Manufacturing synthetic rubber and wool and experimenting to produce petrol from coal in order to reduce dependence on foreign countries.

(viii) Religion was brought under state control, since the churches were a possible source of opposition. At first Hitler proceeded cautiously with both Roman Catholics and Protestants:

The Roman Catholic Church

In 1933 Hitler signed an agreement (known as a Concordat) with the Pope in which he promised not to interfere with German Catholics in any way; in return they agreed to dissolve the Catholic Centre Party and take no further part in politics. But relations soon became strained when the government broke the Concordat by dissolving the Catholic Youth League because it rivalled the Hitler Youth. When Catholics protested their schools were closed down. By 1937 Catholics were completely disillusioned with the Nazis and Pope Pius XI issued an Encyclical (a letter to be read out in all Roman Catholic churches in Germany) in which he condemned the Nazi government for being 'hostile to Christ and his Church'. Hitler was unimpressed, however, and thousands of priests and nuns were arrested and sent to concentration camps.

The Protestant Churches

Since a majority of Germans belonged to one or other of the various Protestant groups, Hitler tried to organise them into a '*Reich* Church' with a Nazi as the first *Reich* bishop. But many pastors (priests) objected and a group of them led by Martin Niemoller protested to Hitler about government interference and about his treatment of the Jews. Again the Nazis were completely ruthless – Niemoller and over 800 other pastors were sent to concentration camps. (Niemoller himself managed to survive for eight years until he was liberated in 1945.) Hundreds more were arrested later and the rest were forced to swear an oath of obedience to the *Führer*.

Eventually the persecutions appeared to bring the churches under control, but resistance survived and the churches were the only organisations to keep up a quiet protest campaign against the Nazi system.

(ix) Above all Germany was a police state. All opposition was ruthlessly sought out by the police, helped by the SS and the *Gestapo*. The law courts were not impartial: 'enemies of the state' rarely received a fair trial, and the concentration camps introduced by Hitler in 1933 were full. The main ones before 1939 were Dachau near Munich, Buchenwald near Weimar and Sachsenhausen near Berlin. They contained 'political' prisoners – communists, Social Democrats, Catholic priests, Protestant pastors and, above all, Jews.

It would be wrong though to give the impression that Hitler hung on to power by terrorising the entire nation. In fact this was not the case at all as far as the great majority of Germans was concerned. Provided you did not mind losing freedom of speech and thought, and did not happen to be a Jew, you could usually exist quite happily under the Nazi system. It was only if you began to protest that you ran into trouble. There can be no doubt that once Hitler was in power he soon won solid support.

(c) Hitler's policies were popular with many sections of the German people:

(i) His arrival in power in January 1933 caused a great wave of enthusiasm and anticipation after the weak and indecisive governments of the Weimar Republic. Hitler seemed to offer promise of action and a great new Germany. He took care to foster this enthusiasm by military parades, torchlight processions and firework displays, the most famous of which were the great rallies held every year in Nuremberg which seemed to appeal to the masses.

illus 8.3   *Hitler and the Sturmabteilung during the Nuremberg rally, 1938*

(ii) Hitler was successful in eliminating unemployment. This was probably the most important reason for his popularity with the masses. When he came to power the unemployment figure still stood at over six million but as early as July 1935 it had dropped to under two million and by 1939 it had disappeared completely. *How was this achieved?* The public works schemes provided thousands of extra jobs. A large party bureaucracy was set up now that the Nazi party was expanding so rapidly, providing thousands of extra office and administrative posts. There were purges of Jews and anti-Nazis from the civil service and many other jobs connected with law, teaching, journalism, broadcasting, the theatre and music, leaving large numbers of vacancies. Conscription was reintroduced in 1935. Rearmament was begun in 1934 and gradually speeded up. Thus Hitler had provided what the unemployed had been demanding in their 1932 marches: work and bread (*Arbeit und Brot*).

(iii) Care was taken to keep the support of the workers once it had been gained by the provision of jobs. This was important because the abolition of trade unions still rankled with many of them. The Strength through Joy Organisation (*Kraft durch Freude*) provided benefits such as subsidised holidays in Germany and abroad, cruises, ski-ing holidays, cheap theatre and concert tickets and convalescent homes. Other benefits were holidays with pay and the control of rents.

(iv) Wealthy industrialists and businessmen were delighted with Hitler and the Nazis in spite of the government's interference with their industries, partly because they now felt safe from a communist revolution and were pleased to be rid of trade unions which had constantly pestered them with demands for shorter working hours and increased wages. In addition they were able to buy back at low prices the shares which they had sold to the state during the crisis of 1929–32, and there was promise of great profits from the public works schemes, rearmament and the orders which the government placed with them.

(v) Farmers, though not impressed at first, gradually warmed towards the Nazis as soon as it became clear that they were in a specially favoured position in the state because of the avowed Nazi aims of self-sufficiency in food production. Prices of agricultural produce were fixed so that they were assured of a reasonable profit. Farms were declared to be hereditary estates, and on the death of the owner had to be passed on to his next of kin. This meant that a farmer could not be forced to sell or mortgage his farm to pay off his debts, and was welcomed by many farmers who were heavily in debt as a result of the financial crisis.

(vi) Hitler gained the support of the *Reichswehr* which was crucial if he was to feel secure in power. The *Reichswehr* was the one organisation which could have removed him by force. Yet by the summer of 1934 Hitler had won it over:

- The officer class was well-disposed towards Hitler because of his declared aim of setting aside the restrictions of the Versailles Treaty by rearmament and expansion of the army to its full strength.
- There had been a steady infiltration of National Socialists into the lower ranks and this was beginning to work through to the lower officer classes.
- The army leaders were greatly impressed by Hitler's handling of the troublesome SA in the notorious *Röhm Purge (Night of the Long Knives)* of 30 June 1934.

The background to this was that the SA, under their leader Ernst Röhm, a personal friend of Hitler from the early days of the movement, was becoming an embarrassment to the new Chancellor. Röhm wanted his brown-shirts to be merged with the *Reichswehr* and himself made a general. Hitler knew that the aristocratic *Reichswehr* generals would not hear of either; they considered the SA to be little more than a bunch of gangsters, while Röhm himself was known to be a homosexual and had criticised the generals in public for their stiff-necked conservatism. Röhm persisted in his demands, forcing Hitler to choose between the SA and the *Reichswehr*.

Hitler's solution to the dilemma was typical of Nazi methods – ruthless but effective. Röhm and other SA leaders were murdered by SS troops and Hitler seized the opportunity to have a number of other enemies and critics murdered who had no connection with the SA. For example, two of Papen's assistants were shot dead by the SS because ten days earlier Papen had made a speech at Marburg criticising Hitler. Papen himself was probably saved only by the fact that he was a close friend of President Hindenburg. It is thought that at least 400 people were murdered during that one night or soon afterwards. Hitler justified his actions on the grounds that they were all plotting against the state.

The purge had important results: the *Reichswehr* were relieved to be rid of the SA and impressed by Hitler's decisive handling of the problem. When President Hindenburg died only a month later, the *Reichswehr* agreed that Hitler should become President as well as Chancellor. (He preferred to use the title *Führer* – leader). The *Reichswehr* took an oath of allegiance to the *Führer*.

(vii) Hitler's anti-Semitic (anti-Jewish) policy was popular with many Germans to begin with. There were only just over half a million Jews in Germany, a tiny proportion of the population, but Hitler decided to use them as scapegoats for everything – the humiliation at Versailles, the depression, unemployment and communism – and claimed that there was a world Jewish plot. Lots of Germans were in such a desperate situation that they were prepared to accept the propaganda about the Jews and were not sorry to see thousands of them removed from their jobs as lawyers, doctors, teachers and journalists. The campaign was given legal status by *the Nuremberg Laws of 1935*, which deprived Jews of their German citizenship, forbade them to marry non-Jews (to preserve the purity of the Aryan race) and ruled that even a person with only one Jewish grandparent must be classed as a Jew.

Later the policy became more extreme. Jews were harassed in every possible way; their property was attacked and burnt, shops looted, synagogues destroyed, and they themselves herded into concentration camps. Eventually the terrible nature of what Hitler called his 'final solution' of the Jewish problem became clear: he intended to exterminate the entire Jewish race. As the Germans occupied countries such as Czechoslovakia, Poland and western Russia, he was able to lay his hands on non-German Jews as well. It is believed that by 1945, out of a total of nine million Jews living in Europe at the outbreak of the Second World War, six million had been murdered, most of them in the gas chambers of the Nazi extermination camps.

(viii) Finally, Hitler's foreign policy was a brilliant success. With each successive triumph, more and more Germans began to think of him as infallible (see Section 14.3).

8.5 NAZISM AND FASCISM

(a) Hitler's Nazi state was in many ways similar to Mussolini's system (see Section 6.3). Both:

 (i) Were intensely anti-communist and because of this drew a solid basis of support from all classes.
 (ii) Attempted to organise a totalitarian state, controlling industry, agriculture, and the way of life of the people, so that personal freedom was limited.
(iii) Attempted to make the country self-sufficient.
(iv) Emphaised the close unity of all classes working together to achieve these ends.
 (v) Emphasised the supremacy of the state, were intensely nationalistic, glorified war, and the cult of the leader.

(b) But there were some important differences:

 (i) Fascism never seemed to take root in Italy as deeply as it did in Germany.
 (ii) The Italian system was not as efficient as that in Germany. They never came anywhere near self-sufficiency and never eliminated unemployment; in fact unemployment rose.
(iii) The Italian system was not as ruthless and brutal as that in Germany and there were no mass atrocities, though there were some unpleasant incidents (the murder of Matteotti).
(iv) Italian fascism was not particularly anti-Jewish until 1938 when Mussolini adopted the policy to emulate Hitler.
 (v) Mussolini was more successful than Hitler with his religious policy after his agreement with the Pope in 1929.

(iv) Finally their constitutional positions were different: the monarchy still remained in Italy, and though Mussolini normally ignored Victor Emmanuel, the king proved useful in 1943 when Mussolini's critics were able to turn to him as the head of state. He was able to announce Mussolini's dismissal and order his arrest. There was nobody in Germany who could dismiss Hitler.

8.6 HOW SUCCESSFUL WAS HITLER IN DOMESTIC AFFAIRS UP TO 1939?

There are conflicting views about this:

(a) One school of thought claims that the Nazis were extremely successful and provided many benefits of the sort mentioned above in Section 8.4(c). If only Hitler had managed to keep out of war, all would have been well and his Third *Reich* might have lasted a thousand years (as he boasted it would).

(b) The other view is that Hitler's policies were only superficially successful and could not stand the test of time; even the superficial success was achieved by methods unacceptable in a modern civilised society:

(i) Full employment was achieved only at the cost of a brutal anti-Jewish campaign and a massive rearmament programme.

(ii) Self-sufficiency was not possible unless Germany was able to take over and exploit large areas of eastern Europe belonging to Poland, Czechoslovakia and Russia.

(iii) Permanent success therefore depended on success in war; thus there was no possibility of Hitler keeping out of war (see also Section 14.3(a)):

The conclusion must be, therefore, as Alan Bullock wrote in his biography of Hitler: 'Recognition of the benefits which Hitler's rule brought to Germany needs to be tempered by the realisation that for the *Führer* – and for a considerable section of the German people – these were by-products of his true purpose, the creation of an instrument of power with which to realise a policy of expansion that in the end was to admit no limits.'

QUESTIONS

1. Why did the Weimar Republic fail to survive in Germany?
2. How did Hitler come to power in Germany? What had he achieved by 1937?
3. 'Doomed from the start.' How far is this an accurate statement about the Weimar Republic?

4. Explain the circumstances in which the Weimar Republic was set up in 1919. What do you consider to have been (a) its main successes and (b) its main failures. What were the chief political changes that took place in Germany between 1931 and 1934?

5. What part did the following play in the rise of Hitler to power?

> The Versailles treaties; economic depression; the National Socialist party programme.

What other factors also played a part?

6. Show how Hitler maintained himself in power and how he endeavoured to build up Germany's strength.

7. Describe the main organisations of the Nazi state in Germany. Outline the policy to 1939 that Hitler pursued towards the SA, the German army, the relief of unemployment, the churches, and racial minorities.

8. Show the effects of Nazi domination on *three* of the following: the trade unions and working classes; the economy; the Jews; the churches; democratic government; education and youth.

9. What were the main similarities and differences between the fascist states in Germany and Italy?

CHAPTER 9

STALIN

AND THE USSR

1924-39

SUMMARY OF EVENTS

Russia during this period was dominated by one man - *Joseph Stalin* - who, as dictator until his death in 1953 at the age of 73, wielded as much power as ever the tsars had done before him. When Lenin died in January 1924 it was widely expected that Trotsky would take over as leader, but a complex power struggle developed from which Stalin had emerged triumphant by the end of 1929. Immense problems faced communist Russia, still only a few years old: industry and agriculture were backward and inefficient, there were constant food shortages, pressing political and social problems, and, many Russians thought, the danger of another attempt by foreign capitalist powers to destroy the new communist state. Stalin made determined efforts to overcome all these problems: there were the Five Year Plans to revolutionise industry, the collectivisation of agriculture and the introduction of a totalitarian regime which was, if anything, more ruthlessly efficient than Hitler's system in Germany. Yet brutal though Stalin's methods were, they seem to have been successful, at least to the extent that when the dreaded attack from the west eventually came in the form of a massive German invasion in June 1941, the Russians were able to hold out and eventually end up on the winning side, though admittedly at terrible cost.

9.1 HOW DID STALIN MANAGE TO GET TO SUPREME POWER?

Joseph Djugashvili (he took the name 'Stalin' - man of steel - some time after joining the Bolsheviks in 1904) was born in 1879 in the small town of Gori in the province of Georgia; his parents were poor peasants; in fact his father, a shoemaker, had been born a serf. Joseph's mother wanted him to become a priest and he was educated for four years at Tiflis Theological Seminary, but he hated its repressive atmosphere and was expelled in 1899 for expounding socialist principles. He became a Bolshevik about 1904 and after 1917, thanks to his brilliance as an administrator, he was quietly able to build up his own position under

illus 9.1 *Joseph Stalin*

Lenin. When Lenin died in 1924 Stalin was Secretary-General of the communist party and a member of the seven-man *Politburo*, the committee which decided government policy. At first it seemed unlikely that Stalin would become the dominant figure; Trotsky called him 'the party's most eminent mediocrity', and Lenin thought him stubborn and rude, and suggested in his will that Stalin be removed from his post. The most obvious successor to Lenin was Trotsky, an inspired orator, an intellectual, and the organiser of the Red Armies. *However, circumstances arose which Stalin was able to use to eliminate his rivals*:

(a) Trotsky's brilliance worked against him by arousing envy and resentment among the other *Politburo* members who combined to prevent his becoming leader: collective action was better than a one-man show.

(b) The *Politburo* members underestimated Stalin, seeing him as nothing more than a competent administrator; they ignored Lenin's advice.

(c) As Secretary-General of the party, Stalin had full powers of appointment and promotion which he used to place his own supporters in key positions while at the same time removing the supporters of others to distant parts of the country.

(d) Stalin used **the disagreements in the Politburo over policy** to his own advantage. These arose partly because Marx had never described in detail exactly how the new communist society should be organised and even Lenin was vague about it, except that 'the dictatorship of the proletariat' would be established, that is workers would run the state and the economy in their own interests. When all opposition had been crushed, the ultimate goal of a classless society would be achieved in which, according to Marx, the ruling principle would be: 'from each according to his ability, to each according to his needs'. With NEP (the New Economic Policy: see Section 3.3(d)) Lenin had departed from socialist principles, though this would only be a temporary measure until the crisis passed. Now the right, led by Bukharin, and the left, whose views were most strongly put by Trotsky, fell out about what to do next:

(i) Bukharin wanted to continue NEP even though it was causing an increase in numbers of *kulaks*. His opponents wanted to abandon NEP and concentrate on rapid industrialisation at the expense of the peasants.

(ii) Bukharin thought it important to consolidate soviet power in Russia, based on a prosperous peasantry and with a very gradual industrialisation: *'socialism in one country'* as it became known. Trotsky believed that they must work for revolution outside Russia, *'permanent revolution'*; when this was achieved the industrialised states of western Europe would help Russia with her industrialisation.

Stalin, quietly ambitious, apparently had no strong views either way at first, but he supported the right simply to isolate Trotsky. Later, when a split occurred between Bukharin and two other *Politburo* members, Zinoviev and Kamenev, who were feeling unhappy about NEP, Stalin supported Bukharin, and one by one Trotsky, Zinoviev and Kamenev were voted off the *Politburo* by Stalin's yes-men and expelled from the party (1927). The following year Stalin decided that NEP must go – the *kulaks* were holding up agricultural progress; when Bukharin protested, he too was expelled (1929) and Stalin was left supreme. Having reached the pinnacle, Stalin attacked the many problems facing Russia, which fell into three categories: economic, political and social, and foreign (see Section 13.3).

9.2 WHAT WERE THE ECONOMIC PROBLEMS AND HOW SUCCESSFUL WAS STALIN IN SOLVING THEM?

(a) The problems

(i) Although Russian industry was recovering from the effects of the war, production from heavy industry was still surprisingly low; in 1929 for example, France, not a major industrial power, produced more coal and steel than Russia, while Germany, Britain and especially the USA were streets ahead. Stalin believed that a rapid expansion of heavy industry was essential so that Russia would be able to survive the attack which he was convinced would come sooner or later from the western capitalist powers who hated communism. Industrialisation would have the added advantage of increasing support for the government, because it was the industrial workers who were the communists' greatest allies: the more industrial workers, the more secure the communist state would be. One serious obstacle to overcome, though, was lack of capital to finance expansion, since foreigners were unwilling to invest in a communist state.

(ii) More food would have to be produced both to feed the growing industrial population and to provide a surplus for export which would bring in foreign capital and profits for investment in industry. Yet the primitive agricultural system was incapable of providing such increases.

(b) The approach

Although he had no economic experience whatsoever, Stalin seems to have had no hesitation in plunging the country into a series of dramatic changes designed to overcome the problems in the shortest possible time. In a speech in February 1931 he explained why: 'We are 50 or 100 years behind the advanced countries. We must make good this distance in 10 years. Either we do it or we shall be crushed'. NEP had been permissible as a temporary measure, but must now be abandoned: both industry and agriculture must be taken under government control.

(i) *Industrial expansion* was tackled by a series of Five Year Plans, the first two of which (1928-32 and 1933-7) were said to have been completed a year ahead of schedule, though in fact neither of them reached the full target. The first plan concentrated on heavy industry – coal, iron, steel, oil and machinery (including tractors), which were scheduled to triple output; the two later plans provided for some increases in consumer goods as well as in heavy industry. It has to be said that in spite of all sorts of mistakes the plans were a remarkable success: by 1940 the USSR had overtaken Britain in iron and steel production, though not yet in coal, and she was within reach of Germany:

Table 9.1
Industrial expansion in Russia : production in millions of tons

	1900	1913	1929	1938	1940
Coal	16.0	36.0	40.1	132.9	164.6
Pig iron	2.7	4.8	8.0	26.3	14.9
Steel	2.5	5.2	4.9	18.0	18.4

Industrial production in Russia compared with other great powers in 1940 (in millions of tons)

	Pig iron	Steel	Coal	Electricity (in billion kilowatts)
USSR	14.9	18.4	164.6	39.6
USA	31.9	47.2	395.0	115.9
Britain	6.7	10.3	227.0	30.7
Germany	18.3	22.7	186.0	55.2
France	6.0	6.1	45.5	19.3

Hundreds of factories were built, many of them in new towns east of the Ural Mountains where they would be safer from invasion. Well-known examples are the iron and steel works at Magnitogorsk, tractor works at Kharkov and Gorki, a hydro-electric dam at Dnepropetrovsk and the oil refineries in the Caucasus.

How was it achieved? The cash was provided almost entirely by the Russians themselves, with no foreign investment; some came from grain exports, some from charging peasants heavily for use of government equipment and the ruthless ploughing back of all profits and surplus. Hundreds of foreign technicians were brought in and great emphasis placed on expanding education in technical colleges and universities and even in factory schools, to provide a whole new generation of skilled workers. In the factories the old capitalist methods of piecework and pay differentials between skilled and unskilled workers were used to encourage production; medals were given to workers who achieved record output; these were known as Stakhanovites after Alexei Stakhanov, a champion miner who in August 1935, supported by a well-organised team, managed to cut 102 tons of coal in a single shift (by ordinary methods even the highly efficient miners of the Ruhr in Germany were managing only 10 tons per shift). Ordinary workers were ruthlessly disciplined: there were severe punishments for bad workmanship, accusations of being a 'saboteur' when targets were not met and often a spell in a forced labour camp. Primitive housing conditions and a severe shortage of consumer goods (because of the concentration on heavy industry) on top of all the regimentation must have made life grim for most workers. As Richard Freeborn points out: 'It is probably no exaggeration to claim that the First Five Year Plan represented a declaration of war by the state machine against the workers and peasants of the USSR who were subjected to a greater exploitation than any they had known under capitalism.' However, by the mid-1930s things were improving as benefits such as education, medical care and holidays with pay became available.

(b) The problems of agriculture were dealt with by the process known as *collectivisation.* The idea was that the small farms and holdings belonging to the peasants should be merged to form large collective farms jointly owned by the peasants. There were two main reasons for Stalin's decision to collectivise:

(i) The existing system of small farms was inefficient, whereas large farms, under state direction and using tractors and combine harvesters, would vastly increase grain production.

(ii) He wanted to eliminate the class of prosperous peasants (*kulaks* or nepmen) which NEP had encouraged because, he claimed, they were standing in the way of progress. But the real reason was probably political: Stalin saw the *kulak* as the enemy of communism: 'we must smash the *kulaks* so hard that they will never rise to their feet again.'

illus 9.2   *Russian peasants admire the first tractor in their village, 1926*

The policy was launched in earnest in 1929 and had to be carried through by sheer brute force, so determined was the resistance in the countryside. It was a complete disaster from which, it is probably no exaggeration to claim, Russia has not fully recovered even today. There was no problem in collectivising landless labourers, but all peasants who owned any property at all, whether they were *kulaks* or not, were hostile and had to be forced to join by armies of party members who urged poorer peasants to seize cattle and machinery from the *kulaks* to be handed over to the collectives. *Kulaks* often reacted by slaughtering cattle and burning crops rather than allow the state to take them. Peasants who refused to join collective farms were arrested and deported to labour camps or shot; when newly collectivised peasants tried to sabotage the system by producing only enough for their own needs, local officials insisted on seizing the required quotas, resulting in large-scale famine during 1932-3, especially in the Ukraine. Yet one and three-quarter million tons of grain were exported during that period while over five million peasants died of starvation. Some historians have even claimed that Stalin welcomed the famine, since, along with the 10 million *kulaks* who were removed or executed, it helped to break peasant resistance. In this way well over 90 per cent of all farmland had been collectivised by 1937. In one sense Stalin could claim that collectivisation was a success: it allowed greater mechanisation, which gradually increased grain output until by 1940 it was over 80 per cent higher than in 1913. On the other hand, so many animals had been slaughtered that it was 1953 before livestock production recovered to the 1928 figure and the cost in human life and suffering was enormous.

9.3 POLITICAL AND SOCIAL PROBLEMS AND STALIN'S SOLUTIONS

(a) **The problems** were to some extent of Stalin's own making; he obviously felt that under his totalitarian regime, political and social activities must be controlled just as much as economic life; he aimed at complete and unchallenged power for himself and became increasingly suspicious and intolerant of criticism.

(i) Starting in 1930, there was growing opposition within the party which aimed to slow down industrialisation, allow peasants to leave collective farms, and remove Stalin from the leadership if necessary. However, Stalin was equally determined that political opponents and critics must be eliminated once and for all.

(ii) A new constitution was needed to consolidate the hold of Stalin and the communist party over the whole country.

(iii) Social and cultural aspects of life needed to be brought into line and harnessed to the service of the state.

(b) **Stalin's methods** were typically dramatic.

(i) Using the murder of Sergei Kirov (December 1934), one of his supporters on the *Politburo*, as an excuse Stalin launched what became known as *the purges*. It seems fairly certain that Stalin himself organised Kirov's murder, 'the crime of the century,' as Robert Conquest calls it, 'the keystone of the entire edifice of terror and suffering by which Stalin secured his grip on the Soviet peoples', but it was blamed on Stalin's critics. Over the next four years hundreds of important officials were arrested, tortured, made to confess to all sorts of crimes of which they were largely innocent (such as plotting with the exiled Trotsky or with capitalist governments to overthrow the soviet state) and forced to appear in a series of 'show trials' at which they were invariably found guilty and sentenced to death or labour camp. Those executed included all the 'Old Bolsheviks' - Zinoviev, Kamenev, Bukharin and Radek - who had helped to make the 1917 revolution, the Commander-in-Chief of the Red Army, Tukhachevsky, thirteen other generals and about two-thirds of the top officers; millions of innocent people ended up in labour camps (Conquest puts the figure at about eight million by 1938). Even Trotsky was sought out and murdered in exile in Mexico City, though he managed to survive until 1940. The purges were successful in eliminating possible alternative leaders and in terrorising the masses into obedience, but the consequences were serious: many of the best brains in the government, the army and in industry had disappeared, and in a country where the highly educated class was still small, this was bound to hinder progress.

(ii) In 1936, after much discussion, a new and apparently more democratic constitution was introduced in which everyone was allowed to vote by secret ballot for members of a national assembly known as the Supreme Soviet. However, this met for only about two weeks in the year, when it elected a smaller body, the *Praesidium,* to act on its behalf, and when it also chose the Union Soviet of Commissars, a small group of ministers of which Stalin was the Secretary, and which wielded the real power. In fact the democracy was an illusion: the constitution merely underlined the fact that Stalin and the party ran things, and though there was mention of freedom of speech, anybody who ventured to criticise Stalin was quickly 'purged'.

(iii) Writers, artists and musicians were expected to produce works of realism glorifying soviet achievements; anybody who did not conform was persecuted, and even those who tried often still fell foul of Stalin. The young composer Shostakovich was condemned when his new opera, *Lady Macbeth of Mtsensk*, failed to please Stalin, even though the music critics had at first praised it. Further performances were banned with the result, according to the American ambassador, that 'half the artists and musicians in Moscow are having nervous prostration and the others are trying to imagine how to write and compose in a manner to please Stalin.' Education like everything else was closely watched by the secret police, and although it was compulsory and free it tended to deteriorate into indoctrination; but at least literacy was increased, which along with the improvement in social services, was an unprecedented achievement. Finally an attempt was made to clamp down on the Orthodox Church: churches were closed and clergy persecuted; but this was one of Stalin's failures: in 1940 probably half the population were still convinced believers, and during the war the persecution was relaxed to help maintain morale.

9.4 WAS THE STALIN APPROACH NECESSARY?

Historians have failed to agree about the extent of his achievement or indeed whether he achieved any more with his brutality than could have been managed by less drastic methods. Stalin's defenders, who include many soviet historians, argue that the situation was so desperate that only the pressures of brute force could have produced such a rapid industrialisation together with the necessary food; for them, the supreme justification is that thanks to Stalin Russia was strong enough to defeat the Germans. The opposing view is that Stalin's policies, though superficially successful, actually weakened Russia: ridiculously high targets for industrial production placed unnecessary pressure on the workers and caused slipshod work and poor-quality products; the brutal enforcement of collectivisation vastly reduced the amount of meat available and made peasants so bitter that in the Ukraine the German invaders were welcomed; the purges slowed economic progress by removing many of the most experienced men, and almost caused military defeat during the first months of the war by depriving the army of all its experienced generals; in fact Russia won the war in spite of Stalin, not because of him.

Whichever view one accepts, a final point to bear in mind is that many Marxists outside Russia feel that Stalin betrayed the idealism of Marx and Lenin: instead of a new classless society in which everybody was free and equal, ordinary workers and peasants were just as exploited as under the tsars, whereas skilled workers were an élite; the party had taken the place of the capitalists, and enjoyed all the privileges – the best houses, country retreats and cars. Instead of Marx's 'dictatorship of the proletariat' there was merely the dictatorship of Stalin.

QUESTIONS

1. How was Stalin able to come to power in Russia after the death of Lenin? What were his achievements in the period 1924–39?
2. Identify the main political, social and economic features of Stalinist communism.
3. In what ways and with what success did Stalin attempt to promote economic growth in Russia?
4. Why was Stalin so sensitive to political opposition and criticism? Describe the ways in which he (a) reacted to his political opponents and (b) discouraged criticism by writers, artists and musicians.
5. 'He had not trusted his fellow party workers . . . nor his comrades in exile. He did not trust the peasants to sow their own grain and harvest the wheat unless he forced them to do it. He did not trust the workers to work unless he laid down their production targets.' (Solzhenitsyn). Discuss this verdict on Stalin's rule in Russia.
6. Write two obituary notices for Stalin such as would have been suitable for publication in (a) a USA newspaper and (b) an official Russian newspaper.

CHAPTER 10

TURKEY, JAPAN AND SPAIN BETWEEN THE WARS

SUMMARY OF EVENTS

These three countries are interesting in their own ways because each illustrates a different reaction to the problems which faced most countries during the 1920s and 1930s, though all three found themselves with undemocratic nationalist governments. *Turkey* provides a good example of a government achieving success with a minimum of fuss and violence; Mustafa Kemal, President of the Turkish republic from 1923 until his death in 1938, became so popular that in 1934 he was able to take the title or surname of Ataturk (father of Turks). The other two countries were much less successful: in *Japan* the government, increasingly embarrassed by economic, financial and political problems, fell under the influence of the military in the early 1930s, with unfortunate consequences for the rest of the world. In *Spain* an incompetent parliamentary government was replaced by General Primo de Rivera who ruled from 1923 until 1930 as a sort of benevolent dictator; the world economic crisis brought him down, and in an atmosphere of growing republicanism King Alfonso XIII abdicated (1931). Various republican governments failed to solve the array of problems facing them and the situation deteriorated into a civil war (1936-9) which was won by the right-wing nationalists; their leader, General Franco, became head of the government, a position he held until his death in 1975.

10.1 TURKEY

(a) In 1919 Turkey was a defeated nation, further humiliated by the Treaty of Sèvres, which compelled them to hand over large areas of the country to the Allies (see Section 2.10). This provoked a strong nationalist reaction especially among the educated classes and the army; the lead was taken by Mustafa Kemal, a young general who had made a reputation for himself as the commander who beat the British at Gallipoli in 1915. He and his supporters were determined not to accept defeat, and denouncing the Sultan and his government at Constantinople (Istanbul) as 'prisoners of the Allies', they set up a rival government at Ankara with Kemal as president. By September 1922 all foreign occupying troops had been removed though the crisis at Chanak almost caused war with Britain (see Section 4.1 (b) (vii)), the Sultan fled, the monarchy was abolished and the Treaty of Lausanne (1923) allowed Turkey more favourable terms. In October 1923 Kemal, leader of the Republican People's Party which he had himself created, was elected first president of the Turkish republic.

(b) What were the problems facing the new president and how successfully did he deal with them?

The fundamental problem was that Turkey was backward in almost every conceivable way, and though Kemal believed in democracy, the necessary reforms were so drastic that serious opposition was bound to occur. This obliged him to rule as a dictator for most of his presidency; his policies had considerable success:

(i) As soon as the drastic nature of Kemal's proposed reforms became known, there was strong opposition both inside and outside the National Assembly (parliament), especially from Muslim clerics. A rebellion broke out in 1925 led by a conservative sheikh; Kemal swiftly suppressed it and used it as an excuse to ban all political parties except his own and to take control of the press. This enabled the first batch of reforms to be carried through successfully. By 1929 Kemal was ready to relax controls and an opposition party was allowed to form; unfortunately after several demonstrations organised by the new party had deteriorated into riots, Kemal decided that his experiment in democracy was premature, and he again banned all opposition parties. Not until 1946 were the Turks allowed another attempt at democracy. However, Kemal's dictatorship, though strict, was not brutal or aggressive.

(ii) The country was backward socially and legally because of the influence of the Muslim (Islamic) religion which pervaded all aspects of Turkish life including education and law, and held up Turkey's development into a modern state. To bring Turkey into the twentieth century meant an attack on the powers of Islam and the introduction of western methods and customs. After 1928 Islam was no longer the state religion and played no part in politics; Turkey was a secular state (one free from religious control). New codes of civil and criminal law, the Roman alphabet, western calendar and the weekend were introduced; thousands of new schools were built. The status of women was much improved: polygamy was prohibited, the wearing of the veil discouraged, civil marriage and divorce made legal and in 1934 women were given the vote. Another law compelled Turks to wear western-style clothes, banned the fez and required that all men's hats must have brims. The burden of taxation on the peasants was reduced and primary education made free and compulsory.

illus 10.1 *Kemal Ataturk reviewing troops, 1922*

(iii) To cure Turkey's economic weaknesses Kemal adopted a policy known as *statism* – state interference in as many areas as possible. Farmers were encouraged with government subsidies to use the latest techniques and equipment and to join co-operatives; during the great depression of the early 1930s they were directed to produce those crops which were still exportable; consequently peasant farmers came through the depression reasonably well. The government took over railways, harbours and shipping and provided funds to expand industries such as textiles, mining, iron and steel, paper, glass and sugar; again, with the help of tariffs and state control of foreign exchange, Turkish industry weathered the depression better than most European countries.

By a curious mixture of measures which his critics variously denounced as communist or fascist and by a foreign policy which aimed at friendship with all, Kemal transformed Turkey. Of course there was still a long way to go: in 1938 she could hardly be classed as a wealthy industrial state, and her farming remained largely primitive. But his achievement was threefold: he had rid Turkey of the ineffective monarchy, restored her national pride, and brought her part of the way along the road to being a modern, westernised state. It is no exaggeration to call him 'the father of modern Turkey'.

10.2 JAPAN

(a) In 1918 Japan was in a strong position in the Far East; she had a powerful navy, a great deal of influence in China, and had benefited economically from the First World War, while the states of Europe were preoccupied with fighting each other. Japan took advantage of the situation both by providing the Allies with shipping and other goods, and by stepping in to supply orders, especially in Asia, which the Europeans could not fulfil. During the war years her exports of cotton cloth almost trebled, while her merchant fleet doubled in tonnage. Politically the course seemed set fair for democracy when in 1925 all adult males were given the vote. Hopes were soon dashed: at the beginning of the 1930s the army assumed control of the government.

(b) Why did Japan become a military dictatorship?

During the 1920s problems developed, as they did in Italy and Germany, which democratically elected governments seemed incapable of solving:

(i) From the beginning democracy was not popular with many influential groups in Japanese society, such as the army and the conservatives who were strongly entrenched in the upper house of parliament (the Peers) and in the Privy Council. They seized every opportunity to discredit the government, criticising for example Baron Shidehara Kijuro (Foreign Minister 1924–7) for his conciliatory approach to China, which he thought was the best way to strengthen Japan's economic hold over that country. The army was itching to inter-fere in China, which was torn by civil war, and considered Shidehara's policy to be 'soft'. They were strong enough to bring the government down in 1927 and reverse his policy.

(ii) Many politicians were corrupt and regularly accepted bribes from big business; sometimes fighting broke out in the lower house (the Diet) as charges and counter-charges of corruption were flung about. The system was not one to inspire confidence and parliamentary prestige suffered accordingly. Neither (i) nor (ii) made military dictatorship inevitable, but when economic problems were added to the political ones the situation became serious.

(iii) The great trading boom of the war years lasted only until the middle of 1921 when Europe began to revive and recover lost markets. Unemployment and industrial unrest developed, and at the same time farmers were hit by the rapidly falling price of rice caused by a series of bumper harvests. When farmers and industrial workers tried to organise themselves into a political party, they were ruth-lessly suppressed by the police. Thus the workers, as well as the army and the right, gradually became hostile to a parliament which posed as democratic but allowed the left to be suppressed and accepted bribes from big business.

(iv) The world economic crisis beginning in 1929 (see Section 7.2) affected Japan severely; her exports shrank disastrously and other countries introduced or raised tariffs against her to safeguard their own industries. One of the worst affected trades was the export of raw silk which went mostly to the USA. The period after the Wall Street Crash was no time for luxuries and the Americans drastically reduced their imports of raw silk, so that by 1932 the price had fallen to less than one-fifth of the 1923 figure. This was a further blow for Japanese farmers, since about half of them relied for their livelihood on the production of raw silk as well as rice. There was desperate poverty, especially in the north, for which peasants and factory workers blamed the government and big business. Most of the army recruits were peasants; consequently the rank-and-file as well as the officer class were disgusted with what they took to be weak parliamentary government. Many officers, attracted by fascism, were as early as 1927 planning to seize power and introduce a strong nationalist government.

(v) Matters were brought to a head in 1931 by the situation in Manchuria where the Chinese were trying to squeeze out Japanese trade and business, which would have been a severe blow to a Japanese economy already hard hit by the depression. To preserve their economic advantages Japanese army units invaded and occupied Manchuria (September 1931) without permission from their government. When Prime Minister Inukai criticised extremist action he was assassinated by a group of army officers (May 1932); his successor felt he had to support the army's actions. For the next 13 years the army more or less ran the country, introducing similar measures to those adopted in Germany and Italy: ruthless suppression of Marxists, assassination of opponents, tight control of education, a build-up of armaments, and an aggressive foreign policy which aimed to capture territory in Asia as markets for Japanese exports. This led to an attack on China (1937) and participation in the Second World War in the Pacific (see Section 15.2(c)). Some historians blame the Emperor Hirohito who, though he deplored the attack on Manchuria, refused to become involved in political controversy, afraid to risk his orders for a withdrawal being ignored. Richard Storry claims that 'it would have been better for Japan and for the world if the risk had been taken'; he believes that Hirohito's prestige was such that the majority of officers would have obeyed him if he had tried to restrain the attacks on Manchuria and China.

10.3 SPAIN

(a) The constitutional monarchy under Alfonso XIII (king since 1885) was never very efficient and reached rock bottom in 1921 when a Spanish army sent to put down a revolt led by Abd-el-Krim in Spanish Morocco was massacred by the Moors. In 1923 *General Primo de Rivera* seized power in a bloodless coup, with Alfonso's approval, and ruled for the next seven years. The king called him 'my Mussolini', but though Primo was a military dictator, he was not a fascist. He was responsible for a number of public works – railways, roads and irrigation schemes; industrial production developed at three times the rate before 1923; most impressive of all, he managed to end the war in Morocco (1925). When the illus 10.2 *Japanese troops invade Manchuria, 1931*

world economic crisis reached Spain in 1930 unemployment rose, Primo and his advisers bungled the finances, causing depreciation of the peseta, and the army withdrew support, whereupon Primo resigned. In April 1931 municipal elections were held in which the republicans won all the large cities; as huge crowds gathered on the streets of Madrid, Alfonso decided to abdicate to avoid bloodshed, and *a republic was proclaimed.* The monarchy had been overthrown without bloodshed, but unfortunately the slaughter had merely been postponed until 1936.

(b) Why did civil war break out in Spain?

(i) The new republic was faced by a number of serious problems: Catalonia and the Basque provinces wanted independence; the Roman Catholic Church was bitterly hostile to the republic, which in return disliked the church and was determined to reduce its power; it was felt that the army had too much influence in politics and might attempt another coup; there were the additional problems caused by the depression: agricultural prices were falling, wine and olive oil exports declined, land went out of cultivation and peasant unemployment rose; in industry iron production fell by a third and steel production by almost half; it was a time of falling wages, unemployment and falling standards of living. Unless it could make some headway with this final problem, the republic was likely to lose the support of the workers.

(ii) The left's solutions to these problems were not acceptable to the right, which became increasingly alarmed at the prospect of social revolution. The dominant group in the *Cortes* (parliament), the socialists and middle-class radicals, began energetically: Catalonia was allowed some self-government; an attack was made on the church (church and state were separated, priests would not be paid by the government, Jesuits were expelled, other orders could be dissolved, and religious education ceased); a large number of army officers were compulsorily retired; a start was made on the nationalisation of large estates; and attempts were made to raise industrial wages. Each of these measures infuriated one or other of the right-wing groups (church, army, landowners and industrialists); in 1932 some army officers tried to overthrow the Prime Minister, *Manuel Azana*, but the rising was easily suppressed, as the majority of the army remained loyal at this stage. A new right-wing party, the *Ceda*, was formed to defend the church and the landlords.

(iii) The republic was further weakened by opposition from two powerful left-wing groups, the anarchists and the syndicalists (certain powerful trade unions) who favoured a general strike and the overthrow of the capitalist system; they despised the socialists for co-operating with the middle-class groups. They organised strikes, riots and assassinations; matters came to a head in January 1933 when government guards set fire to some houses in the village of Casas Viejas near

Cadiz, to smoke out some anarchists; 25 people were killed, which lost the government much working-class support, and caused even the socialists to withdraw support from Azana, who resigned. In the following elections (November 1933) the right-wing parties won a majority, the largest group being the new Catholic *Ceda* under its leader *Gil Robles.*

(iv) The actions of the new right-wing government aroused the left to fury: they cancelled most of Azana's reforms, interfered with the working of the new Catalan government and refused to allow the Basques self-government, a serious error since the Basques had supported the right in the elections, but now switched to the left. As the government moved further right, the left-wing groups (socialists, anarchists, syndicalists and now communists) drew closer together to form a Popular Front. Revolutionary violence grew: anarchists derailed the Barcelona–Seville express killing 19 people; there was a general strike in 1934, as well as rebellions in Catalonia and Asturias. The miners of Asturias fought bravely but were crushed ruthlessly by troops under the command of General Franco. In the words of Hugh Thomas, 'after the manner in which the revolution had been quelled, it would have required a superhuman effort to avoid the culminating disaster of civil war. But no such effort was forthcoming.' Instead, as the financial situation deteriorated as well as the political one, the right fell apart, and in the elections of February 1936 the Popular Front emerged victorious.

(v) The new government turned out to be ineffective, since the socialists decided not to support it, hoping to seize power when the middle-class republican government failed. The government seemed incapable of keeping order, the climax coming in July 1936, when Calvo Sotelo, the leading right-wing politician, was murdered by police. This terrified the right and convinced them that the only way to restore order was by a military dictatorship. A number of generals conspiring with the right, especially with the new fascist *Falange* party of José Antonio de Rivera (Primo's son), had already planned a military takeover. Using Calvo Sotelo's murder as an excuse, they began a revolt in Morocco, where General Franco soon assumed the leadership. The civil war had begun.

(c) The civil war 1936–9

By the end of July 1936, the right (calling themselves nationalists) controlled most of the north, while the republicans controlled most of the south, including Madrid. The following struggle was a bitter one in which both sides committed terrible atrocities. The nationalists were helped by Italy and Germany who sent arms and men; the republicans received some help from Russia but France and Britain refused to intervene, merely allowing volunteers to fight in Spain. The war ended in March 1939 when the nationalists captured Madrid. *Reasons for the nationalist victory* were that Franco was extremely skilful in holding together the various right-wing groups (army, church, monarchists and Falangists); the republicans were much less united (anarchists and communists actually fought each other for a time in Barcelona). The extent of foreign help was probably decisive: this included 60,000 Italian troops, a large Italian air force, and hundreds of German planes and tanks. One of the most notorious actions was the German bombing of the defenceless Basque town of Guernica, in which over 1,600 people were killed.

Franco, taking the title *Caudillo* (leader), set up a government on the fascist model, marked by repression and at first mass executions; he was shrewd enough to remain neutral in the Second World War, and consequently survived his supporters, Hitler and Mussolini. He ruled until his death in 1975.

QUESTIONS

1. How far would you agree with the description of Kemal Ataturk as the 'father of modern Turkey'?
2. What problems faced Mustafa Kemal when he became president of Turkey in 1922 and how successful was he in dealing with them?
3. Explain why Japan became a military dictatorship in the early 1930s.
4. Outline the main problems and developments in Spain during the 1920s and 1930s.
5. What were the causes of the civil war in Spain (1936 to 1939) and why were Franco's forces victorious?

CHAPTER 11

THE EMPIRES

BETWEEN THE WARS

SUMMARY OF EVENTS

Most of the states of Europe had overseas empires, built up during the nineteenth century or earlier, of which the greatest in area was the British empire; it included vast tracts of Africa, Malaya, India, Burma, the West Indies, and a special feature which no other empire could boast – the white dominions – Canada, Australia, New Zealand and South Africa. France had the second largest empire, with territories in Africa, Indo-China and the West Indies. Both empires had been swelled by the mandates taken from Germany and Turkey in the peace settlement at the end of the First World War (see Sections 2.8 and 2.10). Other important empires were those of Holland (East Indies), Belgium (Congo), and Portugal (Mozambique, Angola and Guinea). Italy and Spain also had territory in Africa (see Fig 2.4).

After 1918 nationalist movements aiming at independence developed in many of these empires. Britain had trouble in India, Egypt, the Arab mandates and Ireland; even the white dominions were unhappy about exactly what the term 'dominion status' involved, and pressed for a clear definition. France faced revolutionary nationalism in Indo-china and the Arab mandates as did the Dutch in the East Indies. On the whole Africa remained quiet between the wars and nationalism scarcely existed in the Belgian Congo and the Portuguese colonies; however, the Spanish had to deal with a troublesome revolt in Morocco led by Abd-el-Krim. All these territories eventually gained independence, a few before 1939, but most of them after the Second World War.

It is interesting to compare the attitudes of the three main colonial powers to the growth of nationalism. Britain compromised, claiming that her territories would be allowed to proceed to independence in gradual stages; and indeed southern Ireland was granted dominion status (1922), Egypt semi-independence (1922) and Iraq full independence (1932); the Statute of Westminster (1931) satisfied the dominions about their relationship with Britain and saw the formation of the British commonwealth; however, progress in India was far too gradual for the nationalists' liking. France took quite a different view and refused to make any concessions to nationalist feeling which was ruthlessly suppressed in Syria and Indo-China. The Dutch attitude lay somewhere between: there was talk of independence for the Dutch East Indies, but when slow progress caused revolts in Java (1926–7), determined repression followed. Finally against the general trend, when nineteeth-century-style imperialism was out of fashion, two countries, Italy (in Abyssinia) and Japan (in China), were trying to extend their overseas empires during the 1930s.

11.1 BRITAIN AND THE COMMONWEALTH

(a) Britain's white dominions, Canada, Australia and New Zealand, as well as South Africa, and the Irish Free State (since 1922), were already self-governing as far as internal affairs were concerned, but had to act along with Britain for foreign policy, which was one of the reasons why they all fought on Britain's side in the First World War. By the end of the war a desire to run their own foreign affairs had developed, partly because the war had made them more aware of their importance as separate nations (together they had put over a million men in the field); in addition they were encouraged by Woodrow Wilson's support for the principle of national independence, and they were worried in case Britain should drag them into another war. Consequently Canada and South Africa refused to help Britain during the Chanak incident (see Section 4.1(b) (vii)), and they all refused to sign the treaties of Lausanne in 1923 (see Section 2.10) and Locarno in 1925 (see Section 13.1(e)). South Africa in particular became increasingly hostile to Britain and seemed determined to leave the empire. Clearly some initiative was needed, and happily for the future of the commonwealth, as it was beginning to be called, this was taken at:

(b) The Imperial Conference of 1926. Under the chairmanship of Balfour, the former Conservative Prime Minister, the conference showed that Britain was prepared to conciliate the dominions. Balfour produced a famous formula which defined the dominions as free countries, equal to each other and to Britain, and in complete control of their own internal and foreign affairs; they were to be 'freely associated as members of the British Commonwealth of Nations'. This satisfied the dominions (even South Africa for the time being) and was passed through the British parliament as the Statute of Westminster (1931). The commonwealth was a unique experiment in international organisation but because of the degree of independence enjoyed by the dominions, the achievements of the new 'white man's club', as it was described, were often something of a disappointment. There was no commonwealth parliament or other set machinery for co-operation to take place, though during the depression of the 1930s some trading agreements were made. In addition the Irish Free State under de Valera was unco-operative.

11.2 BRITAIN AND IRELAND 1916–39

In the summer of 1914 the Third Irish Home Rule Bill, which would have given self-government to Ireland, was about to become law. Unfortunately this was no solution to the problems of Ireland since Ulster in the north (with its Protestant majority) wanted to remain with Britain, and it was only the outbreak of war in 1914 which put the situation on ice for the time being. The operation of the act was postponed until the end of the war. The British government hoped that Ireland would remain quiet for the duration of the war, but their hopes were dashed when violence broke out again at Easter 1916.

(a) What were the problems in Ireland between 1916 and 1923, and how did British governments try to solve them?

(i) Though the majority of the Irish seemed prepared to wait until the war was over for Home Rule (thousands actually volunteered to fight for Britain against the Germans), a minority, mainly a group called *Sinn Fein* (meaning 'ourselves alone' – freedom from British rule), hoped to seize independence while Britain was preoccupied with the war. In 1916 they launched *the Easter Rebellion* proclaiming a republic and seizing several strong points in Dublin, including the General Post Office, in the hope that the rest of the country would rise in sympathy and force the British to withdraw. However, no sympathetic rising took place and British troops soon put an end to the rebellion which was militarily a total failure.

(ii) Though the rebellion was over within a few days, British treatment of the rebels caused a wave of disgust throughout Ireland and the USA with its large Irish population. Fifteen of the leaders were shot; one of them, James Connolly, was already dying of gunshot wounds and, being unable to stand, was shot sitting in a chair. This caused many more people to want a complete break with Britain, not just Home Rule, and there was a rush of support for *Sinn Fein*, which set about organising the powerful IRA (Irish Republican Army).

(iii) There was still a chance that the Irish might be pacified if Home Rule could be introduced immediately. Lloyd George got the Ulstermen and Home Rule supporters together (1917) and persuaded them to agree to a Home Rule scheme, thus detaching the Home Rulers from *Sinn Fein*. Unfortunately the British Conservatives (Unionists) who were against Home Rule and wanted the Irish to be repressed refused to accept the scheme; consequently what was probably the last chance of settling the Irish problem peacefully was lost.

(iv) The problem developed a stage further when in the British general election of December 1918 *Sinn Fein* won 73 out of the 105 Irish seats, but instead of going to the British parliament at Westminster they proclaimed an independent Irish republic with their own parliament (*Dail Eireann* - Assembly of Ireland) in Dublin, and elected Eamonn de Valera as leader. He was one of the few surviving leaders of the Easter Rising and became the symbol of Irish republicanism. Together with Michael Collins and Arthur Griffith, he organised an effective government which ignored the British and ran the country in its own way, collecting taxes and setting up law courts. The British Prime Minister, Lloyd George, hoped that the Government of Ireland Act (February 1920) would win moderate support back to the British. This was a revised version of the original Home Rule Bill of 1912, delayed by the Lords and then by the war; this time Ireland was partitioned, with one parliament for the south at Dublin and another for the six counties of Ulster at Belfast. The Belfast parliament was for the benefit of the Ulster Protestants, who still refused to be ruled by a Dublin-based Roman Catholic government. Although Ulster reluctantly accepted their parliament, *Sinn Fein* rejected the entire act, because it gave them control only of certain domestic matters, whereas they were determined on a complete break with Britain; also they wanted control of Ulster.

(v) Violence continued as the IRA pursued a campaign of terrorism against the police (Royal Irish Constabulary). Lloyd George retaliated by letting loose the notorious Black and Tans (recently demobilised British soldiers) against the IRA, and both sides committed terrible atrocities. By the summer of 1921 Lloyd George realised that such a situation could not continue; under pressure from Labour, from many Liberals and from King George V, who hated the British campaign of violence and pleaded for peace and common sense, Lloyd George decided to try negotiations. The IRA, close to exhaustion, responded, and Lloyd George managed to persuade both *Sinn Fein* and the British Conservatives to sign a treaty (December 1921). Southern Ireland became independent with the same status as the dominions, and accepted membership of the commonwealth; the British navy was to be allowed to use three ports.

(vi) The troubles were still not over: a section of *Sinn Fein*, led by de Valera, refused to accept the settlement because of the partition and the remaining connection with Britain, and civil war broke out between the two *Sinn Fein* factions. This ended in April 1923 with a victory for supporters of the treaty. The Irish Free State came into existence officially in December 1922.

(b) **The relationship between Britain and the Irish Free State** after 1923 continued to change gradually. De Valera formed a new party, *Fianna Fail* (Soldiers of Destiny) which won the election of 1932, mainly because the slump and unemployment had made the government of William Cosgrave highly unpopular. De Valera, Prime Minister for the next 16 years, set about destroying the links with Britain, though without taking the final step of declaring a republic. The oath of allegiance to the British monarch was ignored and in 1937 a new constitution was introduced illus 11.1 *Sinn Feiners held up at pistol point by the Black and Tans, 1920*

making Eire completely independent in practice. Neville Chamberlain, the British Prime Minister, made concessions in the hope of winning Eire's friendship. Debts amounting to £100 million still owing by Eire were written off, and the three naval bases handed back. However, Eire remained unco-operative: de Valera would never be satisfied until he controlled Ulster. Consequently Eire took no part in the commonwealth, remained neutral during the Second World War, and in 1949 finally declared itself an independent republic.

11.3 THE INDIAN STRUGGLE FOR INDEPENDENCE

(a) Indian nationalism began in the late nineteenth century when many middle-class Indians, having received a British-style education, often at Oxford or Cambridge, felt frustrated that their country continued to be·run by the British while they were allowed no say in government and only a very minor role in local affairs. They founded a party called *the Indian National Congress* (1885) to press for greater participation by Indians in government, in response to which the British introduced the 1909 *Morley–Minto reforms* (Morley was the Secretary of State for India, Lord Minto the Viceroy, who ruled India on behalf of the King). Indians were allowed to sit on the executive councils which advised the provincial governors, and for the time being the Indians seemed satisfied. After 1914 nationalist feeling intensified, probably encouraged by the important contribution made by Indians to the war effort, and perhaps by the successful revolutions in Russia and by Woodrow Wilson's talk of self-determination for subject peoples.

(b) How did the British government deal with the demands for Indian independence?

The British were slowly coming round to the idea that India would have to be given a measure of self-government; in 1917 the Indians were promised 'the gradual development of self-governing institutions with a view to the progressive realisation of responsible government in India as an integral part of the British Empire.' However, many Conservatives, including Winston Churchill and Lord Birkenhead (Secretary of State for India from 1924 to 1928) were utterly opposed to the idea, although the pace was far too slow for the impatient nationalists, whose leaders, Mahatma Gandhi and Jawaharlal Nehru, both lawyers educated in London, organised the anti–British campaign. The stages in the gradual move towards independence were:

(i) In 1918 Montagu (Secretary of State for India) and Lord Chelmsford (Viceroy), put forward plans which eventually became *the Government of India Act* (1919). There was to be a national parliament with two houses; about five million of the wealthiest Indians were given the vote; in the provincial governments the ministers of education, health and public works could now be Indians; a commission would be held ten years later to decide whether India was ready for further concessions. Congress was bitterly disappointed because the British kept complete control of the central government and of the key provincial ministries such as law and order and taxation. Moreover the Indians were enraged at the slowness with which the British put even these limited advances into operation. Rioting broke out and at *Amritsar* in the Punjab, after 5 Europeans had been murdered, General Dyer dispersed an excited crowd of over 5,000 Indians with machinegun fire, killing 379. Order was soon restored, illus 11.2 *Mahatma Gandhi addressing a crowd in Bombay*

but the Amritsar massacre was an important turning point: it provoked so much fury that Congress was transformed from a middleclass party to a mass movement. 'After Amritsar,' writes Martin Gilbert, 'no matter what compromises and concessions the British might suggest, British rule would ultimately be swept away.' By this time *Gandhi* was the leading figure of Congress. He believed in non-violent protest and the equality of all classes. Always dressed as a simple peasant, he somehow managed by sheer force of personality to persuade Indians to refuse to work, stage sit-down strikes, fast, stop paying taxes and boycott elections. Unfortunately he was unable to control his more extreme supporters and violence often developed; in 1922 he called off his first non-co-operation campaign.

(ii) The next British move, apart from putting Gandhi in gaol, was to appoint *the Simon Commission* (1928), as mentioned in the 1919 Act. In 1930 this proposed self-government for the provinces but was treated with contempt by the Indians, who were not even represented on the commission and who were demanding immediate dominion status. As soon as he was out of gaol Gandhi began his second civil disobedience campaign by breaking the law that only the government could manufacture salt. After a symbolic 250-mile march to the sea, he produced salt from seawater; but again violent incidents developed and again Gandhi was arrested.

(iii) *Lord Irwin* (Viceroy 1926–31) was a humane and enlightened politician, sympathetic to the Indians; before the Simon Report appeared in 1930 he had expressed the view that dominion status must come, so that the Indians felt even more let down when the report made no mention of it. Irwin was convinced that negotiations must take place and consequently two *Round Table Conferences* (1930 and 1931) were held in London. The first was unsatisfactory because, although the Indian princes were represented and accepted the idea of an Indian federation, no Congress representatives were there: most of them were in prison. Irwin had them released and prevailed upon Gandhi to travel to London to attend the second conference, much to the horror of Churchill who described Gandhi as 'this malignant and subversive fanatic'. Again little progress was made, this time because of disagreements about Muslim representation in an independent Indian parliament.

(iv) A major step towards independence was *the Government of India Act of 1935*, introduced as a result of co-operation between MacDonald and Baldwin, and in spite of bitter oppostion from Churchill. The elected Indian assembly was to have a say in everything except defence and foreign affairs; the eleven provincial assemblies were to have more or less full control over local affairs. The nationalists were still not satisfied: the act fell short of dominion status (the white dominions controlled their own defence and foreign policies), and the princes who still ruled certain areas of India refused to co-operate; thus their areas remained outside the system. Another failure of the act was that it ignored the religious rivalry between Hindus and Muslims. Roughly two-thirds of the Indians were Hindus, and the next largest group, the Muslims (who believed in the Islamic religion) were afraid that in a democratic India they would be dominated and unfairly treated by the Hindus. When Nehru's Congress party, which was overwhelmingly Hindu, won control of eight out of the eleven provinces in the 1937 elections, the Muslim League under its leader M. A. Jinnah demanded a separate state of their own called Pakistan, while Congress and Gandhi were determined to preserve a united India. No further developments took place before the Second World War, but mounting Hindu/Muslim hostility boded ill for the future, and provided some justification for the British reluctance to grant full self-government.

11.4 BRITAIN AND HER MIDDLE EAST MANDATES

In 1916 the Arabs in the Turkish empire rose in revolt, and helped by the British Colonel T. E. Lawrence (Lawrence of Arabia) and later by

British troops under Allenby, they played an important part in liberating the Arab territories from Turkish control. As a bribe to win Arab support against Turkey, the British had made vague promises that when the war was over, the Arabs would be allowed to set up independent states; but about the same time (1916) doubtless under the pressures of war, the British had also made the contradictory Sykes-Picot agreement with France, whereby Turkey's Arab lands would be divided between the two of them. In 1919 therefore, to their intense disappointment, the Arabs found their territories handed over as mandates (to be 'looked after' and prepared for self-government) to Britain (Iraq, Transjordan and Palestine) and France (Syria and Lebanon). Again Britain was reluctant to sever all connections with her mandates because of the Middle East oil resources, particularly in Iraq, and wanted to be allowed to station troops there to guarantee a sure source of oil. On the other hand the British dared not offend the Arabs too deeply or oil supplies might equally be threatened. Consequently steady progress towards independence was made in Iraq and Transjordan, though with strings attached; however the situation in Palestine was complicated by the Jewish/Arab problem.

(a) **In Iraq**, after some initial nationalist rioting, the British set up an Iraqi national government in which each minister had a British adviser. The *Amir Feisal* (who had just been driven out of Syria by the French) was accepted as king. Although extreme nationalists did not approve, this set-up was agreed by the Anglo-Iraqi Treaty of 1922 and worked well. An elected parliament was introduced in 1924 and Feisal, a man of great personal charm and political ability, proved to be an excellent ruler. With British help, industry and agriculture were organised and an efficient administrative system introduced; the British won Iraqi support by successfully opposing Turkish claims to the province of Mosul with its vast oil resources. In 1932 Iraq became fully independent, though Britain was allowed to keep two air bases; according to one Arab nationalist, George Antonius, 'the modern state of Iraq owes its existence largely to the efforts and devotion of its British officials.'

(b) **In Transjordan** the British set up Feisal's brother Abdullah as king, and allowed him to run the country's internal affairs, which he did competently. However, Transjordan was a poor state, lacking in resources and with no oil, and was therefore dependent on Britain for subsidies and for defence. In 1946 it was given complete independence, though Abdullah kept on the British officers who led his army.

(c) **Palestine** proved to be the most troublesome mandate because of the growing hostility between Jews and Arabs. The problem originated about two thousand years earlier in AD 71 when most of the Jews were driven out of Palestine, their homeland, by the Romans. In fact small communities of Jews remained behind in Palestine and over the following seventeen hundred years there was a gradual trickle of Jews returning from exile, though until the end of the nineteeth century there were never enough to cause the Palestinian Arabs to fell threatened. However, in 1897 some European Jews founded *the World Zionist Organisation* at Basle in Switzerland, an event which was to be of profound importance for the Middle East. Greatly disturbed by the recent persecutions of Jews in Russia, Germany and France, the Zionists demanded a Jewish national home in Palestine. Even before they received the mandate over Palestine, the British had become involved in the controversy and must take much of the blame for the chaos that followed, especially after 1945.

How did Britain become involved and how did the situation develop up to 1939?

(i) During the First World War the British had made three contradictory promises, which were bound to lead to frustration and hostility. There were the two already mentioned: independent states for the Arabs and the partition of the Arab territories between Britain and France; the third was *the Balfour Declaration* (November 1917) in which the British Foreign Minister pledged British support for a Jewish 'national home' in Palestine. The British motive, apart from genuine sympathy with the Zionists, was a belief that the Jews would help to safeguard the Suez Canal and provide a buffer between the canal zone and the French in Syria.

(ii) Faced with bitter Arab protests both against the British failure to grant independence and against the arrival of increasing numbers of Jews, the British government stated (1922) that there was no intention that the Jews should occupy the whole of Palestine and that there would be no interference with the rights of the Arabs in Palestine. The British hoped to persuade Jews and Arabs to live together peacefully in the same state and they failed to understand the deep religious gulf between the two.

(iii) Jews continued to arrive complete with Zionist money, bought land from Arabs who were at first willing to sell, started industries and reclaimed land. It was soon clear that they intended to develop not just a national home but a Jewish national state; by 1928 there were 150,000 of them. The Arabs rioted and began murdering Jews and consequently in 1930 the British Labour government decided that Jewish immigration must cease for the time being. Now it was the turn of the Zionists to rage against the British to such an extent that MacDonald felt obliged to allow immigration to continue.

(iv) The situation took a turn for the worse after Hitler came to power in Germany (1933): Nazi persecution caused a flood of refugees until by 1935 about a quarter of the total population of Palestine was Jewish. Arabs again began to attack Jews while British troops struggled to keep order.

(v) In 1937 the British Peel Commission suggested dividing Palestine into two separate states, one Jewish, one Arab, but the Arabs rejected the idea.

(vi) As war loomed in 1939 the British felt the need to win Arab support, and in a White Paper they agreed to limit Jewish immigration to 10,000 a year and promised to set up an independent Arab state in ten years, thus guaranteeing an Arab majority in the new state. At this point, with nothing resolved, the British hoped to shelve the problem until after the war (see Chapter 25).

QUESTIONS

1. What developments took place in the relationship between Britain, her empire and the commonwealth between 1919 and 1939?

2. Outline the changing relationship between Britain and Ireland between 1916 and 1939.

3. What were the problems in Ireland between 1916 and 1923 and how did British governments try to solve them?

4. How did British governments try to deal with Indian demands for independence between 1919 and 1947?

5. Describe the criticisms an Indian nationalist would have made of:

    (a) The Government of India Act (1919);
    (b) The Simon Commission Report (1930);
    (c) Round Table Conferences (1930-1);
    (d) The Government of India Act (1935).

6. Outline the history of Palestine under the British mandate. In what circumstances did Britain decide to abandon the mandate? Describe the results of this decision over the following two years (see Chapter 25 for second part of this question).

7. In what ways was Britain's policy in the Near and Middle East between 1917 and 1939 influenced by the following factors: Arab dislike of Turkish rule; growth of Zionism; Britain's sea routes to India; increasing interest in oil resources?

CHAPTER 12

THE LEAGUE OF NATIONS

SUMMARY OF EVENTS

The League of Nations formally came into existence on 10 January 1920, the same day that the Versailles Treaty came into operation. With headquarters at Geneva in Switzerland, one of its main aims was to settle international disputes and so prevent war from ever breaking out again. After some initial teething troubles, the League seemed to be functioning successfully during the 1920s: not only did it solve a number of minor international disputes, it also achieved valuable economic and social work, such as helping thousands of refugees and former prisoners of war to find their way home again. In 1930 supporters of the League felt optimistic about its future; indeed the South African statesman, Jan Smuts, was moved to remark that 'we are witnessing one of the great miracles of history.' However, during the 1930s the authority of the League was several times challenged, first by the Japanese invasion of Manchuria (1931) and later by the Italian attack on Abyssinia (1935). Both aggressors ignored the League's orders to withdraw, and for a variety of reasons it proved impossible to force them to comply. After 1935 respect for the League declined as its weaknesses became more apparent. In Germany's disputes with Czechoslovakia and Poland which led on to the Second World War the League was not consulted, and it was unable to exert the slightest influence to prevent the outbreak of war. After December 1939 it did not meet again and it was dissolved in 1946 – a total failure, at least as far as preventing war was concerned.

12.1 WHAT WERE THE ORIGINS OF THE LEAGUE?

The League is often spoken of as being the brainchild of the American president Woodrow Wilson. Although Wilson was certainly a great supporter of the idea of an international organisation for peace, the League was in reality the result of a coming together of similar suggestions (made during the First World War) by a number of world statesmen. Lord Robert Cecil of Britain, Jan Smuts of South Africa and Léon Bourgeois of France put forward detailed schemes as to how such an organisation might be set up; Lloyd George referred to it as one of Britain's war aims, and Wilson included it as the last of his 14 points (see Section 2.7(a)). Wilson's great contribution was to insist that the League Covenant (the list of rules by which the League was to operate), which had been drawn up by an international committee including Cecil, Smuts and Bourgeois as well as Wilson himself, should be included in each of the separate peace treaties. This ensured that the League actually came into existence instead of merely remaining a topic for discussion.

It had two main aims:

(a) To maintain peace through **collective security**: if one state attacked another, the member states of the League would act together, collectively, to restrain the aggressor, either by economic or by military sanctions.

(b) To encourage **international co-operation** in order to solve economic and social problems.

12.2 HOW WAS THE LEAGUE ORGANISED?

There were 42 member states at the beginning and 55 by 1926 when Germany was admitted. Its main organs were:

(a) **The General Assembly**: this met annually and contained representatives of all the member states, each of which had one vote. Its function was to decide general policy: it could, for example, propose a revision of peace treaties, and it handled the finances of the League. Any decisions taken had to be unanimous.

(b) **The Council**: this was a much smaller body which met more often, at least three times a year, and contained four permanent members – Britain, France, Italy and Japan (USA was to have been a permanent member but declined to join the League) – and four other members to be elected by the Assembly for periods of three years. The number of non-permanent members had increased to nine by 1926. It was the Council's task to deal with specific political disputes as they arose and again decisions had to be unanimous.

(c) **The Permanent Court of International Justice**: this was based at the Hague in Holland and consisted of 15 judges of different nationalities; it dealt with legal disputes between states as opposed to political ones.

(d) **The Secretariat**: this looked after all the paperwork, preparing agendas, and writing resolutions and reports for carrying out the decisions of the League.

(e) In addition there were a number of commissions and committees to deal with specific problems. The main commissions were those which handled the mandates, military affairs, minority groups and disarmaments, while there were committees for international labour, health, economic and financial organisation, child welfare, drug problems and women's rights.

(f) In its function of peace-keeping it was expected that the League would operate as follows: all disputes threatening war would be submitted to the League and any member which resorted to war, thus breaking the covenant, would face action by the rest; the council would recommend 'what effective military, naval or air force the members should contribute to the armed forces'.

12.3 THE SUCCESSES OF THE LEAGUE

(a) It would be unfair to dismiss the League as a total failure; in fact many of the commissions and committees achieved valuable results and much was done to foster international co-operation. One of the most successful was *the International Labour Organisation* under its French socialist director, Albert Thomas. Its purpose was to improve conditions of labour all over the world by persuading governments to fix a maximum working day and week, specify adequate minimum wages and introduce sickness and unemployment benefit and old age pensions. It collected and published a vast amount of information and many governments were prevailed upon to take action. *The Refugee Organisation* led by Fridtjof Nansen, the Norwegian explorer, solved the problem of thousands of former prisoners of war marooned in Russia at the end of the war; about half a million were returned home. After 1933 valuable help was given to thousands fleeing from the Nazi persecution in Germany. *The Health Organisation* did good work in investigating the causes of epidemics and was particularly successful in combating a typhus epidemic in Russia which at one time seemed likely to spread across Europe. *The Mandates Commission* supervised the government of the territories taken from Germany and Turkey, while yet another commission was responsible for administering the Saar, which it did most efficiently, concluding by organising the 1935 plebiscite in which a large majority voted for the Saar to be returned to Germany. Not all were successful, however; *the Disarmament Commission* made no progress in the near impossible task of persuading member states to reduce armaments, though they had all undertaken to do so when they agreed to the covenant.

(b) Several political disputes were referred to the League in the early 1920s; in all but two the League's decisions were accepted. For example in the quarrel between Sweden and Finland over the Aaland Islands, the verdict went in favour of Finland (1920); over the rival claims of Germany and Poland to the important industrial area of Upper Silesia, the League decided that it should be partitioned between the two (1921);

when the Greeks invaded Bulgaria after some shooting incidents on the frontier, the League swiftly intervened: Greek troops were withdrawn and damages paid to Bulgaria (1925). When Turkey claimed the province of Mosul, part of the British mandated territory of Iraq, the League decided in favour of Iraq. Even further afield, squabbles were settled between Peru and Colombia and between Bolivia and Paraguay. It is significant, however, that none of these decisions went against a major state, which might have challenged the League's verdict. In fact during this same period the League twice found itself overruled by the Conference of Ambassadors based in Paris, which was intended to deal with problems arising out of the Versailles treaties. There were first the rival claims of Poland and Lithuania to Vilna (1920) followed by the Corfu Incident, a quarrel between Italy under Mussolini and Greece (1923). The fact that the League seemed unable or unwilling to respond to these affronts was not a promising sign.

12.4 WHY DID THE LEAGUE FAIL TO PRESERVE PEACE?

At the time of the Corfu Incident in 1923, many people wondered what would happen if a powerful state were to challenge the League on a matter of major importance, for example, by invading an innocent country. How effective would the League be then? Unfortunately several such challenges occurred during the 1930s, and on every occasion the League was found wanting. Reasons suggested for its failure are:

(a) An initial disadvantage was that it was too closely linked with the Versailles treaties, giving it the air of being an organisation for the benefit of the victorious powers. In addition it had to defend the peace settlement which was far from perfect. Some of its provisions were bound to cause trouble - for example, the disappointment of Italy and the inclusion of Germans in Poland and Czechoslovakia.

(b) The League was dealt a serious blow in March 1920 when the United States Senate rejected both the Versailles Settlement and the League. The reasons behind their decision were varied: many Americans wanted to return to a policy of isolation and feared that membership of the League might cause them to be embroiled in another war; the Republicans, now in a majority in the Senate, strongly opposed Woodrow Wilson (a Democrat), but Wilson refused to compromise one iota over either the terms of the Treaties or the League Covenant. Indeed he was so obstinate that many of his own party lost patience and deserted him. The League was deprived of a powerful member whose presence would have been of great psychological and financial benefit.

(c) Germany was not allowed to join until 1926 and the USSR became a member only in 1934 (when Germany left), so that for the first few years of its existence the League was deprived of three of the world's most important powers.

(d) In the early years the Conference of Ambassadors in Paris was an embarrassment. It was intended to function only until the League machinery was established, but it lingered on, and on several occasions took precedence over the League. In 1920 the League supported Lithuania in her claim to Vilna which had just been seized from her by the Poles, but then allowed the Ambassadors to award Vilna to Poland. A later example was the Corfu Incident (1923) which arose from a boundary dispute between Greece and Albania, in which three Italian officers working on the boundary commission were killed. Mussolini blamed the Greeks, demanded huge compensation and bombarded and occupied the Greek island of Corfu. Greece appealed to the League, but Mussolini refused to recognise its competence to deal with the problem and threatened to withdraw from the League, whereupon the Ambassadors ordered Greece to pay the full amount demanded. At this early stage, however, supporters of the League dismissed these incidents as teething troubles.

(e) There were serious weaknesses in the covenant making it difficult to ensure that decisive action was taken against any aggressor. It was difficult to achieve unanimous decisions; the League had no military force of its own, and though Article 16 expected member states to supply troops if necessary, a resolution was passed in 1923 that each member would decide for itself whether or not to fight in a crisis. This clearly made nonsense of the idea of collective security. Several attempts were made to strengthen the covenant but these failed because a unanimous vote was needed to change it and this was never achieved. The most notable attempt was made in 1924 by the British Labour Prime Minister, Ramsay MacDonald, in a resolution known as the Geneva Protocol which pledged members to accept arbitration and help any victim of unprovoked aggression. With supreme irony, the Conservative government which followed MacDonald informed the League that they could not agree to the Protocol; they were reluctant to commit Britain and the dominions to the defence of all the 1919 frontiers. Unfortunately this left the League, as its critics remarked, 'lacking teeth'.

(f) The continued absence of the USA and the USSR plus the hostility of Italy made the League very much a Franco–British affair, but as their rejection of the Geneva Protocol showed, the British Conservatives were never enthusiastic about the League and preferred to sign the Locarno Treaties (1925) outside the League instead of conducting negotiations within it (see Section 13.1(e)). None of these weaknesses necessarily doomed the League to failure, however, provided all the members were prepared to refrain from aggression and accept League decisions; between 1925 and 1930 events ran fairly smoothly. Unfortunately:

(g) The world economic crisis which began in 1929 contributed to the League's decline. It brought unemployment and falling living standards to most countries, and caused extreme right-wing governments to come to power in Japan and Germany; together with Mussolini, they refused to keep to the rules and pursued a series of actions which revealed the League's weaknesses:

(h) In 1931 Japanese troops invaded the Chinese territory of Manchuria (see Section 14.1); China appealed to the League which condemned Japan and ordered her troops to be withdrawn. When Japan refused the League appointed a commission under Lord Lytton which decided (1932) that there were faults on both sides and suggested that Manchuria be governed by the League. However, Japan rejected this and withdrew from the League (March 1933). The question of economic sanctions let alone military ones was not raised, because Britain and France had serious economic problems and were reluctant to apply a trade boycott of Japan in case it led to war, which they were ill-equipped to win, especially without American help. Japan had successfully defied the League, and its prestige was damaged though not yet fatally.

(i) The failure of the World Disarmament Conference (1932-3) which met under the auspices of the League was a grave disappointment. The Germans asked for equality of armaments with France, but when the French demanded that this should be postponed for at least eight years, Hitler was able to use the French attitude as an excuse to withdraw Germany from the conference and later from the League.

(j) The most serious blow was the Italian invasion of Abyssinia in October 1935 (see Section 14.2(b)). The League condemned Italy and introduced economic sanctions which, however, did not include a ban on exports of oil, coal and steel to Italy. So half-hearted were the sanctions that Italy was able to complete the conquest of Abyssinia without too much inconvenience (May 1936). A few weeks later sanctions were abandoned and Mussolini had flouted the League. Again Britain and France must share the blame for the League's failure. Their motives were the desire not to antagonise Mussolini too much so as to keep him as an ally against the real danger - Germany. But the results were disastrous: Mussolini was annoyed by the sanctions anyway and began to draw closer to Hitler; small states lost all faith in the League; and Hitler himself was encouraged to break the Versailles treaties. After 1935 therefore the League was not taken seriously again.

The real explanation for the failure of the League was simple: when aggressive states such as Japan, Italy and Germany defied it, the League members, especially Britain and France, were not prepared to support it either by decisive economic measures or by war. The League was only as strong as the determination of its leading members to stand up to aggression; unfortunately determination of that sort was sadly lacking during the 1930s.

QUESTIONS

1. Give an account of the origins and organisation of the League of Nations. Identify and describe *three* of the successes, general or particular, which the League achieved during its existence.

2. Show how the following contributed to the decline of the League of Nations: The League Covenant; rejection of the Geneva Protocol (1924); the Manchuria Crisis (1931–3); failure to secure disarmament (1932–3); the Abyssinian War (1935–6). What other factors contributed towards the League's failure?

3. 'Only small powers had anything to fear from the League of Nations; the big powers had nothing to fear.' By a brief description of the League's activities between 1919 and 1939, show how such a statement came to be made. 1930

4 The accompanying cartoon was published in the early 1930s. Study it and then answer the following questions:

Fig 12.1

(i) Why is 'Geneva' written on the pillar on the right? (1 mark)

(ii) Which country does the man entering the building represent? (1 mark)

(iii) The news-poster lying by the side of the prostrate figure refers to 'Invasion of Manchuria'. Briefly describe the immediate events which led to the invasion. (3 marks)

(iv) The figure kneeling on the right depicts the British Minister at that time. What was his name? (1 mark)

(v) Explain the cartoonist's idea in printing the words, 'Face-Saving Outfit', on the side of the box, by the kneeling figure. (2 marks)

(vi) Who led the commission sent by the League of Nations to investigate the invasion? (1 mark)

(vii) State briefly the main points of the commission's report. (3 marks)

(viii) What other commissions, permanent and temporary, were set up by the League and how successful were they? (8 marks)

CHAPTER 13

FOREIGN AFFAIRS AND INTERNATIONAL RELATIONS 1919-33

SUMMARY OF EVENTS

International relations between the two world wars fall into two distinct phases with the division at January 1933, the fateful month in which Adolf Hitler came to power in Germany. Before that there seemed a good chance that world peace could be maintained, in spite of the failure of the League of Nations to curb Japanese aggression in Manchuria; once Hitler was firmly in control there seemed little chance of preventing a war of some sort, either limited or full-scale, depending on one's interpretation of Hitler's intentions (see Section 14.3). The first phase can be divided roughly into three:

(a) **1919 to 1923.** In the aftermath of the First World War, relations were disturbed by problems arising from the Paris peace settlement, while the newborn League of Nations struggled to sort things out. Both Turkey and Italy were dissatisfied with their treatment, Turkey being prepared to defy the settlement (see Section 2.10). The Italians, soon to come under the rule of Mussolini (1922), showed their resentment first by the seizure of Fiume which had been awarded to Yugoslavia and then in the Corfu Incident; later Italian aggression was turned against Abyssinia (1935). The problem of German reparations and whether or not she could afford to pay caused strained relations between France and Britain, on account of their differing attitudes towards German recovery. Lloyd George's attempt to reconcile France and Germany at the 1922 Genoa Conference failed miserably, and relations deteriorated still further in 1923 when French troops occupied the Ruhr (an important German industrial region) in an attempt to seize what the Germans were refusing to pay in reparations; this succeeded only in bringing about the collapse of the German currency. Meanwhile the USA, though choosing to remain politically isolated, exercised considerable economic influence on Europe by, among other things, insisting on full payment of European war debts. The USSR, now communist, was viewed with suspicion by the western countries, several of which, along with Japan, intervened against the Bolsheviks in the civil war which ravaged the USSR during 1918-20.

(b) 1924 to 1929 saw a general improvement in the international atmosphere brought about partly by changes in political leadership. In France Edouard Herriot and Aristide Briand, in Germany Gustav Stresemann and in Britain Ramsay MacDonald came to power, and all were keen to improve relations. The result was the Dawes Plan worked out in 1924 with American participation, which eased the situation with regard to German reparations. 1925 saw the signing of the Locarno Treaties which guaranteed the frontiers in western Europe fixed at Versailles; this seemed to remove French suspicions of German intentions. Germany was allowed to join the League in 1926 and two years later 65 nations signed the Kellogg-Briand Pact renouncing war. The 1929 Young Plan reduced German reparations to a more manageable figure; all seemed set fair for a peaceful future.

(c) 1930 to 1933. Towards the end of 1929 the world began to run into economic difficulties which helped to cause a deterioration in international relations. It was partly for economic reasons that Japanese troops invaded the Chinese province of Manchuria in 1931; mass unemployment in Germany played an important role in enabling Hitler to come to power. In this unpromising climate the World Disarmament Conference met (1932) only to break up in failure when the German delegates walked out (1933). With such a complex period, it will be best to treat the various themes separately.

13.1 WHAT ATTEMPTS WERE MADE TO IMPROVE INTERNATIONAL RELATIONS AND HOW SUCCESSFUL WERE THEY?

(a) The League of Nations played an important role, settling a number of international disputes and problems (see Section 12.3). However, its authority tended to be weakened by the fact that many states seemed to prefer signing agreements independently of the League, which suggests that they were not brimming with confidence at the League's prospects.

(b) The Washington Conferences (1921-2) tried to improve relations between the USA and Japan. The USA was increasingly suspicious of growing Japanese power in the Far East and of Japanese influence in China, especially as during the First World War Japan had seized Kiaochow and all the German islands in the Pacific. To prevent a naval building race, it was agreed that the Japanese navy would be limited to three-fifths the size of the American and British navies; Japan also agreed to withdraw from Kiaochow and the Shantung province of China which she had occupied since 1914. In return she was allowed to keep the former German Pacific islands as mandates, and the western powers promised not to build any more naval bases within striking distance of Japan. In addition, the USA, Japan, Britain and France agreed to guarantee the neutrality of China and to respect each other's possessions in the Far East. At the time the agreements were regarded as a great success and relations between the powers involved improved. In reality, however, Japan was left supreme in the Far

East, possessor of the world's third largest navy, which she could concentrate in the Pacific, whereas the navies of Britain and the USA, though larger, were spread more widely. This was to have unfortunate consequences for China in the 1930s when the USA refused to become involved in checking Japanese aggression.

(c) **The Genoa Conference** (1922) was the brainchild of the British Prime Minister, Lloyd George, who hoped it would solve the pressing problems of Franco-German hostility (the Germans were threatening to stop paying reparations), European war debts to the USA, and the need to resume proper diplomatic relations with soviet Russia. Unfortunately the conference failed: the French refused all compromise and insisted on full reparations payments; the Americans refused even to attend, and the Germans and Russians withdrew and signed a mutual agreement at Rapallo. When, the following year, the Germans failed to pay the amount due, French troops occupied the Ruhr, and deadlock quickly developed when the Germans replied with passive resistance.

(d) It was in an attempt to break this deadlock that **the Dawes Plan** was drawn up and finally accepted at a conference in London (1924). The three newcomers to international politics, Ramsay MacDonald, Edouard Herriot and Gustav Stresemann, were eager for reconciliation; the Americans were persuaded to take part and the conference was chaired for part of the time by the American representative, General Dawes. No reduction was made in the total amount Germany was expected to pay, but it was agreed that she should pay annually only what she could reasonably afford until she became more prosperous; a foreign loan of 800 million gold marks, mainly from the USA, was to be made to Germany; France, now assured of at least some reparations from Germany, agreed to withdraw her troops from the Ruhr. The plan was successful: the German economy began to recover on the basis of the American loans and international tensions gradually relaxed, preparing the way for the next agreements:

(e) **The Locarno Treaties** of 1925 were a number of different agreements involving Germany, France, Britain, Italy, Belgium, Poland and Czechoslovakia. The most important one was that Germany, France and Belgium promised to respect their joint frontiers; if one of the three broke this agreement, Britain and Italy would assist the state which was being attacked. Germany signed agreements with Poland and Czechoslovakia providing for arbitration over possible disputes. The agreements were greeted with wild enthusiasm all over Europe, and the reconciliation between Germany and France was referred to as the 'Locarno honeymoon'. Later, historians were not so enthusiastic about Locarno: there was one notable omission from the agreements – no guarantees were given about Germany's eastern frontiers with Poland and Czechoslovakia. By ignoring this problem, the signatories at Locarno were also ignoring the fact that by signing the League of Nations Covenant they had undertaken to guarantee all members against aggression. Locarno gave the impression that no action need necessarily be taken if Germany attacked Poland and Czechoslovakia and that Britain had perhaps turned her back on eastern Europe. For the time being though, as the world enjoyed a period of great economic prosperity, such uneasy thoughts were pushed into the background, and Germany was admitted to the League in 1926 and Stresemann and Briand (French Foreign Minister from 1925 to 1932) met regularly and had friendly discussions; often Austen Chamberlain (British Foreign Minister from 1924 until 1929) joined them. This 'Locarno spirit' culminated in the next piece of paper signing:

(f) The Kellogg–Briand Pact (1928) originated in an idea of Briand who proposed that France and the USA should sign a pact renouncing war. Frank B. Kellogg, the American Secretary of State, proposed that the whole world should be involved; eventually 65 states signed, agreeing to renounce war as an instrument of national policy. This sounded impressive, but was completely useless because no mention was made of sanctions against any state which broke its pledge. Japan for example signed the pact, but was not prevented from waging war against China only three years later.

(g) The Young Plan (1929) aimed to settle the remaining problem of reparations – the Dawes Plan had left uncertain the total amount payable. In the improved atmosphere the French were willing to compromise, and a committee chaired by an American banker, Owen Young, decided to reduce reparations from £6,600 million to £2,000 million, to be paid on a graded scale over the next 59 years. This was the figure that Keynes had urged at Versailles, and its acceptance ten years later was an admission of error by the Allies. The plan was welcomed in Germany, but before there was time to put it into operation a series of events following in rapid succession destroyed the fragile harmony of Locarno: the death of Stresemann (October 1929) removed one of the outstanding 'men of Locarno'; the Wall Street Crash in the same month soon developed into the great depression, and by 1932 there were over six million unemployed in Germany. Hope was kept alive by the Lausanne Conference (1932) at which Britain and France released Germany from most of her remaining reparations payments. However, in January 1933 Hitler became German Chancellor and after that, international tension mounted.

(h) The World Disarmament Conference (1932-3) met at Geneva to try and work out a formula for scaling down armaments, which all members of the League had undertaken to do when they accepted the covenant. In fact Germany was the only state to disarm, as Stresemann regularly pointed out, but the rest shrank from being the first to reduce armaments. If no progress could be made during the Locarno honeymoon, there was little chance of success in the disturbed atmosphere of the early 1930s. The

French, alarmed at the rapid increase of support for the Nazis in Germany, refused either to disarm or to allow Germany equality of armaments. Hitler, knowing that Britain and Italy sympathised with Germany, withdrew from the conference (October 1933) which was dead from that moment; a week later Germany also withdrew from the League.

In retrospect it could be seen that the statesmen of the world had only a limited success in improving international relations; even the 'Locarno spirit' proved illusory because so much depended on economic prosperity; when this evaporated, all the old hostilities and suspicions surfaced again, and authoritarian regimes which were prepared to risk aggression came to power.

13.2 HOW DID FRANCE TRY TO DEAL WITH THE PROBLEM OF GERMANY BETWEEN 1919 AND 1933?

As soon as the First World War ended, the French, after all they had suffered in two German invasions in less than 50 years, wanted to make sure that the Germans never again violated the sacred soil of France; this remained the major preoccupation of French foreign policy throughout the inter-war period. At different times, depending who was in charge of foreign affairs, the French tried several different methods of dealing with the problem: trying to keep Germany economically and militarily weak, signing alliances with other states to isolate Germany, and extending the hand of reconciliation and friendship. In the end they all failed.

illus 13.1 *French troops occupy a factory in the Ruhr, 1923*

(a) At the Paris peace conference the French premier, Clemenceau, insisted on a harsh settlement; in order to strengthen French security, the German army was to number no more than 100,000 men and there were to be severe limitations on armaments (see Section 2.8(a)). The German Rhineland was to be demilitarised to a distance of 50 kilometres east of the river, and France was to have the use of the Saar for 15 years. Britain and the USA promised to help France if the Germans attacked her again. Although many Frenchmen were disappointed (Foch, for example, wanted France to be given the whole of the German Rhineland west of the river but they were allowed to occupy it only for 15 years), it looked at first as though security was guaranteed. Unfortunately French satisfaction was short-lived: when the Americans rejected the entire peace settlement (March 1920) they abandoned their guarantee of assistance; the British used this as an excuse to cancel their obligations and the French felt betrayed.

(b) Clemenceau also demanded that the Germans should pay reparations (money to help repair damages). The figure was fixed in 1921 at £6,600 million, payment of which, it was thought, would keep Germany economically weak for the next 66 years (the period over which reparations were to be paid in annual instalments) and make another attack on France less likely. However, financial troubles in Germany soon caused the government to fall behind with its payments, and the French, who needed reparations to balance their budget and pay their own debt to the USA, became desperate.

(c) The next Prime Minister, the anti-German Raymond Poincaré, decided that drastic methods were needed to force the Germans to pay. French and Belgian troops occupied the Ruhr (the main German industrial area which includes the cities of Essen and Dusseldorf), but the Germans replied with passive resistance, strikes and sabotage. A number of nasty incidents between troops and civilians resulted in the deaths of over a hundred people; although the French managed to extract goods worth about £40 million, the whole episode caused galloping inflation and the collapse of the German mark, which by November 1923 was completely valueless. It also revealed the basic difference between the French and British attitudes towards Germany: while France adopted a hard line and wanted a Germany permanently crippled, Britain now saw moderation and reconciliation with Germany as the best security and believed that an economically healthy Germany would be good for the stability of Europe (as well as for British exports). Consequently the British government strongly disapproved of the Ruhr occupation and sympathised with Germany.

(d) At the same time the French tried to increase their security by building up a network of alliances, first with Poland (1921), and later with Czechoslovakia (1924), Rumania (1926) and Yugoslavia (1927). This network, known as the 'Little Entente', though impressive on paper, did not amount to much because the states involved were comparatively weak; what was needed was a renewal of the old alliance with Russia, which had served the French well during the First World War, but this seemed out of the question now that Russia had become communist.

(e) The French worked for a strong League of Nations with the victorious powers acting as a military police force compelling aggressive states to behave themselves. However, in the end it was the much more vague Wilson version of the League that was adopted. French disappointment was bitter when Britain took the lead in rejecting the Geneva Protocol which might well have strengthened the League; clearly there was no point in expecting much guarantee of security from that direction.

(f) By the summer of 1924 when the failure of Poincaré's Ruhr occupation was obvious, the new premier Herriot was prepared to accept a compromise solution to the still pressing problem of German reparations. This was the Dawes Plan (see previous section).

(g) During the Briand era (he was Foreign Minister in eleven successive governments between 1925 and 1932), the French approach to the German problem was one of reconciliation. Briand persevered with great skill to build up genuinely good relations with Germany, as well as to improve relations with Britain and strengthen the League. Fortunately Stresemann, who was in charge of German foreign policy from November 1923 until 1929, believed that the best way to foster German recovery was by co-operation with Britain and France; the result was the Locarno Treaties, the Kellogg-Briand Pact, the Young Plan and the cancellation of most of the remaining reparations payments (see previous section). There is some debate among historians about how genuine this apparent reconciliation between France and Germany really was. Taylor suggests that though Briand and Stresemann were sincere, 'they did not carry their peoples with them', so strong was nationalist feeling in the two countries that both men were limited in the concessions they could offer. The fact that Stresemann was privately determined to get the frontier with Poland redrawn to Germany's advantage would have caused friction later, since Poland was France's ally; he was equally determined to work for union with Austria and a revision of the Versailles terms.

(h) Even before that happened though, the death of Stresemann, the world economic crisis and the subsequent growth of support for the Nazis alarmed the French, causing their attitude towards Germany to harden. When in 1931 plans were produced for an Austro-German customs union to ease the economic crisis, the French insisted that the matter be referred to the Court of International Justice at the Hague on the grounds that it was a violation of the Paris peace agreements. Though it made economic sense, the court ruled against it, and the plan was blocked. At the World Disarmament Conference (1932-3) relations worsened (see previous section) and when, with Hitler in power, the Germans walked out of the conference and the League, all Briand's work was ruined. The German problem was as far from solution as ever.

13.3 HOW DID RELATIONS BETWEEN THE USSR AND BRITAIN, GERMANY AND FRANCE DEVELOP BETWEEN 1919 AND 1933?

For the first three years after the Bolsheviks came to power (November 1917) relations between the new government and the western countries deteriorated to the point of open war. This was mainly because the Bolsheviks tried to spread the revolution further, especially in Germany. As early as December 1917 floods of propaganda attempted to turn the masses against their capitalist masters; after the Russian defeat Karl Radek, one of the Bolshevik leaders, went secretly to Berlin to plan the revolution, while other agents did the same in Austria and Hungary; it was hoped that world-wide revolution would follow. This sort of behaviour did not endear the communists to the western governments, Britain, France, Czechoslovakia and the USA, who (together with Japan) tried rather half-heartedly to destroy the Bolsheviks by intervening in the civil war to help the Whites (see Section 3.5(c)). Nor were the Russians invited to the Versailles conference in 1919. By the middle of 1920, however, circumstances were gradually changing: the interventionist countries had acknowledged failure and withdrawn their troops; communist revolutions in Germany and Hungary had failed; and Russia was too exhausted by the civil war to contemplate stirring up any more revolutions for the time being. The way was open for communications to be re-established.

(a) USSR and Britain
Relations blew hot and cold according to which government was in power in Britain; the two Labour governments (1924 and 1929–31) were much more sympathetic to Russia than the others.

(i) After the interventionist fiasco, Lloyd George (British Prime Minister from 1916 to 1922) was prepared for reconciliation, and this corresponded with Lenin's desire for improved relations with the west in order to acquire foreign trade and capital. The result was an Anglo-Russian trade treaty (March 1921) which was important for Russia not only commercially, but also because Britain was the first of the powers to acknowledge the existence of the Bolshevik government; it was to lead to similar agreements with other countries and to full political recognition. The new rapprochement was soon shaken, however, when at the Genoa conference (1922) Lloyd George suggested that the Bolsheviks pay war debts incurred by the tsarist regime. The affronted Russians left the conference and signed the Treaty of Rapallo with the Germans; this greatly alarmed Britain and France who could see no good coming from what Lloyd George called this 'fierce friendship'.

(ii)   Relations improved briefly in 1924 when Ramsay MacDonald and the new Labour government gave full diplomatic recognition to the communists, signed another trade treaty and proposed a British loan. However, this was unpopular with British Conservatives and Liberals who soon brought MacDonald's government down.

(iii) Under the Conservative government (1924-9) relations with Russia deteriorated. British Conservatives had no love for the communists, even less after the affair of the Zinoviev Letter (see Section 4.4(c)). There was evidence that Russian propaganda was responsible for part of the trouble in India. Police raided the British Communist Party headquarters in London (1925) and the premises of Arcos, a soviet trading organisation based in London (1927), and claimed to have found evidence of Russian plotting with British communists to overthrow the system. The government expelled the mission and broke off diplomatic relations with the Russians, who replied by arresting some British residents in Moscow.

(iv)   Matters took a turn for the better in 1929 when Labour, encouraged by the new pro-western Foreign Minister, Maxim Litvinov, resumed diplomatic relations with Russia and signed another trade agreement the following year; but the improvement was only short-lived.

(v)   The Conservative-dominated National government cancelled the trade agreement (1932) and in retaliation the Russians arrested four Metropolitan-Vickers engineers working in Moscow; they were tried and given sentences ranging from two to three years for 'spying and wrecking'. However, when Britain placed an embargo on imports from Russia, Stalin released them (June 1933). By this time Stalin was becoming nervous about the possible threat from Hitler and was therefore prepared to take pains to improve relations with Britain.

(b) USSR and Germany

Russian relations with Germany were more consistent and more friendly than with Britain. This was because the Germans saw certain advantages to be gained from exploiting friendship with the USSR and because the Bolsheviks were anxious to have stable relations with at least one capitalist power.

(i)   A trade treaty was signed (May 1921) followed by the granting of Russian trade and mineral concessions to some German industrialists.

(ii)   The Rapallo Treaty signed on Easter Sunday 1922 after both Germany and Russia had withdrawn from the Genoa conference was an important step forward. Full diplomatic relations were resumed and mutual claims for reparations cancelled. Thereafter both enjoyed advantages from the new friendship: they could co-operate to keep Poland weak, which was in both their interests; Russia had Germany as a buffer against any future attack from the west; the Germans were allowed to build factories in Russia for the manufacture of aeroplanes and ammunition, enabling them to get round the

Versailles disarmament terms; German officers trained in Russia in the use of the new forbidden weapons.

(iii) The Treaty of Berlin (1926) renewed the Rapallo agreement for a further five years; it was understood that Germany would remain neutral if Russia were attacked by another power and neither would use economic sanctions against the other.

(iv) About 1930 relations began to cool somewhat as some Russians expressed concern at the growing power of the recovered Germany: the German attempt at a customs union with Austria in 1931 was taken as an ominous sign of increasing German nationalism. Russian concern changed to alarm at the growth of the Nazi party which was strongly anti-communist, and though Stalin and Litvinov tried to continue the friendship with Germany, they also began approaches to Poland, France and Britain. In January 1934 Hitler abruptly ended Germany's special relationship with the soviets by signing a non-aggression pact with Poland (see Section 14.5(b)).

(c) USSR and France

The Bolshevik takeover in 1917 was a serious blow for France because Russia had been an important ally whom she relied on to keep Germany in check. Now her former ally was calling for revolution in all capitalist states and could only be regarded as a menace to be destroyed as soon as possible. The French sent troops to help the Whites in the civil war, and it was because of French insistence that the Bolsheviks were not invited to Versailles. The French also intervened in the war between Russia and Poland in 1920: troops commanded by General Weygand helped to drive back a Russian advance on Warsaw, and afterwards the French government claimed to have stemmed the westward spread of Bolshevism. The subsequent alliance between France and Poland (1921) seemed to be directed as much against Russia as against Germany. Relations improved in 1924 when the moderate Herriot government resumed diplomatic relations, but the French were never enthusiastic especially as the French Communist Party was under orders from Moscow not to co-operate with other left-wing parties. Not until the early 1930s did the rise of the German Nazis cause a change of heart on both sides.

13.4 UNITED STATES FOREIGN POLICY 1919-33

The USA had been deeply involved in the First World War and when hostilities ceased she seemed likely to play an important role in world affairs. President Woodrow Wilson was a crucial figure at the Paris peace conference; his great dream was the League of Nations through which the USA would maintain world peace. However, the American people, tired of the war and suspicious of Europe, rejected Wilson and his League of Nations. From 1921 until early 1933 the USA was ruled by Republican governments which believed in a policy of isolation: she never joined the League and she tried to avoid political disputes with other states and the signing of treaties. Some historians still blame the failure of the League on the absence of the USA. In spite of this desire for isolation, the Americans found it impossible to avoid some involvement in world affairs, because of overseas trade, investment and the thorny problem of European war debts and reparations.

(a) During the prosperous years of the 1920s, Americans tried to increase trade and profits by investment abroad, in Europe, Canada and in Central and South America, and it was inevitable that the USA should take an interest in what was happening in these areas. There was, for example, a serious dispute with Mexico whose government was threatening to seize American-owned oil wells, but a compromise solution was reached.

(b) President Harding called the Washington Conferences (1921-2) because of concern at Japanese power in the Far East (see Section 13.1).

(c) Allied war debts to the USA caused much ill-feeling. During the war the American government had organised loans to Britain and her allies amounting to almost 12 billion dollars at 5 per cent interest. The Europeans hoped that the Americans would cancel the debts since the USA had done well out of the war (by taking over former European markets) but both Harding and Coolidge insisted that repayments be made in full. The Allies claimed that their ability to pay depended on whether Germany paid her reparations to them, but the Americans would not acknowledge any connection between the two. Eventually Britain was the first to agree to pay the full amount, over 62 years at the reduced interest rate of 3.3 per cent. Other states followed, the USA allowing much lower interest rates depending on the poverty of the country concerned: Italy, for example, got away with 0.4 per cent but this caused strong objections from Britain.

(d) With the German financial crisis of 1923 the Americans had to change their attitude and admit the connection between reparations and war debts; they agreed to take part in the Dawes and Young Plans (1924 and 1929) which enabled Germany to pay reparations. However, this caused the ludicrous situation in which America lent money to Germany so that she could pay reparations to Britain, France and Belgium, so that they could pay their war debts to the USA. The whole set-up, together with the American insistence on keeping high tariffs, was a contributory cause of the world economic crisis (see Section 7.2), with all its far-reaching consequences.

(e) The Kellogg-Briand Pact (1928) was another notable though useless American foray into world affairs.

(f) Relations with Britain were uneasy not only because of war debts but also because the Conservatives resented the limitations on British naval expansion imposed by the earlier Washington agreement. MacDonald, anxious to improve relations, organised a conference in London (1930), attended also by the Japanese, at which the three states reaffirmed the 5:5:3 ratio in cruisers, destroyers and submarines agreed at Washington. This was successful in re-establishing friendship between USA and Britain, but the Japanese soon exceeded their limits.

(g) The USA reverted to a policy of strict isolation when the Japanese invaded Manchuria in 1931. Although Hoover condemned the Japanese action, he refused to join in economic sanctions or make any move which might lead to war with Japan. Consequently Britain and France felt unable to act and the League was shown to be helpless. Throughout the 1930s, though acts of aggression mounted, the Americans remained determined not to be drawn into a conflict.

13.5 THE TROUBLE-MAKERS: POLAND, ITALY AND JAPAN

(a) It is perhaps unfair to describe **Poland** as a trouble-maker, sandwiched as she was between Germany and Russia, both of which bitterly resented the loss of their territory to make up the new state of Poland in 1919. However, the Poles had grievances arising from Versailles: they believed they ought to have been awarded the important industrial area of Teschen (given to Czechoslovakia) and parts of Lithuania and the Ukraine; they were determined to be as uncompromising as possible in relations with Germany and Russia and to seize every opportunity of furthering their interests.

- (i) They took advantage of Bolshevik exhaustion at the end of the civil war to invade the Ukraine, and though close to disaster as the Russians counter-attacked, the Poles, thanks to French help, were able to force the Russians to sign the Treaty of Riga (1921) ceding a large slice of the Ukraine to Poland. The west ignored it because it was a blow at communism.
- (ii) They seized the city of Vilna from Lithuania (1920) and hung on to it even though the League of Nations believed it should be returned to Lithuania. In 1923 the Conference of Ambassadors reluctantly agreed that Vilna should remain Polish. The French particularly were anxious to strengthen Poland as much as possible to take the place of Russia as her eastern ally against Germany.

(b) **Italy** also felt cheated by Versailles, and though many Italians were tired of war, nationalists felt that violent gestures were needed for the sake of national pride:

- (i) In September 1919 d'Annunzio occupied Fiume (see Section 6.1(a)); by an agreement signed at Rapallo in 1920 Fiume was to be a free city, but Italy was given the Istrian peninsula instead.
- (ii) Mussolini (who came to power October 1922) believed that aggression paid dividends. In 1923 Fiume was occupied again and the following

year the Yugoslavs agreed that it should remain Italian. 1923 also saw the Corfu Incident, another example of Italian aggression (see Section 12.4(d)). After 1923 both Poland and Italy calmed down and it was Japan which took over the role of aggressor-in-chief.

(c) **Japan** had emerged from the First World War in a strong position but after 1929 she was severely affected by the world economic crisis, which led the army to occupy the Chinese province of Manchuria (see Section 10.2). The League of Nations failed to control the Japanese (see Section 12.4(h)) who withdrew from the League in 1933. It was clear that international relations were moving into a new phase dominated not by the Locarno spirit but by major acts of aggression and violence.

QUESTIONS

1. How and with what success did the great powers seek to improve international relations between 1920 and 1933?
2. What problems threatened international relations between 1919 and 1933 and how successfully did the world's statesmen deal with them?
3. Explain the following attempts to improve international relations: Washington Conferences (1921-2); Dawes and Young Plans (1924 and 1929); Locarno Treaties (1925); Kellogg-Briand Pact (1928); Disarmament Conference (1932-3).
4. Using the following material, describe the changing ways in which France tried to deal with Germany between 1919 and 1933:
    reparations (1919-20); occupation of the Ruhr (1923); Dawes and Young Plans (1924 and 1929); Locarno Treaties (1925); the increase in Nazi support (1929-33); proposed Austro-German customs union (1931).
5. Describe and comment on French foreign policy between 1919 and 1936.
6. Show how British and French policy towards Germany differed between 1919 and 1923.
7. Describe Anglo-Soviet relations between the wars, using the following material and any additional material you think relevant:
    British intervention in the Russian Civil War (1918-20); recognition of Soviet regime by Britain (1924); Zinoviev Letter (1924); British appeasement of Hitler (1936-9); Nazi-Soviet non-aggression pact (1939). (See also next chapter.)
8. Write an account of relations between Germany and the USSR in the 1920s and 1930s. (See also next chapter.)

9. Trace the relations between the USA and Europe between 1919 and 1939 and explain why she followed a policy of isolation.

10. Describe the foreign policy of the Republican administrations in the USA between 1921 and 1933.

CHAPTER 14

FOREIGN AFFAIRS AND INTERNATIONAL RELATIONS 1933-9

SUMMARY OF EVENTS

This short period is of crucial importance in world history because it culminated in the Second World War. Economic problems caused the Locarno spirit to evaporate and the new rule seemed to be each country for itself. Affairs were dominated by the three arch-aggressors – Japan, Italy and Germany – whose extreme nationalism led them to commit so many acts of violence and breaches of international agreements that in the end the world was plunged into the ordeal of total war.

Japan became the first aggressor, as we have already seen, with her successful invasion of Manchuria (1931); both Hitler and Mussolini took note of the failure of the League to curb Japanese aggression. Hitler, much the most subtle of the three, began cautiously by announcing the reintroduction of conscription (March 1935). This breach of Versailles caused Britain, France and Italy to draw together briefly in suspicion of Germany. At a meeting held at Stresa (on Lake Maggiore, northern Italy) they condemned Hitler's action and soon afterwards in May the French, obviously nervous, signed a treaty of mutual assistance with Russia. However the Stresa Front, as it was called, was only short-lived: it was broken in June 1935 when the British, ignoring their two partners, signed the Anglo–German Naval Agreement allowing the Germans to build submarines – another breach of Versailles. This astonishing move by Britain disgusted France and Italy and destroyed any trust which had existed between the three of them. Mussolini, encouraged by Japanese and German successes, now followed suit with his successful invasion of Abyssinia (October 1935) which met only half-hearted resistance from the League and from Britain and France.

March 1936 saw Hitler sending troops into the Rhineland which had been demilitarised by the Versailles treaties: Britain and France again protested but took no action to expel the Germans. An understanding then followed (October 1936) between Germany and Italy, Mussolini having decided to throw in his lot with Hitler; it was known as the Rome-Berlin Axis. The following month Hitler signed the Anti-Comintern

Pact with Japan. (The Comintern or Communist International was an organisation set up in 1919 by Lenin with the aim of starting communist parties in other countries to work for revolution.) During the summer of 1936 the Spanish Civil War broke out and quickly developed an international significance when both Hitler and Mussolini, flexing their military muscles, sent help to Franco, while the republicans received soviet help. Predictably Britain and France refused to intervene and by 1939 Franco was victorious.

In 1937 the Japanese took advantage of Europe's preoccupation with events in Spain to embark on a full-scale invasion of northern China. The resulting Sino–Japanese War eventually became part of the Second World War.

By this time it was clear that the League of Nations working through collective security was totally ineffective; consequently Hitler, now assured of Italian acquiescence, carried out his most ambitious project to date – the annexation of Austria (known as the *Anschluss* – March 1938). Next he turned his attentions to Czechoslovakia and demanded the Sudetenland, an area containing three million Germans adjoining the frontier with Germany. When the Czechs refused Hitler's demands, the British Prime Minister, Chamberlain, anxious to avoid war at all costs, was instrumental in the calling of a conference at Munich (September 1938) at which it was agreed that Germany should have the Sudetenland, but no more of Czechoslovakia. War seemed to have been averted. However, the following March Hitler broke this agreement and sent German troops to occupy Prague, the Czech capital. At this Chamberlain decided that Hitler had gone too far and must be stopped. When the Poles rejected Hitler's demands for Danzig, Britain and France promised to help Poland if the Germans attacked. Hitler was not sufficiently impressed by these British and French threats and grew tired of waiting for Poland to negotiate. Having first secured a non-aggression pact with Russia (August 1939), the Germans invaded Poland on 1 September. Britain and France accordingly declared war on Germany.

14.1 RELATIONS BETWEEN JAPAN AND CHINA

We have already seen (see Section 10.2(e)) the motives behind the Japanese invasion of Manchuria in 1931: it was essential to keep control of the province as a valuable trade outlet; China seemed to be growing stronger under the rule of Chiang Kai-shek and the Japanese feared this might result in their being excluded from Manchuria. In fact it is possible to present a good defence of Japanese actions, as indeed Sir John Simon, the British Foreign Minister, did at the League of Nations. Japan had been involved in the province since the 1890s and was given Port Arthur and a privileged position in south Manchuria as a result of the Russo-Japanese War. Since then the Japanese had invested millions of pounds in Manchuria in the development of industry and railways. By 1931 they controlled the south Manchurian Railway and the banking system, and could not stand by and see themselves gradually squeezed out of such a valuable province with a population of 30 million, especially when they were suffering economic hardship because of the great depression. Although nobody was fooled when the Japanese announced that they had turned Manchuria into the independent state of Manchukuo under Pu Yi, the last of the Chinese emperors, no action was taken against them. However, what followed could not be justified and could only be described as flagrant aggression.

(a) In 1933 the Japanese began to advance from Manchuria into the rest of north-eastern China to which she had no claim whatsoever. By the end of 1935 a large area of China as far as Peking had fallen under Japanese political and commercial control, while the Chinese themselves were torn by civil war between Chiang Kai-shek's *Kuomintang* government and the communists led by Mao Tse-tung (see Section 17.2).

(b) After signing the Anti-Comintern Pact with Germany (1936), the Japanese army seized the excuse provided by an incident between Chinese and Japanese troops in Peking to begin an invasion of other parts of China (July 1937). Although the Prime Minister, Prince Konoye, was against such massive intervention, he had to bow to the wishes of General Sugiyama, the War Minister. By the autumn of 1938 the Japanese had captured the cities of Shanghai, Nanking (Chiang Kai-shek's capital) and Hankow, committing terrible atrocities against Chinese civilians. However, complete victory eluded the Japanese: Chiang had reached an understanding with his communist enemies whereby both co-operated against the invaders; a new capital was established well inland at Chungking and spirited Chinese resistance mounted with help from the Russians.

(c) Japanese troops landed in the south of China and quickly captured Canton, but Chiang still refused to surrender or accept Japanese terms.

Meanwhile the League of Nations had again condemned Japanese aggression but was powerless to act, since Japan was no longer a member and refused to attend a conference about the China situation. Britain and France were too preoccupied with Hitler to take much notice of China, and the Russians did not want full-scale war with Japan. The USA, the only power capable of effectively resisting Japan, was still bent on isolation. Thus, on the eve of the Second World War, the Japanese were in control of most of eastern China (though outside the cities their hold was shaky) while Chiang held out in the centre and west.

14.2 MUSSOLINI'S FOREIGN POLICY

To begin with, Italian foreign policy was somewhat confused: Mussolini knew what he wanted, which was 'to make Italy great, respected and feared', but he was not sure how to achieve it, beyond agitating for a revision of the 1919 peace settlement in Italy's favour. At first, as we have already seen, he seemed to think an adventurous policy was his best line of action, hence the Corfu Incident and the occupation of Fiume in 1923. After these early successes he became more cautious, perhaps alarmed by Italy's isolation at the time of Corfu. After 1923 his policy falls roughly into two phases:

(a) 1923-34. At this stage Mussolini's policy was determined by rivalry with the French in the Mediterranean and the Balkans, where Italian relations with Yugoslavia, France's ally and protégé, were usually strained. Another factor was the Italian fear that the weak state of Austria along her north-eastern frontier might fall too much under the influence of Germany; Mussolini was nervous about a possible German threat via the Brenner Pass. He tried to deal with both problems mainly by diplomatic means:

 (i) He attended the Locarno Conference (1925) but was disappointed when the agreements signed did not guarantee the Italian frontier with Austria.
 (ii) He was friendly towards Greece, Hungary and especially Albania, the southern neighbour and rival of Yugoslavia. Economic and defence agreements were signed with the result that Albania was virtually controlled by Italy, which now had a strong position around the Adriatic.
 (iii) He cultivated good relations with Britain: he supported her demand that Turkey should hand over Mosul province to Iraq and in return the British gave Italy a small part of Somaliland.
 (iv) Italy became the first state after Britain to recognise the USSR and signed a non-aggression pact with her in September 1933.
 (v) He tried to bolster up Austria against the threat from Nazi Germany by supporting the anti-Nazi government of Dollfuss and by signing trade agreements with Austria and Hungary. When Dollfuss was murdered by Austrian Nazis (July 1934) the *Duce* sent three Italian divisions to the frontier in case the Germans invaded Austria; consequently the Nazis called off their attempt to seize power in Austria. This decisive anti-German stand improved relations between Italy and France. However, though he was highly respected abroad, Mussolini was growing impatient; his successes were not spectacular enough.

(b) After 1934 he gradually drifted from extreme suspicion of Hitler's designs on Austria to grudging admiration of Hitler's achievements and a desire to imitate him. After their first meeting (June 1934) Mussolini described Hitler contemptuously as 'that mad little clown', but he later came to believe that there was more to be gained from friendship with Germany than with Britain and France. The more he fell under Hitler's influence, the more aggressive he became. His changing attitude is illustrated by events:

(i) When Hitler announced the reintroduction of conscription (March 1935), Mussolini joined the British and French in condemning the German action and guaranteeing Austria (the Stresa Front, April 1935). Both the British and French carefully avoided discussion of the Abyssinian crisis which was already brewing, and Mussolini took this to mean that they would turn a blind eye to an Italian attack on Abyssinia, regarding it as a bit of old-fashioned colonial expansion. The Anglo–German Naval Agreement (June 1935), which broke the Stresa Front, only served to convince Mussolini of British cynicism and self-interest.

(ii) *The invasion of Abyssinia (October 1935)* was the great turning point in Mussolini's career. Italian involvement in the country, the only remaining independent state left in Africa, went back to 1896 when an Italian attempt to colonise it had ended in ignominious defeat at Adowa. Mussolini's motives for the 1935 attack were obvious: Italy's existing colonies in East Africa (Eritrea and Somaliland) were not rewarding, and his attempts (by a treaty of friendship signed in 1928) to reduce Abyssinia to the position of Albania had failed. The Emperor Haile Selassie had strongly resisted falling under Italian economic domination. In addition Italy was suffering from the depression, and a victorious war would divert attention from internal troubles, provide a new market for Italian exports, please the nationalists and colonialists, and boost Mussolini's sagging popularity. The Italian victory over the ill-equipped and unprepared Ethiopians was a foregone conclusion. Its real significance was how it demonstrated the ineffectiveness of collective security. The League condemned Italy as an aggressor and applied economic sanctions, but these were useless because they did not include preventing sales of oil and coal to Italy, even though the resulting oil shortage would have seriously hampered the Italian war effort. The League's prestige suffered a further blow when it emerged that the British Foreign Secretary, Hoare, had made a secret deal with Laval the French Prime Minister (December 1935) to hand over a large section of Abyssinia to Italy; this was more than the Italians had managed to capture at the time. Public opinion in Britain and France was so outraged that the idea was dropped. *Reasons for this weak stand against Italy* were that Britain and France were economically and militarily unprepared for war and were anxious to avoid any action (such as oil sanctions) which might provoke Mussolini into declaring war on them; both were hoping to resurrect the Stresa Front and use Italy as an ally against the real threat to European peace – Germany; hence their aim was to appease Mussolini. *Unfortunately the results were disastrous*: the League and the idea of collective security were discredited; Mussolini was annoyed by the sanctions and began to be drawn towards friendship with Hitler, who had not criticised the invasion and refused to apply sanctions; in return Mussolini dropped his objections to a German takeover of Austria; Hitler took advantage of the preoccupation with Abyssinia to send troops into the Rhineland.

(iii) When the Spanish Civil War broke out in 1936 Mussolini sent extensive help to Franco in the hope of establishing a third fascist state in Europe and of gaining naval bases in Spain from which he could threaten France; his excuse was that he wanted to prevent the spread of communism.

(iv) An understanding was reached with Hitler known as the Rome-Berlin Axis, around which, in the *Duce*'s words, 'all European states that desire peace can revolve', and in 1937 Italy joined the Anti-Comintern Pact with Germany and Japan, in which all three pledged themselves to stand side by side against Bolshevism. When the Germans occupied Austria (March 1938) Mussolini accepted it without protest. This reversal of his previous policy and his friendship with Germany were not popular in Italy, and disillusionment with Mussolini spread rapidly.

(v) His popularity revived temporarily with his part in the Munich settlement (September 1938) which seemed to have secured peace, but Mussolini failed to draw the right conclusions from his people's relief and committed another act of aggression:

(vi) In April 1939 Italian troops suddenly occupied Albania with very little resistance. This was a pointless operation since Albania was already under Italian economic control, but Mussolini wanted a triumph to imitate Hitler's recent occupation of Czechoslovakia.

(vii) Carried away by his successes, Mussolini signed a full alliance with Germany, the Pact of Steel (May 1939), in which Italy promised full military support if war came. Mussolini was committing Italy to deeper and deeper involvement with Germany, which would in the end ruin him.

14.3 WHAT WERE HITLER'S AIMS IN FOREIGN POLICY AND HOW SUCCESSFUL HAD HE BEEN BY THE END OF 1938?

(a) Hitler aimed to make Germany into a great power again and this he hoped to achieve by destroying the hated Versailles settlement, building up the army, recovering lost territory such as the Saar and the Polish Corridor, and bringing all Germans within the *Reich*. This last aim would involve the annexation of Austria and the acquisition of territory from Czechoslovakia and Poland, both of which had large German minorities as a result of Versailles. There is some disagreement about what, if anything, Hitler intended beyond these aims. Most historians believe that the annexation of Austria and parts of Czechoslovakia and Poland was only a beginning, to be followed by the seizure of the rest of Czechoslovakia and Poland and by the conquest and permanent occupation of Russia as far east as the Ural Mountains. This would give him what the Germans called *Lebensraum* (living space) which would provide food for the German people and an area in which the excess German population could settle

Fig 14.1 *Hitler's gains before the Second World War*

and colonise. An additional advantage was that communism would be destroyed. However, not all historians agree about these further aims; A. J. P. Taylor, for example, claims that Hitler never intended a major war and at most was prepared only for a limited war against Poland.

(b) Whatever the truth about his long-term intentions, Hitler began his foreign policy with a series of brilliant successes, one of the main reasons for his popularity in Germany). By the end of 1938 almost every one of the first set of aims had been achieved, without war and with the approval of Britain. Only the Germans of Poland remained to be brought within the *Reich*. Unfortunately it was when he failed to achieve this by peaceful means that Hitler took his fateful decision to invade Poland.

   (i) Given that Germany was still militarily weak in 1933, Hitler had to move cautiously at first. He withdrew Germany from the World Disarmament Conference and from the League of Nations on the grounds that France would not agree to German equality of armaments. At the same time he insisted that Germany was willing to disarm if other states agreed to do the same, and that he wanted only peace. This was one of his favourite techniques: to act boldly while soothing his opponents with the sort of conciliatory speeches he knew they wanted to hear.

  (ii) Next Hitler signed a ten-year non-aggression pact with the Poles (January 1934), who were showing alarm in case the Germans tried to take back the Polish corridor. This was something of a triumph for Hitler: Britain took it as further evidence of his peaceful intentions; it ruined the French Little Entente which depended very much on Poland; and it guaranteed Polish neutrality whenever Germany should move against Austria and Czechoslovakia. On the other hand it improved relations between France and Russia, who were both worried by the apparent threat from Nazi Germany.

(iii) July 1934 saw Hitler suffer a setback to his ambitions of an *Anschluss* (union) between Germany and Austria. The Austrian Nazis, encouraged by Hitler, staged a revolt and murdered the Chancellor, Engelbert Dollfuss, the protégé of Mussolini. However, when Mussolini moved Italian troops to the Austrian frontier and warned the Germans off, the revolt collapsed; Hitler, taken aback, had to accept that Germany was not yet strong enough to force the issue and disclaimed responsibility for the actions of the Austrian Nazis.

(iv) The Saar was returned to Germany (January 1935) after a plebiscite resulting in a 90 per cent vote in favour. Though the plebiscite had been provided for at Versailles, Nazi propaganda made the most of the success, and Hitler announced that now all causes of grievance between France and Germany had been removed.

(v) Hitler's first successful breach of Versailles came in March 1935 when he announced the reintroduction of conscription. His excuse was that Britain had just announced air force increases and France had extended conscription from 12 to 18 months (their justification was German rearmament). Much to their consternation, Hitler told his startled generals and the rest of the world that he would build up his peacetime army to 36 divisions (about 600,000 men). The generals need not have worried: although the Stresa Front condemned this violation of Versailles, no action was taken, the League was helpless, and the Front collapsed anyway as a result of Hitler's next success.

(vi) Shrewdly realising how frail the Stresa Front was, Hitler detached Britain by offering to limit the German navy to 35 per cent of the strength of the British navy. Britain eagerly accepted in the resulting Anglo–German Naval Agreement (June 1935) apparently believing that since the Germans were already breaking Versailles by building a fleet, it would be as well to have it limited. Without consulting her two allies, Britain had condoned German rearmament; from now on it was going to be impossible to prevent that rearmament, which proceeded with gathering momentum. By the end of 1938 the army stood at 51 divisions (about 800,000 men) plus reserves, there were 21 large naval vessels (battleships, cruisers and destroyers), many more under construction, and 47 U-boats. A large air force of over 2000 aircraft had been built up.

(vii) Meanwhile, encouraged by his successes, Hitler took the calculated risk of sending troops into the demilitarised zone of the Rhineland (March 1936) – a breach of both Versailles and Locarno. Though the troops had orders to withdraw at the first sign of French opposition, no resistance was offered beyond the usual protests. At the same time, well aware of the mood of pacifism among his opponents, Hitler soothed them by offering a peace treaty to last for 25 years.

(viii) Later in 1936 Hitler consolidated Germany's position by reaching an understanding with Mussolini (the Rome–Berlin Axis) and by signing the Anti-Comintern Pact with Japan (also joined by Italy in 1937). Germans and Italians gained military experience helping Franco to victory in the Spanish Civil War, one of the most notorious exploits being the bombing of the defenceless Basque market town of Guernica by the German Condor Legion.

(xi) The *Anschluss* with Austria (March 1938) was Hitler's greatest success to date. Matters came to a head when the Austrian Nazis staged huge demonstrations in Vienna, Graz and Linz, which Chancellor Schuschnigg's government could not control. Realising that this could be the prelude to a German invasion, Schuschnigg announced a plebiscite about whether or not Austria should remain independent. Hitler decided to act before this took place, in case the vote went against union; German troops moved in and Austria became part of the Third *Reich*. It was a triumph for Germany: it revealed the weaknesses of Britain and France who again did no more than protest, it demonstrated the value of the new understanding with Italy, and it dealt a severe strategic blow at Czechoslovakia which could now be attacked from the south as well as from the west and north. All was ready for the beginning of Hitler's campaign to acquire the German-speaking Sudetenland, a campaign which ended in triumph at the Munich Conference in September 1938. Before examining the events of Munich and after, we must pause to consider why it was that Hitler was allowed to get away with these violations of the Versailles treaties. The reasons can be summed up in one word – appeasement.

14.4 WHAT IS MEANT BY THE TERM 'APPEASEMENT'? HOW COULD SUCH A POLICY BE JUSTIFIED AND WHAT PART DID IT PLAY IN INTERNATIONAL AFFAIRS BETWEEN 1935 AND 1939?

(a) Appeasement was the policy followed first by the British and later by the French of avoiding war with aggressive powers such as Japan, Italy and Germany, by giving way to their demands provided these were not too unreasonable. There were two distinct phases of appeasement.

(i) From the mid-1920s until 1937 there was a vague feeling that war must be avoided at all costs, and Britain and sometimes France drifted along accepting the various *faits accomplis* (Manchuria, Abyssinia, German rearmament, Rhineland reoccupation).

(ii) When Neville Chamberlain became British Prime Minister in May 1937 he gave appeasement new drive; he believed in taking the initiative: he would find out what Hitler wanted and show him that reasonable claims could be met by negotiation rather than by force.

illus 14.1 Enthusiastic crowds greet Adolf Hitler during his first visit to the ceded Sudetenland, 1938

The origins of appeasement can be seen in British policy during the 1920s with the Dawes and Young Plans, which tried to conciliate the Germans, and also with the Locarno Treaties and their significant omission: Britain did not agree to guarantee Germany's eastern frontiers, which even Stresemann, the 'good German', said must be revised. When Austen Chamberlain, the British Foreign Minister (and Neville's half-brother), remarked at the time of Locarno that no British government would ever risk the bones of a British grenadier in defence of the Polish Corridor, it seemed to the Germans that Britain had turned her back on eastern Europe. Appeasement reached its climax at Munich, where Britain and France were so determined to avoid war with Germany that they made Hitler a present of the Sudetenland and so set in motion the destruction of Czechoslovakia. Even with such concessions as this, appeasement failed.

(b) At the time appeasement was being pursued, however, there seemed much to commend it and the appeasers, who included MacDonald, Baldwin, Simon and Hoare as well as Neville Chamberlain were convinced of the rightness of their policy.

(i) It was essential to avoid war which was likely to be more devastating than ever before, as the horrors of the Spanish Civil War demonstrated. Moreover Britain, still in the throes of the economic crisis, could not afford vast rearmament and the crippling expenses of a major war. British governments seemed to be supported by a strongly pacifist public opinion. In February 1933 the Oxford Union voted that it would not fight for King and Country, and Baldwin and the National government won a huge victory in November 1935 shortly after he had declared: 'I give you my word of honour that there will be no great armaments.'

(ii) Many felt that Italy and Germany had genuine grievances: Italy had been cheated at Versailles, Germany treated too harshly. Therefore Britain should react with sympathy and with regard to Germany, try to revise the most hated clauses of Versailles. This would remove the need for German aggression and lead to Anglo–German friendship.

(iii) Since the League of Nations seemed to be helpless, Chamberlain believed that the only way to settle disputes was by personal contact between leaders; in this way he would be able to control and civilise Hitler, and Mussolini into the bargain, and bring them to respect international law.

(iv) Economic co-operation between Britain and Germany would be good for both; if Britain helped the German economy to recover the internal violence would die down.

(v) Fear of communist Russia was great especially among British Conservatives, many of whom believed the communist threat to be greater than the danger from Hitler. Many British politicians were willing to overlook the unpleasant features of Nazism in the hope that Hitler's Germany would be a guarantee against communist expansion westwards; in fact many admired Hitler's drive and achievements.

(vi) Underlying all these feelings was the belief that Britain ought not to take any military action in case it led to a full-scale war which Britain was totally unprepared for; at the same time the USA was for isolation and France was weak and divided. Chamberlain speeded up British rearmament so that 'nobody should treat her with anything but respect.' The longer appeasement lasted, the stronger Britain would become and the more this would deter aggression.

(c) Appeasement had a profound effect on the way international relations developed. Although it might have worked with some German governments, with Hitler it was doomed to failure. Some historians believe that it convinced Hitler of the complacency and weakness of Britain and France to such an extent that he was willing to risk attacking Poland, thereby starting the Second World War. It is important to emphasise that appeasement was primarily a British policy, with which the French did not always agree. Poincaré stood up to the Germans (see Section 13.2(c)) and although Briand was in favour of conciliation, even he drew the line at a proposed Austro-German customs union in 1931. Louis Barthou, Foreign Minister for a few months in 1934, believed in firmness towards Hitler and aimed to build up a strong anti-German group which would include Italy and Russia. To this end he was largely responsible for Russia's entry into the League of Nations (September 1934); he told the British that France 'refused to legalise German rearmament' contrary to the Versailles treaties. Unfortunately Barthou was assassinated in October 1934 along with King Alexander of Yugoslavia who was on a state visit to France. They were both shot by Croat terrorists shortly after the king had arrived in Marseilles. Barthou's successor, Pierre Laval, signed an alliance with Russia in May 1935, though it was a weak affair – there was no provision in it for military co-operation, since Laval distrusted the communists. He pinned his main hopes on friendship with Mussolini, but these were dashed by the failure of the Hoare-Laval pact. After this the French were so deeply split between left and right that no decisive foreign policy seemed possible, and since the right admired Hitler, France fell in behind the British. *Examples of appeasement at work were*:

(i) No action was taken to check the obvious German rearmament; Lord Lothian, a Liberal, had a revealing comment to make about this after visiting Hitler in January 1935: 'I am convinced that Hitler does not want war ... what the Germans are after is a strong army which will enable them to deal with Russia.'

(ii) The Anglo-German Naval Agreement condoning German naval rearmament was signed without prior consultation with France and Italy. This broke the Stresa Front, gravely shook French confidence in Britain, and encouraged Laval to look for understandings with Mussolini and Hitler.

(iii) There was only half-hearted British action against the Italian invasion of Abyssinia.

(iv) The French, though disturbed at the German reoccupation of the Rhineland (March 1936), did not mobilise; they were deeply divided, ultra-cautious and received no backing from the British, who were impressed by Hitler's offer of a 25-year peace. Indeed Lord Londonderry (a Conservative and Secretary of State for Air from 1931-5) was reported to have sent Hitler a telegram congratulating him on his success, while Lord Lothian remarked that the German troops had merely entered their own 'back garden'.

(v) Neither Britain nor France intervened in the Spanish Civil War, though Italy and Germany sent decisive help to Franco. Britain tried to entice Mussolini to remove his troops by recognising Italian possession of Abyssinia (April 1938); however, Mussolini failed to keep his side of the bargain.

(vi) Though both Britain and France protested strongly at the *Anschluss* between Germany and Austria (March 1938), many in Britain saw it as the natural union of one German group to another. But British passivity encouraged Hitler to make demands on Czechoslovakia, which brought forth Chamberlain's supreme act of appeasement and Hitler's greatest triumph to date : Munich.

14.5 MUNICH TO THE OUTBREAK OF WAR: SEPTEMBER 1938 TO SEPTEMBER 1939

This fateful year saw Hitler waging two pressure campaigns: the first against Czechoslovakia, the second against Poland.

(a) It seems likely that Hitler had decided to destroy Czechoslovakia as part of his *Lebensraum* (living space) policy and because he hated the Czechs for their democracy as well as for the fact that their state had been set up by the hated Versailles Treaty. His excuse for the opening propaganda campaign was that 3.5 million Sudeten Germans under their leader Konrad Henlein were being discriminated against by the Czech government, though in fact they were not being seriously inconvenienced. The Nazis organised huge protest demonstrations in the Sudetenland and clashes occurred between Czechs and Germans. The Czech President, Beneš, feared that Hitler was fomenting the disturbances so that German troops could march in 'to restore order'. Chamberlain and Daladier, the French Prime Minister, feared the same and that war might break out. They determined to go to almost any lengths to avoid war and put tremendous pressure on the Czechs to make concessions to Hitler. Chamberlain twice flew to Germany to confer with Hitler, but no progress could be made. When it seemed that war was inevitable Hitler invited Chamberlain illus 14.2 *Chamberlain and Hitler in Munich, September 1938*

and Daladier to a four-power conference which met at Munich (29 September 1938). Here a plan produced by Mussolini (but drafted by the German Foreign Office) was accepted. The Sudetenland was to be handed over to Germany immediately, but Germany along with the other three powers guaranteed the remainder of Czechoslovakia. Neither the Czechs nor the Russians were invited to the conference; the Czechs were told that if they resisted the Munich decision they would receive no help from Britain or France, even though the latter had guaranteed the Czech frontiers at Locarno. When Chamberlain arrived back in Britain he received a rapturous welcome from the public which ᵛthought war had been averted. Chamberlain himself remarked: 'I believe it is peace for our time.'

However, not everybody was so enthusiastic: Churchill called Munich 'a total and unmitigated defeat' and Duff Cooper, the First Lord of the Admiralty, resigned from the cabinet saying that Hitler could not be trusted to keep the agreement. They were right: Czechoslovakia was crippled by the loss of 70 per cent of her heavy industry and almost all her fortifications to Germany. Slovakia began to demand semi-independence, and when it looked as though the country was about to fall apart, Hitler pressurised President Hacha into requesting German help 'to restore order'. Consequently in March 1939 German troops occupied the rest of Czechoslovakia. Britain and France protested but took no action: according to Chamberlain, the guarantee of Czech frontiers did not apply because technically Czechoslovakia had not been invaded: German troops had entered by invitation. However, the German action caused a great rush of criticism: for the first time even the appeasers were unable to justify what Hitler had done; he had broken his promise and seized non-German territory. Even Chamberlain felt that this was going too far and his attitude hardened.

(b) After taking over the Lithuanian port of Memel (which was admittedly peopled largely by Germans), Hitler turned his attentions to Poland. The Germans resented the loss of Danzig and the Polish Corridor at Versailles, and now that Czechoslovakia was safely out of the way, Polish neutrality was no longer necessary. In April 1939 Hitler demanded the return of Danzig and a road and railway across the corridor. This demand was, in fact, not unreasonable since Danzig was largely German-speaking; but coming so soon after the seizure of Czechoslovakia, the Poles were convinced, probably rightly, that the German demands were only a prelude to invasion. Already fortified by a British promise of help 'in the event of any action which clearly threatened Polish independence', the Foreign Minister, Colonel Beck, rejected the German demands and refused to attend a conference, no doubt afraid of another Munich. British pressure on the Poles to surrender Danzig was to no avail, and the British were so slow in pursuing negotiations for an alliance with Russia, the only way in which their promise of help to Poland could be made effective, that Hitler got in first and signed a non-aggression pact with the USSR. Also agreed was a partition of Poland between Germany and the USSR (24 August). Hitler was convinced that with Russia neutral, Britain and France would not risk intervention; when the British ratified their guarantee to Poland Hitler took it as a bluff. When the Poles still refused to negotiate, a full-scale German invasion began early on 1 September. Chamberlain had still not completely thrown off appeasement and suggested that if German troops were withdrawn, a conference could be held – there was no response from the Germans. Only when pressure mounted in parliament and in the country did Chamberlain send an ultimatum to Germany. When this expired at 11 a.m. on 3 September, Britain was at war with Germany. Soon afterwards, France also declared war.

14.6 WHY DID WAR BREAK OUT? WAS HITLER OR THE APPEASERS TO BLAME?

The debate is still going on about who or what was responsible for the Second World War. The Versailles treaties have been blamed for filling the Germans with bitterness and the desire for revenge; the League of Nations and the idea of collective security have been criticised because they failed to secure general disarmament and to control potential aggressors; the world economic crisis has been mentioned, since without it Hitler would probably never have come to power. While these factors no doubt helped to create the sort of tensions which might well lead to war, something more was needed. It is worth remembering also that by the end of 1938 many of the German grievances had been removed: reparations were largely cancelled, the disarmament clauses had been ignored, the Rhineland was remilitarised, Austria and Germany were united, and 3.5 million Germans had been recovered from Czechoslovakia. Britain had even offered some compensation for lost German colonies. Germany was, in fact, a great power again. What went wrong?

(a) During and immediately after the war **there was general agreement outside Germany that Hitler was to blame.** By attacking Poland on all fronts instead of merely occupying Danzig and the corridor, Hitler showed that he intended not just to recover the Germans lost at Versailles, but to destroy Poland. Martin Gilbert argues that his motive was to remove the stigma of defeat in the First World War; 'for the only antidote to defeat in one war is victory in the next.' Hugh Trevor-Roper and many other historians believe that Hitler intended a major war right from the beginning; they argue that he hated communism and wanted to conquer Russia and control it permanently, and this could be achieved only by a major war; the destruction of Poland was an essential preliminary to the invasion of Russia; the non-aggression pact with Russia was simply a way of lulling Russian suspicions and keeping her neutral until Poland had been dealt with. Their evidence for this theory is taken from statements in Hitler's book *Mein Kampf* (My Struggle) and from the Hossbach Memorandum, a summary made by Hitler's adjutant, Colonel Hossbach, of a meeting held in November 1937, at which Hitler explained his plans to his generals. If this theory is correct, appeasement can be discounted as a cause of war, except insofar as it made Hitler's job easier; war was inevitable anyway sooner or later.

(b) Other historians claim that **appeasement was equally to blame**; Britain and France should have taken a firm line with Hitler before Germany had become too strong: an Anglo-French attack on western Germany in 1936 at the time of the Rhineland occupation would have taught Hitler a lesson. By giving way to him the appeasers increased his prestige at home; as Alan Bullock writes, 'success and the absence of resistance tempted Hitler to reach out further, to take bigger risks.' He may not have had any definite plans for war, but after the surrender at Munich he was so convinced that Britain and France would remain passive again that he decided to gamble on war with Poland. Chamberlain has also been criticised for choosing the wrong issue over which to make a stand against Hitler. It is argued that German claims for Danzig and routes across the corridor were more reasonable than her demands for the Sudetenland (which contained almost a million non-Germans); Poland was difficult for Britain and France to defend and was militarily much weaker than

Czechoslovakia. Chamberlain ought therefore to have made his stand at Munich and backed the Czechs. Chamberlain's defenders claim that his main motive at Munich was to give Britain time to rearm for an eventual fight against Hitler, but his critics argue that if Chamberlain had genuinely intended to curb Hitler, it would have been better to have fought alongside Czechoslovakia, which was militarily and industrially strong and had excellent fortifications.

(c) Characteristically A. J. P. Taylor has produced the most controversial theory about the outbreak of the war. He believes that Hitler did not intend to cause a major war, and expected at the most a short war with Poland. According to Taylor, Hitler's aims were similar to those of previous German rulers – Wilhelm II and Stresemann; only his methods were more ruthless. Hitler was a brilliant opportunist taking advantage of the mistakes of the appeasers and of events such as the crisis in Czechoslovakia in February 1939, the German occupation of which was not the result of a sinister long-term plan; 'it was the unforeseen by-product of events in Slovakia' (the Slovak demand for more independence from the Prague government). Whereas Chamberlain miscalculated when he thought he could make Hitler respectable, Hitler misread the minds of Chamberlain and the British; how could he be expected to foresee that the British and French would be so inconsistent as to support Poland (where his more reasonable claim lay) after appeasing him over Czechoslovakia (where his case was much less valid)? Thus for Taylor, Hitler was lured into the war almost by accident, after the Poles had called his bluff.

(d) The USSR has been accused of making war inevitable by signing the non-aggression pact with Germany. It is argued that she ought to have allied with the west and with Poland, thereby frightening Hitler into keeping the peace. On the other hand, the British were most reluctant to ally with the Russians; Chamberlain distrusted them, as did the Poles, and believed them militarily weak. Russian historians justify the pact on the grounds that it gave the USSR time to prepare their defences against a possible German attack.

What is the unfortunate student to believe then if historians cannot agree? It has to be said that the majority view is that Hitler was largely responsible. Perhaps it is appropriate to allow the German historian, Joachim Fest, the final word: 'There can be no question about whose was the guilt . . . Hitler's urge to bring things to a head so shaped events that any wish to compromise on the part of the western powers was bound to come to nothing. His entire career was oriented towards war.'

QUESTIONS

1. Describe and explain the foreign policy of Mussolini between 1922 and 1940. (See also next chapter.)

2. What were Hitler's aims in foreign affairs and how successful had he been by the end of 1938?

3. Explain the part played by British foreign policy between 1935 and 1939 in the events leading to the outbreak of war.

4. Explain the policy of Neville Chamberlain towards Germany from 1937 until September 1939. What criticisms can be made of it and what defence can be offered?

5. What is meant by the term 'appeasement' and how could such a policy be justified?

6. Explain why Hitler wanted control of Austria, Czechoslovakia and Poland, and show how he achieved his aim.

7. 'Hitler may not have intended war in 1939, but his actions ensured it.' Comment on this statement.

8. 'Hitler wanted the fruits of total victory without total war and thanks to the stupidity of others, he nearly got them.' How and why was Hitler so successful in his foreign policy between 1936 and 1939, and why did war break out in 1939?

9. How far can the responsibility for the outbreak of war in 1939 be attributed to (a) Hitler's aggressive policies; (b) appeasement; (c) mutual suspicions between Russia and the western powers?

CHAPTER 15

THE SECOND WORLD WAR
1939-45

SUMMARY OF EVENTS

Unlike the 1914-18 war, the Second World War was a war of rapid move-ment and was altogether a more complex affair with major campaigns taking place in the Pacific and the Far East, in North Africa and deep in the heart of Russia, as well as in central and western Europe and the Atlantic. The war falls into four fairly clearly defined phases:

(a) **Opening moves: September 1939 to December 1940.** By the end of September the Germans and Russians had occupied Poland; after a five-month pause (known as the 'phoney war') they occupied Denmark and Norway (April 1940). In May attacks were made on Holland, Belgium and France, who were soon defeated, leaving Britain alone to face the dictators (Mussolini had declared war in June, just before the fall of France). Hitler's attempt to bomb Britain into submission was thwarted in the Battle of Britain (July to September), but Mussolini's armies invaded Eygpt and Greece.

(b) **The Axis offensive widens: 1941 to the summer of 1942.** The war now began to develop into a world-wide conflict. First Hitler, confident of victory over Britain, launched an invasion of Russia (June 1941), breaking the non-aggression pact signed less than two years previously; then the Japanese forced the USA into the war by attacking the American naval base at Pearl Harbor (December 1941) and proceeded to occupy territories such as the Philippines, Malaya, Singapore and Burma, scattered over a wide area. At this stage of the war there seemed to be no way of stopping the Germans and Japanese, though the Italians were less successful.

(c) **The offensives held in check: summer 1942 to summer 1943.** This phase of the war saw three important battles in which Axis forces were defeated. In June 1942 the Americans drove off a Japanese attack on Midway Island, inflicting heavy losses. In October the Germans, under Rommel and advancing towards Eygpt, were halted at El Alamein and later driven out of North Africa. The third battle was in Russia where by September 1942 the Germans had penetrated as far as Stalingrad. Here the Russians put up such a fierce resistance that the following February the German army was surrounded and compelled to surrender. Meanwhile the war in the air continued with both sides bombing enemy cities, and at sea where, as in the First World War, the British and Americans gradually got the better of the German submarine menace.

(d) The Axis powers defeated: July 1943 to August 1945. The enormous power and resources of the USA and the USSR combined with an all-out effort from Britain and her empire slowly but surely wore the Axis powers down. Italy was eliminated first and this was followed by an Anglo-American invasion of Normandy (June 1944) which liberated France, Belgium and Holland and crossed the Rhine to capture Cologne. In the east the Russians drove the Germans out and advanced on Berlin via Poland. Germany surrendered in May 1945 and Japan in August after the Americans had dropped atomic bombs on Hiroshima and Nagasaki.

15.1 OPENING MOVES: SEPTEMBER 1939 TO DECEMBER 1940

(a) The Poles were defeated swiftly because of the German *Blitzkrieg* (lightning war) which they were ill-equipped to deal with. It consisted of rapid thrusts by motorised divisions and tanks (*Panzers*) supported by air power: the *Luftwaffe* (the German air force) put the Polish railway system out of action and destroyed the Polish air force. Polish resistance was heroic but pathetic: they had no motorised divisions and attempted to stem the German advance by massed cavalry charges. Britain and France

Fig 15.1 *main German thrusts in 1940*

did little to help their ally directly because French mobilisation procedure was slow and out-of-date and it was difficult to transport sufficient troops to Poland to be effective. When the Russians invaded eastern Poland resistance collapsed. On 29 September Poland was partitioned between Germany and Russia (as agreed in the August pact).

(b) Very little happened in the west for the next five months; in the east the Russians absorbed Estonia, Latvia and Lithuania and invaded Finland (November 1939), forcing her to hand over certain territories which would enable the Russians to defend themselves better against any attack from the west. Meanwhile the French and Germans manned their respective defences – the Maginot and Siegfried Lines. Hitler seems to have hoped that the pause would weaken the resolve of Britain and France and encourage them to negotiate a settlement; in addition it pleased his generals who were not convinced that the German army was strong enough to attack in the west. It was the American press which described this period as the 'phoney war'.

(c) The apparent calm of the 'phoney war' was rudely shattered in April 1940 when Hitler's troops occupied Denmark and landed at the main Norwegian ports. *Control of Norway was important for the Germans* because Narvik was the main outlet for Swedish iron ore to Germany, which was vital for her armaments industry. The British were interfering with this trade by mining Norwegian coastal waters, and the Germans were afraid that they might occupy some of Norway's ports, as they were indeed planning to do. Admiral Raeder, the German navy chief, realised that the fjords would be excellent naval bases from which to attack Britain's trans-Atlantic supply lines. When a British destroyer chased the German vessel *Altmark* into a Norwegian fjord and rescued 300 British prisoners, Hitler decided it was time to act. On 9 April the Germans landed at Oslo, Kristiansand, Stavanger, Bergen and Trondheim, and although British and French troops arrived a few days later, they were unable to dislodge the Germans who were already well-established. After a temporary success at Narvik, all Allied troops were withdrawn by early June because of the growing threat to France itself. *The Germans were successful* because the Norwegian forces were not even mobilised, and local Nazis under their leader Vidkun Quisling gave the invaders every assistance. In addition the British had no air support, whereas the German air force constantly harassed the Allies. *This Norwegian campaign had important results*: Germany was assured of her bases and her iron ore supplies, but had lost three cruisers and ten destroyers, which rendered the navy less effective at Dunkirk than it might have been. The campaign also showed the incompetence of Chamberlain's government; he was forced to resign and Winston Churchill became Prime Minister. Although there has been criticism of Churchill's mistakes there is no doubt that he supplied what was needed at the time – drive, a sense of urgency and the ability to make his coalition cabinet work well together.

(d) The attacks on Holland, Belgium and France were launched simultaneously on 10 May and again *Blitzkrieg* methods brought swift victories. The Dutch, shaken by the bombing of Rotterdam which killed almost a thousand people, surrendered after only four days. Belgium held out longer but her surrender at the end of May left the British and French troops in Belgium perilously exposed as German motorised divisions swept across northern France; only Dunkirk remained in Allied hands. The British navy played the vital role in evacuating over 338,000 troops, two-thirds of them British, from Dunkirk between 27 May and 4 June. Dunkirk was a remarkable achievement in the face of constant *Luftwaffe* attacks on the beaches; it would perhaps have been impossible if Hitler had not ordered the advance towards Dunkirk to halt (24 May) probably because the marshy terrain and numerous canals were unsuitable for tanks. *The events at Dunkirk were important*: a third of a million troops were rescued to fight again and Churchill used it for propaganda purposes to boost British morale with the 'Dunkirk spirit'. In fact it was a serious blow for the Allies: the armies at Dunkirk had lost all their arms and equipment so that it became impossible for Britain to help France. The Germans now swept southwards; Paris was captured on 14 June and France surrendered on the 22nd. At Hitler's insistence the armistice was signed at Compiègne in the same railway coach which had been used for the 1918 armistice (for a full explanation of the French defeat see Section 5.2). The Germans occupied northern France and the Atlantic coast, giving them valuable submarine bases, and the French army was demobilised. Unoccupied France was allowed its own government under Marshall Pétain at Vichy, but it had no real independence and collaborated with the Germans.

(e) The Battle of Britain (12 August to 30 September) was fought in the air when Goering's *Luftwaffe* tried to destroy the RAF as a preliminary to the invasion of Britain. The Germans bombed harbours, radar stations, aerodromes, munitions factories, and in September London itself (in retaliation for a British raid on Berlin). The RAF inflicted heavy losses on the *Luftwaffe* (1,389 German planes were lost as against 792 British) and when it became clear that British air power was far from being destroyed, Hitler called off the invasion. *The British success was partly due* to their chain of radar stations which gave plenty of warning of approaching German attackers, and partly because the German bombers were poorly armed. In addition, though the British fighters (Spitfires and Hurricanes) were not significantly better than the German Messerschmitts, the Germans were hampered by limited range (they could stay in the air only about 90 minutes). The switch to bombing London was a bad mistake because it relieved pressure on the airfields at the critical moment. *The Battle of Britain was probably the first major turning point of the war*: for the first time the Germans had been checked; they were not invincible. Britain was able to remain in the struggle, thus facing Hitler (who was about to attack Russia) with the fatal situation of war on two fronts. As Churchill remarked as he paid tribute to the British fighter pilots: 'Never in the field of human conflict was so much owed by so many to so few.'

(f) Not to be outdone by Hitler, Mussolini sent an army from the Italian colony of Libya which penetrated about 60 miles into Egypt (September 1940) while another army invaded Greece from Albania (October). However, the British soon drove the Italians out of Egypt, pushed them back deeply into Libya and defeated them at Bedafomm, capturing 130,000 prisoners and 400 tanks. They seemed poised to take the whole of Libya. British naval aircraft sank half the Italian fleet in harbour at Taranto and occupied Crete. The Greeks forced the Italians back and invaded Albania. Clearly Mussolini was going to be an embarrassment to Hitler.

15.2 THE AXIS OFFENSIVE WIDENS: 1941 TO THE SUMMER OF 1942

(a) Hitler's first moves in 1941 were to help out his faltering ally. In February he sent Erwin Rommel and the Afrika Korps to Tripoli, and together with the Italians they cleared the British out of Libya; after much advancing and retreating, by June 1942 the Germans were in Egypt approaching El Alamein, only 70 miles from Alexandria. In April 1941 Hitler's forces invaded Greece, the day after 60,000 British, Australian and New Zealand troops had arrived to help the Greeks. The Germans soon captured Athens, forcing the British to withdraw, and after bombing Crete launched a parachute invasion of the island; again the British were forced to evacuate (May 1941). *The campaigns in Greece and Crete had important*

Fig 15.2 *North Africa and the Mediterranean*

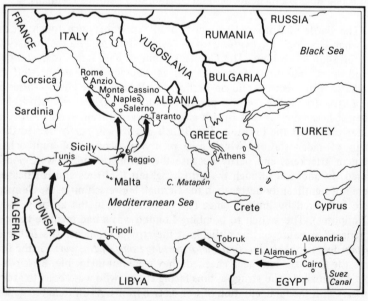

➤ Allied advances and offensives 1942–4

effects: it was depressing for the Allies who lost some 36,000 men; many of the troops had been removed from North Africa, thus weakening British forces there just when they needed to be at their most effective against Rommel. More important in the long run was that Hitler's involvement in Greece and Yugoslavia (which the Germans invaded at the same time as Greece) may well have delayed his attack on Russia (originally planned for 15 May) by five weeks. If the invasion had taken place in May, the Germans might well have taken Moscow before the winter set in.

(b) The German invasion of Russia (Operation Barbarossa) began on 22 June 1941.

(i) *Hitler's motives seem to have been mixed*: fear that the Russians might attack Germany while she was still occupied in the west; hope that the Japanese would attack Russia in the Far East; the more powerful Japan became, the less chance there was of the USA entering the war (or so Hitler thought). But above all there was his hatred of communism and his desire for *Lebensraum*. According to Bullock, 'Hitler invaded Russia for the simple and sufficient reason that he had always meant to establish the foundations of his thousand-year *Reich* by the annexation of the territory lying between the Vistula and the Urals.' It has sometimes been suggested that the attack on Russia was Hitler's greatest mistake, but in fact, as Hugh Trevor-Roper has pointed out, 'to Hitler the Russian campaign was not a luxury: it was the be-all and end-all of Nazism; it could not be delayed. It was now or never.'

(ii) The attack was three-pronged: in the north towards Leningrad, in the centre towards Moscow and in the south through the Ukraine. It was *Blitzkrieg* on an enormous scale involving close on 3.5 million men, and 3,550 tanks supported by 5,000 aircraft. Important cities such as Riga, Smolensk and Kiev were captured; the Russians had been caught off guard, still re-equipping their army and air force, and their generals, thanks to Stalin's purges, were inexperienced. However, the Germans failed to capture Leningrad and Moscow. They were severely hampered by the heavy rains of October which turned the Russian roads into mud and by the severe frosts of November and December when in some places the temperature fell to minus $38°$ Centigrade. The Germans had inadequate winter clothing because Hitler had expected the campaign to be over before winter. Even in the spring of 1942 no progress was made in the north and centre as Hitler decided to concentrate on a major drive south-eastwards towards the Caucasus to seize the oil-fields.

(c) The USA was brought into the war by the Japanese attack on Pearl Harbor (their naval base in the Hawaiian Islands) on 7 December 1941. Until then the Americans, still intent on isolation, had remained neutral, though after the Lend-Lease Act (April 1941) they had provided Britain with massive financial aid.

(i) *Japanese motives for the attack were tied up with her economic situation.* The government believed they would soon run short of raw materials and cast longing eyes towards territories such as Britain's Malaya and Burma which had rubber, oil and tin, and the Dutch East Indies, also rich in oil. Since both Britain and Holland were in no state to defend their possessions, the Japanese prepared to attack, but would probably have preferred to avoid war with the USA. However, relations between the two states deteriorated steadily. The Americans assisted the Chinese who were still at war with Japan; when the Japanese persuaded Vichy France to allow them to occupy French Indo-China (where they set up military bases), President Roosevelt demanded their withdrawal and placed an embargo on oil supplies to Japan (26 July 1941). Long negotiations followed in which the Japanese tried to persuade the Americans to lift the embargo, but stalemate was reached as the Americans insisted on a Japanese withdrawal both from Indo-China and China itself. When the aggressive General Tojo became Prime Minister (16 October) war seemed inevitable.

(ii) The attack was brilliantly organised by Admiral Yamamoto. There was no declaration of war: 353 Japanese planes arrived undetected at Pearl Harbor and in 2 hours destroyed 350 aircraft, 5 battleships and 3,700 men. Roosevelt called 7 December 'a date which will live in infamy'. *Pearl Harbor had important results*: the Japanese now controlled the Pacific and by May 1942 had captured Malaya, Singapore, Burma, Hong Kong, the Dutch East Indies, the Philippines, and two American possessions, Guam and Wake Island. It caused Hitler to declare war on the USA. This was perhaps his most serious mistake: he need not at this stage have committed himself to war with the USA, in which case the Americans might well have concentrated on the Pacific War. As it was, Germany was now faced with the immense potential of the USA which, together with the vast resources of the USSR and the British commonwealth, meant that the longer the war lasted, the less chance there was of an Axis victory. It was essential for them to deliver swift knock-out blows before the American contribution became effective.

(d) The behaviour of both Germans and Japanese in their conquered territories was ruthless and brutal. The Nazis treated the peoples of eastern Europe as sub-humans, fit only to be slaves of the German master race. Jews were even lower – they were to be exterminated. As William Shirer puts it: 'Nazi degradation sank to a level seldom experienced by man in all his time on earth. Millions of decent, innocent men and women were driven into forced labour, millions more tortured in the concentration camps and millions more still (including nearly six million Jews) were massacred in cold blood or deliberately starved to death and their remains burned.' Not only was this immoral, it was also bad tactics; in the Baltic states and the Ukraine the soviet government was so unpopular that decent illus 15.1   *Pearl Harbor, 7 December 1941. U.S. Warships lie in ruins after the Japanese air attack*

treatment would have turned the people into allies of the Germans. The Japanese treated prisoners of war and the Asian peoples badly. Again this was ill-advised: many of the Asians, in Indo-China for example, welcomed the Japanese who were freeing them from European control. The Japanese hoped to organise their new territories into a great economic empire known as a '*Greater East Asia Co-prosperity Sphere*', which would be defended by sea and air power. However, harsh treatment by the Japanese soon turned the Asians against rule from Tokyo, and determined resistance movements began, usually with communist involvement.

15.3 THE OFFENSIVES HELD IN CHECK: SUMMER 1942 TO SUMMER 1943

In three separate theatres of war, Axis forces were defeated and began to lose ground.

(a) At Midway Island (June 1942) in the Pacific the Americans beat off a powerful Japanese attack, which included 5 aircraft carriers, nearly 400 aircraft, 17 large warships and an invasion force of 5,000 troops. The Americans, with only 3 carriers and 233 planes, destroyed 4 of the Japanese carriers and about 330 planes. *There were several reasons for the American victory* against heavier odds: they had broken the Japanese radio code and knew exactly where and when the attack was to be launched; the Japanese were over-confident and made two fatal mistakes: they split their forces, thus allowing the Americans to concentrate on the main carrier force, and they attacked with the aircraft from all four carriers simultaneously, so that when they were all rearming the fleet was extremely vulnerable. At this stage, the Americans launched a counter-attack by dive-bombers which swooped unexpectedly from 19,000 feet, sinking 2 of the carriers and all their planes. *Midway proved to be a crucial turning point* in the battle for the Pacific: the loss of their carriers and strike planes seriously weakened the Japanese, and from then on the Americans maintained their lead in carriers and aircraft, especially dive-bombers. Although the

Fig 15.3 *the war in the Pacific*

Japanese had far more battleships and cruisers, they were mostly in-effective: the only way that war could be waged successfully in the vast expanses of the Pacific was by air power operating from carriers. Gradually the Americans under General ·MacArthur began to recover the Pacific islands beginning in August 1942 with landings in the Solomon Islands. The struggle was long and bitter and continued through 1943 and 1944 by a process known as 'island hopping'.

(b) At El Alamein in Egypt (October 1942) Rommel's *Afrika Korps* were driven back by Montgomery's Eighth Army. This great battle was the culmination of several engagements fought in the El Alamein area: first the Axis advance was temporarily checked (July); when Rommel tried to break through he was halted again at Alam Halfa (September); finally, seven weeks later in the October battle, he was chased out of Egypt for good by the British and New Zealanders. *The Allies were successful* partly because during the seven-week pause massive reinforcements had arrived so that the Germans and Italians were heavily outnumbered (80,000 men and 540 tanks against 230,000 troops and 1,440 tanks); in addition Allied air power was vital, constantly attacking the Axis forces and sinking their supply ships crossing the Mediterranean, so that by October there were serious shortages of food, fuel oil and ammunition; at the same time the air force was strong enough to protect the Eighth Army's own supply routes. Montgomery's skilful preparations probably clinched the issue, though he has been criticised for being over-cautious and for allowing Rommel and half his forces to escape into Libya. However, there is no doubt that the El Alamein victory was another turning point in the war: it prevented Egypt and the Suez Canal from falling into German hands and ended the possibility of a link-up between the Axis forces in the Middle East and those in the Ukraine. More than that, it led on to the complete expulsion of Axis forces from North Africa; it encouraged landings of American and British troops in the French territories of Morocco and Algeria to threaten the Germans and Italians from the west while the Eighth Army closed in on them from Libya. Trapped in Tunisia, 275,000 Germans and Italians were forced to surrender (May 1943) and the Allies were well-placed for an invasion of Italy. The desert war had been a serious drain on German resources which could have been used in Russia where they were badly needed.

(c) At Stalingrad the German southern attack which had penetrated deeply through the Crimea, capturing Rostov, was finally checked. The Germans had reached Stalingrad at the end of August 1942, and though they more or less destroyed the city, the Russians refused to surrender. In November they counter-attacked ferociously, trapping the Germans whose supply lines were dangerously extended in a large pincer movement cutting off their retreat. By 2 February 1943 the German commander von Paulus had no reasonable alternative but to surrender with about 100,000 men. If Stalingrad had fallen, the supply route for Russia's oil from the Caucasus

Fig 15.4 *the Russian Front*

---- Line of the German advance in December 1941

········ German line in November 1942

would have been cut off, and the Germans had hoped to advance up the River Don to attack Moscow from the south-east. This plan had to be abandoned but more than that was at stake: the defeat was a catastrophe for the Germans; it shattered the myth that they were invincible and boosted Russian morale. They followed up with more counter-attacks forcing the Germans to abandon the siege of Leningrad and to retreat from their position west of Moscow. It was only a matter of time before the Germans, now heavily outnumbered and short of tanks and guns, were cleared out of Russia.

15.4 WHAT PART WAS PLAYED BY ALLIED NAVAL FORCES IN THE WAR?

We have already seen how the combination of sea and air power was the key to success in the Pacific War and how, after the initial shock at Pearl

Harbor, the Americans were gradually able to build up that superiority in both departments which was to lead to the eventual defeat of Japan. At the same time the British navy, as in the First World War, had a vital role to play; this included protecting merchant ships bringing food supplies, sinking German submarines and surface raiders, blockading Germany, and transporting and supplying the Allied troops fighting in North Africa and later in Italy. At first success was mixed, mainly because the British failed to understand the importance of air support in naval operations and had few aircraft carriers. Thus they suffered defeats in Norway and Crete where the Germans had strong air superiority. In addition the Germans had numerous naval bases in Norway, Denmark, France and Italy. In spite of this *the British had some successes:*

(a) Aircraft from the carrier *Illustrious* sank half the Italian fleet at Taranto (November 1940); the following March five more warships were destroyed off Cape Matapan.

(b) The threat from surface raiders was removed by the sinking of the *Bismarck*, Germany's only battleship at the time (May 1941).

(c) The navy destroyed the German invasion transports on their way to Crete (May 1941), though they could not prevent the landing of parachute troops.

(d) They provided escorts for convoys carrying supplies to help the Russians; these sailed via the Arctic to Murmansk in the far north of Russia. Beginning in September 1941 the first twelve convoys arrived without incident, but then the Germans began to attack them, until convoy 17 lost 23 ships out of 36 (June 1942). After this disaster Arctic convoys were not fully resumed until November 1943, when stronger escorts could be spared. Altogether 40 convoys sailed: 720 out of a total of 811 merchant ships arrived safely, with valuable cargo for the Russians including 5,000 tanks and 7,000 aircraft as well as thousands of tons of canned meat.

(e) Their most important contribution was their victory in *the Battle of the Atlantic.* This was the struggle against German U-boats attempting to deprive Britain of food and raw materials. At the beginning of 1942 the Germans had 90 U-boats in operation and 250 being built; in the first six months of that year the Allies lost over 4 million tons of merchant shipping and destroyed only 21 U-boats; losses reached a peak of 108 ships in March 1943, almost two-thirds of which were in convoy. However after that the number of sinkings began to fall, while U-boat losses increased; by July 1943 the Allies could produce ships at a faster rate than the U-boats could sink them, and the situation was under control. *The reasons for the Allied success* were that more air protection was provided for convoys by long-range Liberators, both escorts and aircraft protection improved with experience, and the British introduced the new centimetric radar sets which were small enough to be fitted into aircraft, so that submarines could be detected in poor visibility and at night. The victory was just as important as Midway, El Alamein and Stalingrad: Britain could not have continued to sustain the losses of March 1943 and remained in the war.

15.5 WHAT CONTRIBUTION DID AIR POWER MAKE TO THE DEFEAT OF THE AXIS?

(a) The first significant achievement was in the Battle of Britain (1940) when the RAF beat off the *Luftwaffe* attacks, causing Hitler to abandon his invasion plans (see Section 15.1).

(b) In conjunction with the British navy, aircraft played a varied role: the successful attacks on the Italian fleet at Taranto and Cape Matapan, the sinking of the German battleship *Tirpitz* by heavy bombers in Norway (November 1943), the protection of convoys in the Atlantic, and anti-submarine operations. In fact in May 1943 Admiral Doenitz, the German navy chief, complained to Hitler that since the introduction of the new radar devices, more U-boats were being destroyed by aircraft than by naval vessels.

(c) The American air force together with the navy played a vital part in winning the Pacific War against the Japanese. Dive-bombers operating from aircraft carriers won the Battle of Midway Island in June 1942 (see Section 15.3). Later, in the 'island-hopping' campaign, attacks by heavy bombers prepared the way for landings by marines, for example at the Mariana Islands (1944) and the Philippines (1945). American transport planes kept up the vital flow of supplies to the Allies during the campaign to recapture Burma.

(d) The RAF took part in specific campaigns which would have been hopeless without them; for example, during the desert war, operating from bases in Egypt and Palestine, they constantly bombed Rommel's supply ships in the Mediterranean and his armies on land.

(e) British and Americans later flew in parachute troops to aid the landings in Sicily (July 1943) and Normandy (June 1944) and provided air protection for the invading armies. (However, a similar operation at Arnhem in September 1944 was a failure.)

(f) The most controversial aspect was the Allied bombing of German and later Japanese cities. The Germans themselves had bombed London and other important cities and ports during 1940 and 1941, but these raids dwindled after the German attack on Russia which required all the *Luftwaffe*'s strength. The British and Americans retaliated with a 'strategic air offensive' - massive attacks on military and industrial targets in order to hamper the German war effort. The Ruhr, Cologne, Hamburg and Berlin all suffered badly. Sometimes raids seem to have been carried out purely to undermine civilian morale, as when about 40,000 people were killed during a single night raid on Dresden (February 1945). Early in 1945 the Americans launched a series of devastating raids on Japan from bases in the Mariana Islands. In a single raid on Tokyo (March) 80,000 people were killed and a quarter of the city destroyed. There has been argument about how effective the bombing was in hastening the Axis defeat, beyond merely causing inconvenience.

The conclusion now seems to be that the campaign against Germany was not effective until the autumn of 1944. Industrial production continued to increase until as late as July 1944. After that, thanks to the increasing accuracy of the raids, synthetic oil production fell rapidly, causing acute fuel shortages; in October the vital Krupp armaments factories at Essen were put out of action permanently, and the war effort ground to a halt in 1945. By June 1945 the Japanese had been reduced to the same state. In the end, therefore, after much wasted effort early on, the Allied strategic air offensive was one of the decisive reasons for the Axis defeat: besides slowly strangling fuel and armaments production and destroying railway communications, it caused the diversion of many aircraft from the eastern front, thereby helping the Russian advance into Germany.

15.6 THE AXIS POWERS DEFEATED: JULY 1943 TO AUGUST 1945

(a) **The fall of Italy** was the first stage in the Axis collapse. British and American troops landed in Sicily from sea and air (10 July 1943) and quickly captured the whole island. This caused the downfall of Mussolini who was dismissed by the king. Allied troops crossed to Salerno, Reggio and Taranto on the mainland and captured Naples (October 1943) by which time Marshal Badoglio, Mussolini's successor, had signed an armistice and brought Italy into the war on the Allied side. However the Germans, determined to hold on to Italy, rushed troops through the Brenner Pass to occupy Rome and the north. The Allies landed a force at Anzio, 30 miles south of Rome (January 1944) but bitter fighting followed before Monte Cassino (May) and Rome (June) were captured; Milan in the north was not taken until April 1945. The campaign could have been finished much earlier if the Allies had been less cautious in the early stages and if the Americans had not insisted on keeping many divisions back for the invasion of France. Nethertheless the elimination of Italy did contribute towards the final victory: it provided air bases for the bombing of the Germans in central Europe and the Balkans and kept German troops occupied when they were needed to resist the Russians.

(b) **The invasion of France** (known as the Second Front) began on 'D-Day', 6 June 1944. It was felt that the time was ripe now that Italy had been eliminated, the U–boats controlled and Allied air superiority achieved; the Russians had been urging the Allies to start this second front ever since 1941 to relieve pressure on them. The landings took place from sea and air on a 60-mile stretch of Normandy beaches between Cherbourg and Le Havre. There was strong German resistance, but at the end of the first week, aided by prefabricated 'Mulberry' harbours and by PLUTO (pipeline under the ocean) carrying motor fuel, 326,000 men with tanks and heavy lorries had landed safely; eventually over three million Allied troops were landed. Within a few weeks most of northern France was liberated (Paris on 25 August), putting out of action the sites from which the German V1 and V2 rocket missiles had been launched with devastating effects on south-eastern Britain. Brussels and Antwerp were captured in September.

illus **15.2** *D-Day. U.S. assault troops landing in Normandy*

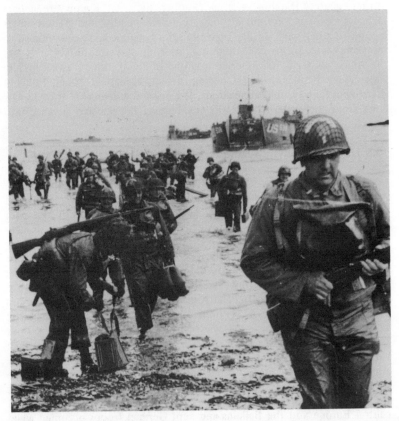

(c) **The assault on Germany** itself followed, but the end was delayed by desperate German resistance and disagreements between the Americans and British. Montgomery wanted a rapid thrust to reach Berlin before the

Fig 15.5 *the Western Front 1944-5*

German Ardennes offensive checked (December 1944), Battle of the Bulge

Allied advances 6 June 1944 – 7 March 1945

·········· Siegfried Line

Russians, but the American General Eisenhower favoured a cautious advance along a broad front. *The British failure at Arnhem* in Holland (September 1944) seemed to support Eisenhower's view, though in fact the Arnhem operation (an attempt by parachute troops to cross the Rhine and outflank the German Siegfried Line) might have worked if the troops had landed nearer the two Rhine bridges.

Consequently Eisenhower had his way and Allied troops were dispersed over a 600-mile front, with unfortunate results: Hitler was able to launch a last offensive through the weakly defended Ardennes towards Antwerp; the Germans broke through the American lines and advanced 60 miles, causing a huge bulge in the front line (December 1944). Determined British and American action stemmed the advance and pushed the Germans back to their original position. But *the Battle of the Bulge*, as it became known, was important because Hitler had risked everything on the attack and had lost 250,000 men and 600 tanks, which at this stage could not be replaced. Early in 1945 Germany was being invaded on both fronts; the British still wanted to push ahead and take Berlin before the Russians, but supreme commander Eisenhower refused to be hurried, and Berlin fell to Stalin's forces in April. Hitler committed suicide and Germany surrendered.

(d) **The defeat of Japan** was still to be achieved. On 6 August 1945 the Americans dropped an atomic bomb on Hiroshima, killing 84,000 people, and one on Nagasaki three days later which killed another 40,000, after which the Japanese government surrendered. The dropping of these bombs was perhaps the most controversial action of the whole war: President Truman's justification was that he was saving American lives, since the war might otherwise drag on for another year. Many historians believe that this bombing was not necessary since, in fact, the Japanese had already put out peace feelers in July via Russia. Liddell-Hart suggests that the real reason was to end the fighting swiftly before the Russians (who had promised to enter the war against Japan) gained too much territory which would entitle them to share the occupation of Japan.

15.7 WHY DID THE AXIS POWERS LOSE THE WAR?

The reasons can be summarised briefly:

(a) A basic weakness was shortage of raw materials: both Italy and Japan had to import supplies and even Germany was short of rubber, cotton, nickel and, after mid-1944, oil. These need not have been fatal, but success depended on a swift end to the war, which indeed seemed likely at first thanks to the speed and efficiency of the German *Blitzkrieg*. However, the survival of Britain in 1940 was important because it kept the western front alive until the USA entered the war.

(b) The Allies soon learned from their early failures: by 1942 they knew how to check *Blitzkrieg* attacks and appreciated the importance of air support and aircraft carriers. Consequently they built up an air and naval superiority which won the battles of the Atlantic and the Pacific and slowly starved their enemies of supplies.

(c) The Axis simply took on too much: Hitler did not understand that war against Britain would involve her empire as well, and that his troops were bound to be spread too thinly – on the Russian front, on both sides of the Mediterranean, and on the western coastline of France. Japan made the same mistake: as Liddell-Hart puts it, 'they became stretched out far beyond their basic capacity for holding their gains. For Japan was a small island state with limited industrial power.' In Germany's case Mussolini was partly to blame: Italian incompetence was a constant drain on Hitler's resources.

(d) The combined resources of the USA and the USSR, not to mention the British empire, were so great that the longer the war lasted the less chance the Axis had of victory. The Russians rapidly moved their industry east of the Ural Mountains and so continued production even though the Germans had occupied vast areas in the west. By 1944 they had four times as many tanks as the Germans and could put twice as many men in the field. When the American war machine reached peak production it could turn out over 70,000 tanks and 120,000 aircraft a year, which the Germans and Japanese could not match.

(e) In addition the Axis made serious tactical mistakes which they could not afford. The Japanese failed to learn the lesson about the importance of aircraft carriers and concentrated too much on producing battleships. Hitler failed to provide for a winter campaign in Russia and became obsessed with the idea that the Germans must not retreat; this led to many disasters in Russia, including Stalingrad, and left his troops badly exposed in Normandy (1944). Perhaps most serious of all was Hitler's decision to concentrate on producing V–rockets when he could have been developing jet aircraft which might well have restored German air superiority and prevented the devastating bomb attacks of 1944 and 1945.

15.8 WHAT WERE THE EFFECTS OF THE WAR?

(a) There had been immense destruction of lives, homes, industries and communications both in Europe and Asia. At least 30 million people were killed, over half of whom were Russians; a further 21 million had been up-rooted from their homes (taken to Germany as labourers, placed in con-

illus **15.3** *The devastation of war. Women salvage their personal belongings after a mass air-raid on London*

centration camps or forced to flee before invading armies) leaving the victorious governments with the problem of how to repatriate them. However, it can be argued that the cost was worth it, since it rid the world of Nazism, which among other atrocities had deliberately murdered six million Jews and hundreds of thousands of non-Jews in extermination camps.

(b) There was no all-inclusive peace settlement of the type reached at Versailles at the end of the First World War; this was mainly because the suspicion and distrust, which had re-emerged between Russia and the west in the final months of the war, made a comprehensive settlement impossible. The results of a number of separate treaties can be summarised briefly: Italy lost her African colonies and renounced her claims to Albania and Abyssinia (Ethiopia); Russia took the eastern tip of Czechoslovakia, the Petsamo district and the area round Lake Ladoga from Finland and held on to Estonia, Latvia, Lithuania and eastern Poland which had been occupied in 1939. Russia also took Bessarabia and northern Bukovina from Rumania, who recovered northern Transylvania which the Hungarians had occupied during the war. Trieste, claimed by both Italy and Yugoslavia, was declared free territory protected by the United Nations. Later at San Francisco (1951) Japan agreed to surrender all territory acquired during the previous 90 years, which included a complete withdrawal from China. The Russians refused to agree to any settlement over Germany and Austria beyond that they should be occupied by Allied troops (see Section 16.2(a)), and that East Prussia should be divided between Russia and Poland.

(c) The war stimulated rapid social and scientific developments, the two most quoted examples being the Beveridge Report (1942), a British plan for introducing a welfare state (see Section 20.2(a)), and the production of nuclear weapons, which have a potential so horrifying that they must have acted as a deterrent from another total war.

(d) Other long-term effects which were to set the pattern of world events for the remainder of the century were:

(i) European domination of the world, already in decline before 1939, was now seen to be over; the USA (which had suffered relatively little from the war), and Russia (almost as much an Asian as a European power) became the leading states, with China and Japan (which recovered remarkably quickly) also playing an important role in world affairs.

(ii) Instead of fostering a long period of friendship, the Soviet–American victory was followed by an intensification of their previous suspicions and distrust which became known as *the Cold War* (see Chapter 16). The rivalry of these two super-powers has been the most important feature of international relations since 1945 and apparently a constant threat to world peace.

(iii) The occupation by the Japanese of European-controlled territories such as Malaya and Singapore, French Indo-China and the Dutch East Indies ended the tradition of European invincibility. It could hardly be expected that having fought to rid themselves of the Japanese, the Asiatic peoples would willingly return to the pre-war status quo. Gradually they achieved full independence, though not without a struggle in many cases. This in turn intensified independence demands in Africa and the Middle East, which resulted in the 1960s in a vast array of new states. The leaders of many of these newly emerging nations met in conference at Algiers (1973) and made it clear that they regarded themselves as *a Third World*. By this they meant that they wished to remain neutral or non-aligned in the struggle between the other two worlds – communism and capitalism. Usually poor and underdeveloped industrially, the new nations were often intensely suspicious of the motives of both communism and capitalism and resented their own economic dependence on the world's wealthy powers.

(iv) The United Nations Organisation (UNO) emerged as the successor to the League of Nations to try and maintain world peace; on the whole it has been more successful than its unfortunate predecessor (see Chapter 19).

QUESTIONS

1. Discuss the importance of *four* of the following during the Second World War:
   Dunkirk 1940; German invasion of Norway 1940; invasion of Crete 1941; Pearl Harbor 1941; Midway Island 1942; El Alamein 1942; the surrender of von Paulus at Stalingrad 1943; the Allied strategic air offensive against Germany 1942–5; the Arnhem landing 1944.
2. What part was played by Allied naval forces *or* Allied air forces in securing the defeat of the Axis powers?
3. Describe the contributions made to the defeat of Germany by (a) Britain; (b) the USA, and (c) the USSR.
4. Why did Japan enter the Second World War? Describe and give reasons for her successes between December 1941 and June 1942, and explain why she was eventually defeated.
5. Explain why Hitler attacked Russia and why the attack eventually failed.
6. Why were Germany and Italy defeated in the Second World War?
7. 'Germany lost the Second World War in the waters of the Atlantic, in the deserts of North Africa and in the snows of Russia.' Give reasons for agreeing or disagreeing with this statement.
8. Why were the Germans so successful at first and later so completely defeated in the Second World War?

CHAPTER 16

THE COLD WAR: PROBLEMS OF INTERNATIONAL RELATIONS AFTER THE SECOND WORLD WAR

SUMMARY OF EVENTS

Towards the end of the war the harmony that had existed between the USSR, the USA and the British empire began to evaporate and all the old suspicions came to the fore again. Relations between soviet Russia and the west soon became so difficult that although no actual armed conflict took place directly between the two opposing camps, the decade after 1945 saw the first phase of *the Cold War* which continued, in spite of several 'thaws', into the 1980s. This means that instead of allowing their mutual hostility to express itself in open fighting, the rival powers confined themselves to attacking each other with propaganda and economic measures and with a general policy of non-co-operation. Both super-powers gathered allies about them: between 1945 and 1948 the USSR drew into its orbit most of the states of eastern Europe, as communist governments came to power in Poland, Hungary, Rumania, Bulgaria, Yugoslavia, Albania, Czechoslovakia and East Germany (1949). A communist government was established in North Korea (1948) and the communist bloc seemed to be further strengthened in 1949 when Mao Tse-tung was at last victorious in the long-drawn-out civil war in China. On the other hand the USA hastened the recovery of Japan and fostered her as an ally and worked closely with Britain and 14 other European countries as well as with Turkey, providing them with vast economic aid in order to build up an anti-communist bloc. Whatever one bloc suggested or did was viewed by the other as having only ulterior and aggressive motives; thus, for example, there was a long wrangle over where the frontier between Poland and Germany should be, and no permanent settlement for Germany and Austria could be agreed on. Then in the mid-1950s after the death of Stalin (1953), the new Russian leaders began to talk about 'peaceful co-existence' and the icy atmosphere between the two blocs began to thaw. It was agreed to remove all occupying troops from Austria (1955); however, relations did not warm sufficiently to allow agreement on Germany.

16.1 WHAT CAUSED THE COLD WAR?

The basic cause lay in the differences of principle between the communist states and the capitalist or democratic states which had existed ever since the communists had set up a government in Russia in 1917. Only the need for self-preservation had caused them to sink their differences and as soon as it became clear that the defeat of Germany was only a matter of time, both sides, Stalin in particular, began to plan for the post-war period.

(a) **Stalin's foreign policies contributed to the tensions**: his aim was to take advantage of the military situation to strengthen Russian influence in Europe; this involved occupying as much of Germany as possible as the Nazi armies collapsed and acquiring as much territory as he could get away with from other states such as Finland, Poland and Rumania. In this, as will be seen, he was highly successful but the west was alarmed at what seemed to be Russian aggression. *Was Stalin to blame then for the Cold War?* The motives behind Stalin's aims are still a subject of controversy among historians:

(i)   Many western historians still believe, as they did at the time, that Stalin was either continuing the traditional expansionist policies of the tsars or, worse still, was determined to spread communism over as much of the world as possible now that 'socialism in one country' had been established.

(ii) The Russians themselves, and since the mid-1960s some western historians as well, claim that Stalin's motives were purely defensive: he wanted a wide buffer zone to protect Russia from any further invasion from the capitalist west. There had been much to arouse his suspicions that the USA and Britain were still as keen to destroy communism as they had been at the time of their intervention in the civil war (1918–20): their delay in opening the second front against the Germans in France seemed deliberately calculated to keep most of the pressure on the Russians and bring them to exhaustion. Stalin was not informed about the existence of the atomic bomb until shortly before its use on Japan, and his request that Russia should share in the occupation of Japan was rejected. Above all, the west had the atomic bomb and Russia did not. Unfortunately it is impossible to be sure which motive was uppermost in Stalin's mind.

(b) **Leading American and British politicians were deeply hostile to the soviet government** as they had been since 1917. Harry S. Truman, who became US President in April 1945 on the death of Roosevelt, was much more suspicious of the Russians than Roosevelt who was inclined to trust Stalin. Churchill's views were well known: towards the end of the war he had wanted the British and Americans to make a dash for Berlin before the Russians took it; and in May 1945 he had written in a letter to Truman: 'What is to happen about Russia? Like you I feel deep anxiety . . . an iron curtain is drawn down upon their front.' Both were prepared to take a hard line.

Historians must try to ignore their own bias and be guided only by the evidence; the conclusion has to be that both sides were to some extent to blame for the Cold War. If somehow mutual confidence could have been created between the two sides, the conflict might have been avoided, but given their entrenched positions and deep suspicion of each other, perhaps it was inevitable. In this atmosphere almost every international act could be interpreted in two different ways: what was claimed as necessary for self-defence by one side was taken by the other as evidence of aggressive intent, as the events described in the next section show. But at least open war was avoided because the Americans were reluctant to use the atomic bomb again unless attacked directly, while the Russians dare not risk such an attack.

16.2 HOW DID THE COLD WAR DEVELOP BETWEEN 1945 AND 1953?

(a) The Yalta Conference (February 1945) held in the Crimea was attended by Stalin, Roosevelt and Churchill. At the time it was generally thought to be a success, agreement being reached on several points: the United Nations Organisation should be set up; Germany was to be divided into zones – Russian, American and British (a French zone was included later) – while Berlin (which would be in the Russian zone) would be split into corresponding zones; similar arrangements were to be made for Austria; free elections would be allowed in the states of eastern Europe; Stalin promised to join the war against Japan on condition that Russia received the whole of Sakhalin Island and some territory in Manchuria. However, there were ominous signs over Poland: when the Russians swept through Poland, pushing the Germans back, they had set up a communist government in Lublin, even though there was a Polish government-in-exile in London. It was agreed at Yalta that some members (non-communists) of the London-based government should be allowed to join the Lublin government, while in return Russia would be allowed to keep the strip of eastern Poland which she had occupied in 1939; but Roosevelt and Churchill refused to agree to Stalin's demands that Poland should be given all German territory east of the Rivers Oder and Neisse.

(b) The Potsdam Conference (July 1945) revealed a distinct cooling-off in relations. The main representatives were Stalin, Truman and Churchill (replaced by Clement Attlee who became British Prime Minister after Labour's election victory). The war with Germany was over but no agree-

Fig 16.1 *Europe after 1945*

Land taken by Poland from Germany: territory east of the *Oder–Neisse* Line and part of East Prussia

Land acquired by the USSR during the war

Occupation zones in Germany and Austria:
1 Russian   3 French
2 British   4 American

ment was reached about her long-term future beyond what had been decided at Yalta (it was understood that she should be disarmed, the Nazi party disbanded and its leaders tried as 'war criminals'). Moreover Truman and Churchill were annoyed because Germany east of the Oder–Neisse Line had been occupied by Russian troops and was being run by the pro-communist Polish government which expelled some five million Germans living there; this had not been agreed to at Yalta! Truman did not inform Stalin about the nature of the atomic bomb, though Churchill was told about it during the conference. A few days after the conference closed the two atomic bombs were dropped on Japan and the war ended quickly on 10 August without the need for Russian aid (though the Russians declared war on Japan on 8 August and invaded Manchuria). Though they annexed south Sakhalin as agreed at Yalta they were allowed no part in the occupation of Japan.

(c) **Churchill's 'Iron Curtain' speech** (March 1946) was made at Fulton, Missouri (USA) in response to the spread of communism in eastern Europe. By this time pro-communist coalition governments had been established under Russian influence in Poland, Hungary, Rumania, Bulgaria and Albania. In some cases their opponents were imprisoned or murdered; in Hungary, for example, the Russians allowed free elections and, though the communists won less than 20 per cent of the votes (November 1945), saw to it that a majority of the cabinet were communists. Repeating the same phrase that he had used earlier, Churchill declared: 'From Stettin in the Baltic to Trieste in the Adriatic an *iron curtain* has descended across the continent'; claiming that the Russians were bent on 'indefinite expansion of their power and doctrines', he called for a western alliance which would stand firm against the communist threat. The speech helped to widen the rift between east and west: Stalin was able to denounce Churchill as a warmonger while over a hundred British Labour MPs signed a motion criticising the Conservative leader; but he was only expressing what most leading American politicians felt.

(d) Undeterred by the Fulton Speech **the Russians continued to tighten their grip on eastern Europe**; by the end of 1947 every state in that area with the exception of Czechoslovakia had a fully communist government. Elections were rigged, non-communist members of the coalition governments were expelled, many being arrested and executed, and eventually all other political parties were dissolved; all this took place under the watchful eyes of secret police and Russian troops. In addition Stalin treated the Russian zone of Germany as if it belonged to Russia, allowing only the communist party and draining it of vital resources. (Yugoslavia did not quite fit the pattern: the communist government of Marshal Tito had been legally elected in 1945. He had immense prestige as a leader of the anti-German resistance; it was Tito's forces, not the Russians, who had liberated Yugoslavia from the Nazi occupation, and Tito resented Russian interference.) The west was profoundly irritated by Russia's attitude which seemed to disregard Stalin's promise of free elections made at Yalta; the Russians could argue that friendly governments in her neighbouring states were essential for self-defence, that these states had never had democratic governments anyway and that communism would bring much-needed progress to backward countries. Even Churchill had agreed with Stalin in their 1944 discussions that much of eastern Europe should be a Russian 'sphere of influence'.

(e) The next major development was the appearance of **the 'Truman Doctrine' which soon became closely associated with the Marshall Plan.**

(i) *The 'Truman Doctrine'* sprang from events in Greece where communists were trying to overthrow the monarchy. British troops, who had helped liberate Greece from the Germans in 1944, had restored the monarchy but were now feeling the strain of supporting it against the communists who were receiving help from Albania, Bulgaria and Yugoslavia. Ernest Bevin, the British Foreign Minister, appealed to the USA and Truman announced (March 1947) that the USA would 'support free peoples who are resisting subjugation by armed minorities or by outside pressures.' Greece immediately received massive amounts of arms and other supplies and by 1949 the communists were defeated. Turkey, which also seemed under threat, received aid worth about 60 million dollars. The 'Truman Doctrine' made it clear that the US had no intention of returning to isolation as she had after the First World War; she was committed to a policy of containing the spread of communism, not just in Europe but throughout the world, including Korea and Vietnam.

(ii) *The Marshall Plan* (announced June 1947) was an economic extension of the 'Truman Doctrine'. American Secretary of State George Marshall produced his European Recovery Programme (ERP) which offered economic and financial help wherever it was needed. 'Our policy', he declared, 'is directed not against any country or doctrine but against hunger, poverty, desperation and chaos.' Its aim was to promote the economic recovery of Europe, thus ensuring markets for American exports; in addition, communism was less likely to gain control in a prosperous western Europe. By September 16 nations (Britain, France, Italy, Belgium, Luxembourg, Netherlands, Portugal, Austria, Switzerland, Greece, Turkey, Iceland, Norway, Sweden, Denmark, and the 3 western zones of Germany) had drawn up a joint plan for using American aid; over the next 4 years over 13,000 million dollars of Marshall Aid flowed into western Europe, fostering the recovery of agriculture and industry which in many countries were in chaos as a result of war devastation. The Russians on the other hand were well aware that there was more to Marshall Aid than benevolence. Although aid was in theory available to eastern Europe, Molotov, the Russian Foreign Minister, denounced the whole idea as 'dollar imperialism', seeing it as a blatant American device for gaining control of western Europe, and worse still, for interfering in eastern Europe, which Stalin considered to be in the Russian 'sphere of influence'. Russia rejected the offer and neither her satellite states nor Czechoslovakia, which was showing interest, were allowed to take advantage of it. The 'iron curtain' seemed a reality and the next development only served to strengthen it:

(f) The Cominform was set up by Stalin (September 1947). This was an organisation to draw together the various European communist parties. All the satellite states were members and the French and Italian communist parties were represented. Stalin's aim was to tighten his grip on the satellites: to be communist was not enough; it must be Russian-style communism. Eastern Europe was to be industrialised, collectivised and centralised; states were expected to trade primarily with Cominform members and all contacts with non-communist countries were discouraged. Only Yugoslavia objected and was consequently expelled from the Cominform in 1948, though she remained communist. In 1949 *the Molotov Plan* was introduced, offering Russian aid to the satellites, and another organisation known as *Comecon* (Council of Mutual Economic Assistance) was set up to co-ordinate their economic policies.

(g) The communist takeover in Czechoslovakia (February 1948) came as a great blow to the western bloc because it was the only remaining democratic state in eastern Europe. There was a coalition government freely elected in 1946. The communists had won 38 per cent of the votes and held a third of the cabinet posts. The Prime Minister, Klement Gottwald, was a communist; President Beneš and Foreign Minister Jan Masaryk were not, and they hoped that Czechoslovakia with its highly developed industries would remain as a bridge between east and west. However, a crisis arose early in 1948. Elections were due in May and all the signs were that the communists would lose ground: they were blamed for the Czech rejection of Marshall Aid which might have alleviated the continuing food shortages. The communists decided to act before the elections; already in control of the unions and the police, they seized power in an armed coup, while thousands of armed workers paraded through Prague. All non-communist ministers, with the exception of Beneš and Masaryk, resigned. A few days later Masaryk's body was found under the windows of his offices; his death was described officially as suicide, but Dubcek's (see Section 18.2 (f)) opening of the archives in 1968 proved it was murder. The elections were duly held in May but there was only a single list of candidates – all communists. Beneš resigned and Gottwald became President. The western powers and the UN protested but could hardly take any action because they could not prove Russian involvement; the coup was purely an internal affair. However, there can be little doubt that Stalin, disapproving of Czech connections with the west and of their interest in Marshall Aid, had prodded the Czech communists into action; nor was it just coincidence that several of the Russian divisions occupying Austria were moved up to the Czech frontier. The bridge between east and west was gone; the 'iron curtain' was complete.

(h) The Berlin blockade and airlift (June 1948 – May 1949) brought the Cold War to its first climax. The crisis arose out of disagreements over the treatment of Germany:

(i)   At the end of the war, as agreed at Yalta and Potsdam, Germany and Berlin were each divided into four zones. While the three western powers set about organising the economic and political recovery of their zones, Stalin, determined to make the Germans pay for the damage inflicted on Russia, continued to treat his zone as a satellite, draining its resources away to Russia.

(ii) Early in 1948 the three western zones were merged to form a single economic unit whose prosperity, thanks to Marshall Aid, was in marked contrast to the poverty of the Russian zone. At the same time the west began to prepare a constitution for a self-governing West Germany, since the Russians had no intention of allowing complete German reunification. However, the Russians were alarmed at the prospect of a strong independent West Germany which would be part of the American bloc.

(iii) When in June 1948 the west introduced a new currency and ended price controls and rationing in their zone and in West Berlin, the Russians decided that the situation in Berlin had become impossible. Already irritated by the island of capitalism deep in the communist zone, they felt it impossible to have two different currencies in the same city and were embarrassed by the contrast between the prosperity of West Berlin and the poverty of the surrounding area.

The Russian response was immediate: all road, rail and canal links between West Berlin and West Germany were closed; their aim was to force the west to withdraw from West Berlin by reducing it to starvation point. The western powers, convinced that a retreat would be the prelude to a Russian attack on West Germany, were determined to hold on; they decided to fly supplies in, rightly judging that the Russians would not risk shooting down the transport planes. Over the next 10 months 2 million tons of supplies were airlifted to the blockaded city in a remarkable operation which kept the 2.5 million West Berliners fed and warmed right through the winter. In May 1949 the Russians admitted failure by lifting the blockade. *The affair had important results*: the outcome provided a great psychological boost for the western powers, though it brought relations with Russia to their worst ever; it caused the western powers to co-ordinate their defences by the formation of NATO. In addition it meant that since no compromise seemed possible, Germany was doomed to be permanently divided.

(i) The formation of NATO (North Atlantic Treaty Organisation) took place in April 1949. The Berlin blockade demonstrated the west's military illus 16.1 *The Berlin Wall.* Left – *an eighteen-year-old East Berliner lies dying after being shot during an escape attempt.* Right – *he is carried away by East Berlin guards*

unreadiness and frightened them into making definite preparations. Already in March 1948 Britain, France, Belgium, Holland and Luxembourg had signed *the Brussels Defence Treaty* promising military collaboration in case of war. Now they were joined by the USA, Canada, Portugal, Denmark, Ireland, Italy and Norway. All signed *the North Atlantic Treaty,* agreeing to regard an attack on any one of them as an attack on them all, and placing their defence forces under a joint NATO Command Organisation which would co-ordinate the defence of the west. This was a highly significant development: the Americans had abandoned their traditional policy of 'no entangling alliances' and for the first time had pledged themselves in advance to military action. Predictably Stalin took it as a challenge, and tension remained high, especially when it became known in September 1949 that the Russians had developed their own atomic bomb.

(j) **The two Germanies.** Since there was no prospect of the Russians allowing a united Germany, the western powers went ahead alone and set up *the German Federal Republic, known as West Germany* (August 1949). Elections were held and Konrad Adenauer became the first Federal Chancellor. The Russians replied by setting up their zone as *the German Democratic Republic or East Germany* (October 1949). Even in the 1980s Germany remains divided and it is difficult to imagine the circumstances in which she could become united again.

(k) Though tension remained high in Europe, the Cold War spotlight now shifted to **the war in Korea** (1950-3) (see Section 17.2), at the end of which tensions began to relax and it was possible to talk of a 'thaw' in the Cold War.

16.3 WHY WAS THERE A 'THAW' IN THE COLD WAR AFTER 1953 AND WHAT FORM DID IT TAKE?

(a) **The death of Stalin** (March 1953) was probably the starting point of the 'thaw', because it brought to the forefront new leaders -- Malenkov, Bulganin and Khrushchev - who wanted to improve relations with the USA. Their reasons were possibly connected with the fact that by August 1953 the Russians as well as the Americans had developed the hydrogen bomb: the two sides were now so finely balanced that international tensions must be relaxed if nuclear war were to be avoided. *Nikita Khrushchev* explained the new policy in a famous speech (February 1956) in which he criticised Stalin and said that 'peaceful co-existence' with the west was not only possible but essential: 'there are only two ways - either peaceful co-existence or the most destructive war in history. There is no third way.' This did not mean that Khrushchev had given up the idea of a communist-dominated world; this would still come, but would be achieved when the western powers appreciated the superiority of the soviet economic system, not when they were defeated in war. In the same way he hoped to win neutral states over to communism by lavish economic aid.

(b) The 'thaw' showed itself in several ways: in a sense the ending of the Korean War in 1953 and of the war in Indo-China the following year (see Section 17.4(a)) were the earliest signs. In 1955 the Russians agreed to give up their military bases in Finland, Bulganin attended a summit meeting in Geneva where he met US President Eisenhower, and in December the Russian veto on the admittance of 16 new member states to the United Nations was lifted. The quarrel with Yugoslavia was healed when Khrushchev paid a visit to Tito and the Cominform was abandoned, suggesting more freedom for the satellite states (April 1956). Most satisfying of all, at least for the west, was that agreement was at last reached over Austria by *the Austrian State Treaty* (May 1955). At the end of the war in 1945 the country was divided into four occupied zones with the capital, Vienna, in the Russian zone, but unlike Germany she was allowed her own government, because she was viewed not as a defeated enemy but as a state liberated from the Nazis. The Austrian government had only limited powers and the problem was similar to the one in Germany: whereas the three western occupying powers set about organising the recovery of their zones, the Russians insisted on squeezing reparations, mainly in the form of food supplies, from theirs. No permanent settlement seemed likely, but early in 1955 the Russians unexpectedly became co-operative, possibly because they feared a merger between West Germany and western Austria, and agreement was reached. All occupying troops were withdrawn and Austria became independent with her 1937 frontiers. She was not to unite with Germany, her armed forces were strictly limited and she was to remain neutral in any dispute between east and west, which meant that she joined neither NATO nor the European Economic Community. Since then the country has developed successfully though the Austrians were not happy about the loss of the German-speaking people in the south Tyrol, which Italy was allowed to keep.

(c) In fact though, **the 'thaw' was only partial:** Khrushchev's policy was a curious mixture which western leaders often found difficult to understand. While making the apparently conciliatory moves just described, he was quick to respond to anything which seemed to be a threat to the east and had no intention of relaxing his overall grip on the satellites, as the Hungarians discovered to their cost when a rising in Budapest was ruthlessly crushed by Russian tanks (1956) (see Section 18.2(c)). Sometimes he seemed prepared to see how far he could push the Americans before they stood up to him, as when he made the provocative move of installing soviet missiles in Cuba (1962).

(i) *The Warsaw Pact* (1955) was signed between Russia and her satellite states shortly after West Germany was admitted to NATO. The pact was a mutual defence agreement which the west took as a gesture against German membership of NATO.

(ii) *The Russians continued to build up nuclear armaments:* by 1957 they had successfully tested an intercontinental ballistic missile and had also launched the first space satellite, Sputnik 1, none of which made the west feel any more secure.

(iii) *The situation in Berlin caused more tension.* In 1958, perhaps encouraged by Russia's apparent lead in the nuclear arms race, Khrushchev announced that Russia no longer recognised the rights of the western powers in West Berlin; when the Americans made it clear that they would resist any attempt to push them out, Khrushchev did not press the point. In 1960 it was Khrushchev's turn to feel aggrieved when an American U-2 spy plane was shot down over a thousand miles inside Russia. President Eisenhower declined to apologise, defending America's right to make reconnaissance flights and the affair ruined the summit conference which was about to begin in Paris. In 1961 Khrushchev again suggested, this time to the new American President John F. Kennedy, that the west should withdraw from West Berlin. The communists were embarrassed at the large numbers of refugees escaping from East Germany into West Berlin – these averaged about 200,000 a year and totalled over 3 million since 1945. When Kennedy refused, *the Berlin Wall* was erected (August 1961), a 28-mile-long monstrosity across the entire city effectively blocking the escape route.

(iv) *The Cuban missile crisis* (1962) was the most tense incident of the entire Cold War. It occurred when Kennedy demanded the removal of Russian missiles from Cuba, which is less than 100 miles from the American coast. The two powers seemed on the brink of nuclear war, but Khrushchev agreed to remove the missiles (see Section 17.3(b)). *The crisis had important results:* the enormity of what might have happened seemed to bring both sides to their senses and produced a marked relaxation of tension. A telephone link (*the 'hot line'*) was introduced between Moscow and Washington to allow swift consultations and in July 1963, Russia, USA and Britain signed a *Nuclear Test Ban Treaty* agreeing to carry out nuclear tests only underground to avoid polluting the atmosphere. (For further developments in east–west relations see Chapter 17).

QUESTIONS

1. What do you understand by the phrase the 'Cold War'? Explain why it developed and describe the significance in the struggle of the Truman Doctrine, the Berlin Airlift and the Cuban Missile Crisis.

2. Describe Stalin's foreign policy after 1945 showing how and why a 'Cold War' developed.

3. What were the main causes of tension between east and west in Europe between 1945 and 1965?

4. Show how Berlin fell into the hands of the Allied powers. What arrangements did the powers make for the control of the city? Explain how Berlin became the focus of international crises in (a) 1948/49 and (b) 1961.

5. With the aid of the following and any other material you wish to use, describe how the problem of Germany affected relations between the great powers between 1945 and 1961: Potsdam Conference 1945; Berlin blockade 1948-9; formation of German Federal and Democratic Republics 1949; admission of Federal Republic to NATO 1955; Berlin Wall 1961.

6. Explain and illustrate to what extent Nikita Khrushchev's foreign policies changed Russia's relations with the outside world.

7. Trace how a gradual 'thaw' in relations took place between the USA and the USSR following the death of Stalin. Describe the course of these relations up to the time of President Nixon's visit to Moscow in 1972. (See also Chapter 17).

8. Study the cartoon below and then answer the questions which follow.

Fig 16.2

  (i) Suggest a title for the cartoon. (1 mark)
 (ii) Name the character depicted kneeling in the foreground. (1 mark)
(iii) To whom does 'Joe' refer? (1 mark)
 (iv) Where was the speech made which led to this cartoon being published? (1 mark)
  (v) In which year did this cartoon appear? (1 mark)
 (vi) Name the two ports which are supposed to mark the northern and southern ends of the barrier depicted. (2 marks)
(vii) How did this picture forecast what happened in August 1961. (1 mark)
(viii) Why did a 'Cold War' develop between the western powers and the USSR after the Second World War? (8 marks)
 (ix) Write a paragraph to describe what happened in and around Berlin between May 1948 and June 1949. (4 marks)

[AEB]

CHAPTER 17

THE SPREAD OF COMMUNISM OUTSIDE EUROPE AND ITS EFFECT ON INTERNATIONAL RELATIONS

SUMMARY OF EVENTS

Communism was not confined to Europe: several other communist states emerged each with its own particular brand of Marxism. As early as 1921, encouraged by the Russian Revolution, *the Chinese Communist Party* (CCP) had been founded. At first it co-operated with the *Kuomintang* (KMT), the party trying to govern China and control the generals who were struggling among themselves for power. The *Kuomintang* leaders were Dr Sun Yat-sen and, after his death in 1925, General Chiang Kai-shek. As the KMT established its control over more of China, it felt strong enough to dispense with the communists and tried to destroy them. The communists reacted vigorously and, after escaping from surrounding KMT forces, embarked on the famous 6,000-mile *Long March* (1934–5) to form a new power base in northern China. Civil war dragged on, complicated by Japanese interference which culminated in the full-scale invasion of 1937. When the Second World War ended in the defeat and withdrawal of the Japanese, Chiang, with American help, and the communists under their leader Mao Tse-tung were still fighting it out. At last in 1949 Mao triumphed, and Chiang and his supporters fled to the island of Taiwan (Formosa); the second major country had followed Russia into communism.

Meanwhile communism had also gained a hold in *Korea*, which had been controlled by Japan since 1910. After the Japanese defeat in 1945 the country was divided into two zones: the north occupied by Russians, the south by Americans. The Russians set up a communist government in their zone, and since no agreement could be reached on what government to have for the whole country, Korea, like Germany, remained divided into two states. In 1950 communist North Korea invaded South Korea. United Nations forces (mostly American) moved in to help the south, while the Chinese helped the north. After much advancing and retreating, the war ended in 1953 with South Korea still non-communist.

In *Cuba* early in 1959 Fidel Castro ousted the corrupt dictator, Batista. Although Castro was not a communist to begin with, the Americans soon turned against him, particularly when they discovered in 1962 that Russian missiles were based on the island; these were later removed after a tense Cold War crisis which brought the world to the brink of nuclear war. In *Vietnam* a similar situation to that in Korea occurred after the Vietnamese had won their independence from the French (1954): the country was divided, temporarily it was thought, into north (communist) and south (non-communist); when a rebellion broke out in the south against a corrupt government, communist North Vietnam gave military assistance to the rebels and the Americans became heavily involved supporting the South Vietnamese government to stop the spread of communism. In 1973 the Americans withdrew from the struggle, following which the South Vietnamese forces rapidly collapsed, and the whole country became united under a communist government (1975). Before the end of the year neighbouring *Cambodia and Laos* had also become communist.

In South America, which had a tradition of right-wing military dictatorships, communism made little headway, except in *Chile*, where in 1970 a Marxist government was democratically elected, with Salvador Allende as President. This was an interesting but short-lived experiment, since in 1973 the government was overthrown by the army and Allende killed. Africa saw the establishment of governments with strong Marxist connections in *Mozambique* (1975) and *Angola* (1976) both of which had just succeeded in winning independence from Portugal. In December 1979 the Russians intervened in an already disturbed *Afghanistan* in support of a communist government, a move which caused a recurrence of the Cold War.

17.1 CHIANG OR MAO? TROUBLED YEARS IN CHINA 1918-49

(a) Soon after a republic was proclaimed (1911) China had dissolved into the chaos known as the Warlord Era (1916-28) during which a number of generals seized control of different provinces, so that China seemed about to break up into many separate empires. The main hope for the survival of a united China lay with *Dr Sun Yat-sen* and his National People's Party or *Kuomintang* (formed 1912) which succeeded in setting up a government at Canton in southern China (1917). The *Kuomintang* was not a communist party, though it was prepared to co-operate with the communists and developed its own party organisation along communist lines as well as building up its own army. Sun himself summarised his aims as the *Three Principles*: nationalism (to rid China of foreign influence and build her into a strong and united power respected abroad), democracy (China should be ruled, not by warlords, but by the people themselves after they had been educated to equip them for democratic self-government) and land reform, sometimes known as 'the people's livelihood' (this was vague:

Fig 17.1 *China after the First World War*

Japanese territory in 1930 ||||||| Territory occupied by the Japanese 1931–9 although Sun announced a long-term policy of economic development and redistribution of land to the peasants and was in favour of rent restraint, he was opposed to the confiscation of landlords' property). Sun gained enormous respect as an intellectual statesman and revolutionary leader, but when he died in 1925 little progress had been made towards achieving the three principles, mainly because he was not himself a general; until the KMT armies were built up, he had to rely on alliances with sympathetic warlords and had trouble exercising any authority outside the south.

(b) General Chiang Kai-shek became leader of the KMT after Sun's death. He had received his military training in Japan before the First World War, and being a strong nationalist, joined the KMT. At this stage the new Russian soviet government was providing help and guidance to the KMT in the hope that nationalist China would be friendly to Russia. In 1923 Chiang spent some time in Moscow studying the organisation of the communist party and the Red Army; the following year he became head of the Whampoa Military Academy (near Canton) which was set up with Russian cash, arms and advisers to train officers for the KMT army. However, in spite of his Russian contacts, Chiang was not a communist; in fact he was more right-wing than Sun Yat-sen and became increasingly anti-communist, his sympathies lying with businessmen and landowners. Soon after becoming party leader he removed all left-wingers from leading positions in the party though for the time being he continued the KMT alliance with the communists. In 1926 he set out on *the Northern March* to destroy the warlords of central and northern China. Starting from Canton, the KMT and the communists had captured Hankow, Shanghai and Nanking by 1927. Peking was taken in 1928. Much of Chiang's success sprang from massive local support among the peasants attracted by communist promises of land; the capture of Shanghai was helped by a rising of industrial workers organised by Chou En-lai, a member of the KMT but also a communist. By April 1927 Chiang decided that the communists were becoming too powerful; in areas where communists were strong, landlords were being attacked and land seized; it was time to destroy an embarrassing ally. All communists were expelled from the KMT, and a terrible 'purification movement' was launched in which thousands of communists, trade union and peasant leaders were massacred; some estimates put the total murdered as high as 250,000. The communists had been checked, the warlords were under control and Chiang was the military and political leader of China. The *Kuomintang* government proved to be a great disappointment for the majority of Chinese. Chiang could claim to have achieved Sun's first principle, nationalism, but relying as he did on the support of wealthy landowners, no moves were made towards democracy or land reform though there was some limited progress with the building of more schools and roads.

(c) Meanwhile Mao Tse-tung and the Chinese Communist Party (CCP) concentrated on survival as Chiang carried out five 'extermination campaigns' against them between 1930 and 1934. The party had been officially founded in 1921, and at first consisted mostly of intellectuals with no military strength, which explains why they were willing to join the KMT. Mao, who was present at the founding meeting, was born in Hunan province (1893) in south-east China, the son of a prosperous peasant farmer. After some time working on the land, Mao trained as a teacher, and then moved northwards to Peking where he worked as a library assistant at the University, a centre of Marxist studies. Later he moved back to Hunan and built up a reputation as a skilful trade union and peasant association organiser. After the communist breach with the KMT, Mao was responsible for changing the party's strategy: they would concentrate on winning mass support among the peasants rather than trying to capture industrial towns where several communist insurrections had failed because of the strength of the KMT. In 1931 Mao was elected chairman of the Central Executive Committee of the party, and from then on he gradually consolidated his position as the real leader of Chinese communism. During the extermination campaigns Mao and his supporters took to the mountains between Hunan and Kiangsi provinces and concentrated on building up the Red Army. However, early in 1934 Mao's base area was surrounded by KMT armies poised for the final destruction of Chinese communism. Mao decided that the only chance of survival was to break through Chiang's lines and found another power base elsewhere. In October 1934 the breakthrough was achieved and almost 100,000 communists set out on the remarkable *Long March* which was to become part of Chinese legend. They covered about 6,000 miles in 368 days and, in the words of Edgar Snow, 'crossed 18 mountain ranges, 5 of which were snow-capped, and 24 rivers. They passed through 12 different provinces, occupied 62 cities, and broke through enveloping armies of 10 different provincial warlords, besides defeating, eluding, or outmanoeuvring the various forces of government troops sent against them.' Eventually the 20,000 survivors found refuge at Yenan in Shensi province, where a new base was organised. Mao was able to control the provinces of Shensi and Kansu. During the next 10 years the communists continued to gain support while Chiang and the KMT steadily lost popularity.

(d) Why did Mao and the communists gain support?

(i) The basic opportunity for them to win support was provided by the inefficiency and corruption of the KMT in government. They had little to offer in the way of reform, spent too much time looking after the interests of industrialists, bankers and landowners, and made no effective attempts to organise mass support.

(ii) There was little improvement in factory conditions, in spite of laws designed to remove the worst abuses such as child labour in textile mills. Often these laws were not applied: there was widespread bribery of inspectors and Chiang himself was not prepared to offend his industrialist supporters.

(iii) There was no improvement in peasant poverty. In the early 1930s there was a series of droughts and bad harvests which caused wide-spread famine in rural areas; at the same time there was often plenty of rice and wheat being hoarded in the cities by profiteering merchants. In addition there were high taxes and forced labour. In contrast, the land policy followed in areas controlled by the communists was much more attractive: at first in the south they seized the estates of rich landlords and redistributed them among the peasants; after the temporary truce with the KMT during the war with Japan, the communists compromised and confined themselves to a policy of restricting rents and making sure that even the poorest labourers got a small piece of land. This less drastic policy had the advantage of winning the support of the smaller landowners as well as the peasants.

(iv) The crucial factor was that the KMT put up no effective resistance to the Japanese, who occupied Manchuria in 1931 and were obviously working to bring the neighbouring provinces of northern China under their control. Chiang seemed to think it was more important to destroy the communists than to resist the Japanese, and moved into south Shensi to attack Mao (1936). Here a remarkable incident took place: Chiang was taken prisoner by some of his own troops, mostly Manchurians who were incensed at the Japanese invasion. They demanded that Chiang turn against the Japanese, but at first he was unwilling. Only after the prominent communist Chou En-lai came to see him at Sian did he agree to a fresh alliance with the CCP and a national front against the Japanese. The new alliance brought great advantages to the CCP: the KMT extermination campaigns ceased for the time being and consequently the CCP was secure in its Shensi base; when full-scale war broke out with Japan in 1937, the KMT forces were quickly defeated and most of eastern China was occupied by the Japanese as Chiang retreated westwards to Chungking; this enabled the communists, undefeated in Shensi, to present themselves as patriotic nationalists, leading an effective guerrilla campaign against the Japanese in the north. This won them massive support among peasants and middle classes, who were appalled at Japanese brutality and arrogance. Whereas in 1937 the CCP had 5 base areas controlling 12 million people, by 1945 this had grown to 19 base areas and 100 million people.

(e) The communist victory in 1949 was still not inevitable, though all the points examined in (d) contributed to it. When the Japanese were defeated in 1945, the KMT and the CCP became locked in the final struggle for power. Many observers, especially in the USA, hoped and expected that Chiang would be victorious. The Americans helped the KMT to take over all areas previously occupied by the Japanese, except Manchuria which had been captured by the Russians a few days before the war ended. Here the Russians obstructed the KMT and allowed CCP guerrillas to move in. In fact the apparent strength of the KMT was deceptive: in 1948 the ever-increasing communist armies were large enough to abandon their guerrilla campaign and challenge Chiang's armies directly. As soon as they came under direct pressure, the KMT armies began to disintegrate. In January 1949 the communists took Peking, and later in the year Chiang and what remained of his forces fled to the island of Taiwan, leaving Mao Tse-tung in command of mainland China.

There were several reasons for the CCP triumph: the communists continued to win popular support by their restrained land policy which varied according to the needs of particular areas – some or all of a land-lord's estates might be confiscated and redistributed among the peasants, or there might simply be rent restriction; communist armies were well-disciplined and communist administration was honest and scrupulously fair. On the other hand the KMT administration was inefficient and corrupt, much of its American aid finding its way into the pockets of officials; its policy of paying for the wars by printing extra money resulted in galloping inflation which caused hardship for the masses and ruined many of the middle class. Its armies were poorly paid and were allowed to loot the countryside; subjected to communist propaganda, they gradually became disillusioned with Chiang and began to desert to the communists. The KMT tried to terrorise the local populations into submission, but this only alienated more areas. Towards the end, Chiang also made some tactical blunders: like Hitler he could not bear to order retreats and consequently his scattered armies were surrounded and often, as at Peking and Shanghai, surrendered without resistance, totally disillusioned. Finally the CCP leaders, Mao Tse-tung and Chou En-lai, were shrewd enough to take advantage of KMT weaknesses and were completely dedicated; the communist generals Lin Piao, Chu Teh and Ch'en Yi, had prepared their armies carefully and were more competent tactically than their KMT counterparts.

17.2 WAR IN KOREA 1950-3

Soon after the communist victory in China civil war broke out in Korea. Its origins lay in the fact that the country had been divided into two zones in 1945 at the end of the Second World War.

(a) **Korea was divided into two at the 38th parallel** by agreement between the USA and the USSR for purely military reasons – so that they could organise the surrender of the occupying Japanese forces; it was not intended to be permanent political division. The United Nations wanted free elections for the whole country and the Americans agreed, believing that since their zone, the south, contained two-thirds of the population, the communist north would be outvoted. However the unification of Korea, like that of Germany, soon became part of Cold War rivalry and no agreement could be reached. Elections were held in the south, supervised by the UN, and the independent Republic of Korea (ROK) or South Korea was

Fig 17.2 *the War in Korea*

set up with Syngman Rhee as president and its capital at Seoul (August 1948). The following month the Russians created The Democratic People's Republic of Korea or North Korea under the communist government of Kim Il Sung, with its capital at Pyongyang. In 1949 Russian and American troops were withdrawn, leaving a potentially dangerous situation: most Koreans bitterly resented the artificial division forced on their country by outsiders, but both leaders claimed the right to rule the whole country. Without warning, North Korean troops invaded South Korea in June 1950.

(b) There is some controversy about the origins of the attack. It is still not clear whether it was Kim Il Sung's idea, perhaps encouraged by General MacArthur's statement in 1949 that Korea was no longer part of the US defence perimeter in the Pacific; or he may have been egged on by the new Chinese communist government who were at the same time massing troops in Fukien province facing Taiwan, as if they were about to attack Chiang Kai-shek; perhaps the Russians were responsible: they had supplied the North Koreans with tanks, planes and other equipment; a communist takeover of the south would strengthen the Russian defensive position in the Pacific and provide a splendid gesture against the Americans to make up for Stalin's failure to squeeze them out of West Berlin. The communists claimed that South Korea had started the war, when troops of the 'bandit traitor' Syngman Rhee had crossed the 38th parallel.

(c) American and UN involvement. President Truman was convinced that the attack on South Korea, coming so soon after Cold War events in Europe, was part of a vast Russian plan to advance communism wherever possible in the world, and believed it essential for the west to take a stand by supporting South Korea. American troops in Japan were ordered to South Korea before the UN had decided what action to take. The UN Security Council called on North Korea to withdraw her troops, and when this was ignored asked member states to send assistance to South Korea. This decision was reached in the absence of the Russian delegation, who were boycotting meetings in protest against the UN refusal to allow Mao's new Chinese regime to be represented, and who would certainly have vetoed such a decision. In the event, the USA and 15 other countries (Australia, Britain, Canada, New Zealand, Nationalist China (Chiang), France, Netherlands, Belgium, Colombia, Greece, Turkey, Panama, Philippines and Thailand) sent troops, though the vast majority were Americans. All forces were under the command of MacArthur.

Their arrival was none too soon: by September communist troops had overrun the whole of South Korea except the south-east, around the port of Pusan. UN reinforcements poured into Pusan and on 15 September American marines landed at Inchon, near Seoul, two hundred miles behind the communist front lines. Then followed an incredibly swift collapse by North Korean forces: by the end of September UN troops had entered Seoul and cleared the south of communists. Instead of calling for a cease-fire now that the original UN objective had been achieved, Truman ordered an invasion of North Korea, with UN approval, aiming to unite the country and hold free elections. Chou En-lai had warned that China would resist if UN troops entered the north, but the warning was ignored; by the end of October UN troops had captured Pyongyang, occupied two-thirds of North Korea, and reached the Yalu River, the frontier between North Korea and China.

The Chinese government was seriously alarmed: the Americans had already placed a fleet between Taiwan and the mainland to prevent an attack on Chiang, and remembering the assistance given to the KMT during the civil war, the Chinese feared an American invasion of Manchuria. In November they launched a massive counter-offensive with over 300,000 troops described as 'volunteers'; by mid-January 1951 they had driven the UN troops out of North Korea and crossed the 38th parallel; Seoul was captured again. MacArthur was shocked at the strength of the Chinese

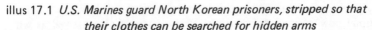

illus 17.1 *U.S. Marines guard North Korean prisoners, stripped so that their clothes can be searched for hidden arms*

forces and argued that the best way to beat them and stop the spread of communism was to attack Manchuria, with atomic bombs if necessary. However, Truman felt this would cause a large-scale war, which the USA did not want, and decided to settle for merely 'containing' communism; MacArthur was removed from his command. In June UN troops cleared the communists out of South Korea again and fortified the frontier; peace talks at Panmunjom lasted for two years, ending in July 1953 with an agreement that the frontier should be roughly along the 38th parallel.

(d) The results of the war were wide-ranging. For Korea herself it was a disaster: the country was devastated, about four million Korean civilians and soldiers had been killed and five million were homeless. The division seemed permanent; both states remained intensely suspicious of each other and heavily armed, and there were constant ceasefire violations. The USA could take satisfaction from having contained communism and could claim that this success, plus American rearmament, dissuaded world communism from further aggression. The United Nations had exerted its authority and reversed an act of aggression (something which the League of Nations had never achieved). On the other hand the communist world denounced the UN as a capitalist tool. The military performance of communist China was impressive; she had prevented the unification of Korea under American influence and was now clearly a world power; the fact that she was still denied a seat in the UN seemed even more unreasonable. The conflict brought a new dimension to the Cold War: American relations now seemed permanently strained with China as well as with Russia; the familiar pattern of both sides trying to build up alliances appeared in Asia as well as Europe. China supported the Indo-Chinese communists in their struggle for independence from France and at the same time offered friendship and aid to underdeveloped 'third world' countries in Asia, Africa and Latin America; 'peaceful co-existence' agreements were signed with India and Burma (1954). Meanwhile the Americans tried to encircle China with bases: in 1951 defensive agreements were signed with Australia and New Zealand and in 1954 these three states together with Britain and France set up the South East Asia Treaty Organisation (SEATO); however, the USA was disappointed when only three Asian states – Pakistan, Thailand and the Philippines – joined SEATO. It was obvious that many states wanted to keep clear of the Cold War and remain uncommitted.

Relations between the USA and China remained poor, mainly because of the Taiwan situation. The communists still hoped to capture the island and destroy Chiang Kai-shek and his Nationalist party for good, but the Americans were committed to defend Chiang and wanted to keep Taiwan. as a military base.

17.3 CUBA: WHY DID FIDEL CASTRO COME TO POWER AND HOW WERE CUBA'S FOREIGN RELATIONS AFFECTED?

(a) The situation which resulted in Fidel Castro coming to power in January 1959 had built up over a number of years:

(i) There was a long-standing resentment among many Cubans of American influence, which dated back to 1898 when the USA had helped wrest Cuba from Spanish control. Although the island became an independent republic, American troops were needed from time to time to maintain stability, and American financial aid and investment kept the Cuban economy ticking over. In fact there was some truth in the claim that the USA controlled the Cuban economy: American companies held controlling interests in all Cuban industries (sugar, tobacco, textiles, iron, nickel, copper, manganese, paper and rum), owned half the land, about three-fifths of the railways, all electricity production and the entire telephone system. The USA was the main market for Cuba's exports, of which sugar was by far the most important. Small wonder that the American ambassador in Havana was usually referred to as the second most important man in Cuba. The American connection need not have been so much resented if it had resulted in an efficiently run country, but this was not so.

(ii) Though Cuba was prosperous compared with other Latin American countries, she was too dependent on the export of sugar, and the wealth of the country was concentrated in the hands of a few. Unemployment was an insoluble problem: it varied from about 8 per cent of the labour force during the 5 months of the sugar harvest to over 30 per cent during the rest of the year. Yet there was no unemployment benefit, and the trade unions, dominated by workers who had all-the-year-round jobs in sugar mills, did nothing to help. The poverty of the unemployed was in stark contrast to the wealth in Havana, the capital, and in the hands of corrupt government officials; consequently social tensions were high.

(iii) No effective democratic political system had been developed. In 1952 *Fulgencio Batista*, who had been in the forefront of politics since 1933, seized power illegally and began to rule as a dictator. He introduced no reforms and according to Hugh Thomas, 'spent a lot of time dealing with his private affairs and his foreign fortunes, leaving himself too little time for affairs of state'. As well as being corrupt, his regime was also brutal.

(iv) Since there was no prospect of a peaceful social revolution, the feeling grew that violent revolution was necessary. The leading exponent of this view was Fidel Castro, a young lawyer from a middle-class background. Before he came to power, Castro was more of a liberal nationalist than a communist: he wanted to rid Cuba of Batista and corruption and to introduce limited land reforms so that all peasants should receive some land. After an unsuccessful attempt to overthrow Batista in 1953, which earned him two years in gaol, Castro began a campaign of guerrilla warfare and sabotage in the cities. The rebels soon controlled the mountainous areas of the east and north and won popular support there by carrying through Castro's land reform policy.

(v) Batista's reaction played into Castro's hands. He took savage reprisals against the guerrillas, torturing and murdering suspects, which polarised the struggle; even many of the middle class began to support Castro as the most likely way of ousting a brutal dictator. Morale in Batista's poorly paid army began to crumble in the summer of 1958 after an unsuccessful attempt to destroy Castro's forces. The USA began to feel embarrassment at Batista's behaviour and cut off arms supplies, a serious blow to the dictator's prestige. In September a small rebel force under *Che Guevara*, an Argentinian supporter of Castro, gained control of the main road across the island and prepared to move on Santa Clara. On 1 January 1959 Batista fled from Cuba, and a liberal government was set up with Castro at its head.

(b) Cuban relations with the USA did not deteriorate immediately; Castro was thought to be, at worst, a social democrat, and consequently most Americans were prepared to give him a chance. Before long, however, he had outraged the USA by nationalising American-owned estates and factories. President Eisenhower threatened to stop importing Cuban sugar, forcing Castro to sign a trade agreement with Russia. In July 1960 when the Americans carried out their threat, the USSR promised to buy Cuba's sugar, and Castro confiscated all remaining American property. As Cuba's relations with the USA worsened, those with Russia improved: in January 1961 the USA broke off diplomatic relations with Cuba, but the Russians were already supplying economic aid. Convinced that Cuba was now a communist state in all but name, the new American president, John F. Kennedy, approved a plan by a group of Batista supporters to invade Cuba from American bases in Guatemala. The American Central Intelligence Agency (CIA), a kind of secret service, was deeply involved. The small invading force landed at *the Bay of Pigs* in April 1961, but the operation was so badly planned and executed that Castro's forces and his two jet planes had no difficulty in crushing it. Later the same year Castro announced that he was a Marxist and that Cuba was now a socialist country.

The missile crisis (1962) brought Cuba into the Cold War forefront and the world to the brink of nuclear war. During the summer Russia supplied Cuba with large quantities of arms and on 22 October Kennedy announced that U-2 spy planes had photographed Russian missile bases being built in Cuba; he alerted American troops, began a blockade of Cuba to keep out further arms (several Russian ships carrying missiles were en route for Cuba) and demanded that Russia withdraw the missiles. On 28 October Khrushchev agreed to remove the offending missiles and in return Kennedy promised not to invade Cuba. The crisis had passed and thereafter the Cold War thawed somewhat (see Section 16.3(c)); but relations between Cuba and the USA remained cool. The attitude of other Latin American states, most of which had right-wing governments, was one of extreme suspicion; in 1962 they expelled Cuba from the Organisation of American States (OAS), which only made her more dependent on Russia (for Castro's domestic policies see Section 18.4).

17.4 THE WARS IN VIETNAM: 1946-54 AND 1961-75

(a) From 1946 until 1954 the Vietnamese were fighting for independence from France. Vietnam together with Laos and Cambodia made up Indo-China which had been part of the French empire since the late nineteenth century. During the Second World War the area was occupied by the Japanese; resistance to both Japanese and French was organised by *the League for Vietnamese Independence* (Vietminh), led by the communist *Ho Chi Minh* who had spent many years in Russia learning how to organise revolutions. The Vietminh, though led by communists, was an alliance of all shades of political opinion which wanted to see the end of foreign control. At the end of the war in 1945 Ho Chi Minh declared the whole of Vietnam independent; when it became clear that the French had no intention of agreeing to full independence, the Vietminh attacked the French in Hanoi, beginning an eight-year struggle which ended with the French defeat at Dien Bien Phu (May 1954). The Vietminh were successful partly because they were masters of guerrilla tactics and had massive support from the Vietnamese people and because the French, still suffering the after-effects of world war, failed to send enough troops. The decisive

Fig 17.3 *the wars in Vietnam*

...... Ho Chi Minh Trail

■ American bases

factor was probably that from 1950 the new Chinese communist government supplied the rebels with arms and equipment. The USA also became
involved: seeing the struggle as part of the Cold War and the fight against
communism, she supplied the French with military and economic aid; but
it was not enough. By *the Geneva Agreement* (1954) Laos and Cambodia
were to be independent; Vietnam was temporarily divided into two states
at the 17th parallel: Ho Chi Minh's Vietminh government was recognised
in North Vietnam; South Vietnam was to have a separate government for
the time being, but elections were to be held by 1956 for the whole
country, which would then become united. Ho Chi Minh was disappointed
at the partition, but was confident that the communists would win the

national elections. As it turned out the elections were never held and a repeat performance of the Korean situation seemed likely. A civil war gradually developed in South Vietnam which involved the north and the USA.

(b) What caused the war and why was the USA involved?

(i) The South Vietnamese government under *President Ngo Dinh Diem* (chosen by a national referendum in 1955) refused to make preparations for the elections for the whole of Vietnam, and the USA, which was backing his regime, did not press him for fear of a communist victory if the elections were held.

(ii) Although Diem began energetically, his government soon lost popularity: he came from a wealthy Roman Catholic family, whereas three-quarters of the population were Buddhist peasants who thought themselves discriminated against; they demanded land reform of the type carried through in China and North Vietnam, but none was forthcoming. He also gained a reputation, perhaps not wholly deserved, for corruption and was unpopular with nationalists who thought he was too much under American influence.

(iii) In 1960 various opposition groups which included many former communist members of the Viet Minh, formed the *National Liberation Front (NLF)*. They demanded a democratic national coalition government which would introduce reforms and negotiate peacefully for a united Vietnam. A guerrilla campaign was started, attacking government officials and buildings, while Buddhist monks had their own special brand of protest, committing suicide in public by setting fire to themselves. Diem's credibility declined further when he dismissed all criticism and opposition as communist inspired whereas the communists were only one section of the NLF; he also introduced harsh security measures. He was overthrown and murdered by an army coup (1963) and the country was ruled by a series of generals of which *President Nguyen Van Thieu* survived longest (1967-75). The removal of Diem left the basic situation unchanged and the guerrilla war continued.

(iv) When it became clear that Diem could not cope with the situation the USA decided to increase her military presence in South Vietnam. Under Eisenhower she had been supporting the regime since 1954 with economic aid and military advisers and accepted Diem's claim that communists were behind all the trouble. Kennedy and Johnson saw it as another Korea: if a strong enough stand were made, South Vietnam could be saved from communism.

(v) The Americans were strengthened in their determination by the knowledge that the Vietcong (as the guerrillas were now known) were receiving supplies, equipment and troops from North Vietnam. Ho Chi Minh believed that such aid was justified: given South Vietnam's refusal to agree to the national elections, only force could unite the two halves of Vietnam.

(c) **The phases of the war** correspond to successive American presidencies which each saw the introduction of new policies:

(i) *Kennedy* (1961-3) tried to keep American involvement down to an anti-guerrilla campaign. He sent about 16,000 advisers plus equipment and helicopters and introduced *the 'safe village' policy*, in which local peasants were moved en masse into fortified villages, leaving the Vietcong isolated outside. This was a failure because most of the Vietcong were peasants who simply continued to operate inside the villages.

(ii) *Johnson* (1963-9) was not deterred by reports from American advisers in 1964 that the Vietcong and the NLF controlled about 40 per cent of South Vietnamese villages and that the peasant population seemed to support them. He assumed that the Vietcong were controlled by Ho Chi Minh and decided to bomb North Vietnam (1965) in the hope that he would call off the campaign. Over the next seven years North Vietnamese cities suffered an even greater tonnage of bombs than the Germans during the Second World War. In addition over half a million American troops arrived in the south. In spite of these massive efforts the Vietcong still managed to unleash an offensive in February 1968 which captured something like 80 per cent of all towns and villages; although much ground was lost later, this offensive convinced many Americans of the hopelessness of the situation, and great pressure was brought on the government to withdraw from Vietnam. This Johnson had no intention of doing, though he did suspend the bombing of North Vietnam (March 1968).

(iii) *Nixon* (1969-74) realised that a new approach was needed since public opinion would hardly allow him to commit any more American troops (early in 1969 there were 500,000 Americans, 50,000 South Koreans and 750,000 South Vietnamese against 450,000 Vietcong plus perhaps 70,000 North Vietnamese). His new idea was *Vietnamisation*: the Americans would rearm and train the South Vietnamese army to look after the defence of South Vietnam; this would allow a gradual withdrawal of American troops (in fact about half had been sent home by mid-1971). On the other hand Nixon began the heavy bombing of North Vietnam again and also began to bomb the Ho Chi Minh Trail through Laos and Cambodia along which supplies and troops came from North Vietnam. All was to no avail: at the end of 1972 the Vietcong controlled the entire western half of the country. By now Nixon was under pressure both at home and from world opinion to withdraw; apart from the terrible bombing of North Vietnam, the use of chemicals to destroy jungle foliage and of inflammable napalm jelly which burned people alive, plus the deaths of thousands of innocent civilians, caused a revulsion of feeling against continuing the war. Even Russia and China who were helping the Vietcong with supplies and equipment were looking round for a way out. Consequently *a cease-fire was arranged for January 1973.* It was agreed that all American troops would be withdrawn from Vietnam and both north and south would respect the frontier along the 17th parallel. However, the Vietcong continued their campaign and without the Americans, President Thieu's government in Saigon soon collapsed. In April 1975 Saigon was occupied by the North Vietnamese and Vietcong; at last Vietnam was united and free from foreign intervention - under a communist government. In the same year communist governments were also established in Laos and Cambodia. American policy of preventing the spread of communism in south-east Asia had ended in complete failure and humiliation.

(d) Why did the Americans fail?

(i) The main reason was that the Vietcong and the NLF had widespread support among ordinary peasants who had genuine grievances against an inefficient government which failed to introduce necessary reforms. When the NLF was formed in 1960 the communists were only one of several opposition groups; by ignoring the rightness of the NLF case and choosing instead to prop up such an obviously deficient regime in their obsession with the fight against communism, the Americans actually encouraged the spread of communism in the south.

(ii) The Vietcong, like the Vietminh before them, were experts at guerrilla warfare and were fighting on familiar territory; the Americans found them much more difficult to deal with than the conventional armies they had faced in Korea: with no distinguishing uniform, guerrillas could easily merge into the local peasant population. It proved impossible to stop supplies and reinforcements moving down the Ho Chi Minh Trail.

(iii) The Vietcong received important help from North Vietnam in the way of troops, while China and Russia supplied arms. After 1970 the Russian contribution was vitally important and included rifles, machineguns, long-range artillery, anti-aircraft missiles and tanks.

(iv) The North Vietnamese were dedicated to eventual victory and the unification of their country and showed amazing resilience; in spite of appalling damage and casualties during the bombings, they responded by evacuating city populations and rebuilding factories outside the cities.

The effects of the war were wide-reaching: Vietnam was united but the problems of reconstruction were enormous, and the new government's policies had unpleasant aspects such as concentration camps for opponents, and loss of freedom of speech. As well as being a blow to American prestige, her failure had a profound effect on American society: involvement in the war was seen in many circles as a terrible mistake and this, together with the Watergate scandal (see Section 21.1(f)) which forced Nixon to resign (August 1974), shook confidence in a political system which could allow such things to happen. Future American governments would have to think carefully before committing themselves so deeply to any similar situation. The war was a victory for the communist world, though both the Russians and Chinese reacted with restraint and did not boast about it to any great extent, indicating perhaps that they wanted to relax international tensions; however, the communist world now had another powerful military force in the Vietnamese army.

17.5 CHILE UNDER SALVADOR ALLENDE 1970-3

In September 1970 Salvador Allende, a Marxist doctor of medicine from a middle class background, won the presidential election as the leader of a left-wing coalition of communists, socialists, radicals and social democrats; it called itself Unidad Popular (UP). It was a narrow victory, Allende gaining 36 per cent of the poll against the 35 per cent of his nearest rival. But it was enough to make him president, the world's first Marxist president to be voted in through a democratic election. Although it lasted only three years Allende's government is worth looking at in some detail because it is still the only one of its kind and it illustrates the problems faced by a Marxist government trying to function within a democratic system.

(a) How did Allende come to be elected?
Chile, unlike most other South American states, had a tradition of democracy. There were three main parties or groups of parties: the Unidad Popular on the left, the Christian Democrats (also left-inclined) and the National Party (a liberal/conservative coalition). The army played little part in politics and the democratic constitution (similar to that of the USA except that the president could not stand for re-election immediately) was usually respected. The election of 1964 was won by *Eduardo Frei*, leader of the Christian Democrats, who believed in social reform. Frei began vigorously: inflation was brought down from 38 per cent to 25 per cent, the rich were made to pay their taxes instead of evading them, 360,000 new houses were built, the number of schools was more than doubled and some limited land reform introduced: over 1,200 private holdings which were being run inefficiently were confiscated and redistributed to landless peasants. He also took over about half the holdings in the American-owned Chilean copper mines, with suitable compensation. The American government admired his reforms and poured in lavish economic aid.

By 1967, however, the tide was beginning to turn against Frei: the left thought his land reforms too cautious and wanted full nationalisation of the copper industry (Chile's most important export), whereas the right thought he had gone too far as it was. In 1969 there was a serious drought in which a third of the harvest was lost; large quantities of food had to be imported, causing inflation to soar again. There were strikes of copper miners demanding higher wages and several miners were killed by government troops. *Allende* made skilful use of this ammunition during the 1970 election campaign, pointing out that Frei's achievements fell far short of his promises. Allende's coalition had a much better campaign organisation than the other parties and could get thousands of supporters out on the streets. Allende himself inspired confidence: elegant and cultured, he appeared the very opposite of the violent revolutionary; appearances were not deceptive: he believed that communism could succeed without a violent revolution. In the 1970 election 36 per cent of the voters were in favour of trying his policies.

(b) Allende's problems and policies. The problems facing the new government were enormous: inflation was running at over 30 per cent, unemployment at 20 per cent, industry was stagnating, and 90 per cent of the population lived in such poverty that half the children under 15 suffered from malnutrition. Allende believed in a redistribution of income, which would enable the poor to buy more and thereby stimulate the economy. All-round wage increases of about 40 per cent were introduced and firms were not allowed to increase prices. The remainder of the copper industry, textiles and banks were nationalised, and Frei's land redistribution speeded up. The army was awarded an even bigger pay rise than anybody else to make sure of retaining its support. In foreign affairs he restored diplomatic relations with Castro's Cuba, China and East Germany. Whether Allende's policies would have succeeded in the long run is open to argument. Certainly he retained his popularity sufficiently for the UP to win 49 per cent of the votes in the 1972 municipal elections and to increase slightly their seats in the 1973 congressional elections. However, the Allende experiment came to an abrupt and violent end in September 1973.

(c) Why was he overthrown?
Criticism of the government gradually built up as Allende's policies began to cause problems: land redistribution caused a fall in agricultural production, mainly because farmers whose land was due to be taken stopped sowing and often slaughtered their cattle (like the Russian *kulaks* during collectivisation); this caused food shortages and further inflation. Private investors were frightened off and the government became short of funds to implement social reforms (housing, education, social services) as rapidly as it would have liked. Copper nationalisation was disappointing: there were long strikes for higher wages, production fell, and the world price of copper fell suddenly by about 30 per cent causing a further drop in government revenue. Some communists who wanted a more drastic Castro-style approach to Chile's problems grew impatient with Allende's caution, refusing to make allowances for the fact that he did not have a stable parliamentary majority; they founded the Movement of the Revolutionary Left (MIR) which embarrassed the non-violent UP by seizing farms and evicting the owners. In addition the USA disapproved strongly of Allende's policies and other South American governments were nervous in case the Chileans tried to export their 'revolution'.

Looming above all else was the question of what would happen in September 1976 when the next presidential election was due; under the constitution Allende would not be able to stand, but no Marxist regime had ever allowed itself to be voted out of power. The opposition feared, perhaps with justification, that Allende was planning to change the constitution. As things stood, any president finding his legislation blocked by congress could appeal to the nation by means of referendum. With sufficient support Allende might be able to use the referendum device to postpone the election. It was this fear, or so they afterwards claimed, that caused the opposition groups to draw together and take action before Allende did. They organised a massive strike and having won the support of the army, the right staged a military coup organised by leading generals, and set up a military dictatorship in which General Pinochet came to the fore. Left-wing leaders were murdered or imprisoned; Allende himself was killed in the coup. It has been suggested that the American CIA, helped by the Brazilian government (a repressive military government), played an important role in the preparations for the coup as part of its policy of preventing the spread of communism in Latin America. The new regime provoked great criticism from the outside world for its brutal treatment of political prisoners; however the American government, which had greatly reduced its economic aid while Allende was in power, stepped up its assistance again. The Pinochet government had some economic success and by 1980 had brought the annual inflation rate down from around 1,000 per cent to manageable proportions.

17.6 DETENTE: INTERNATIONAL RELATIONS IN THE 1970s

The word *'détente'* is used to mean a permanent relaxation of international tensions rather than just a 'thaw' in the Cold War. The first signs of real *détente* between east and west came in the early 1970s, stimulated probably by the continuing fear of nuclear war and the horrors of Vietnam.

(a) **The motives of the individual powers** in pursuing *détente* were mixed: *the Chinese* were anxious about their isolation, nervous about American intentions in Vietnam (after what had happened in Korea) and not happy about their worsening relations with Russia. *The Americans* were realising that there must be a better way of coping with communism than the one they were trying in Vietnam; perhaps peaceful co-existence was the way after all. *The Russians* wanted to reduce defence spending so as to devote more energy to bringing living standards up to western levels; nor did they want to be left out when they saw relations between China and the USA improving.

(b) **The USSR and the USA** had already made progress with the 'hot line' telephone link and the agreement to carry out only underground nuclear tests (both 1963); further steps were taken in 1969 with the beginning of

Strategic Arms Limitation Talks (SALT). Nixon twice visited Moscow (1972 and 1974) while Brezhnev went to Washington in 1973. The USA began to export wheat to Russia. Most important of all was *the Helsinki Agreement* (July 1975) in which the USA, the USSR, Canada and almost all the European states accepted the European frontiers which had been drawn up after the Second World War (thus recognising the permanent division of Germany). The communist countries undertook to allow their peoples 'human rights' (including freedom of speech and freedom to leave the country).

(c) **China and the USA** had been extremely hostile towards each other since the Korean War and seemed likely to remain so while the Americans backed Chiang Kai-shek and the Chinese Nationalists in Taiwan and while the Chinese backed Ho Chi Minh. However the Chinese made the first move in 1971, and an unlikely one at that: they invited an American table tennis team to visit China, and following the success of that visit the USA responded by calling off her veto of Chinese entry into the United Nations. Communist China was admitted in October 1971 and the Nationalist representatives from Taiwan left. Presidents Nixon and Ford both paid successful visits to Peking (1972 and 1975). However, Taiwan still remained to sour the relationship: though Chiang himself died in 1975, the KMT still occupied the island and the communists will not be satisfied until it is brought under their control. Relations improved further in December 1978, when Carter decided to withdraw recognition of Nationalist China; however, this caused a row in the USA where Carter was accused of betraying his ally.

(d) **Relations between the USSR and China** on the other hand have deteriorated steadily since about 1956. In 1950 they had signed a treaty of mutual friendship and assistance, but later the Chinese disapproved of Khrushchev's policies, particularly his belief in 'peaceful co-existence' and his claim that it was possible to achieve communism by methods other than violent revolution (see Section 18.1). This was not what Lenin had said and consequently the Chinese accused the Russians of '*revisionism*', revising or reinterpreting the teachings of Marx and Lenin to suit their own ends. They were incensed at Khruschchev's 'soft' line towards the USA. In retaliation the Russians sharply reduced economic aid to China. The ideological argument is not the only source of trouble: there is also a frontier dispute; during the nineteenth century Russia took over large areas of Chinese territory north of Vladivostok and in Sinkiang province which the Chinese are now demanding back, so far without success. Now that China herself is following a 'softer' policy towards the USA it seems that the territorial problem is the main bone of contention between them. At the end of the 1970s it seemed that both Russia and China were vying for American support against each other in the struggle for the leadership of world communism, in which, to complicate matters further, Vietnam now supports Russia.

(e) Is the Cold War over? This was a familiar question throughout the 1970s which many optimists in the west were inclined to answer in the affirmative. On the other hand there were several not very hopeful signs: in spite of the Helsinki Agreement neither free speech nor free travel is allowed in eastern Europe where dissidents (people who criticise the government) are harassed in all sorts of ways. Western military experts allege that the Russians are still building up massive armaments and ask why. Most serious of all was *the Russian invasion of Afghanistan* in December 1979 on the pretext of supporting the new communist government of Babrak Karmal. President Carter reacted angrily, announcing a grain embargo, breaking off SALT talks and calling for a boycott of the Olympic Games to be held in Moscow in the summer of 1980. However the western European response disappointed the USA and although no American athletes attended the Moscow Olympics, Russian troops stayed in Afghanistan. All the old American suspicions have revived: are the Russians in Afghanistan in order to secure their own frontier or as part of the march of world communism? Some western politicians have compared *détente* with appeasement in the 1930s suggesting that all the compromise was being made by the west while, as Margaret Thatcher put it in the Commons (February 1980), 'for the Russians it has meant the chance to extend, by overt and covert means, their influence and political control wherever opportunity offered.'

QUESTIONS

1. Explain how Chiang Kai-shek (a) came to power in China; (b) tried to consolidate his power; (c) misused his power; (d) finally lost power on the Chinese mainland.

2. Show how the influence of Mao Tse-tung spread in mainland China (1934–48) and explain the successful culmination of his bid for power in 1949.

3. Explain how and with what results the USA became involved in Korea after the Second World War.

4. What circumstances in Cuba led to the accession to power of Fidel Castro. Explain the American attitude towards his government and describe the events which led to the missiles crisis of 1962.

5. Describe how President Allende came to power in Chile in 1970. What were the political and economic problems confronting him. Explain the attitude of the other American states towards him. Why was his regime overthrown in 1973?

6. Account for the division after 1945 of (a) Korea and (b) Vietnam. Show how the division of Korea began to appear permanent in the 1950s

and 1960s but how Vietnam gained a measure of unity in the 1970s.

7. Account for the success of the communists in the Vietnam wars of 1946-54 and 1961-75.

8. Describe (a) the increasing involvement of the USA in Vietnam under Eisenhower, Kennedy and Johnson; (b) the closing stages under Nixon.

9. Write an account of the changing relations between China, the USA and the USSR since 1949.

CHAPTER 18

INTERNAL AFFAIRS

OF

THE COMMUNIST STATES

SUMMARY OF EVENTS

The theories of Marx and Lenin are so vague that many different interpretations of them are possible; consequently there is a great deal of variation in what actually happens in communist countries and a communist system of government need not be identical to the Russian system. Of course Stalin tried to keep it that way, but after his death in 1953 the states of eastern Europe began to show more independence. Yugoslavia under Tito had already developed a more decentralised system in which the communes were an important element. Poland and Rumania successfully introduced variations, but the Hungarians (1956) and Czechs (1968) went too far and found themselves invaded by Russian troops and brought to heel. Meanwhile Mao Tse-tung was setting about rebuilding a shattered China with Russian help and advice, but later introduced the 'Great Leap Forward' (1958) in which communism was adapted to meet the Chinese situation, with the emphasis on decentralisation, agriculture, communes and contact with the masses. Mao became highly critical of the Russians who, in his view, were straying from strict Marxist/Leninist principles and following the 'capitalist road' in both foreign and domestic affairs. In the early 1960s these disagreements caused a serious split in world communism. Finally there was Cuba where Fidel Castro followed, with mixed success, socialist policies designed to cure the island's own peculiar problems.

18.1 THE USSR

(a) **Joseph Stalin** continued to rule Russia after 1945 for a further eight years until his death in March 1953. The western half of European Russia was devastated by the war: roads, railways and industries were shattered and 25 million people were homeless. Stalin was determined that there would be no relaxation of government controls: the economy must be reconstructed. The Fourth Five Year Plan was started in 1946 and, incredibly in the circumstances, succeeded in restoring industrial production to its 1940 levels. And then, just as he was about to launch another set of purges, Stalin died, to the immense relief of his close associates.

(b) The rise of Khrushchev 1953-7

With the departure of Stalin, the situation was similar to that after Lenin's death in 1924: there was no obvious candidate to take over the reins; Stalin had allowed no one to show any initiative in case he developed into a dangerous rival. The leading members of the *Politburo* or *Praesidium* (as it was now called) decided to share power and rule as a group: Malenkov became Chairman of the Council of Ministers, Khrushchev Party Secretary, and Voroshilov Chairman of the *Praesidium*; also involved were Beria (Chief of the Secret Police), Bulganin and Molotov. Gradually, however, Nikita Khrushchev began to emerge as the dominant personality. The son of a peasant farmer, he had worked as a farm labourer and then as a mechanic in a coalmine before going to technical college and joining the communist party. Beria, who had an atrocious record of cruelty as police chief, was executed, probably because the others were nervous in case he turned against them. Malenkov resigned in 1955 after disagreeing with Khrushchev about industrial policies, but it was significant that in the new relaxed climate he was not executed or imprisoned. Khrushchev's position was further strengthened by an amazing speech which he delivered at the *Twentieth Communist Party Congress* (1956) strongly criticising various aspects of Stalin's policies. He condemned Stalin for encouraging the cult of his own personality instead of allowing the party to rule, revealed details about Stalin's purges of the 1930s, criticised his conduct of the war, claimed that socialism could be developed in ways other than those insisted on by Stalin, and suggested that peaceful coexistence with the west was not only possible but essential if nuclear war were to be avoided. Khrushchev was not quite supreme yet: Molotov and Malenkov believed his speech was too drastic and would encourage unrest (they blamed him for the Hungarian revolution of October 1956); they tried to force him out of office. However as Party Secretary, Khrushchev, like Stalin before him, had been quietly filling key positions with his own supporters, and since he could rely on the army, it was Molotov and Malenkov who found themselves compulsorily retired (June 1957). After that Khrushchev was fully responsible for all Russian policy until 1964; but he never wielded as much power as Stalin; the Central Committee of the party was ultimately in charge and it was the party which voted him out in 1964.

(c) Khrushchev's problems and policies

In spite of Russia's recovery during Stalin's last years there were a number of serious problems including the low standard of living among industrial and agricultural works, and the inefficiency of her agriculture which was still a long way from providing all Russia's needs. Khrushchev was fully aware of the problems both at home and abroad and was determined to introduce important changes as part of *a general de-Stalinisation policy*:

(i) *Industry* was still organised on the Five Year Plans but for the first time these concentrated more on light industries producing consumer goods (radios, television sets, washing machines, sewing machines) in an attempt to raise living standards. To reduce over-centralisation and encourage efficiency a hundred Regional Economic Councils were set up to make decisions about and organise their local industries. Managers were encouraged to make profits instead of merely meeting quotas, and wages depended on output. All this certainly led to an improvement in living standards: a vast housing programme was started in 1958; between 1955 and 1966 the number of radios per thousand of the population increased from 66 to 171, television sets from 4 to 82, refrigerators from 4 to 40, and washing machines from 1 to 77. However, this was way behind the USA which in 1966 could boast per thousand of the population no fewer than 1,300 radios, 376 television sets, 293 refrigerators and 259 washing machines. Of course much depends on how one measures progress, but it was Khrushchev himself who had rashly claimed that the gap between Russia and America would be closed within a few years. Another more spectacular piece of technological progress was the first manned orbit of the earth by Yuri Gagarin (1961).

(ii) *In agriculture* there was a drive to increase food production. Khrushchev's special brainchild was *the virgin lands scheme* (started 1954) which involved cultivating for the first time huge areas of land in Siberia and Kazakhstan. Peasants on collective farms were allowed to keep or sell crops produced on their private plots and the government increased its payments for crops from the collectives, thus providing incentives to produce more. By 1958 total farm output had risen by 56 per cent; between 1953 and 1962 grain production rose from 82 million tons to 147 million. But then things began to go wrong: the 1963 grain output was down to 110 million tons, mainly because of the failure of the virgin lands scheme. The trouble was that much of the land was of poor quality, not enough fertilisers were used, and the exhausted soil began to blow away in dust storms. In general there is still too much interference in agriculture from local party officials, and it remains the least efficient sector of the economy; the Russians have to rely on grain imports, often from USA.

(iii) *Political changes* (the thaw) included the return to party control instead of Stalin's personality cult, a reduction in secret police activities (deposed politicians and officials retired into obscurity instead of being tortured and executed), more freedom for ordinary Russians, more tourism, and a slight relaxation of press controls.

(iv) *In foreign affairs*, following his Twentieth Congress speech, Khrushchev aimed for *peaceful coexistence* and a thaw in the Cold War (see Section 16.3) and seemed prepared to allow different 'roads to socialism' among the satellites. However, these departures from strict Marxist/Leninist ideas (including his encouragement of profit and wage incentives) laid him open to Chinese accusations of *'revisionism'* (see Section 17.6(d)); moreover, encouraged by his speech, Poland and Hungary tried to break Moscow's grip; Khrushchev's reaction to these attempts showed how limited his toleration was.

(d) Khrushchev's fall. In October 1964 the Central Committee of the party voted him into retirement on the grounds of ill health; although he was 70 his health was perfectly good. The real reasons were probably the failure of his agricultural policy (though he had been no less successful than previous governments in this), his loss of prestige over the Cuban missile crisis and the widening breach with China which he made no attempt to heal. Perhaps his colleagues were tired of his extrovert personality (once in a heated moment at the United Nations he took off his shoe and hammered the table with it) and felt he was taking too much on himself (without consulting them he had just tried to win the friendship of President Nasser of Egypt by awarding him the Order of Lenin at a time when he was busy arresting Egyptian communists). Khrushchev was a man of outstanding personality: a tough politician and yet impulsive and full of warmth and humour. He deserves to be remembered for his foreign policy innovations, for the return to comparatively civilised politics (at least inside Russia) and for the improved living standards of the masses.

(e) Kosygin and Brezhnev, Khrushchev's successors, continued broadly similar policies including wage differentials and profit incentives, so that Russia was not the sort of socialist state that Marx and Lenin had in mind (hence the continued friction with China). And the same weaknesses were still there: the 1980 harvest fell well short of self-sufficiency. The government's attitude to criticism hardened again and press controls became as tight as ever; dissidents now tended to be certified as insane and put in mental hospitals rather than in labour camps. Most disturbing for the non-communist world were the Russian interventions in Czechoslovakia (see below) in 1968 and in Afghanistan (1979).

18.2 THE USSR AND THE STATES OF EASTERN EUROPE

When fully communist governments had been established in Russia's satellite states (Poland, Hungary, Czechoslovakia, Rumania, Bulgaria, Albania and East Germany) Stalin set about making them into carbon copies of Russia through the Cominform and Comecon (see Section 16.1(f)). All had the same political and educational systems, and the same Five Year Plans (involving nationalisation of industries and ruthless collectivisation of agriculture); all had to carry out the bulk of their trade with Russia, and their foreign policies and armed forces were controlled by Moscow. Politicians who protested were shot or imprisoned. Once Stalin was dead there was likely to be a reaction against such close control; Khrushchev's Twentieth Congress speech also encouraged the desire for more independence.

(a) Yugoslavia was the only east European state that refused to be browbeaten by the Russians. Occupied by the Germans during the war, the Yugoslavs organised a successful resistance campaign which liberated the country in 1945. One of the resistance leaders, Marshal Tito, who had been head of the Yugoslav Communist Party since 1937, was elected leader of the new republic (1945) and was President from 1953 until his death in 1980. The establishment of communism owed nothing to the Russians; like Mao in China, Tito owed much of his popularity to his successful resistance against a hated enemy. By 1948 he had fallen out with Stalin: he was determined to follow his own road to communism, not Stalin's; he was against over-centralisation, and objected to Stalin's plan for the Yugoslav economy and to the constant Russian interference; he wanted to be free to trade with the west as well as with Russia. Consequently Stalin expelled Yugoslavia from the Cominform and cut off economic aid, expecting that the country would soon be ruined economically and Tito forced to resign. However, Stalin miscalculated: Tito was much too popular to be toppled by such outside pressures; he continued to apply communism in his own way, which included full contact and trade with the west and the acceptance of aid from the International Monetary Fund (IMF). Relations with Russia remained non-existent until 1955 when Khrushchev visited Belgrade and apologised for Stalin's attitude. The breach was fully healed the following year during Khrushchev's second visit (June 1956) when he gave approval to Tito's successful brand of socialism (with important effects for the Russian satellites).

What was special about Yugoslav communism? The Yugoslavs soon realised that the Russian system of control from the centre was too rigid, too distant and inefficient; it took away the rights and initiatives of ordinary local people; the officials at the centre became corrupt and workers became bored and apathetic. In 1950 the Yugoslavs began to reverse the process of centralisation: industries were denationalised and instead of being state-owned became public property, managed by workers' representatives through councils and assemblies. The same applied in agriculture. *The communes* were and still are the most important unit in the state: these are groups of families (501 of them in 1973) each containing between 5,000 and 100,000 people; the elected Commune Assembly takes decisions about and organises matters to do with the economy, education, health, culture and welfare. The whole system is a remarkable example of ordinary people playing a part in making the decisions which closely affect their own lives, both at work and in the community; it has achieved much because workers have a personal stake in the success of their firm and their commune. There were some weaknesses, however, such as workers' unwillingness to sack colleagues and a tendency to pay themselves too much (leading to over-employment and high costs and prices). Nevertheless with its capitalist elements (wage differentials and a free market) it was an alternative Marxist system which many developing African states, especially Tanzania, found attractive.

(b) Poland was the first of the satellite states to come out in open protest against the Russians (except for East Berlin where in May 1953 100,000 workers demonstrating for better pay were dispersed by Russian tanks). The Polish communist leader, *Wladyslaw Gomulka*, had been expelled from the party and imprisoned because Stalin disapproved of his support of Tito (1948). But as soon as Stalin was dead discontent began to build up among the Poles, who had a long tradition of anti-Russian hostility. Spurred on by Khrushchev's Twentieth Congress speech, it burst out at Posen (Poznan) in June 1956 in a massive anti-government and anti-Russian demonstration; their banners demanded 'bread and freedom' and they protested against poor living standards, wage restrictions and high taxes; they were dispersed by Russian tanks. However, the Russians were prepared to compromise: Khrushchev went to Warsaw for discussions and it was decided that Gomulka should be reappointed as First Secretary of the Party and that Polish communism could develop in its own special way provided that the Poles went along with Russia in foreign affairs. The Russians obviously felt that Gomulka could be trusted not to stray too far. Relations between the two states were fairly smooth, though Poland was quite 'revisionist' in her application of communism (only about 10 per cent of farmland was collectivised and she traded extensively outside the communist bloc). The Polish government was more susceptible to public opinion than the Russian government: in 1970 Gomulka resigned in favour of Gierek after riots in Gdynia; in 1980 food shortages and industrial unrest again led to strikes in Gdansk (Danzig) and other cities and caused Gierek's resignation; the government was forced to allow the formation of an independent trade union movement (Solidarity). This acted with admirable restraint, insisting on the sacking of corrupt party officials responsible for the country's economic plight (almost bankrupt and heavily in debt to the west) but not demanding an end to press censorship or the introduction of free elections. Nevertheless the situation was extremely delicate; one step too far could mean Russian military intervention.

(c) **Hungary**, which had fought on Germany's side during the war, was viewed as a defeated enemy by the Russians and treated harshly, being made to pay reparations. Although the communists gained less than 20 per cent of the votes in the free elections held in November 1945, the Russians saw to it that communists filled all important posts, and under their leader Rakosi, they were soon running the country. When protests developed against the Moscow hard line, Laszlo Rajk, the leading anti-Stalin communist was hanged (1949) and over 200,000 expelled from the party. Rakosi toed the Stalin line, but after Stalin's death he was replaced by *Imre Nagy*, a more moderate communist. However, Rakosi continued to interfere and overthrew Nagy (1955); from then on resentment steadily built up until it exploded in the *Hungarian Rising* (October 1956). *Its causes were many*: hatred of Rakosi's brutal and repressive regime which executed at least 2,000 people and put 200,000 others in prisons and concentration camps; falling living standards for the masses while hated party leaders were comfortably off; intense anti-Russian feeling; Khrushchev's Twentieth Congress speech and the return to power of Gomulka in Poland stimulated the demonstrators to greater efforts. At first the

Russians seemed prepared to compromise and Nagy, ecstatically received, was allowed to become Prime Minister. The demonstrations soon swelled into a national rising against the hated Russians; Cardinal Mindszenty, who had been in prison for six years for anti-communist views, was released and plans were afoot to allow other political parties and to withdraw from the Warsaw Pact. At this point the Russian army moved in and blasted Budapest into submission; 20,000 people were killed, a similar number imprisoned and Nagy executed after being promised a safe-conduct; about 20,000 people fled the country. Janos Kadar, a reliable communist, was made Prime Minister by the Russians.

The rising was important because it showed how limited Khrushchev's new tolerance was: Gomulka could be stomached in Poland because Poland would remain a close Russian ally; but Nagy had gone too far and was threatening Russian control of eastern Europe; if he had his way, Hungary might become non-communist and neutral instead of a Russian ally. The rest of eastern Europe was very quiet after 1956. Although both Rumania and Albania showed some independence there was no fundamental attempt to change relationships with Russia until 1968 in Czechoslovakia. The Russians also took heed of the lesson and allowed the Kadar government to provide more consumer goods. In 1962 when Khrushchev suggested that each satellite state should concentrate on a particular commodity, the Hungarians along with the Rumanians and Poles who wanted to develop an all-round economy objected strongly, and the idea was not pressed. After 1966 the government gradually began to decentralise control of industry, but not quite so drastically as the ill-fated Czechs.

(d) In Albania the communist resistance movement seized power and set up a republic in 1945, so that as in Yugoslavia the Russians were not responsible for the introduction of communism. Nevertheless they insisted on the Albanian government following their line and executed the communist leader Koze Xoxe when he seemed reluctant to do so. His successor Enver Hoxha was an admirer of Stalin and copied his system faithfully. With Russian aid and their own oil supplies, the Albanians began to industrialise, with particular success in textiles. After Stalin's death Hoxha did not approve of Khrushchev's revisionist policies, feeling more in sympathy with what was happening in China. Diplomatic relations with Moscow were severed in 1961 and Albania left the Warsaw Pact in 1968. However, since there was no question of her ceasing to be communist (and strict Marxist/Leninist communist at that) and since she had a powerful ally in China, the Russians took no action.

(e) Rumania provides the best example (apart from Yugoslavia) of a satellite state pushing revisionist policies to the absolute limit that the Russians would accept without military intervention. Like Hungary she had been occupied by the Russians in 1945, forced to pay reparations and had a communist government thrust upon her. Patrascanu, a communist leader unco-operative to the Russians, was expelled (1949) and later shot, and another, Anna Pauker, removed in 1952. However, in the early 1960s Rumania, a comparatively prosperous country with her oil wells, wheatlands and great potential for tourism, took the lead under President Ceauşescu in opposing the Russian desire to organise the economy of the entire communist bloc. She insisted on adopting plans for decentralised industrial development whereas the Russians wanted to use Rumania as a source of raw materials and food; she was keen to expand her trade with countries outside the soviet bloc, which the Russians did not encourage; to show their attitude the Rumanians dropped Russian as a compulsory school subject (1962). Although she made it plain that she would remain in the Warsaw Pact she began to cultivate friendship with Yugoslavia, with western states and even with China. The Russians angrily condemned these trends (1963), but since the Rumanians pointed out that they were merely trying to develop their economy in the best national interest and were not threatening the unity of the communist bloc, no military action took place. Unfortunately this was not the case with Czechoslovakia which in 1968 pushed matters too far.

(f) Czechoslovakia was the last of the satellites to go communist, in 1948 (see Section 16.2(g)). This was followed by the usual executions of 'unreliable' communist leaders (Clementis and Slansky) following which she was a fully obedient satellite under Novotny until 1968. It was in the mid-1960s that *opposition to the government* began to come out into the open. The Czechs, industrially and culturally the most advanced of the satellites, objected to the over-centralised Russian control of their economy; it seemed senseless, for example, that they should have to put up with poor quality Siberian iron-ore when they could have been more conveniently using high-grade Swedish ore. Having enjoyed great freedom between 1918 and 1938, they resented the restrictions on personal liberty, particularly the press censorship and the loss of freedom of speech; protest marches were brutally suppressed by the police. Matters came to a head in January 1968 when Novotny was forced to resign and *Alexander Dubcek* became First Secretary of the Party with Svoboda as President and Cernik as Prime Minister.

Then followed what later became known nostalgically as *the 'Dubcek Spring'*. They had a completely new programme: the communist party would no longer dictate policy; industry would be decentralised with factories run by works councils and with independent farming co-operatives encouraged; there were to be wider powers for trade unions, expansion of trade with the west and freedom to travel abroad (the frontier with West Germany was immediately thrown open); there was to be freedom of speech and press, and criticism of the government was encouraged. Dubcek believed that although the country would remain communist, the government should earn the right to be in power by responding to the people's wishes; it was what he called 'socialism with a human face'. He was most careful to assure the Russians that Czechoslovakia would stay in the Warsaw Pact and remain a reliable ally. As the spring and summer progressed, the illus 18.1 *Prague 1968. Czechs implore and argue with a Russian tank commander*

Russians became increasingly disturbed as this programme was carried into operation. In August a massive invasion of Czechoslovakia took place by Russian, Polish, Bulgarian and East German troops. The Czech government decided not to resist and although the Czech people resisted passively for a time, the government was compelled eventually to abandon its reforms; the following year Dubcek was replaced by the more amenable Husak.

Why did the Russians intervene in Czechoslovakia but not in Rumania? In fact as we have seen, many similar developments were taking place in Rumania. Where the Czechs went too far for the Russians was in allowing freedom of speech and press, which was bound to lead to similar demands throughout the soviet bloc; this the Russians dare not risk since it might cause the downfall of Kosygin and Brezhnev as well as Novotny. There was pressure for Russian action from other communist leaders, especially Ulbricht of East Germany. The Russians were also suspicious of increasing Czech contact with West Germany. This sad end to the 'Dubcek Spring' showed that prospects for a drawing together of the two blocs are remote and that, as Derek Morgan puts it, 'even domestic reform in a soviet satellite must be carried out with the greatest care and prudence'.

18.3 CHINA: WHAT WERE THE PROBLMES FACING MAO TSE-TUNG AND HOW SUCCESSFUL WAS HE IN DEALING WITH THEM?

(a) **The problems** facing the People's Republic in 1949 were complex to say the least. The country was devastated after the long civil war and the war with Japan: railways, roads, canals and dykes had been destroyed and there were chronic food shortages. Industry was backward, agriculture was inefficient and incapable of feeding the poverty-stricken masses, and inflation seemed out of control. Mao had the support of the peasants and many of the middle class, disgusted by the miserable performance of the KMT, but it was essential for him to improve conditions if he were to hold on to their support. To control and organise such a vast country with a population of at least 600 million must have been a superhuman task; yet Mao managed it, and China today, whatever its faults, is his creation. He began by looking closely at Stalin's methods and experimented by a process of trial and error to find which would work in China and where a special Chinese approach was necessary.

(b) **The constitution of 1950** (officially adopted 1954) included the National People's Congress (the final authority for legislation), whose members were elected for four years by people over 18, the State Council and the Chairman of the Republic (both elected by the Congress), whose function was to make sure that laws were carried out and the administration of the country went ahead; the whole system was, of course, dominated by the communist party. The constitution was important because it provided China with a strong central government for the first time for many years, and it has remained more or less unchanged.

(c) **Agricultural changes** transformed China from a country of small, inefficient private farms into one of large co-operative farms like those in Russia (1950–6). In the first stage land was taken from large landowners and redistributed among the peasants, no doubt with violence in places; some sources mention as many as two million people killed, though Jack Gray believes that 'the redistribution of China's land was carried out with a remarkable degree of attention to legality and the minimum of physical violence against landlords.' The next step was achieved without violence: peasants were persuaded (not forced as they were in Russia) to join together in co-operative (collective) farms in order to increase food production. By 1956 about 95 per cent of all peasants were in such co-operatives (consisting of between 100 and 300 families) with joint ownership of the farm and its equipment.

(d) **Industrial changes** began with the government nationalising most businesses; in 1953 it embarked on a Five Year Plan concentrating on the development of heavy industry (iron, steel, chemicals and coal). The Russians helped with cash, equipment and advisers, and the plan had some success. Before it was complete, however, Mao began to have grave doubts as to whether China was suited to this sort of heavy industrialisation. On the other hand he could claim that under his leadership the country had recovered from the ravages of the wars: full communications had been restored, inflation was under control and the economy was looking much healthier.

(e) **The Hundred Flowers Campaign** (1957) seems to have developed to some extent out of industrialisation which produced a vast new class of technicians and engineers. The party *cadres* (groups who organised the masses politically and economically; the collectivisation of the farms for example was carried out by cadres) believed that this new class of experts would threaten their authority. The government, feeling pleased with its progress so far, decided that open discussion of the problems might improve relations between cadres and experts or intellectuals; 'let a hundred flowers bloom and a hundred schools of thought contend', said Mao, calling for constructive criticism. Unfortunately he got more than he had anticipated: critics attacked the cadres for incompetence and over-enthusiasm, the government for over-centralisation and the party itself; some suggested that opposition parties should be allowed. Mao hurriedly called off the campaign and clamped down on his critics, insisting that his policies were right. The campaign showed how much opposition there still was to communism and to the uneducated cadres, and convinced Mao that a drive was necessary to consolidate the advance of socialism; hence in 1958 he called for:

(f) **The Great Leap Forward**, a policy designed to meet the Chinese situation and not based on Russian experience; it involved further important developments in both agriculture and industry, in order to increase output (agriculture particularly was still not providing the required food) and to adapt industry to Chinese conditions. Its most important features were:

(i) The introduction of *communes*, units larger than collective farms, containing up to 75,000 people, divided into brigades and work teams and with an elected council. They ran their own collective farms and factories, carried out most of the functions of local government within the commune and undertook special local projects. One typical commune, for example, in 1965 contained 30,000 people of which a third were children at school or in creches, a third were housewives or elderly and the rest the workforce (which included a science team of 32 graduates and 43 technicians). Each family received a share-out of profits and also had a small private plot of land.

illus **18.2** *China – building a canal by mass labour*

(ii) A complete change of emphasis in industry: instead of aiming for large-scale works of the type seen in Russia and the west, much smaller factories were set up in the countryside to provide machinery for agriculture; Mao talked of 600,000 'backyard steel furnaces' springing up, organised and managed by the communes, which also undertook to build roads, dams, reservoirs and irrigation channels.

At first it looked as though the Great Leap might be a failure: there was some opposition to the communes, a series of bad harvests (1959-61) and the withdrawal of all Russian aid following the breach between the two; all this coupled with the lack of experience among the cadres caused hardship in the years 1959 to 1963. Even Mao's prestige suffered and he was forced to resign as Chairman of the People's Congress (to be succeeded by Liu Shao-chi) though he remained Chairman of the communist party. However, in the long term *the importance of the Great Leap* became clear: eventually both agricultural and industrial production increased substantially, and China was managing at least to feed its massive population without famine (which rarely happened under the KMT); the commune proved to be a remarkably successful innovation – much more than merely collective farms, they are perhaps the ideal solution to the problem of running a vast country while at the same time avoiding the over-centralisation that stifles initiative; the crucial decision had been taken that China would remain predominantly an agricultural country with small-scale industry scattered about the countryside; the economy would be labour-intensive (relying on massive numbers of workers instead of introducing labour-saving machines). Given the country's enormous population, this seems sensible, and so far China has avoided the growing unemployment problems of the highly industrialised western nations. Other benefits were the spread of education and welfare services and the improvement of the position of women in society.

(g) The Cultural Revolution (1966–9) was Mao's attempt to keep the revolution and the Great Leap on a pure Marxist–Leninist course. In the early 1960s when the success of the Great Leap was by no means certain, opposition to Mao grew. Right-wing members of the party believed that more incentives (piecework, greater wage differentials and larger private plots, which had been creeping in in some areas) were necessary if the communes were to function efficiently; also there should be an expert managerial class to push forward with industrialisation on the Russian model, instead of relying on the cadres. But to the Maoists this was totally unacceptable; it was exactly what Mao was condemning among the Russians whom he dismissed as 'revisionists' taking the capitalist road. The party must avoid the emergence of a privileged class and keep in touch with the masses. Between 1963 and 1966 there was a great public debate about which course to follow, between the rightists (who included Liu Shao-chi and Deng Xiaoping) and the Maoists. Mao, using his position as chairman of the party to rouse the young people, launched a desperate campaign to 'save' the revolution. In this Great Proletarian Cultural Revolution, as he called it, Mao appealed to the masses. His supporters, *the Red Guards*, (mostly students) toured the country arguing Mao's case, while schools and, later on, factories were closed down. It was an incredible propaganda exercise in which Mao was trying to renew revolutionary fervour and even to create a new kind of socialist person whose aim was to serve others. At times fighting broke out between the two factions and the country seemed likely to descend into chaos. In the end the Maoists were successful thanks to the army under the command of Lin Piao; order was restored and the

248

illus 18.3 A mass demonstration of 700,000 people in Peking at the time of the cultural revolution .

'revisionists' disgraced (1969). Afterwards the Maoist approach was followed until 1976 when both Mao and his reliable ally Chou En-lai died.

Accurate information was difficult to come by but most visitors seemed to agree that the regime's achievements were impressive. It remained to be seen how China would develop under her new party chairman *Hua Kuo-feng*, and vice-chairman Deng Xiao-ping. In 1980 she seemed stable and more friendly towards the west, and the government was veering towards 'revisionism' again. Four over-enthusiastic Maoists during the Cultural Revolution were put on trial for 'evil, monstrous and unpardonable crimes'; this trial of the so-called 'Gang of Four' was in fact open criticism of Mao and his policies.

18.4 CUBA: CASTRO'S PROBLEMS, MEASURES, SUCCESSES AND FAILURES

(a) Some of Castro's most **serious difficulties** were special to Cuba: how would the other Latin American states and above all the USA react to this new socialist threat on their doorsteps? Cuba was dependent on the USA's taking most of her sugar exports; the economy relied far too heavily on the sugar industry and was at the mercy of fluctuations in world sugar prices. The whole of government and administration was riddled with corruption and in addition there was serious unemployment and poverty.

(b) Details of Cuba's problems with the USA are given in Section 17.3(b). For the internal problems Castro had the help of *Ernesto 'Che' Guevara*, an Argentinian Marxist who had played an important part in the revolution and was a member of Castro's government until 1965. (Guevara believed, wrongly as it turned out, that the peasants of South America were ready to burst out into revolution. He became an expert in guerrilla warfare and wrote a book about it which had a great impact on Latin America, stirring up guerrilla campaigns in a number of states. He soon became frustrated in government and, believing that his real mission was to organise further revolutions, he left Cuba in 1965 and was killed by troops of the Bolivian government in 1967.)

The new government set about the problems with enthusiasm and dedication; David Harkness writes that during his first ten years Castro took this poor and backward country by the scruff of the neck and shook it into new and radically different patterns of life. Agricultural land was taken over by the government and collective farms introduced; factories and businesses were nationalised; attempts were made to modernise sugar production and increase output, and to introduce new industries to reduce Cuba's dependence on sugar. Social reforms included attempts to improve education, housing, health, medical facilities and communications; there was equality for negroes and more rights for women; there were touring cinemas, theatres, concerts and art exhibitions. Castro himself seemed to have boundless energy, constantly touring the island, making speeches and urging people to greater efforts.

(c) **The government could claim considerable success**, especially in the sphere of social reform: all children were now receiving some education, instead of fewer than half before 1959; sanitation and hygiene were much improved, unemployment and corruption reduced, and there was a greater sense of equality and stability than ever before. At the end of its first decade in power the government seemed to be popular with the vast majority of people.

On the other hand *there were some significant failures*: the attempt to diversify industrial and agricultural output met with very little success; consequently the island's economy still depended dangerously on the quality of the sugar harvest, the world price of sugar, and the willingness of the USSR and her satellites to absorb her exports. In the late 1970s sugar production actually began to decline and in 1980 the crop was further reduced by a fungus infection, while the tobacco crop was also seriously affected by another fungus. This plunged the country into an economic crisis, unemployment rose again, and thousands of people began to emigrate to the USA. Food rationing was in operation and the whole economy was being heavily subsidised by the Soviet Union.

It is probably too early to write Castro's regime off as a failure, but after a promising start, its progress is certainly faltering.

QUESTIONS

1. Trace the steps by which Nikita Khrushchev climbed to supreme power; what were his main achievements for Russia and why did he fall from power in 1964?
2. What problems faced Khrushchev in Russia after 1956 and how effectively did he handle them?
3. Nikita Khrushchev tried to make major changes (a) within Russia and (b) in Russia's relations with the outside world. Illustrate the truth of this statement and identify two lasting results of his leadership of the USSR.
4. Describe the main developments in the USSR since the death of Stalin in 1953.
5. Describe and comment on relations since 1945 between the USSR and *three* of the following – Albania, Hungary, Yugoslavia, Poland, Rumania.
6. Explain how Czechoslovakia came into soviet control in 1948. Trace its history under the communists over the next 20 years. Why was there an uprising in 1968 and why did it fail?
7. Outline the history since 1939 of either Poland or Yugoslavia mentioning the importance of the war, the establishment of communism and relations with the USSR.

8. Describe and give reasons for the crises in Hungary (1956) and Czechoslovakia (1968).

9. Show how the communists in China have successfully contributed to the modernisation of their country.

10. Explain the importance of the constitution of 1950, the Hundred Flowers Campaign, the break with Russia, the Great Leap Forward and the Cultural Revolution in the development of China since 1949.

11. What problems faced Fidel Castro and how successfully did he deal with them in his first 20 years as Cuba's leader?

CHAPTER 19

THE UNITED NATIONS ORGANISATION

SUMMARY OF EVENTS

The United Nations Organisation (UNO) was formed in 1945 to replace the discredited League of Nations which had failed so dismally. The United Nations Charter was drawn up at San Francisco during 1945 based on proposals made at an earlier meeting between Russia, the USA, China and Britain held at Dumbarton Oaks (USA) in 1944. The aim of the UN was to preserve peace and to remove the causes of conflict by encouraging economic, social, educational and cultural progress throughout the world, especially in under-developed nations. It was hoped that the careful framing of the charter would have eliminated some of the weaknesses which dogged the League, but in fact the UN was unable to solve many of the most important problems of international relations, particularly those caused by the Cold War. On the other hand it played an important role in a number of international crises by arranging ceasefires, negotiations and peace-keeping forces; its successes in non-political work (such as care of refugees, protection of human rights, dealing with health and population problems and economic planning) have been enormous.

19.1 THE STRUCTURE OF THE UNITED NATIONS ORGANISATION

The basic structure of UNO with its six main organs (General Assembly, Security Council, Secretariat, International Court of Justice, Economic and Social Council, and Trusteeship Council) looks remarkably similar to that of the League, though the last two did not appear in the same form in the League, and there were important changes of procedure in the Assembly and the Council designed to produce more decisive action.

(a) **The General Assembly** includes representatives from every member state and each member has one vote. It meets once a year in September but special sessions can be called in times of crisis by the members them-illus 19.1 *The headquarters of the United Nations Organisation, New York*

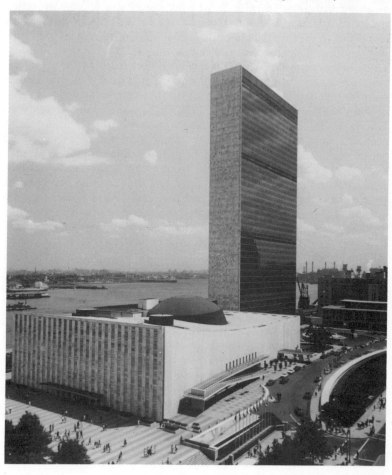

selves or by the Security Council. Its function is to debate and make proposals about international problems, to consider the budget and what amounts each member state should pay, to elect the Security Council members and generally to supervise the work of the many other UN bodies. Decisions do not require a unanimous vote as they did in the League Assembly: sometimes a simple majority is enough though on issues which the Assembly deems to be of major importance a two-thirds majority is needed.

(b) The Security Council began with eleven members, five of them permanent (China, France, Britain, USA and Russia) and the other six elected by the General Assembly for two-year terms; in 1965 the number of non-permanent members was increased to ten. Its function is to deal with crises as they arise, by whatever action seems appropriate, and if necessary by calling on members to take economic or military action against an aggressor. Decisions require at least nine of the fifteen members to vote in favour, but these must include all five permanent members; thus any one of the permanent members can veto a decision and prevent action being taken. In practice it has gradually been accepted that abstention by a permanent member does not amount to a veto, but this has not been written into the charter. In order to secure some action in case of veto, the General Assembly in 1950 (at the time of the Korean War) introduced the *'Uniting for Peace' resolution*, stating that if the Council's proposals were vetoed the Assembly could meet within 24 hours and decide what action to take (even military intervention if necessary); such a decision by the Assembly would require only a two-thirds majority. Again this was not added to the charter, and the Russians, who used the veto more often than any other member, have always maintained that a Security Council veto should take precedence over a General Assembly decision. Nevertheless the Assembly has acted in this way many times.

(c) **The Secretariat** looks after the administrative work, preparing minutes, translations and information; it is headed by the *Secretary–General*, appointed for a five-year term by the Assembly on the recommendation of the Security Council. He has much greater responsibility and influence than his counterpart in the League had: he has the power to bring before the Security Council any matter he wishes. The UN has been fortunate in having four Secretaries–General of outstanding ability and dedication: Trygvie Lie of Norway (1946–52), Dag Hammarskjöld of Sweden (1952–61), U Thant of Burma (1961–71) and Kurt Waldheim of Austria (1971–81).

(d) **The International Court of Justice at the Hague** has fifteen judges, all of different nationality, elected for three-year terms by the Assembly and Council jointly. It has dealt successfully with a number of disputes that could be settled judicially, including a frontier dispute between Holland and Belgium and a disagreement between Britain and Norway over fishing limits.

(e) **The Trusteeship Council** replaced the League Mandates Commission, its main function being to see that all states looking after trust territories prepared them as soon as possible for independence. By 1970 its job was almost completed, but there are still some trouble spots, particularly South West Africa, the territory given to South Africa as a mandate by the Versailles treaties in 1919. South Africa refused to grant independence to the territory (now known as Namibia), though by 1980 there were signs that she was prepared to do so.

(f) **The Economic and Social Council** has 27 members elected by the Assembly, with one-third retiring each year; it organises projects concerned with health, education and other social and economic matters.

Its task is so enormous that it has appointed four regional commissions (for Europe, Latin America, Africa, and Asia and the Far East), as well as commissions on population problems, drugs problems, human rights and the status of women. The Council also supervises and co-ordinates the work of an astonishing array of other commissions and *specialised agencies,* approaching 30 in all. Among the best known are *the International Labour Organisation* (ILO), founded originally in 1919, which continues its successful work of trying to secure basic minimum standards of employment; *the World Health Organisation* (WHO) which has achieved excellent results, fighting epidemics, promoting maternal and child welfare, and generally improving living standards, and whose most celebrated breakthrough was the eradication of smallpox; and *the Food and Agriculture Organisation* (FAO) which aims to raise living standards by encouraging improvements in agricultural production, and which has had particular success in India and Pakistan. *The United Nations Educational, Scientific and Cultural Organisation* (UNESCO) encourages not simply the spread of education but also international co-operation between artists, scientists and scholars in all fields, working on the assumption that the best way of avoiding war is to educate people's minds in the pursuit of peace. *The United Nations Children's Fund* (UNICEF) was founded originally in 1946 to help children left in difficulties by the war; nowadays its scope has widened to include relief work for children suffering as a result of disasters – famine, earthquakes and tornadoes. To deal with the specific problem of Arab refugees from Palestine (see Section 25.2), *the United Nations Relief and Works Agency* (UNRWA) was set up (1950). Its achievement has been remarkable: it began by providing basic food, clothing and shelter, and later went on to provide schools and medical services; it is not difficult to imagine the chaos that would have developed without the work of UNRWA; as it is, although some camps are still unsatisfactory, others are gradually becoming self-supporting. Finally there are a number of financial agencies; the one which the general public hears most about is the *International Monetary Fund* (IMF) which provides short-term loans to countries in financial difficulties to enable them to avoid devaluation, while *the World Bank* provides larger and longer loans to help countries undertake economic development.

19.2 WHAT ARE THE MAIN DIFFERENCES BETWEEN UNO AND THE LEAGUE?

Obviously the vastly enlarged scope of its activities (all the specialised agencies mentioned in the previous section, with the exception of the ILO, were founded in 1945 or later) is one of the major differences between UNO and the League. Others already mentioned are the changes in procedure of the Assembly and the Council, and the increased power of the Secretary–General, all designed to secure more decisive action than the League achieved. UNO has a much wider membership and is therefore more of a genuine world organisation than the League, with all the extra prestige that this entails. Both the USA and the USSR were founder-members of UNO which in 1980 contained over 150 member states whereas the League never had more than 50. Between 1963 and 1968 no fewer than 43 new members joined, mainly the emerging states of Africa and Asia. This meant that the combined Afro–Asian bloc had a majority in the General Assembly, making it more difficult for the east-west power blocs to control the voting. The increased importance of the Assembly resulting from the 'Uniting for Peace' resolution meant that these new Third World states could often determine the outcome of important issues. Some of the great powers found this alarming since many of the new members were inexperienced, and the rival blocs began to spend a lot of time and energy intriguing to win the support of each new member.

19.3 HOW SUCCESSFUL HAS UNO BEEN AS A PEACE-KEEPING BODY?

Although it has had mixed success, it is probably fair to say that UNO has been rather more successful than the League in its peace-keeping efforts, especially in crises which did not directly involve the interests of the great powers, such as the civil war in the Congo and the dispute between Holland and Indonesia over West New Guinea. On the other hand it has often been just as ineffective as the League in situations such as the Hungarian and Czech crises, when the interests of one of the great powers, in this case Russia, seemed to be threatened and where the great power chose to ignore or defy UNO. The best way to illustrate the organisation's varying degrees of success is to examine some of the major disputes in which it has been involved.

(a) In 1946 UNO helped to arrange the granting of independence by Holland to the Dutch East Indies which became *Indonesia* (see Section 22.4(a) and Fig 23.3). However, no agreement was reached about the future of *West New Guinea (West Irian)* which both countries claimed. In 1961 fighting broke out; after U Thant had appealed to both sides to reopen negotiations, it was agreed (1962) that the territory should become part of Indonesia. The transfer was organised and policed by a UN force. In this case the UN played a vital role in getting successful negotiations going, though it did not itself make the decision about West Irian's future.

(b) The problem of the warring **Jews and Arabs in Palestine** was brought before the UN by Britain in 1947, and the resulting UN investigation decided to partition Palestine, setting up the Jewish state of Israel (see Section 25.2). The UN was unable to prevent a series of wars between Israel and various Arab states (1948-9, 1956, 1967 and 1973) though it did useful work arranging cease-fires and providing supervisory forces while UNRWA cared for the Arab refugees.

(c) **The Korean War** (1950-3) was the only occasion on which the UN was able to take decisive action in a crisis directly involving the interests of the great powers; when South Korea was invaded by communist North Korea in June 1950, the Security Council immediately passed a resolution condemning North Korea and called on member states to send help to the south. However, this was only possible because of the temporary absence of the Russian delegates who would certainly have vetoed the resolution if they had not been boycotting Council meetings since January in protest against the failure to admit communist China to UN membership. Although the Russian delegates returned smartly, it was too late for them to prevent action going ahead. Troops of 16 countries were able to repel the invasion and preserve the frontier between the two Koreas along the 38th parallel (see Section 17.2). Though this was claimed by the west as a great UN success, it was in fact overwhelmingly an American operation; the vast majority of troops and the commander-in-chief, General MacArthur, were American, and the US government had already decided to intervene with force the day before the Security Council decision was taken. Only the absence of the Russians enabled the USA to turn it into a UN operation, a situation not likely to be repeated since the Russians would take good care to be present at all future Council sessions.

The Korean War had important results for the future of the UN: one was the passing of the 'Uniting for Peace' resolution which would permit a Security Council veto to be bypassed by a General Assembly vote; another was the launching of a bitter attack by the Russians on Trygvie Lie for what they considered to be his biased role in the crisis; as a result his position became impossible so that he eventually agreed to retire early and was replaced by Dag Hammarskjöld.

(d) **The Suez Crisis** (1956) showed the UN at its best. When President Nasser of Egypt suddenly nationalised the Suez Canal, many of the shares in which were British- and French-owned, both these powers protested strongly and sent troops 'to protect their interests' (see Section 25.3). At the same time the Israelis invaded Egypt from the east; the real aim was to destroy Nasser. A Security Council resolution condemning force was vetoed by Britain and France, whereupon the matter passed to the Assembly which by a majority of 64 votes to 5 condemned the invasions and called for a withdrawal of troops. In view of the weight of opinion against them the aggressors agreed to withdraw provided the UN ensured a reasonable settlement over the canal and kept the Arabs and Israelis from slaughtering each other. A United Nations Emergency Force of 5,000 made up of troops from 10 different countries moved in while British, French and Israelis went home. The prestige of the UN and of Hammarskjöld himself, who conducted the operation with consummate skill, was greatly enhanced, though American and Russian pressure were important in bringing about a cease-fire. However, the UN was not so successful in the 1967 Arab-Israeli conflict (see Section 25.4).

illus 19.2 *United Nations truce supervision in Palestine*

(e) The Hungarian Rising (1956), which occurred at the same time as the Suez Crisis, showed the UN at its most ineffective. When the Hungarians tried to exert their independence from Russian control, soviet troops entered Hungary to crush the revolt (see Section 18.2(c)). The Hungarian government appealed to the UN, but the Russians vetoed a Security Council resolution calling for a withdrawal of their forces. The Assembly passed the same resolution and set up a committee to investigate the problem; but the Russians refused to co-operate with the committee and no progress could be made. The contrast with Suez was striking: there Britain and France had been willing to bow to international pressure; the Russians, not so susceptible, simply ignored the UN, and nothing could be done.

(f) In the Belgian Congo Civil War which dragged on from 1960 until 1964 (see Section 24.1) the UN mounted its most complex operation so far (excepting Korea). When the Congo (known as Zaire since 1971) dissolved into chaos immediately after gaining independence, a UN force numbering over 20,000 at its largest managed to restore some sort of precarious order; a special UN Congo Fund was established to help with the recovery and development of the ravaged country. But the financial cost of the operation was so high that the UN was brought close to bankruptcy, especially when Russia, France and Belgium refused to pay their contributions towards the cost of the operations, because they disapproved of the way the UN was handling the situation. The crisis also cost the life of Dag Hammarskjöld who was killed in a plane crash in the Congo.

(g) Cyprus has kept the UN busy since 1964. A British colony since 1878, the island was granted independence in 1960; in 1963 civil war broke out between the Greeks, who made up about 80 per cent of the island's population, and the Turks. A UN peace-keeping force arrived in March 1964; an uneasy peace was restored but it required 3,000 troops permanently stationed in Cyprus to prevent Greeks and Turks tearing each other apart. Even this was not enough for in 1974 the Greek Cypriots tried to unite the island with Greece; this prompted the Turkish Cypriots, helped by invading Turkish regular troops, to seize the north of the island as their own territory and to expel all the Greeks who happened to be living in that area. Again UN forces achieved a cease-fire and are still policing the frontier between Greeks and Turks. However the UN has not been successful in finding an acceptable constitution or any other compromise and dare not risk withdrawing its troops.

(h) In Kashmir the UN found itself in a similar situation to that in Cyprus. After 1947 this large province lying between India and Pakistan (see Fig 23.2) was claimed by both states. Already in 1948 the UN had negotiated a cease-fire after fighting had broken out. At this point the Indians were occupying the southern part of Kashmir, the Pakistanis the northern part, and for the next 16 years the UN policed the cease-fire line between the 2 zones. When Pakistani troops invaded the Indian zone in 1965, a short war developed between India and Pakistan, but once again the UN successfully intervened and hostilities ceased. The original dispute still remained though and even in 1980 there seemed little prospect of the UN or any other agency finding a permanent solution.

(i) The Czechoslovakia crisis (1968) was almost a repeat performance of the Hungarian Rising twelve years earlier. When the Czechs showed what Moscow judged to be too much independence, Russian and other Warsaw Pact troops were sent in to enforce obedience (see Section 18.2(f)). The Security Council tried to pass a motion condemning this action but the Russians vetoed it, claiming that the Czech government had asked for their intervention. Although the Czechs denied this, there was nothing the UN could do in view of the Russian refusal to co-operate.

(j) **The Russian invasion of Afghanistan** (December 1979) to replace one communist government with another (that of Babrak Karmal) posed similar problems for the UN: a motion condemning Russian intervention and calling for a withdrawal of troops was predictably vetoed by the Russians in the Security Council (January 1980), and although a similar motion passed the General Assembly with a large majority, Russian troops stayed put; it seemed that yet another satellite had been brought into the soviet orbit.

19.4 WHAT ARE THE WEAKNESSES OF UNO?

Obviously one of its major problems is the difficulty of prevailing upon great powers to accept its decisions if they chose to put self-interest first. This has meant that some states put more faith in their own regional organisations, such as NATO, than in the UN which, among its other weaknesses, is always short of cash. There is the problem of exactly when during the course of a dispute the UN should become involved; sometimes it hangs back, as it did in the case of Uganda, too long, so that the problem becomes much more difficult to handle; sometimes it hesitates so long that it scarcely becomes involved at all, which happened with the Vietnam War and the Cuban missile crisis. Another difficulty is that the preponderance of Third World members means that only they can be certain of having their resolutions passed and it is increasingly difficult for the other blocs to get resolutions through the General Assembly. Some delegates become disillusioned because member states usually vote by bloc rather than on the merits of each case; it has proved impossible, for example, to have a motion condemning terrorism passed in the General Assembly: on its last appearance (September 1979) such a motion was defeated by the Arab states and their supporters.

Chaim Weissman, the former Israeli ambassador to the UN, speaking on BBC radio in August 1980, was pessimistic about the future of the UN, suggesting that as more and more international agreements are reached outside the UN (he mentioned SALT, Vietnam, the Camp David peace between Israel and Egypt, and the settlement of the Rhodesia/Zimbabwe problem), the organisation is becoming irrelevant, and is little more than an arena for propaganda speeches.

On the other hand, Brian Urqhart, the British Assistant Secretary-General of the UN, was much more optimistic believing that there will be a gradual improvement in the way governments use the UN, as new members gain experience. The hopeful sign of the UN is that at least it brings together over 150 nations, keeps them talking, and provides even the smallest of them with a world forum. Though it may not produce dramatic solutions, the UN with its peace-keeping forces and its care of refugees has prevented and is still preventing bloodshed and suffering on a colossal scale.

QUESTIONS

1. For what purpose was the UN founded in 1945? How was it organised? Describe three of its specialised agencies and the work they do.

2. Describe the organisation of the UN and the importance of the part it played in Korea *or* Cyprus.

3. Describe the composition and functions of the General Assembly and the Security Council and give an account of the UN's work in economic, social, educational and similar fields through its specialised agencies.

4. Explain how the UN resembled and differed from the League of Nations.

5. Illustrate and explain the development of the UN's peace-keeping role, from the time of the Korean War onwards.

6. 'The successes of the UN far outweigh its failures.' How far would you agree?

7. Which nations have dominated the UN and how does its machinery make this possible? How far has it become possible for the Third World to influence UN decisions, and what prospects do you see for the success of the organisation during the coming years?

CHAPTER 20

WESTERN EUROPE SINCE 1945

SUMMARY OF EVENTS

In 1945 much of Europe lay in ruins; it no longer dominated the world and seemed about to be engulfed by the tide of communism spreading from Russia. In this situation many people felt that the continent could only be rebuilt and defended by a common military, economic and political effort; this *move towards a united Western Europe*, which involved the setting up of *NATO* and *the Council of Europe* (both in 1949) as well as the *European Economic Community (EEC) or the Common Market* (1957), has been the most striking development of the post-war period. In Britain enthusiasm for such co-operation developed more slowly than in other countries through fear that it would threaten British sovereignty. She declined to join the EEC in 1957; when she changed her mind in 1961 the French vetoed her entry, and it was 1972 before she finally became a member.

The states of western Europe recovered surprisingly quickly from the effects of the war, thanks to a combination of American aid under the Marshall Plan (see Section 16.2(e)), an increase in world demand for European products, technological improvements and careful planning by governments. During the 1960s, however, inflation became a serious problem and during the mid–1970s rising oil prices worsened inflation and combined with unemployment as Europe began to move into a trade recession (a temporary reduction in demand for goods, but not as serious as a slump).

In Britain the Labour governments (1945-51) introduced important nationalisation and social welfare measures. Under the Conservatives (1951-64) the British people had 'never had it so good', as the Prime Minister, Macmillan, told them; but in fact inflation and a worsening balance of payments (when the value of goods imported is greater than that of goods being exported, causing a drain on gold and foreign currency reserves) caused growing concern. After 1964 governments alternated and all of them wrestled with the same economic problems, apparently without any lasting success.

In France the Fourth Republic (1946-58) suffered from most of the political weaknesses of the Third; it was further troubled by inflation and by defeat in Indo-China (1954) and was brought down by a rebellion in Algeria. At the height of the crisis General de Gaulle stepped in to become President of the Fifth Republic, under which the President had much more power than before. Though de Gaulle gradually lost much of his popularity and resigned in 1969, the Fifth Republic continued with right-wing governments under Pompidou (1969-74) and Giscard d'Estaing (1974-1981).

The German Federal Republic (West Germany), set up in 1949, enjoyed a remarkable economic recovery under the conservative government of Chancellor Adenauer (1949-63), though there were some setbacks and a rise in unemployment under his successors Erhard (1963-6) and Kiesinger (1966-9). Since 1969 the left-wing Social Democrats have been in power, with Liberal support, first under Brandt (1969-74) and then under Schmidt.

The new *Republic of Italy* began with a period of prosperity and stable government under de Gasperi (1946-53) but then many of the old problems of the pre-Mussolini era reappeared; weak coalition governments failed to solve problems of inflation and unemployment so that support for the communist party grew rapidly. Meanwhile *Spain* played little part in European affairs; outwardly quiet, she was kept under the tight fascist rein of Franco who ruled until his death in 1975 whereupon the monarchy was restored under King Juan Carlos. There was a return to democracy as there was in neighbouring Portugal after the overthrow of the fascist regime in 1974.

20.1 THE GROWTH OF UNITY IN WESTERN EUROPE

(a) In every country in western Europe there were people from all parts of the political spectrum who believed in closer co-operation between the states, while some thought in terms of a united federal Europe on the same lines as the United States of America. *Their reasoning was simple*: only by a co-operative effort and a pooling of resources could Europe recover from the ravages of war; the countries were too small to be economically and militarily viable separately in a world dominated by the super-powers, the USA and the USSR; there would be less likelihood of war between the countries; the threat from Russia could be met only by joint action. West Germany especially supported the idea because it would gain her early acceptance as a responsible nation, and *Winston Churchill* was one of its most eloquent advocates: in March 1943 he spoke of the need for a Council of Europe, and in a speech at Zurich in 1946 he argued that only as a United States of Europe could the countries count for anything in the world.

(b) Although federalists have been bitterly disappointed by their failure to achieve complete integration, some progress has been made:

(i) *The Organisation for European Co-operation (OEEC)* was the first initiative towards unity; it was set up in 1947 in response to the American offer of Marshall Aid (see Section 16.2(e)), with 16 European nations involved. Its first function, successfully achieved over the next four years, was to apportion American aid among its members, after which it went on, again with great success, to encourage trade among its members by reducing restrictions. It was helped by a United Nations *General Agreement on Tariffs and Trade* (GATT) whose function was to reduce tariffs and by *the European Payments Union* (EPU) which encouraged trade by improving the system of payments between member states so that each state could use its own currency. OEEC was so successful that trade between its members doubled during the first six years; when the USA and Canada joined in 1961 it became *the Organisation for Economic Co-operation and Development* (OECD); later Japan and Australia joined.

(ii) *The North Atlantic Treaty Organisation* (NATO) was established in 1949 (see Section 16.2(i)) as a mutual defence in case one of the member states should be attacked. The Korean war (1950-3) caused the USA to press successfully for the integration of NATO forces under a centralised command; a Supreme Headquarters Allied Powers Europe (SHAPE) was established near Paris. Until the end of 1955 NATO seemed to be developing impressively: the forces available for the defence of western Europe had been increased fourfold; it was claimed by some that it had deterred the Russians from attacking West Germany. However, problems soon arose: the French were not happy about the dominant American role; in 1966 de Gaulle withdrew from NATO so that French forces and nuclear policy would not be controlled by a foreigner. Moreover, compared with the Warsaw Pact countries, NATO was weak: with 60 divisions in 1980 it fell far short of its target of 96 divisions, whereas the communist bloc boasted 102 divisions and 3 times as many tanks as NATO.

(iii) *The Council of Europe* (1949) was an attempt at political unity. By 1971 all the states of western Europe (except Spain and Portugal) had joined and Turkey was included (making 16 members in all). Based at Strasbourg, it consists of the foreign ministers of the member states and an Assembly of representatives chosen by the parliaments of the states. It has no powers, however, since several states, particularly Britain, refused to join any organisation which threatened their own sovereignty. It can make recommendations and has achieved useful work sponsoring human rights agreements, but it has been a grave disappointment to the federalists.

(iv) *The European Economic Community* had the most direct impact on the majority of ordinary people in Europe:

(c) **The European Economic Community** (EEC), known in Britain as *the Common Market*, was established by the Treaty of Rome (1957) and in spite of many difficulties it has been the most successful of the attempts at co-operation. The stages in its evolution were:

(i) In 1944 the exiled governments of Belgium, Netherlands and Luxembourg formed *the Benelux Union*, a customs and trading association which came into operation in 1947.

(ii) *By the Treaty of Brussels* (1948) Britain and France joined the three Benelux countries in pledging 'military, economic, social and cultural collaboration'. While the military collaboration eventually resulted in NATO, the next step in economic co-operation was:

(iii) *The European Coal and Steel Community* (ECSC) (1951). It was the brainchild of Robert Schuman, the French Foreign Minister, who hoped by involving West Germany to improve Franco–German relations as well as to make European industry more efficient. Six countries joined: France, West Germany, Italy, Belgium, Netherlands and Luxembourg. All duties and restrictions on trade in coal, iron and steel between the six were removed, and a High Authority created to administer the community and organise a joint programme of expansion. The only disappointment for the federalists was that Britain refused to join because she objected to handing over control of her industries to a supranational authority. Nevertheless the ECSC was such an outstanding success, with steel production rising by almost 50 per cent during the first five years that the six decided to extend it to include all production. The agreements setting up the full EEC were signed in Rome (1957) and came into operation on 1 January 1958.

The six countries would gradually remove all customs duties and quotas so that there would be free competition and a common market. Tariffs would be kept against non-members, though even these were reduced. The treaty also spoke of improving living and working conditions, expanding industry, encouraging the development of the world's backward areas, safeguarding peace and liberty, and working for a closer union of European peoples; obviously something much wider than just a common market was in the minds of the statesmen of the six countries. By 1967 the machinery to run the EEC had been refined to include the Commission (which manages the EEC), the Council of Ministers, an Assembly or Parliament (containing representatives since 1979 directly elected by voters in all member states), a Secretaria and a Court of Justice Associated with the EEC was EURATOM, an organisation in which the six pooled their efforts towards the development of atomic energy. Like the ECSC, the EEC was soon off to a flying start; within five years it was the world's biggest exporter and buyer of raw materials and was second only to the USA in steel production. Once again, however, Britain had declined to join.

(d) Why did Britain refuse membership of the EEC? It was ironic that though Churchill (who retired as Prime Minister in 1955) was one of the strongest supporters of a united Europe, both Labour and Conservative governments drew back from committing themselves too far; their main objection was that Britain would no longer be in complete control of her own economy which would be at the mercy of a supranational authority – the EEC Commission in Brussels. There was also the fear that Britain's relationship with the commonwealth might be ruined if she were no longer able to give preference to commonwealth goods such as New Zealand lamb and butter; the commonwealth with its population of over 800 million seemed a more promising market than the EEC with its 165 million. Nor did Britain want to risk upsetting her special relationship with the USA by becoming too deeply involved in economic integration with Europe which many Europeans wanted to see extended into political integration.

Britain and other countries outside the EEC were worried about being excluded from trade with the six by their high external tariffs. Consequently Britain took the lead in organising *the European Free Trade Area* (EFTA) in 1959. Britain, Denmark, Norway, Sweden, Switzerland, Austria and Portugal agreed gradually to abolish tariffs between each other, but there was no mention of common economic policies. By 1961, however, the British had had a complete change of mind, and Macmillan announced that they wished to join the EEC.

(e) Why did the British attitude to the EEC change? In the first place it was clear that by 1961 the EEC was an outstanding success – without Britain. Since 1953 French production had risen by 75 per cent while German production had increased by almost 90 per cent; Britain's, however, was only 30 per cent up. EFTA had been successful in increasing the trade of its members, but to nothing like the same extent as the EEC. In fact the British economy seemed to be stagnating in comparison with that of the six. The commonwealth, in spite of its size, could not compare with the purchasing power of the EEC, and Macmillan pointed out that there was no clash of interest between Britain's membership of the EEC and trade with the commonwealth: there were signs that the EEC was willing to make special arrangements for the commonwealth countries to become associate members and to allow Britain's EFTA partners to join as well. Another argument was that once Britain was in, competition from the other EEC members would stimulate British industry to greater effort and efficiency. Macmillan even made the point that Britain could not afford to be left out if the EEC developed into a political union.

Negotiations opened in October 1961, and though there were some difficulties it came as a shock when in January 1963 de Gaulle broke off the talks and announced that Britain was not ready for membership.

(f) Why did the French oppose British entry to the EEC? At the time de Gaulle claimed that Britain had too many economic problems and would therefore weaken the EEC. Though the French colonies were associate members, he objected to any concessions being made for the commonwealth since this would be a drain on Europe's resources. It was suggested in Britain that de Gaulle wanted to continue dominating Europe;

if Britain came in she would be a serious rival, while her close ties with the USA would bring unwelcome American influence producing, as he himself said, 'a colossal Atlantic grouping under American dependence and control'. He was perhaps annoyed that Britain had just agreed to receive American Polaris missiles without first consulting France, while he was determined to prove that France was a great power and in no need of American assistance. Finally there was the problem of French agriculture: the EEC protected its farmers with high tariffs so that prices were much higher than in Britain whose agriculture was highly efficient and subsidised to keep prices relatively low. If this continued after Britain's entry, French farmers, with their small and inefficient farms, would be exposed to competition from Britain and perhaps from the commonwealth.

Britain's entry was eventually secured from 1 January 1973 by two factors: after de Gaulle's resignation in 1969, his successor Pompidou was more amenable to Britain while the new British Conservative Prime Minister, Edward Heath, a committed European, negotiated with obstinate determination for British admission. Eire and Denmark also joined. In 1975 a referendum was held in Britain in which 67 per cent of those who voted expressed approval of British membership.

(g) What have been the EEC's main problems?
The EEC has faced several crises and problems. During the 1960s de Gaulle caused tensions first by his high-handed attitude towards British entry and later by his hostility to the Commission which was becoming too powerful for his liking. In 1965 he threatened to withdraw from the EEC if the Commission's powers were not reduced. He got his own way but held up progress for almost a decade. There was, and still is, the problem of producing a common agricultural policy acceptable to all members. France objected to imports of cheap wine from Italy and lamb from Britain, and on occasion refused them entry, though this was a breach of the community rules. A major crisis blew up in 1980 when Britain protested about her budget contribution for that year which seemed unreasonably high at £1,209 million compared with £699 million from Germany and only £13 million from France. The difference was so marked because the contribution was calculated partly as a levy on each country's duties received from imports from outside the EEC. Since Britain imported much more from the outside world than the other members, her contribution soared. Fortunately, after some ruthless bargaining by the British Prime Minister, Margaret Thatcher, a compromise was reached whereby Britain's contribution was reduced to a total of £1,346 million over the next three years. As the EEC moved into the 1980s the major challenge was how it would react to the deepening world recession. Three new members – Greece (joined January 1981), Spain and Portugal (probably joining 1984) – all have relatively poor economies, which could place further strain on the other members. The British Labour party was becoming disillusioned with the EEC and there is a distinct possibility of a future Labour government withdrawing Britain.

20.2 BRITAIN

(a) **Labour in power, 1945-51**. The Labour Party won an overwhelming majority in the General Election of July 1945, with 393 seats against 213 Conservatives, 12 Liberals and 22 others. It was the first time Labour had won an overall majority. Their victory was surprising after Churchill's success as a war leader, but though Churchill himself was popular, the Conservatives were not - too many people remembered the unemployment of the 1930s, appeasement, and the early disasters in the war; Labour promised social reform and more housing. The new government faced enormous economic problems in the aftermath of the war, but the Prime Minister, Clement Attlee, though mild in appearance (Churchill once described him as 'a sheep in sheep's clothing'), was shrewd and determined. With its large majority Labour was able to push ahead with a programme of drastic changes amounting to a social revolution. *What were Labour's achievements?*

(i) *A major expansion of the welfare state* based on *the Beveridge Report* (1942). William Henry Beveridge was a liberal who believed the time was ripe for social revolution. The great evils to be overcome, as the report explained, were want, disease, ignorance, squalor and idleness. The government should fight them with insurance schemes, child allowances, a national health service and a policy of full employment. The wartime coalition government had already made a start with *R. A. Butler's Education Act* (1944) which introduced free secondary education for all and raised the leaving age to 15 (from 1947); it had also introduced family allowances at the rate of 5s. a week for each child after the first. The first of Labour's major contributions was *the National Insurance Act* (1946). This extended the previous schemes so that the whole adult population was insured for unemployment and sickness benefit, retirement, widows' and orphans' pensions, and maternity and death grants. As in the original 1911 scheme, all workers and employers as well as the government had to pay weekly contributions. *The National Health Service Act* (1946), mainly the work of Aneurin Bevan, the Minister of Health, was a remarkable achievement. Most hospitals were brought under state control and everyone was entitled to free medical, dental and ophthalmic treatment including free teeth and spectacles. It was financed partly from taxation and partly from revenue received from National Insurance payments. It resulted in a marked improvement in the health of the working class, while deaths from tuberculosis, pneumonia and diphtheria were greatly reduced. *The National Assistance Act* (1948) gave financial help to those not covered by the National Insurance Act and introduced old people's homes. In the same year *the Children's Act* provided child care officers and the Youth Employment Service. *The Industrial Injuries Act* (1946) set up tribunals to decide the amount of benefit to be paid for injuries suffered at work. The government encouraged council house building; by 1951 over 800,000 had been completed, though this was well below target (it was estimated in 1945 that there was a shortage of at least a million houses). New towns such as Stevenage, Harlow and Hatfield were built and tenants protected by rent controls.

(ii) *Nationalisation* of the Bank of England, the coal industry, civil aviation, railways, canals, road haulage, gas and electricity, and iron and steel. The justification for this was that government control would lead to more efficient planning and better conditions for the workers. Nationalisation has always been a controversial issue and not everybody, certainly not the Conservatives, would agree that it was an achievement. However, both the coal industry and the railways were inefficient and using obsolete equipment and needed the drastic modernisation that nationalisation was expected to provide. The National Coal Board increased output after the serious coal shortages of 1947, but results in some of the other industries were often disappointing because the government was unwilling to invest in them sufficiently.

(iii) *Help for agriculture.* It was important in a time of world food shortages that farmers produced the maximum amount possible. The government encouraged them by price guarantees, subsidies for modernisation, and the National Agricultural Advisory Service to provide the expertise. The results were highly successful: a 20 per cent increase in output between 1947 and 1952 and one of the most mechanised and efficient farming industries in the world.

(iv) Miscellaneous reforms included the repeal of Baldwin's 1927 Trade Disputes Act so that sympathetic strikes and the political levy were legal again (see Section 4.6(e)); the reduction of the delaying power of the House of Lords to one year; and the abolition of plural voting.

(v) *Recovery and full employment.* This was not achieved without setbacks such as the serious coal shortage during the bitterly cold winter of 1946-7 when over a million workers had to be laid off for a time, and the 1949 financial crisis which led to a devaluation of the pound. However, by the end of 1950 industry was booming: exports were 77 per cent above the 1938 level, the most spectacular success being in the car industry, with tractors, motorcycles, engineering, shipbuilding and chemicals not far behind. Success was achieved by a combination of factors: a high demand for goods at home to repair wartime shortages and damage; Marshall Aid; low interest rates to stimulate house-building and industrial expansion; strict government control of the economy. The Chancellor of the Exchequer, Sir Stafford Cripps, became famous for his 'austerity' policies; he restricted imports, persuaded the trade unions to accept a wage freeze (1948-50), continued wartime rationing and exhorted businessmen to export as much as possible. The devaluation of the pound from 4.03 to 2.80 American dollars made British exports cheaper abroad. Prospects for the future seemed bright in 1950 when there was a healthier balance of payments than at any time since 1918.

Behind the dramatic social revolution and the return to full employment, the government was plagued by the inter-linked *problems of inflation and the balance of payments.* From 1945-7, partly because of high interest payments on loans from the USA and the loss of many overseas assets during the war, the balance was unfavourable. The only way to earn was to increase exports which in 1945 stood at less than half the 1938 figure. But this concentration on exports meant a shortage of consumer goods for the home market and consequently rising prices and demands for wage increases which in a time of full employment and even labour shortage, employers were forced to meet. By 1950, as we have seen, the government seemed to have both problems under control, thanks to Cripps's wage freeze and the boom in exports after the devaluation; but this proved to be short-lived: in 1951 the balance was back in the red again mainly because of the Korean War which disrupted trade. As the USA frantically rearmed, prices of raw materials were forced up on the world market so that goods imported by Britain rose sharply in price; when Britain also decided to increase her rearmament programme this caused more economies and shortages. When the new Chancellor, Hugh Gaitskell, tried to save money by the introduction of charges for spectacles and dental treatment, Bevan resigned, along with Harold Wilson, the President of the Board of Trade, causing a serious split in the party. As Seaman says, 'the gains so painfully achieved between 1945 and 1950 were almost entirely eclipsed in the public mind, and the Conservatives were returned to power in 1951.' (Labour's overall majority had already been reduced to 7 in the election 1950.)

(b) The Conservatives in power, 1951-64. The Conservatives won only a small overall majority of 15 in the 1951 General Election; this increased to over 60 in 1955 and to over 100 in 1959. Churchill was Prime Minister until his retirement shortly before the 1955 election, when he was replaced by Anthony Eden, who resigned through ill health in 1957 soon after the failure of his Suez policy (see Section 25.3). Harold Macmillan, one of the most progressive of the Conservatives and on the left wing of the party, was Prime Minister from 1957 until 1963 when Sir Alec Douglas-Home took over for the final year.

During the 1950s there was no dramatic change in policies, and the term *'Butskellism'* was coined from the surnames of R. A. Butler (Churchill's Chancellor of the Exchequer) and Hugh Gaitskell of the Labour Party, implying that there was little to chose between the parties. This was not strictly true, of course, but certainly the Conservatives accepted most of Labour's nationalisation (only iron and steel and road transport were denationalised), the welfare state and full employment.

There have been widely differing assessments of the 13 years of Tory rule. Some, pointing to the steady increase in living standards - the affluent society - claimed that they were successful years, an attitude summed up by one of the slogans during the 1959 election campaign - 'Life's better under the Conservatives'. Critics dismissed them as years of missed opportunities.

What did the Conservatives achieve?

(i) *A marked increase in living standards.* Between 1951 and 1963 wages rose by 72 per cent while prices rose only 45 per cent so that people could afford more consumer goods than ever before: the number of cars rose from under 3 million to 7.5 million and licensed televisions from 340,000 to almost 13 million. The rate of house-building increased from about 200,000 a year under Labour to around 320,000. In 1961 the working week was reduced from 48 to 42 hours.

(ii) *Some important extensions of the welfare state*, including the raising of benefits (though a 2s. prescription charge was introduced) and the Mental Health Act (1959) by which mental illness was to be regarded no differently from physical illness.

(iii) *Help for agriculture* in the form of grants for improvements so that production continued to rise.

(iv) *Education expansion* with about 6,000 new schools, 11 new universities and the introduction of colleges of advanced technology.

On what grounds could the Conservatives be criticised?

(i) Like Labour before them the Conservatives did not find a permanent solution to *the triple problems of economic growth, inflation and the balance of payments.* Successive Chancellors tried different methods, sometimes completely reversing the policy of the previous Chancellor, an approach which came to be called '*stop-go*'. Under Butler the economy was stable: exports boomed and the balance of payments was so favourable that he reduced income tax. By 1955, however, rising wages caused increased demand for goods at home (and therefore inflation) which was met by increasing imports; at the same time exports were adversely affected by strikes and consequently the balance of payments (with imports increasing while exports decreased) became unfavourable. Butler tried to reduce home demand by raising purchase tax and hire purchase deposits, while his successor, Macmillan, raised the bank rate to 5.5 per cent, making it more expensive to borrow cash. This is known as a *credit squeeze*: an attempt to reduce spending, thereby checking inflation and reducing imports in order to improve the balance of payments. This successfully produced a favourable balance for 1956. Unfortunately this was a 'stop' period after the 'go' of 1952-4; the difficulty with squeezes is that when credit is restricted, investment is reduced and industry cannot expand as rapidly as is necessary to sustain exports. Consequently governments dare not risk continuing 'stop' periods too long because this slows the economic growth rate and industry is in danger of stagnating. The dilemma facing the

Tories and all governments into the 1980s was how to maintain the economic growth rate while at the same time avoiding inflation and an un-healthy balance of payments.

This is what led Thorneycroft (Chancellor 1957-8) to relax the squeeze and risk a 'go': taxes and credit restrictions were reduced and an export boom followed; but at the same time more cash was available to spend at home, causing an increase in demand and a consequent rise in prices and imports. Price rises led to wage demands and strikes, so that exports were soon affected and the balance of payments threatened again. The next Chancellor, Heathcoat Amory, tried to hold down wage increases and began a further credit squeeze in 1960, but this was not enough and his successor, Selwyn Lloyd, took tougher measures: he raised interest rates, put 10 per cent on purchase tax and raised import duties. He also tried a new idea – a pay pause which managed to hold wages of government employees down for almost a year, but was repeatedly breached after that; this was the first attempt at a definite pay policy: it failed. By the early 1960s the repeated 'stops' were holding back industrial expansion and Britain was lagging behind her competitors in Europe.

The Conservatives realised that a new approach was needed: first, in 1961, they applied for membership of the EEC, but the application was turned down by France: later the same year they set up the National Economic Development Council (Neddy) followed by a National Incomes Commission (1962) to try and plan the economy centrally; finally the latest Tory Chancellor, Reginald Maudling, aimed for growth with another 'go' period: there were generous tax reductions and encouragement for investors.

(ii) The Conservatives can be criticised for failing to join the EEC at the outset in 1957, with unfortunate consequences for British production and exports (see Section 20.1(e)).

(iii) Certain industries declined, particularly textiles (hampered by competition from Portugal, Japan and India) and shipbuilding (competition from Japan); although other industries were expanding (aircraft, cars and chemicals), production costs were high which often made British goods expensive; in the face of some strong foreign competition, exports did not boom as much as they might; consequently there was a constant struggle to keep costs down. Unemployment became more of a problem in the 1960s especially in the north of England and in Scotland; early in 1963 there were almost 900,000 out of work.

(iv) A combination of failure to enter the EEC, economic stagnation and Maudling's final 'go' period which caused a sudden surge in imports, resulted in a record balance of payments deficit of £748 million for 1964.

In addition to its economic problems the government's reputation was somewhat tarnished after the War Minister, John Profumo had resigned following a scandal involving call girls and spies, and after a rather unseemly squabble over Macmillan's successor as Prime Minister. Labour won a small overall majority of four (October 1964) and Harold Wilson became Prime Minister.

(c) Labour and Wilson (1964–70) faced a number of serious problems:

(i) Most pressing was the balance of payments deficit inherited from the Conservatives. James Callaghan, the Chancellor, borrowed heavily from the International Monetary Fund to replenish dwindling gold reserves (which were being used up to cover the deficit); in yet another squeeze he tried to cut spending by holding wages down and raising import duties. In 1967 the pound was devalued from 2.80 to 2.40 dollars, making exports cheaper. The next Chancellor, Roy Jenkins, cut government spending by £750 million and tightened the wages policy. These drastic measures gradually worked and by 1969 there was a favourable balance of payments which lasted until 1972. However, by 1970 as the wages policy ended, wages began to rise steeply and so did prices.

(ii) Unemployment, which had fallen to under 400,000 in 1964, gradually rose to just over 600,000 in 1970, because of the contraction of coal-mining, shipbuilding, textiles and railways, and increasing automation in other industries.

(iii) The economy was damaged by large numbers of strikes, many of which seemed irresponsible; but when Wilson tried to introduce a bill to reform trade unions and curb unofficial strikes, both the Labour Party and the TUC rejected it and it was dropped.

(iv) There was serious violence in Northern Ireland which had been comparatively calm since Lloyd George's 1922 settlement (see Section 11.2). However, the IRA (Irish Republican Army) would never rest until the north was united with Eire; this the Protestant-dominated Northern Ireland parliament would never agree to. Since the mid-1950s, there had been sporadic terrorist outrages and the situation suddenly deteriorated in 1969. The Northern Ireland Catholics (about one-third of the population) claimed that they were being deprived of full civil rights: they were being discriminated against in jobs, housing and voting. Protestant extremists began disrupting civil rights marches and the IRA used the situation to launch a series of riots and attacks on Protestants which threatened to plunge the province into civil war. Wilson sent troops to Northern Ireland to protect both Catholics and Protestants; this calmed the situation, though not for long. (For the Rhodesia problem see Section 24.2.)

In spite of its preoccupation with the economy, the government found time for some *valuable reforms*: rent rebates, votes at 18, abolition of the death penalty, creation of the Ombudsman (to investigate complaints against inefficient administrators) and the

Race Relations Act which made it illegal to discriminate in jobs, housing and other areas. More controversial were Labour's renationalisation of the steel industry and moves towards comprehensive schools.

(d) Heath and the Conservatives (1970–4). The Conservatives won the 1970 election with a comfortable overall majority of 31 after Edward Heath had conducted a skilful campaign dwelling on Wilson's failures. Heath believed it was possible to escape from the 'stop–go' trap by reducing controls to a minimum and taking Britain into the EEC, which would stimulate British industry. *Very little went right for the government*:

(i) The Chancellor, Anthony Barber, began decisively, cutting taxes and reducing restrictions on hire purchase and credit; Britain's entry into the EEC was secured in 1972, Heath's greatest achievement. However, the hoped-for investment in industry failed to materialise and inflation became serious again, causing Heath to introduce a sharp about-turn: a three-stage policy holding wages down, and the return of controls; but there was no rapid improvement: 1973 showed a balance of payments deficit of over £900 million, unemployment hovering at over 850,000 and inflation still rising (partly because of a 70 per cent increase in oil prices imposed by Arab producers).

(ii) The Family Income Supplement and rate and fuel rebates helped poor families but were criticised by many Conservatives as being too much like socialism.

(iii) The Industrial Relations Act (1971) reformed trade union law in an attempt to cut down strikes and curb extremists. It set up a National Industrial Relations Court and introduced a 'cooling-off period' and ballots for strikes. Although in many quarters this was seen as a moderate and sensible measure, the unions opposed it bitterly with a wave of strikes, the most serious of which was the miners' strike (1974) which led to a three-day working week to conserve fuel.

(iv) Disturbances continued in Ireland where the British army soon found itself in the impossible situation of trying to prevent Catholics and Protestants slaughtering each other while at the same time having to endure attacks from the IRA and another group calling itself the Provisional IRA. The government decided to suspend the Northern Ireland parliament and bring the province under direct rule from Westminster. When early in 1974 a new coalition government was set up in which the Catholics had more say than ever before, Protestant extremists organised massive strikes which quickly paralysed the country; after only a few weeks parliament was again suspended. Since then no government has been able to make any progress, and a solution seems as far away as ever.

(v) Heath decided to hold an election (February 1974) hoping to win public support for his stand against the miners' wage demands; but

Labour with a programme of ending wage policies and reducing taxes won 301 seats against 296 Conservatives, 14 Liberals and 24 assorted Nationalists.

(e) What was wrong with the British economy? The simple fact was that British industry was not producing enough goods for export at the right prices; foreign competitors could produce more cheaply and secured a larger share of the market. The reasons for the inefficiency are a matter of controversy: management blamed unions for excessive wage demands; unions blamed poor management and insufficient investment on new equipment and automation; management were criticised for being so greedy for profit that too little was ploughed back for development. It was also suggested that governments should have spent more on grants to develop industry and less on social services.

(f) Labour in power (1974–9). The new government did nothing to remedy the basic weakness of the economy, and after Wilson allowed the miners' full claim, a rash of other wage increases followed. By 1976 inflation was increasing at a rate of over 20 per cent a year and 1.3 million people were out of work; the high cost of oil imports contributed to the enormous balance of payments deficit. Labour's main weapon for controlling inflation was to persuade the unions to co-operate and accept limited wage increases; this was known as the '*social contract*'. Under Callaghan who became Prime Minister in 1976 after Wilson's retirement, Labour's policies, plus the increasing output of oil from British fields in the North Sea, began to have an impact, and by the end of 1978 the annual rate of inflation had fallen below 10 per cent. Unfortunately for Callaghan, the unions at this point refused to accept his proposal to extend the social contract for a further period by limiting wage increases to 5 per cent, and a number of damaging strikes followed in what became known as the 'winter of discontent'. In the election of May 1979 the Conservatives won an overall majority of 43 and their new leader, Margaret Thatcher, became Britain's first woman Prime Minister.

(g) Thatcher and the Conservatives (1979–). This was the first government since the war to try a completely new remedy for Britain's economic ills – *the monetarist approach*. Monetarists believe in keeping a tight hold on the money supply via the Bank of England by maintaining high rates of interest, so that firms and individuals are forced to reduce borrowing. Management must therefore keep costs down by laying off workers and streamlining operations for greater efficiency. There would be no government grants to prop up inefficient firms, so that only those which made themselves competitive would survive. Such a policy meant a high unemployment level, but its supporters claimed that it was like a major surgical operation – drastic but effective in the long run: British industry, though much contracted, would be efficient and competitive overseas. With purchasing power reduced as unemployment rose, inflation would be controlled and wage demands moderated accordingly. Another side effect, particularly attractive to the Conservatives, was that trade unions would be less powerful: workers, thankful to be in a job, would be less willing to strike.

Thatcher and her Chancellor, Howe, stuck resolutely to this policy with a cripplingly high minimum lending rate of 17 per cent early in 1980 (though this was reduced to 14 per cent by the end of the year) and massive spending cuts affecting housing, education and transport. They confidently predicted that by the end of 1981, the rate of inflation, which had soared to 20 per cent again early in 1980, would be down to 10 per cent and still falling. However, unemployment which reached 2.8 million in January 1981 was disturbing; with world recession deepening, this figure was increasing daily, and some critics were beginning to wonder whether the surgery was in danger of killing off the patient.

20.3 FRANCE

As soon as France was liberated in 1944, General de Gaulle took over the government. The old constitution, which had produced weak government for so many years, was scrapped, a new one introduced and the title changed to the Fourth Republic. De Gaulle resigned in disgust because he felt the president ought to have more power. Though it was born out of the euphoria of liberation the Fourth Republic found its support gradually dwindling until its fortunes reached rock bottom in 1958.

(a) Why did the Fourth Republic lose popularity?

(i) There was constant inflation which produced demands for wage increases and in 1947 widespread strikes. In fact the economy recovered well from the war, because of Marshall Aid and some efficient government planning (largely the work of Jean Monnet). By 1954 industrial production was 50 per cent higher than in 1938 and the steel industry was now fully modernised. The government had the vision to take France into the EEC in 1957. However agriculture still stagnated, and as inflation continued, there was unrest among the small craftsmen, employers, peasants and shop-keepers who did not seem to be sharing in the general progress.

(ii) Governments were still weak since the new constitution retained proportional representation and gave the president no more power. There were five major parties; from left to right they were: communists, socialists, radicals, *Mouvement Républicain Populaire* (MRP) - a new party which stood for Christian democratic principles - and de Gaulle's party, *Rassemblement du Peuple Française* (RPF). The communists and the RPF were hostile to the republic; consequently governments were coalitions made up of ministers from the other three parties; they were constantly changing: in the 12 years which the Fourth Republic lasted there were 25 different governments which were mostly too weak to rule effectively. It was not a system that inspired confidence, and its ineptness was demonstrated by a number of disasters.

(iii) In the eight-year struggle to hold on to Indo-China the government finally had to admit defeat after the military disaster at Dien Bien Phu (1954) (see Section 17.4(a)). Soon afterwards nationalist agitation caused independence to be given to Tunisia and Morocco.

(iv) French intervention in Suez (1956) turned out to be a fiasco (see Section 25.3).

(v) Troubles in Algeria reached a climax in 1958 and the crisis brought de Gaulle back to power. The problem was similar to that in Tunisia and Morocco - the nationalists wanted independence from France and began anti-French riots as early as 1945. By 1954 the National Liberation Front (FLN) led by Ben Bella was ready for a full-scale military revolt. Many French people were prepared to give the Algerians independence, but the situation was complicated by the fact that over a million French settlers lived in Algeria who were flatly opposed to any such move. In addition the 400,000 French troops fighting the rebels were determined not to suffer another Dien Bien Phu. When in 1958 it was suspected that the government was about to give way, French troops and civilians occupied government buildings in Algiers in open revolt against the politicians in Paris and demanded that de Gaulle be called in to head a new government. They were convinced that the general, a great patriot, would never agree to Algerian independence. Civil war seemed imminent; the government could see no way out of the deadlock and consequently resigned. President Coty called upon de Gaulle who agreed to become Prime Minister on condition that he could draw up a new constitution. This was in effect the end of the Fourth Republic.

De Gaulle soon produced his new constitution (approved in a referendum by almost 80 per cent of the electorate) and was elected President of the Fifth Republic (December 1958), a position he held until his resignation in April 1969.

(b) What were de Gaulle's achievements?

(i) The new constitution was a marked improvement on the previous one since it allowed strong and decisive government for the first time since 1871. It transferred the power to make laws from parliament to the President who could chose his own Prime Minsiter and other ministers. The Assembly and the Senate had to agree to laws before they could be carried out, but the President, elected by a national referendum for seven years, could dissolve the Assembly. He controlled foreign policy and defence and could hold referendums on important questions, thus reducing the influence of parliament. Proportional representation was replaced by single member constituencies in which the winning candidate had to poll half the votes; if he failed, a second ballot was held for which the candidates with fewest votes in the first ballot dropped out, so that voters would switch to one of the other candidates. Although this system worked against left-wing parties and enabled the Gaullists to remain the largest party in the Assembly, it provided France with a period of much-needed stability.

(ii) He settled the Algerian problem though not in the way the Europeans and the French army in Algeria had expected. Vicious fighting continued with the FLN and the army both committing atrocities; de Gaulle soon realised that military victory was out of the question and opened negotiations with the FLN, offering them independence. When some French generals defied him and seized power in Algeria, de Gaulle, appearing on television in his general's uniform, denounced them, and the rebellion collapsed. Public opinion in France was now sick of the war and when it was agreed (March 1962) that Algeria should become independent, the decision was approved by a 90 per cent vote in a referendum. The Algerian settlement was probably de Gaulle's greatest achievement after 1945, but it was bitterly resented by the French settlers who felt that the general had betrayed them.

(iii) The economy continued to expand steadily between 1958 and 1963 with many new industries established and moves made to modernise agriculture. However, this was due as much to the planning that had taken place under the Fourth Republic as it was to de Gaulle's efforts, and also to France's membership of the EEC.

De Gaulle was at the height of his popularity in 1962 at the end of the Algerian war. By 1965 his prestige was already waning and in that year, although he defeated the socialist François Mitterand in the presidential election, the margin was much smaller than in 1958 – 54 per cent to 46 per cent. This trend continued until in 1969 he failed to win a referendum and retired into private life.

(c) Why did de Gaulle lose power?

(i) His foreign policy aroused criticism. In his quest to make France a great power again, he pursued an anti-American, anti-NATO and anti-British line, twice vetoing British entry into the EEC. In 1966 he withdrew France from NATO and insisted on having his own nuclear deterrent. Many people were horrified at the vast expense of this policy and realised that it was absurd of France to be developing her defences in isolation instead of co-operating with other states in western Europe, especially as France's real weakness had been shown up in Indo-China and Algeria. Moreover his attitude towards the EEC held up its development by a decade (see Section 20.1(f) and (g)).

(ii) By 1968 all was not well with the economy: coal, steel and railways seemed to have expanded too far and were showing deficits; about half a million were unemployed and inflation was increasing more rapidly than in the other EEC countries.

(iii) Pressing social problems had been ignored by de Gaulle: there was a serious housing shortage making it almost impossible for young married couples to find homes; very few hospitals and schools had been built.

(iv) In February 1968 there was a wave of student strikes and demonstrations; they were objecting to poor accommodation, irrelevancy of courses and the authoritarian and undemocratic nature of the regime. In May ten million workers joined the students and there seemed a real danger of revolution developing. However, de Gaulle was able to weather the storm by promises of wage increases and shorter hours and by playing on the danger of a communist takeover if he fell.

(v) The economic problem and inflation still remained and de Gaulle tried to revive his prestige by allowing the Senate more power. In April 1969 he held a referendum seeking approval of the changes and indicated that he would treat the result as a vote of confidence. Nearly 11 million voted in favour but 12.5 million voted against; consequently the general resigned.

He died in 1970, a controversial figure who, as Walter Lacqueur says, 'outlasted his usefulness. By clinging to power too long, he put in question the achievements of the earlier years of his rule.'

(d) After de Gaulle's departure the Fifth Republic continued to provide stable government under the next two Presidents. Pompidou, though a Gaullist, was more realistic and more moderate than the general, approving of British entry to the EEC, devaluing the franc, paying more attention to social reform and improving relations with the USA. After Pompidou's death in 1974, Giscard d'Estaing (who called himself a liberal rather than a Gaullist) was very narrowly elected President. Like Pompidou he realised the importance of keeping working-class support and sought this by lowering the voting age to 18 and increasing worker participation in industry. By 1980 France, like the rest of western Europe, was suffering from the world recession; there was growing impatience with Giscard's autocratic style of government and the blatant appointment of his supporters as prefects, and in the police and in the media. In May 1981 François Mitterrand, the socialist leader, was elected president in the first left-wing victory since 1956.

20.4 WEST GERMANY

(a) Adenauer in charge (1949–63)

The new German Federal Republic came into being in 1949 (see Section 16.2(h) and (j)) with the 73-year-old Konrad Adenauer as Chancellor. He illus 20.1 *Konrad Adenauer and Charles de Gaulle, 1963*

had acquired his reputation as a successful mayor of Cologne (1919–33) who had been dismissed for opposing Hitler. Under Adenauer's leadership West Germany recovered quickly from the ruin and destruction of the war and was soon enjoying remarkable prosperity. *Reasons for the German success were :*

(i) There was stable government because although the new constitution was similar to that of the Weimar Republic, there was one crucial difference: a party had to receive 5 per cent of the total votes before it could be represented in the *Bundestag* (the lower house). Thus the trend was towards a two-party system: Christian Democrats (CDU - Adenauer's conservative party) and Social Democrats (SPD) with the liberals (FDP) a poor third. The CDU was the dominant party for the first 20 years and Adenauer brought sanity and tranquillity back to German life.

(ii) Guided by the Minister of Economics, Ludwig Erhard, the country enjoyed an 'economic miracle'. It was achieved by a high rate of investment in new plant and equipment and the ploughing of profits back into industry rather than distributing them as higher dividends or higher wages (which happened in Britain). Through fear of inflation, unions did not press high wage demands and therefore prices were kept under control. Industrial recovery was so complete that by 1960 West Germany was producing 50 per cent more steel than the united Germany in 1938. All classes enjoyed prosperity;

pensions and children's allowances were geared to the cost of living and 10 million new dwellings had been provided.

(iii) Adenauer's foreign policies were successful and popular on the whole. The occupation by foreign troops ended in 1952 and West Germany was recognised as an equal member of NATO (1955). He believed strongly in European unity and took Germany into the European Coal and Steel Community and the EEC, providing industry with new opportunities for expansion. He worked hard for reconciliation with France and signed a treaty of co-operation with her (January 1963).

During the early 1960s Adenauer was increasingly criticised for his authoritarian methods, his refusal to recognise East Germany and his apparent determination to hang on to power at all costs. In addition there were the first signs of the end of the economic boom. At last he was manoeuvred into retiring at the age of 87.

(b) Erhard (of the CDU) led a coalition with the liberals; problems occurred in 1965 as domestic orders began to level out and unemployment appeared. Although this was through no fault of Erhard's, the liberals withdrew support and he was forced to resign (1966). He was replaced by another CDU member, *Kurt Kiesinger,* who headed a coalition, this time with the Social Democrats. This would have been out of the question a few years earlier, but in 1959 the SPD had abandoned its Marxist outlook and was attracting middle-class support. The coalition soon dealt with unemployment, but *by 1969 other problems were causing concern*: inflation was developing because full employment caused demand for goods to exceed the capacity of industry to meet it; there were outbursts of violence from left-wing students protesting against their lack of say in the running of universities, against the materialistic society and against the German connection with the Americans who were felt to have been discredited by their involvement in Vietnam; a new extreme right-wing party, the National Democrats (NDP), also caused anxiety.

(c) The Social Democrats in power (1969-)
The SPD narrowly defeated the CDU in the 1969 elections but needed liberal support for a majority. *Willi Brandt,* an efficient administrator and mayor of West Berlin, became Chancellor; he introduced several new policies:

(i) He worked for friendly relations with eastern Europe, including East Germany, a policy known as *Ostpolitik*. Treaties were signed with Russia and Poland (1970) renouncing the use of force and recognising Polish possession of the former German lands east of the Oder–Neisse line (see Section 16.2(a) and (b)). In 1971 agreement was reached with Russia that access to Berlin was still a four-power responsibility and that West Berliners could visit relatives over in the east. These were courageous and statesmanlike policies which aimed, in the long run, at the reunification of Germany. In the short term, *Ostpolitik* contributed towards *détente* and prepared the way for the Helsinki Agreement of 1975 (see Section 17.6(b)).

(ii) He tried to control inflation by revaluing the mark upwards, thereby making more goods available through cheaper imports. This had a fair amount of success but was risky because it made German exports, already expensive because of the strong mark, even more so.

Brandt resigned unexpectedly in 1974 after one of his aides confessed to being an East German spy. In fact Brandt need not have resigned on account of this, since his personal prestige remained high. It is believed that his real motive was his disappointment at the bitter criticism aroused at home by his *Ostpolitik*, his failure to secure educational reforms and the worsening economy.

The SPD remained in power with *Helmut Schmidt* as Chancellor. His main problem was a sudden surge in unemployment which reached one million in 1975. Schmidt acted decisively, giving government aid to new firms, and successfully encouraging modest wage increases. Unemployment gradually fell and inflation was kept at no more than 6 per cent. As West Germany moved into the 1980s, she suffered increasingly from the world recession, though less severely than the other states of western Europe. Even so there was an adverse balance of payments in 1980, for almost the first time since the Federal Republic's formation. The *Ostpolitik* received a setback late in 1980 when the East Germans suddenly became much less co-operative because of the difficult situation in Poland (see Section 19.2(b)). However, none of these problems was serious enough to prevent Schmidt from being convincingly re-elected as Chancellor in October 1980.

QUESTIONS

1. Trace the main steps towards European economic and political unity between 1945 and 1973.

2. Why did Britain fail to join the EEC in 1957, find herself refused entry in the 1960s, join in 1972, and seem unhappy about membership after 1978?

3. How successful has the EEC been in achieving its aims? What problems has it had to face?

4. What did the Labour governments achieve in British domestic affairs, 1945–51?

5. 'You've never had it so good.' '13 wasted years.' Explain the apparent contradiction of these comments on the British Conservative governments 1951–64.

6. Identify and describe the main social evils in Britain named in the Beveridge Report. Describe the measures to implement the recommendations of the Report since 1944.

7. 'All British governments since the Second World War have failed to maintain adequate economic growth rates.' What does this mean and how far is it true? Refer to balance of payments, credit squeeze, stop--go, devaluation, prices and incomes policies.

8. Explain the reasons for the diminishing popularity within France of the Fourth Republic and the government of de Gaulle.

9. What circumstances combined to bring de Gaulle to power in France in 1958. Identify and describe two of his lasting achievements.

10. Outline the main problems and trace the chief historical developments in France during the 1950s.

11. Explain why France was more politically stable in the 20 years after 1958 than in the 20 years before it.

12. Give an account of the successes and show the importance for West Germany of the work of Adenauer and Brandt.

13. Outline the main problems and trace the chief historical developments in West Germany during the 1960s.

14. Study the cartoon below and then answer the questions which follow.

Fig 20.1

"VOILA, THIS IS WHAT YOU CALL 'HIT FOR SIX, NON' . . ."

(i) Who is the character holding the bat? (1 mark)
(ii) Who is the bowler? (1 mark)
(iii) What do the letters forming the wicket stand for? (1 mark)

  (iv) What is the significance of the notice 'England collapses'? (2 marks)
   (v) In what year was this cartoon published?   (1 mark)
  (vi) What is the significance of 'six' in the phrase, 'Hit for six'? (2 marks)
 (vii) Why did the character represented by the batsman, on two occasions, oppose Britain's attempts to join his 'team'? Give *three* reasons.

                                                          (3 marks)
(viii) In what year was the 'batsman' replaced and who was his successor?   (2 marks)
  (ix) Give the arguments that were put forward in Britain *for* and *against* her joining the 'team' represented by the batsman.   (6 marks)
   (x) After Britain had joined this 'team', what happened in 1975 concerning her membership?   (1 mark)

[AEB Nov 1980]

CHAPTER 21

THE USA, THE AMERICAS AND JAPAN AFTER 1945

SUMMARY OF EVENTS

The USA continued to be the world's largest industrial power and the world's richest nation. In spite of this the country was racked by serious problems, outlined below, some of which still remain unsolved in the 1980s. There have been unhappy experiences such as the assassination of President Kennedy (1963), the failure of American policy in Vietnam, and the forced resignation of President Nixon (1974) as a result of the Watergate scandal, all of which have shaken confidence in American society and values and in the American system. Both political parties have taken turns in power: Democrats (Truman 1945-53), Republicans (Eisenhower 1953-61), Democrats (Kennedy 1961-3 and Johnson 1963-9), Republicans (Nixon 1969-74 and Ford 1974-7), Democrats (Carter 1977-81) and Republicans again (Reagan since 1981). Latin America was by comparison underdeveloped both industrially and agriculturally with massive problems of poverty, illiteracy and unstable political systems. Revolutions, military coups and assassinations were common and there had been no significant improvement by 1980 when dictators such as Pinochet (Chile) and Videla (Argentina) headed repressive military regimes. The great success story was provided by Japan which recovered remarkably swiftly from defeat in 1945 to become one of the world's leading industrial and exporting powers. The USA provided economic aid for both Latin America and Japan though, as we shall see, her motives were not entirely selfless.

21.1 THE UNITED STATES OF AMERICA

(a) What were the problems?

(i) The USA took upon herself the world role of preventing the spread of communism, causing her to become deeply involved in Europe, Korea, Vietnam, Latin America and Cuba (see Chapters 16 and 17).

(ii) At home many Americans were obsessed with anti-communist feelings which sometimes bordered on hysteria. This was at its most serious from 1949–54 when Republican Senator Joseph McCarthy led a campaign to root out suspected communists; unfortunately the operation got out of hand: socialists, liberals, intellectuals, artists, pacifists and anyone whose views did not appear orthodox were liable to be hounded out of their jobs for 'un–American activities' and McCarthy became the most feared man in the country. Even after McCarthy overreached himself and was disgraced in 1954, right-wing extremism continued.

(iii) Ironically in the world's richest country, poverty remained a problem. Although the economy was on the whole a spectacular success story with industry flourishing and exports booming, there was constant unemployment: in 1960 the figure stood at 5.5 million, about 7 per cent of the labour force. In 1945 social welfare and pensions were still limited: there was, for example, no national health system. More people shared in the general prosperity than ever before but as late as 1966 it was calculated that 30 million Americans were living below the poverty line, a large proportion of them over 65.

(iv) The colour issue has passed through several phases: in 1977 there were 24 million Negroes in the USA, about 12 per cent of the population. After the war, Negroes were still being treated as second-class citizens, deprived of full civil rights, particularly in the southern states where they were not allowed to vote and were segregated into separate schools, buses, restaurants and other facilities. Although Negroes had the vote in the north and official segregation was much less, they were still under-privileged and discriminated against in employment. There was increasing pressure on the Federal government to grant full civil rights and Martin Luther King, a coloured Baptist Minister, emerged as the outstanding leader of the non-violent protest movement. He organised a boycott of buses in Montgomery, Alabama, so that segregated seating was abandoned (1955–6). However, progress was so painfully slow that in the mid-1960s some Negroes broke away from the non-violent protest movement to form militant organisations such as the Black Panthers, leading to riots, arson and murder. By the mid-1970s (when Negroes had full civil rights, at least by law) the race problem was largely one of poverty: there was still discrimination in jobs and housing which left millions of poor Negroes living in ghettoes in decaying city centres; at the same time thousands of Indians were living a meagre existence on reservations.

(v) In the late 1960s there was a strong reaction against American activities in Vietnam, the power of the state, poverty and what was seen as a moral decline in American society; this led to the New Left movement which did not fit in with either of the major parties and expressed itself in demonstrations and student sit-ins.

The following sections examine how the presidents dealt with whichever of these problems loomed largest during their years in office.

(b) Harry S. Truman (1945–53) (Democrat)

(i) Truman, a man of great courage and common sense, once compared by a reporter to a bantam-weight prize fighter, had to face the special problem of returning the country to normal after the war. This was achieved though not without difficulties: removal of wartime price controls caused inflation and strikes, and the Republicans won control of Congress in 1946.

(ii) Abroad he took up the anti-communist crusade: the Truman Doctrine and Marshall Aid (see Section 16.2(e)), help for the *Kuomintang* in China (see Section 17.1) and intervention in Korea (see Section 17.2).

(iii) In the fight against poverty his programme was known as *the Fair Deal*: a national health scheme, maternal and child benefits, a national old age pensions scheme, a higher minimum wage, slum clearance and full employment. However, the Republican majority in Congress threw out his proposals, and even passed over his veto the *Taft-Hartley Act* (1947) reducing trade union powers. The attitude of Congress gained Truman working-class support and enabled him to win the 1948 Presidential election together with a Democrat majority in Congress. Some of the Fair Deal then became law (extension of social security benefits and an increase in the minimum wage), but Congress still refused to pass his national health and old age pensions schemes, which was a bitter disappointment. Many southern Democrats voted against Truman because they disapproved of his support for Negro civil rights. Again Congress prevented progress in that direction except that segregation in the army was ended (1948).

(iv) Truman had to face the full impact of McCarthyism, and although he did much to tone down the movement's hysteria, it was an embarrassment when Congress passed over the President's veto *the McCarran Act* (1950) which required organisations suspected of being communist to supply lists of members who were then likely to be dismissed from their jobs – a serious infringement of personal liberties. The pervading attitude which regarded social welfare as socialism – only one step removed from communism – helps to explain why much of the Fair Deal failed to pass Congress.

(c) Dwight D. Eisenhower (1953–61) (Republican)

Eisenhower was chosen as Republican candidate because of his popularity as a victorious general, although he had no previous party connections. He won a decisive victory, but disappointed the right-wing Republicans who expected him to reverse the New Deal and Fair Deal reforms; in fact he made no attempt to do so and in his affable way often seemed to have more in common with moderate Democrats (who supported his policies in Congress) than with conservative Republicans.

(i) Problems of foreign affairs were mostly handled by Secretary of State John Foster Dulles who continued the anti-communist stand.

The Korean War was brought to an end but the USA became involved in Vietnam with economic aid and military advisers (see Section 17.4(b)). After the death of Dulles (1959) Eisenhower was able to appear more moderate, favouring peaceful coexistence. Unfortunately his summit meeting with Khrushchev (1960) was a failure because of the U-2 affair (see Section 16.3(c)).

(ii) McCarthyism reached a climax soon after Eisenhower's election. Though McCarthy had probably won many votes for the Republicans among those who took his wild accusations seriously, he went too far when he began to accuse leading generals of communist sympathies. The Senate condemned him by a large majority and he foolishly attacked the President for supporting the Senate. After that his reputation was ruined; but at least nine million people had been 'investigated', thousands of innocent people had lost their jobs, and an atmosphere of suspicion and insecurity had been created.

(iii) For dealing with poverty Eisenhower had no particular programme, though some slight progress was made: insurance for long-term disabled, financial help towards medical bills for people over 65, federal cash for housing, and more spending on education to encourage study in science and mathematics (it was feared that Americans were falling behind the Russians who in 1957 launched the first space satellite – Sputnik). Farmers faced problems during the 1950s because increased production kept agricultural prices and therefore incomes low. The government spent massive sums paying farmers to take land out of production, but this was not a success: farm incomes did not rise rapidly and poorer farmers hardly benefited at all; many of them sold up and moved into the cities. Much remained to be done, but the Republicans were totally against national schemes such as Truman's health service which smacked of socialism.

(iv) The government itself did a little to ease the racial problem by passing two Civil Rights Acts: one (1957) established a Commission to investigate the denial of voting rights to Negroes; the second (1960) provided help for Negroes to register as voters, but this was ineffective. More important than government action were a number of decisions by the Supreme Court which showed itself pro-Negro. It ruled that some Negroes must be included on juries, that separate schools for blacks and whites were illegal (1954) and that desegregation in education must take place (1955). The problem was that whites in the southern states refused to carry this out, and to his credit, Eisenhower sent federal troops to escort Negro children into the high school at Little Rock, Arkansas, where the governor had defied the Supreme Court order (1957). This was a symbolic victory, but southern whites continued to defy the law and by 1961 only a tiny fraction of schools and colleges in the south were desegregated. Negroes were already turning impatiently to more violent methods of protest.

illus 21.1 *Little Rock, 1957. A group of black students leave the school under trooper escort*

(d) John F. Kennedy (1961–3) (Democrat)

Kennedy was the first Roman Catholic and, at the age of 42, the youngest President ever to be elected. He won because the Republicans were blamed for inflation, unemployment and for their unsatisfactory handling of foreign affairs (particularly the U–2 affair and the Paris summit), and because Kennedy ran a brilliant campaign accusing them of neglecting education and social services. He came over as elegant, articulate, witty and dynamic, and though his margin of victory was very slim, his election seemed to many to be the beginning of a new era. He faced enormous problems in foreign affairs, as well as poverty, unemployment and the civil rights situation at home; his policies showed great vigour and promise, but his presidency was tragically cut short after less than three years when he was shot dead in Dallas, Texas.

(i) Kennedy's handling of foreign affairs met with mixed success: he acted decisively over the Russian threat to Berlin (see Section 16.3(c)) and in the Cuban missile crisis in 1962 (see Section 17.3(b)) but his attempt to keep American involvement in Vietnam to a minimum failed (see Section 17.4(c)). The setting up of the telephone link with Moscow and the Partial Test Ban Treaty (1963) were constructive achievements. He began a policy of economic co-operation with Latin America and founded the Peace Corps consisting of skilled volunteers who would work abroad bringing much-needed expertise to underdeveloped countries. His Trade Expansion Act reduced tariffs and encouraged international trade.

(ii) The poverty problem was pressing, with over 4.5 million unemployed when Kennedy took office. He had a detailed programme: medical payments for the poor and aged, more federal aid for education and housing, increased unemployment and social security benefits. 'We stand today on the edge of a New Frontier', he said, and implied that only when these reforms were introduced would the frontier be crossed and poverty eliminated. From this his policy became known as *the New Frontier*. Unfortunately for Kennedy, he had to face strong opposition from Congress where many Democrats as well as Republicans viewed his proposals as 'creeping socialism'; hardly a single one was passed without some watering down and many were rejected altogether. Congress would allow no extra federal cash for education and rejected his scheme to pay hospital bills for old people. His successes were: an extension of social security benefits to each child whose father was unemployed; raising of the minimum wage from a dollar to 1.25 an hour; federal loans to enable people to buy houses; federal grants to the states enabling them to extend the period covered by unemployment benefit. Kennedy's overall achievement was limited: unemployment benefit was only enough for subsistence and even that for a limited period; unemployment still stood at 4.5 million in 1962, and soup kitchens had to be set up to feed poor families.

(iii) The New Frontier also included full civil rights and equality for Negroes; just how far there was still to go on this issue was summed up by Kennedy himself when he said (1963) that an American Negro had 'half as much chance of completing high school as a white, one-third as much chance of completing college, twice as much chance of becoming unemployed, one-seventh as much chance of earning 10,000 dollars a year, and a life expectancy which is seven years less.' Kennedy showed his intentions by appointing the first Negro ambassador and presenting a Civil Rights Bill to Congress; this was delayed at first by the conservative Congress but passed in 1964 after a debate lasting 736 hours. It was a far-reaching measure, guaranteeing the vote for Negroes and making racial discrimination in public facilities (such as hotels, restaurants and stores) and in jobs illegal. Again the act was not always carried out especially in the south where Negroes were afraid to vote.

(e) Lyndon B. Johnson (1963–9) (Democrat)

Johnson, Kennedy's Vice-President, became President under the terms of the constitution on Kennedy's assassination. Coming from a humble illus 21.2 *The assassination of John F Kennedy, 1963. Here the President slumps forward seconds after having been shot*

background in Texas, Johnson was just as committed as Kennedy to social reform, and achieved enough in his first year to enable him to win a landslide victory in the 1964 election. In 1963, as well as facing a nation in deep shock, appalled at the growing violence, he inherited all Kennedy's problems.

(i) In Vietnam Johnson decided to commit the USA far more deeply than Kennedy had done and he began the bombing of North Vietnamese cities (see Section 17.4(c)). These policies brought no success and eventually ruined his popularity within America.

(ii) In 1964 Johnson's economic advisers fixed an annual income of 3,000 dollars for a family of two or more as *the poverty line* and estimated that over 9 million families (30 million people, approaching 20 per cent of the population) were on or below the line. Many of them were Negroes, Puerto Ricans, Red Indians and Mexicans; the problems of poverty and racial discrimination were closely connected. Johnson announced that he wanted to move America towards *the Great Society* where there would be an end to poverty and racial injustice and 'abundance and liberty for all'. Many of his measures became law partly because after the 1964 elections the Democrats had a huge majority in Congress and partly because Johnson was more skilful and persuasive in handling Congress than Kennedy had been. The Economic Opportunity Act (1964) provided a number of schemes whereby young people from poor homes could receive job training and higher education. Other reforms were: federal money for special education schemes in slum areas, including help in paying for books and transport; financial aid for clearing slums and rebuilding city areas; and the Appalachian Regional Development Act (1965) which created new jobs in one of the poorest regions. Perhaps his most important innovation was the Social Security Amendment Act (1965), also known as *Medicare*: this was a partial national health scheme, though it applied only to people over 65. This is an impressive list and yet the overall results were not as successful as Johnson would have hoped, for a number of reasons: it has been suggested that the whole programme was under-financed because of the enormous expenditure on the war in Vietnam; on the other hand there was a lack of public support because of the strong American tradition of self-help: it was up to the poor to help themselves and wrong to use the taxpayers' money on such a scheme which would only make the poor lazier; thus many state governments failed to take advantage of federal offers of help.

(iii) Civil rights were an important aspect of the Great Society. Johnson began by steering Kennedy's Civil Rights Bill through Congress, and followed it with the Voting Rights Act (1965) to try and make sure that Negroes exercised their right to vote, and another Civil Rights Act (1968) which made it illegal to discriminate in selling property or letting accommodation. Again the problem was to make sure that these acts were applied in the face of bitter white prejudice; much progress was made especially in the voting field (by 1975 there were 18 Negroes in Congress, 278 in various state governments, and 120 had been elected mayors). However, there can never be full equality until black poverty and the black ghettoes disappear.

(iv) In the mid-1960s violence seemed to be getting out of hand: riots in Negro ghettoes where the sense of injustice was strongest; student riots in the universities, protesting, among other things, at Vietnam; political assassinations (President Kennedy in 1963, Martin Luther King and Senator Robert Kennedy in 1968). Between 1960 and 1967 the number of violent crimes rose by 90 per cent. Johnson could only hope that his 'war on poverty' would gradually remove the causes of discontent; beyond that he had no answer to the problem. The general discontent and particularly the student protests about Vietnam (LBJ, LBJ, how many kids have you burnt today?') caused Johnson not to stand for re-election in November 1968, and explain why the Republicans won, on a platform of restoring law and order.

(f) Richard M. Nixon (1969-74) (Republican)

Nixon, who had been Eisenhower's Vice-President from 1956 and had narrowly lost to Kennedy in the 1960 election, faced an unenviable task: what to do about Vietnam, poverty, unemployment, violence and the general crisis of confidence that was afflicting America. How successful was he dealing with these problems?

(i) Overseas problems, particularly Vietnam, dominated his Presidency (until 1973 when Watergate took over). After the Democrat-dominated Congress had refused to vote any further credits for the war, Nixon extricated the USA from Vietnam with a negotiated peace signed in 1973 (see Section 17.4(c)), to the vast relief of the American people who celebrated 'peace with honour'. Yet in April 1975 South Vietnam fell to the communists; the American struggle to prevent the spread of communism in South East Asia had ended in failure and her world reputation was somewhat battered. Nixon was responsible for a radical and constructive change in foreign policy when he sought, with some success, to improve America's relations with Russia and China (see Section 17.6(b) (c)).

(ii) Unemployment became a problem again with over four million out of work in 1971; their plight was worsened by rapidly rising prices. The Republicans were anxious to cut public expenditure and Nixon reduced spending on Johnson's poverty programme, and introduced a wages and prices freeze. However social security benefits were increased, Medicare extended to disabled people under 65, and a Council for Urban Affairs set up to try and deal with the problems of slums and ghettoes.

(iii) A financial crisis and a balance of payments deficit caused Nixon to impose a 10 per cent surcharge on imports and allow a devaluation of the dollar, so that the position improved temporarily.

(iv) Violence seemed to present less of a problem under Nixon partly because protesters could now see the approaching end of the controversial Vietnam involvement and because students were allowed some say in running their colleges and universities.

By the end of his first term Nixon's achievements seemed, if not spectacular, at least full of promise: he had brought the American people within sight of peace, he was following sensible policies of *détente* with the communist world and law and order had returned. The Americans had enjoyed a moment of glory by putting the first men on the moon (Neil Armstrong and Ed Aldrin, 20th July 1969). Nixon won the election of November 1972 overwhelmingly and in January 1973 was inaugurated for a second term. However, his second term was ruined by a new crisis:

(v) *The Watergate scandal* broke in January 1973 when a number of men were charged with breaking into the Democratic Party offices in the Watergate Building, Washington, back in June 1972 during the presidential election campaign. They had planted listening devices and photocopied important documents. It turned out that the burglary had been organised by leading members of Nixon's staff, who were sent to gaol. Nixon insisted that he knew nothing about the affair, but suspicions mounted when he consistently refused to hand over tapes of discussions in the White House which, it was thought, would settle the matter one way or the other. The President was widely accused of having deliberately 'covered up' for the culprits and he received a further blow when his Vice-President, Spiro Agnew, was forced to resign (December 1973) after facing criminal charges of bribery and corruption. (He was replaced by Gerald Ford, a little-known politician but one with an unblemished record.) Nixon was called on to resign but refused even when it was discovered that he had been guilty of tax evasion. He was threatened with impeachment (a formal accusation of his crimes before the Senate, which would then try him for the offences); to avoid this, he resigned (August 1974) and Ford became President. It was a sad end to a presidency which had shown positive achievements especially in foreign affairs, but the scandal shook people's faith in politicians and in a system which could allow such happenings. Ford won admiration for the way in which he restored dignity to American politics, but given recession, unemployment and inflation, it was no surprise when he lost the 1976 election to the Democrat Carter.

(g) Jimmy Carter (1977–81) (Democrat)

Carter's presidency was a disappointment. He was elected as an outsider (peanut farmer, ex-governor of Georgia, and a man of deep religious convictions), the newcomer to Washington who would restore the public's faith in politicians. He managed some significant achievements: he stopped giving automatic American aid to right-wing authoritarian governments merely in order to keep communism out; he co-operated with Britain to bring about black majority rule in Zimbabwe (see Section 24.2(d)); he signed a second Strategic Arms Limitation Treaty (SALT II) with the USSR; and he played a vital role in the Camp David talks bringing peace between Egypt and Israel (see Section 25.6).

Unfortunately his lack of experience of handling Congress meant that he had the same difficulties as Kennedy, and he failed to pilot the majority of his reforming programme into law. By 1980 the world recession was biting deeply, with factory closures, rising unemployment and oil shortages. Apart from Camp David, Democratic foreign policy seemed unimpressive; there was the American inability to take effective action against the Russian occupation of Afghanistan (see Section 17.6(e)). Just as frustrating was their failure to free a number of American hostages seized in Teheran by Iranian students (November 1979) and held for over a year. The Iranians were trying to force the American government to return the exiled Shah and his fortune, but stalemate persisted even after the Shah's death. A combination of these problems and frustrations resulted in a decisive Republican victory in the election of November 1980. Ironically the hostages were set free minutes after the inauguration of Carter's successor (January 1981). The new president, former film star Ronald Reagan, seemed likely to provide right-wing government: a reduction in government spending on social services and foreign aid, an increased defence budget, and an aggressive stand against communism abroad.

21.2 LATIN AMERICA

(a) The area known as Latin America consists of the countries of South America, Central America including Mexico and islands in the Caribbean Sea such as Cuba and Hispaniola (divided into two states, Haiti and the Dominican Republic). These states gained independence from Spain or Portugal in the early nineteenth century and had much in common: Spanish is spoken in most of them, though in Brazil Portuguese is the main language; in the period after 1945 they shared similar problems:

(i) *They were economically underdeveloped* both industrially and agriculturally. Factory industries did exist (the Second World War acted as a stimulus to industrial development because manufactured goods from Europe and the USA were impossible to come by), but for all sorts of reasons Latin American industry is still well below the level of industry in the developed countries of Europe, the USA and Japan: there was a shortage of capital, equipment and technical knowledge; home markets were unpredictable because the vast majority of people were too poverty-stricken to provide enough purchasing power; and it was difficult to export in competition with advanced industrial nations. Thus states found themselves heavily dependent for exports on a limited range of products, sometimes even a single commodity; a fall in the world price of that commodity would be a major disaster: Chile relied on copper, Cuba on sugar and tobacco, Bolivia on tin; in fact 80 per cent of all Bolivian revenue came from tin in the 1950s. Agriculture remained backward because peasant labour was so plentiful and cheap that wealthy estate owners had no need to bother about modernisation; Peru was dominated by huge estates whose owners were all-powerful, ruling their peasants like feudal monarchs.

(ii) *There was a massive rise in population* due mainly to advances in medicine and hygiene and the refusal of the Roman Catholic church to promote birth control. The population is still increasing at a rate of 3 per cent per year, faster than in any other area of the world: between 1945 and 1962 it rose from 130 million to 216 million and by 1980 to over 500 million. Whenever it seemed that a country might be making some progress, for example by land reform in which a peasant received land of his own, this was neutralised by the population growth. Peasant holdings were too small to support large

Fig 21.1 *Latin America*

families; many left for the cities but found jobs hard to come by; almost all the major cities were surrounded by filthy improvised slums without water, sewage disposal or electricity. The gap between rich and poor grew wider and little progress was made in eliminating poverty and illiteracy.

(iii) *Latin American political systems were, for the most part, inadequate* for dealing with such enormous problems. There was no tradition of democracy (except in Chile) and states were run by groups of wealthy landowners supporting *caudillos* (military dictators). When democratic systems were introduced in some of the states after the

Second World War and governments tried to effect reforms, it was common for the army to intervene on behalf of the disapproving landowners, either to block the reforms or to overthrow the government; this happened in Guatemala (1950), Bolivia (1964), Brazil (1964, after only eight years of democracy), Argentina (1966) and Chile (1973).

(iv) Heavy investment by foreigners in industry and agriculture was a problem, because much of the profit was taken out of the countries: most of the oil in Bolivia and Venezuela (potentially rich countries) is got out by American-owned companies; the US United Fruit Company was the biggest landowner in Guatemala; Chilean copper mines and Cuban sugar plantations were also American controlled.

(b) What was done about the problems?

(i) Several international organisations were set up: the Organisation of American States (OAS), founded in 1948, included most of the Latin American countries and the USA, and aimed to bring about inter–American co-operation and to settle disputes. The Central American Common Market (1960) had some success in bringing about a reduction of tariffs. However, the Latin American Free Trade Association (LAFTA) formed in 1961 has had little success.

(ii) The United Nations helped by sending technical experts and by holding conferences to consider how underdeveloped nations might increase exports.

(iii) The USA has sent massive economic aid. Kennedy started the Alliance for Progress which aimed to pump billions of dollars into Latin America to enable economic and social reform to be carried out. However, this sort of aid did not always work out for the best, sometimes creating extra problems. American motives were mixed: they hoped, by solving economic problems, to encourage moderate reforming governments which would be popular enough to keep communism out. Sometimes the loans were provided on condition that a high proportion was spent on American products, which hardly helped native industries to develop and involved governments in large interest payments. Often, as with Castro's Cuba and Allende's Chile, aid would be cut short if a government unacceptable to the USA came to power, to be resumed later when the government changed. The USA therefore could exert political influence via economic control. Sometimes there was more direct influence: in 1954 Washington supplied arms to Guatemalan rebels who overthrew a reforming government and replaced it with a right-wing military dictatorship; more blatant was US intervention in the Dominican Republic (1965) where 20,000 American troops crushed an attempted comeback by former President Bosch who had an extensive programme of social reform and was therefore suspected of being a communist.

The conclusion must be that the problems of Latin America have not been solved, and in 1980, with the world in deep recession, prospects looked gloomy. The poverty-stricken masses feel helpless and many join guerrilla terrorist movements such as the *Tupamaros* in Uruguay, who operate in cities and specialise in kidnapping foreign diplomats and businessmen for whom they can secure large ransoms. The Roman Catholic Church has become increasingly critical of military dictators who neglect social justice.

We have already seen how these problems manifested themselves and with what results in Cuba (see Sections 17.3 and 18.4) and Chile (see Section 17.5). Two other interesting examples are Venezuela and Guatemala.

(c) Venezuela

Venezuela is one of the wealthiest states of Latin America because of its oil resources, but until 1945 profits went to foreign oil companies (mainly American and British) or to the small group of wealthy people who ran the country through a military dictatorship. The great mass of the population received no benefit and remained poor and illiterate. In 1945 Romulo Betancourt, leader of a progressive left-wing party called *Accion Democratica*, was placed in power by a group of young army officers after fierce fighting in Caracas, the capital, had overthrown the military government. Betancourt introduced a new constitution which allowed full civil rights to all citizens; land reform was started, heavy taxes placed on the foreign oil companies, and plans prepared to exclude the army from politics. These reforms were bitterly opposed by foreign companies and rich landowners and in 1948 Betancourt was driven out by an army coup.

For the next ten years the country was under ruthless military dictatorship. American dollars flowed in and some progress was made with the building of steel plants to exploit local iron ore deposits. Iron and steel soon became Venezuela's most valuable export. In 1957 Archbishop Blanco of Caracas publicly condemned the government's wealth and corruption while the majority of Venezuelans lived in sub-human conditions. In 1958 a general strike broke out and a section of the army removed the dictator, Jimenez. Democracy was restored and Betancourt was voted back to power. Immediately he raised Venezuela's share of oil revenues to 60 per cent, but this disappointed the growing communist party who had expected him to nationalise all foreign companies. However, Betancourt proceeded cautiously, not wanting to alienate the USA in case aid was stopped, and although measures were introduced to improve education and health and some land redistributed to peasants, Betancourt's popularity gradually waned. Nevertheless democracy survived, the presidency alternating between *Accion Democratica* and the other main group, the Christian Social Party. Venezuela did well out of oil revenues, being the main supplier for the Central American states and to a lesser extent for the USA.

(d) Guatemala

In marked contrast to Venezuela, Guatemala is one of the poorest states of Latin America and its history is an excellent illustration of US involvement. Largely an agricultural state, its economy depended on exports of bananas and coffee. The population consisted mainly of landless peasants and the economy was dominated by American firms, particularly the United Fruit Company. The country's military dictator was overthrown by revolution in 1945, elections were held and the Christian Socialist Juan José Arevalo became President for five years. Much-needed reforms were introduced: many foreign estates were confiscated and redistributed to peasants; there was a minimum wage, new houses, hospitals and schools, and landowners were required to provide adequate housing for their workers. The next President, Jacobo Arbenz, took uncultivated land from large estates, to be redistributed among peasants and legalised the communist party. This was too much for the USA: all aid was immediately stopped, Arbenz was accused of being a communist, and his opponents were supplied with arms and trained in neighbouring Honduras. In 1954 American backed forces led by Castillo Armas invaded Guatemala and overthrew Arbenz. Armas became military dictator; he was assassinated in 1955 only to be replaced by another dictator, Miguel Ydigoras. US aid was resumed and a revolution against Ydigoras was put down in 1960 with American help.

In 1978 Lucas Garcia was elected President, leading a right-wing coalition, but after the election the situation deteriorated. The government planned to distribute uncultivated land in the north of the country to the landless peasants but large areas somehow fell into the hands of rich landowners. There were many peasant protests leading to violent clashes between left and right, in which the Roman Catholic Church came out in support of the peasants. In January 1980 the Jesuits announced that since the previous October, 3,252 political murders had been committed. They blamed the forces of the right, whereupon the 52 Jesuit priests in Guatemala received death threats from the Secret Anti-Communist Army. The country seemed poised on the verge of civil war, though attention was diverted from internal affairs by the dispute with Britain in which Guatemala claimed possession of British Honduras which was due to become independent (as Belize) later in 1980.

21.3 JAPAN

At the end of the Second World War Japan was defeated; her economy was in ruins with a large proportion of her factories and a quarter of her housing destroyed by bombing. Until 1952 she was occupied by allied troops, mostly American, under the command of General MacArthur. For the first three years the Americans aimed to make sure that Japan could never again start a war; she was forbidden to have armed forces and was given a democratic constitution under which ministers had to be members of the *Diet* (parliament). The Americans did not at this stage seem concerned to restore the Japanese economy. During 1948 the American attitude gradually changed: as the Cold War developed in Europe and the *Kuomintang* crumbled in China, they felt the need for a strong ally in South East Asia and began to encourage Japanese economic recovery. From 1950 industry recovered rapidly and by 1953 production had reached the 1937 level. American occupying forces were withdrawn in April 1952 (as had been agreed by the Treaty of San Francisco the previous September) though some American troops remained for defence purposes.

(a) How was Japan's rapid recovery possible?

(i) American help was vital: Japanese goods were allowed into American markets on favourable terms and the USA supplied aid and new equipment: an economically healthy Japan meant a strong bulwark against communism in South East Asia.

(ii) The Korean War (1950–3) brought orders for military equipment and supplies, and American firms began to co-operate with the Japanese in the development of new industries.

(iii) The alliance with the USA meant that Japan felt well protected and was therefore able to invest in industry money that would otherwise have gone on armaments.

(iv) Profits from exports were ruthlessly ploughed back into industry and this was helped by keeping wages and government expenditure low. Japanese goods (motorcycles, cars, television and hi-fi equipment and ships) were therefore highly competitive on world markets.

(v) Recovery was helped by a series of stable governments, mostly conservative in character, which had the solid support of the farmers who benefited from the land reform carried through by the Americans. Enjoying plots of their own for the first time they were afraid that their land would be nationalised if the socialists came to power.

(b) Japanese recovery was not without its problems however. There was a good deal of anti-American feeling in some quarters; many Japanese felt inhibited by their close ties with the USA; they felt that the Americans exaggerated the threat from communist China. They wanted good relations with China and the USSR but this was difficult with Japan in the American camp. The renewal of the defence treaty with the USA in 1960 caused strikes and demonstrations. The Japanese gradually restored good relations with Russia and in the early 1970s reached an understanding with their old enemy China. Another problem was working class unrest at low wages and overcrowded living conditions. Stability depends on economic prosperity; as Japan moves into the 1980s and begins to experience recession for the first time since the 1930s, it remains to be seen whether the democratic system can survive a fall in exports and the consequent social hardship.

QUESTIONS

1. What have been the main internal problems in the USA since 1945 and how successfully have governments dealt with them?

2. What were the main problems which confronted *either* Eisenhower *or* Kennedy? Give an account of the major achievements of the President you have chosen.

3. Explain the 'New Frontier' ideal of Kennedy and compare it with Johnson's 'Great Society'. What obstacles stood in the way of these Presidents in the realisation of their ideals?

4. In what circumstances did Johnson come to power? What were the chief problems which faced him and how successfully did he deal with them?

5. What are the main features of the colour problem in the USA? Describe the efforts made by successive Presidents since 1945 to deal with the problem. Which President, in your opinion, has dealt with the problem most successfully?

6. How far would you agree that 'but for Watergate Nixon was an extremely successful President both at home and abroad'?

7. Give an account of the main social, economic and political problems which have been experienced since 1945 by Latin American countries. Illustrate your answer by references to specific countries.

8. In what ways and with what results has the USA been concerned with Latin America since 1945?

9. Show how Japan was able to recover from her defeat in the Second World War.

10. Refer to the two Nixon cartoons below and then answer questions (*a*) to (*i*) which follow.

(*a*) Supply the name in Cartoon 1 which President Nixon had momentarily forgotten. (1)

(*b*) In what circumstances was Spiro dumped in the dustbin? (1)

(*c*) What principal event at the time of his re-election campaign of 1972 resulted in scandals which brought about the downfall of President Nixon? (2)

(*d*) What part did the tapes illustrated in Cartoon 2 play in the case against President Nixon at the time of his suggested impeachment in 1974? (3)

(*e*) In what circumstances was President Nixon as suggested in Cartoon 2, forced to 'eat his words'? What was the significance of his public 'eating of his words' to his position as President? (2)

(*f*) Give brief details of *one* other charge commonly put forward against President Nixon at the time when his impeachment was being considered. (2)

(*g*) Why did it prove unnecessary to proceed with the impeachment of President Nixon? (1)

(*h*) In Cartoon 1, President Nixon holds a paper on which there is the name of a politician relatively unknown in 1973-4. Name the offices to which this candidate succeeded (i) in 1973 and (ii) in 1974.   (1 + 1)

(*i*) Describe and explain *two* positive achievements of the Nixon Administrations.   (6)

Fig 21.2   *London Board June 1976*

Cartoon 1 for Question 10

Cartoon 2 for Question 10

CHAPTER 22

THE END OF THE EMPIRES

SUMMARY OF EVENTS

The 20 years after 1945 saw remarkable changes taking place in Asia and Africa as the European states gradually released their hold over their empires, which broke free to form a large number of independent states. The pace of nationalist aspirations was accelerated by the Second World War: the prestige of Europe was badly damaged by the failure to defend Asian possessions against the Japanese and the myth of European invincibility was destroyed; Asians in areas such as the Dutch East Indies, French Indo-China and the British territories of Burma and Malaya had no wish to return to the pre-war status quo after stubbornly resisting the Japanese occupation. Their success in gaining independence encouraged similar demands in the Middle East and Africa. Many Africans, who had left their homeland for the first time to fight in the war, were appalled at the contrast between the primitive conditions in Africa and their relatively comfortable existence even in the armed forces. Nationalists were also encouraged by the Russians who constantly denounced 'imperialism'.

The colonial powers had to decide first whether and then how to grant independence. The problems involved were often complex; for example in India there were bitter religious differences to resolve; in some areas large numbers of whites had settled (Algeria, Kenya, Uganda, Tanganyika and Rhodesia) who were relentlessly hostile to independence which would place them under black majority rule. Britain was prepared to concede independence as soon as she felt individual territories were ready for it; by 1964 most of her empire had become independent though the majority of the new states retained a link with Britain by remaining in the commonwealth. The main territories gaining independence (some of which changed their name) were India and Pakistan (1947), Burma and Ceylon (1948), Malaysia (1957), Gold Coast (Ghana, 1957), Nigeria (1960), Cyprus (1960), Tanganyika and Zanzibar (together forming Tanzania, 1961), Uganda (1962), Kenya (1963), Nyasaland (Malawi, 1964), Northern Rhodesia (Zambia, 1964), British Guiana (Guyana, 1964), Malta (1964), Bechuanaland (Botswana, 1966) and Aden (South Yemen, 1967).

The French were at first determined to hold on to their empire, but strong nationalist resistance in Indo-China (see Section 17.4(a)) and Algeria (see Section 20.3) forced a change of heart. They withdrew from Indo-China in 1954, from Morocco and Tunisia in 1956, and by 1962 from most of their other African possessions, including Equatorial and West Africa. Belgium granted independence to the Congo (1960) with insufficient preparation, leading immediately to a terrible civil war (see Section 24.1). The Dutch were forced against their will to accept the independence of the East Indies (Indonesia, 1949) and the Spanish withdrew from Spanish Morocco (1956), Ifni (1969) and Spanish Sahara (1978). Portugal held out stubbornly against the general trend but the new left-wing government decided to withdraw from her African colonies, Guinea (became Guinea-Bissau, 1974), Mozambique and Angola (1975).

22.1 WHY AND HOW WAS INDIA PARTITIONED IN 1947?

By 1945 Indian independence could not be delayed much longer after the long nationalist campaign (see Section 11.3). The British had promised to allow dominion status once the war was over and the new Labour government was anxious to go ahead. Unfortunately there was more to it than simply granting independence: there were complex problems which resulted in India being divided into two separate states, India and Pakistan.

(a) Why was partition necessary?

(i) The problem sprang from religious hostilities between Hindus who made up about two-thirds of the population and the rest who were mostly Muslims. After their victories in the elections of 1937 (see Section 11.3(b)), the Hindu Congress party unwisely called on the Muslim League to merge with Congress; this alarmed the League who were now convinced that an independent India would be dominated by Hindus. Jinnah, the Muslim leader, demanded a separate Muslim state of Pakistan.

(ii) Attempts to draw up a compromise constitution acceptable to Hindu leaders (Nehru and Gandhi) and to Jinnah, failed. The British proposed a federal scheme in which the central government would have only limited powers while those of the provincial governments would be extensive; thus provinces with a Muslim majority would be able to control their own affairs, and there would be no need of a separate state. Both sides accepted the principle but could not agree on details.

(iii) Violence broke out in August 1946 when the Governor-General, Lord Wavell, invited Nehru to form an interim government, still hoping that details could be worked out later. Nehru formed a cabinet which included two Muslims, but Jinnah, convinced that the Hindus could not be trusted, called for 'direct action' to achieve Pakistan. Fierce rioting followed in Calcutta where 5,000 people were killed, and spread to Bengal where Muslims set about slaughter-

illus 22.1 *New Delhi, 1947. During a lull in the rioting, victims of the
many clashes are removed from the streets*

ing Hindus. As Hindus retaliated the country seemed on the verge of
civil war.

(iv) To try and force the Indians into a more responsible attitude, Attlee
announced early in 1947 that the British would leave no later than
June 1948. The new Viceroy, Lord Mountbatten, realised that
partition was the only way to avoid civil war, and by this time the
majority of Congress (though not Gandhi) agreed with him. Afraid
that delay would cause more violence, Mountbatten advanced the
date for British withdrawal to August 1947.

(b) How was partition carried out?

The Indian Independence Act was rushed through the British parliament
(August 1947) separating the Muslim majority areas (the north-west and
north-east of India) from the rest of India as the independent state of
Pakistan, which was in two sections, over a thousand miles apart. But it
was not easy to operate the act:

(i) It had been necessary to split the provinces of the Punjab and
Bengal which had mixed Hindu/Muslim populations and inevitably
millions of people found themselves on the wrong side of the new
frontiers.

(ii) Fearing persecution, millions made for the frontier, Muslims trying
to get into Pakistan and Hindus into India. Clashes occurred developing into near-hysterical mob violence, especially in the Punjab, in
which about 250,000 people were murdered. Violence was not
quite so widespread in Bengal where Gandhi, still preaching non-
violence and toleration, managed to calm the situation.

(iii) Violence began to die down before the end of 1947, but in January
1948 Gandhi was shot dead by a Hindu fanatic who detested his
tolerance towards Muslims. It was a tragic end to a disastrous set of
circumstances, but the shock seemed to bring people to their senses,
so that India and Pakistan could begin to think about their other
problems.

22.2 MALAYA AND CYPRUS

(a) Malaya was liberated from the Japanese occupation in 1945 but there
were two difficult problems to be faced before the British could think of
withdrawing:

(i) How could such a complex area be organised? It consisted of nine
states each ruled by a sultan, two British settlements, Malacca and
Penang, and Singapore, a small island less than a mile from the mainland. The population was multi-racial: mostly Malays and Chinese
but with Indians and Europeans as well. It was decided to group the
states and the settlements into *the Federation of Malaya* (1948)
while Singapore remained a separate colony. Each state had its
own legislature for local affairs, the sultans retained some power,
but the central government had firm overall control. Since everybody
had the vote, the Malays, the largest group, usually dominated affairs.

(ii) Chinese communist guerrillas who had led the resistance to the
Japanese, now began to stir up strikes and violence against the
British, and the situation was serious enough for a state of emergency to be declared in 1948. The British dealt with the problem
successfully, though it took time: all Chinese suspected of helping
the guerrillas were re-settled into specially guarded villages; it was
made clear that independence would follow as soon as the country
was ready for it; this ensured that the Malays remained firmly pro-
British and gave little help to the communists, who were Chinese.
Even so the emergency remained in force until 1960.

The move towards independence was accelerated when the
Malay party under their able leader Tunku Abdul Rahman, joined
forces with the main Chinese and Indian groups to form *the Alliance
Party*, which won 51 out of 52 seats in the 1955 elections. This
seemed to suggest stability and the British were persuaded to grant
full independence in 1957 when Malaya was admitted to the commonwealth.

(b) Cyprus

Unlike the Malaya success story, British handling of Cyprus left much to be desired and the island was still troubled and divided in 1980. The problems were:

(i) The population was mixed – about 80 per cent were Greek-speaking Christians of the Orthodox Church, while the rest were Muslims of Turkish origin. The Greek Cypriots wanted union with Greece (*enosis*); the Turks strongly opposed this, but there was no serious trouble until 1954, when:

(ii) Churchill's government produced a new constitution which allowed Cypriots far less power than the previous Labour government had envisaged. There were hostile demonstrations, which had to be dispersed by British troops.

(iii) Eden, Churchill's successor, thought Britain needed Cyprus as a military base to protect her interests in the Middle East, and announced that Cyprus must remain permanently British, though the Greek government promised that they could retain their military bases even if *enosis* took place.

(iv) The Greek Cypriots led by Archbishop Makarios pressed their demands, while a guerrilla organisation called *Eoka*, led by General Grivas, waged a terrorist campaign against the British who declared a state of emergency (1955) and deployed about 35,000 troops to try and keep order. British policy also involved deporting Makarios and executing terrorists.

Eden's successor, Macmillan, adopted a conciliatory approach and appointed the sympathetic and tactful Hugh Foot as governor. He persuaded Makarios to agree to a compromise: the Archbishop dropped *enosis* and in return Cyprus was granted full independence: Turkish interests were safeguarded, Britain retained two military bases and, along with Greece and Turkey, guaranteed the independence of Cyprus; Makarios became first president (1960). It seemed a masterly solution, but unfortunately it lasted only until 1963 (see Section 19.3(g)).

22.3 THE BRITISH IN AFRICA

African nationalism spread rapidly after 1945; this was because more and more Africans were being educated, many of them in Britain and the USA where they were made aware of racial discrimination. Colonialism was seen as the humiliation and exploitation of blacks by whites, and working-class Africans in the new towns were particularly receptive to nationalist ideas. They were greatly encouraged by Indian independence (1947) and by the sympathetic attitude of the British Labour government (1945-51).

(a) West Africa presented comparatively few problems, since the British in that area tended to be administrators rather than permanent settlers with estates to defend.

(i) In the *Gold Coast Kwame Nkrumah*, educated in London and America and since 1949 leader of the Convention People's Party (CPP), organised the campaign for independence. There were demonstrations, some of which got out of hand, and Nkrumah was twice imprisoned. However, the British soon agreed to allow a new constitution which included the vote for all adults, an elected assembly and an eleven-man Executive Council of which eight were chosen by the assembly. In the 1951 elections, the first under the new constitu-

Fig 22.1 *Africa becomes independent*

////. The Central African Federation 1953–63
Northern Rhodesia (Zambia) Southern Rhodesia (Zimbabwe)
Nyasland (Malawi)

R Ruanda 1962
B Burundi 1962

tion, the CPP won 34 out of 38 seats; Nkrumah was released from prison and became Prime Minister in 1952. For the next five years the African politicians gained experience of government under British supervision until in 1957 Ghana, as it was now known, became independent.

(ii) *In Nigeria* the leading nationalist was *Nnamdi Azikiwe*; popularly known as 'Zik', he had been educated in the USA, and after his return to Nigeria in 1937 soon gained enormous prestige. Nigeria was a more difficult proposition than Ghana because of its great size and its regional differences between the huge Muslim north, the western region (dominated by the Yoruba tribe) and the eastern region (the Ibo tribe). However, after Azikiwe had organised an impressive general strike in 1945, the British gradually began to prepare Nigeria for independence. It was decided that a federal system was most suitable; in 1954 a new constitution introduced local assemblies for the three regions with a central (federal) government in Lagos, the capital; the regions assumed self-government first and the country as a whole became independent in 1960.

(b) East Africa included Tanganyika, Uganda and Kenya, and here the problems of independence were complicated by the presence of European and Asian settlers who were afraid of their future under black African government. *The Tanganyika African National Union* (TANU) led by *Dr Julius Nyerere*, who had been educated at Edinburgh University, insisted that the government must be African, and the British, impressed by Nyerere's ability and sincerity, accepted this view and granted independence (1961). *This marked an important change in British policy*: they had begun in 1945 by thinking that independence was not as necessary in East Africa as in the west, and that when it came it would be under multi-racial governments. By 1960 the British Prime Minister, Macmillan, talked of 'the wind of change' in Africa; it was inevitable that Ghana's example would be followed in both East and Central Africa, and Macmillan dropped the idea of multi-racial governments in favour of black majority rule. Independence for *Uganda* was delayed by tribal squabbles; the ruler of the Buganda area (known as the *Kabaka*) objected to the introduction of democracy. Eventually a solution was found in a federal constitution which allowed the *Kabaka* to retain some powers in Buganda. Uganda itself became independent in 1962 with *Dr Milton Obote* as Prime Minister. *Kenya* was the most troublesome area. Here *Jomo Kenyatta* and his Kenya African Union led the struggle for independence and at first made little progress, the only British concession being to allow six Africans on the Legislative Council of 54 members. African impatience burst out in a campaign of terrorist attacks on European farms and African workers, organised by *the Mau Mau* secret society. A state of emergency was declared in 1952, and Kenyatta and other nationalists were arrested; thousands of British troops were used to flush out the terrorists and by 1960 the emergency was over. By this time, no doubt encouraged by the strength of African feeling, the British change of heart had taken place: Kenya became independent under a black African government with Kenyatta as Prime Minister (1963); this was in spite of bitter resistance from the European settlers, many of whom left the country.

(c) **Central Africa** (Nyasaland, Northern and Southern Rhodesia) was the most difficult area to deal with because this was where the white settlers were most strongly entrenched, particularly in Southern Rhodesia. Alarmed at the spread of African nationalism to the north, the whites, with the approval of Churchill's government, set up *the Central African Federation* (1953), a union of the three states. Their aim was to preserve the supremacy of the white minority (about 300,000 Europeans out of a total population of 8.5 million), and the federal parliament at Salisbury (in Southern Rhodesia) was heavily weighted to favour the whites, who hoped the Federation would soon gain full independence from Britain with dominion status. The Africans watched with growing distrust, and as outstanding nationalist leaders emerged, such as Dr Hastings Banda (Nyasaland), Kenneth Kaunda (Norther Rhodesia) and Joshua Nkomo (Southern Rhodesia), they became more militant. As violence spread, states of emergency were declared in Nyasaland and Southern Rhodesia with mass arrests of Africans (1959). However, there was much support for the Africans in Britain, especially in the Labour Party, and the Conservative Colonial Secretary, Iain Macleod, was sympathetic. *The Monckton Commission* (1960) recommended votes for Africans, an end to racial discrimination and the right of territories to leave the Federation. The British introduced new constitutions in Nyasaland and Northern Rhodesia which in effect allowed the Africans their own parliaments (1961-2); both wanted to leave the Federation which was terminated in December 1963. The following year Nyasaland and Northern Rhodesia became fully independent as Malawi and Zambia. There still remained the problem of Southern Rhodesia, or Rhodesia as it was now known. Here the ruling whites, more numerous than in the other two areas, opposed any change in the constitution which would increase African rights; they demanded independence but Harold Wilson, the new British Labour Prime Minister, refused this unless the whites showed a willingness to move towards black majority rule. No compromise could be reached and in 1965 Rhodesia declared itself independent against the wishes of Britain (a unilateral declaration of independence or UDI) (see Section 24.2).

22.4 **PORTUGAL**

The main Portuguese possessions were in Africa: the two large areas of Angola and Mozambique and the small West African colony of Guinea. The Portuguese right-wing government of Dr Salazar for a while blithely ignored nationalist developments in the rest of Africa and their empire seemed likely to survive; it was mainly agricultural, there were few industrial workers, the black populations were almost entirely illiterate, and though nationalist groups were formed in all three colonies in 1956 they remained insignificant. *Several factors changed the situation*: by 1960 the nationalists were greatly encouraged by the large number of other African states winning independence; in alarm the Salazar regime stepped up its repressive policy, but this served only to make the nationalists more resolute. Fighting broke out first in Angola (1961) where Agostinho Neto's MPLA (People's Movement for Angolan Liberation) was the main nationalist movement. Violence soon spread to Guinea where Amilcar Cabral led the resistance and to Mozambique where the Frelimo guerrillas were organised by Eduardo Mondlane. It was an uphill struggle which succeeded only after the Portuguese dictatorship was overthrown by an army coup in 1974. The new president Spinola agreed to all demands: all three states were granted independence in 1975; the transfer of power went smoothly in Guinea-Bissau and Mozambique but in Angola civil war flared up as two rival groups, FNLA (National Front for the Liberation of Angola) and UNITA (National Union for the Total Independence of Angola), tried to seize power from the MPLA. It seems likely that the MPLA had majority support but this did not deter President Mobutu of Zaire, with American backing, from launching an invasion in support of the rival groups; nor did it prevent an invasion by 6,000 white South Africans. By March 1976 the MPLA, with the aid of Russian weapons and a Cuban force, had defeated both invasions and Neto was accepted as president of the new state. The end of Portuguese control in Africa was vitally important: it meant that the white minority regimes in Rhodesia and South Africa were more vulnerable than ever before (see Fig 22.1).

QUESTIONS

1. Why did Britain withdraw from India in 1947? Describe (a) the events from 1945 which brought about the withdrawal and (b) the immediate results.
2. Why and how did India and Pakistan become separate states in 1947?
3. Explain Britain's involvement in Malaya between 1945 and 1966 (see also Section 23.4).
4. Describe the ways in which Britain after 1945 came to terms with the problems of nationalism in Ghana and Nigeria *OR* in Kenya, Uganda and Tanganyika. Why was a solution more complicated in Britain's Central African possessions (Rhodesia, Malawi and Zambia)?
5. Why was a Central African Federation established in 1953? Explain why and how this Federation broke up and trace the subsequent history of *one* of the states which had been part of it (see also Sections 23.5 and 24.2).

CHAPTER 23

THE NEW COMMONWEALTH STATES

SUMMARY OF EVENTS

Having gained independence, all the former British possessions except Burma and Aden chose to remain within the Commonwealth. However, they found that independence was not all plain sailing. Most of them had serious political, social and economic problems. Fighting twice erupted between India and Pakistan over possession of Kashmir (1947 and 1965), and India found herself attacked by China (1962). Malaysia became involved in a long confrontation with Indonesia (1963-6) while Nigeria suffered a bloody civil war (1967-70). Pakistan had a similar experience in 1971 when East Pakistan broke away to become the independent state of Bangladesh. Cyprus was torn by strife between Greeks and Turks and since 1974 a United Nations peace-keeping force has been holding the two factions apart (see Section 19.3(g)). In fact the Commonwealth seemed to be so full of problems of one sort or another that its critics began to question its value.

23.1 WHAT IS THE COMMONWEALTH AND WHAT USE IS IT?

Originally an association of Britain and her dominions (the 'white man's club') drawn up by the 1931 Statute of Westminster (see Section 11.1(b)), the Commonwealth changed, with the admission of the new Asian and African states, into a multi-racial organisation. It is a loose association based on voluntary co-operation in which all member states are equal partners. There is very little formal machinery except the Secretariat (set up only in 1965) and the regular biennial Commonwealth Prime Ministers' Conferences which discuss pressing problems and plan mutual aid. The Commonwealth has done a good deal of unspectacular but valuable work in the way of economic aid. The Colombo Plan (began 1950) provides grants and advisers for projects in the poorer countries of the Commonwealth (and outside); Canadian engineers helped to build a dam in Pakistan; Australia supplied equipment and teachers to develop Malaysian education. The Special Commonwealth African Assistance Plan (1960) provided financial, technical and educational aid for the emerging African nations; Nigeria, for example, received help to develop hydro-electric schemes and Malawi to set up a university. On average Britain spent somewhere approaching £200 million a year in Commonwealth aid.

On the other hand critics of the Commonwealth have plenty of ammunition: many argue that the rich members could have done far more to help the still poverty-striken Third World nations of Africa; the Commonwealth was unable to prevent or solve serious problems such as civil wars in Nigeria and Pakistan, while two of its members, India and Pakistan, have actually fought each other. The rest of the Commonwealth was alarmed at Britain's entry into the EEC (1973) and her special trading relationship with the commonwealth gradually faded as she traded more with Europe; Australia, for example, bitterly attacked Britain and the EEC, blaming them for the declining markets for her beef and lamb (October 1980). However, in spite of the departure of South Africa (1961) because of disapproval of her racial policies (see Section 24.3), and the Rhodesia upheaval (see Section 24.2(b)) the member states chose to remain in the Commonwealth, which would suggest that it still has something to offer.

23.2 INDIA

For all but three years (1977–80) India after independence was ruled by the Congress party, first under Nehru (1947–64), then under Lal Bahadur Shastri (1964–6), followed by Nehru's daughter, Mrs Indira Gandhi (1966–77) who was again elected in 1980 following an anti-Congress coalition government. All these governments had to deal with awe-inspiring problems – racial, social, political and foreign.

(a) What were India's domestic problems and how successfully were they dealt with?

(i)   India had been held together only by British rule and as soon as the British left, the country seemed in grave danger of disintegrating. There were racial, cultural and language differences and the provinces had no sense of loyalty to the central government. Sikhs and Nagas and some of the native princes like the Nizam of Hyderabad, wanted separate states of their own. Nehru's government refused concessions and insisted on unity. The princes were persuaded to surrender their powers and allow their states to be incorporated with the rest of India in return for pensions; by 1952 the initial problem of unity had been solved.

(ii) There were difficulties in working a democractic constitution in a country which had had no real experience of such government, where 80 per cent of the population were illiterate and where large communist groups, encouraged by Stalin, were intent on revolution. Nehru was determined that democracy should be given a chance; communist disorders were suppressed and a new constitution

Fig 23.1 *the Indian subcontinent after 1947*

introduced (1950) with a strong central government at Delhi, two houses of parliament, provincial governments in each of the states, and votes for all adults. The system passed an important test in 1964 when Nehru died and Shastri was appointed smoothly and without violence. In the early 1980s there were tensions between the central and state governments. Three states – West Bengal, Tripura and Kerala – had communist governments, and in September 1980 Mrs Gandhi, beset by enormous problems, gave the government wider powers of arrest and detention without trial, which caused many observers to conclude that this was an admission of failure.

(iii) The caste system stood in the way of progress: Hindu society was divided into four main classes – priests, rulers and soldiers, traders and farmers, and artisans (craftsmen). People outside these groups were regarded as 'untouchables' who were discriminated against in all spheres of activity. Nehru, a strong supporter of human rights, was responsible for a law (1955) banning discrimination against untouchables; he also gave women equal rights; but practices of such long standing would take years to disappear.

(iv) Most serious of all was the state of the economy. Agriculture was primitive, cows, sacred to Hindus, were unproductive, industry was very small and poverty immense; there were horrifying slums in the big cities and in 1958 the average income per person was only £27 a year (£425 in Britain and £880 in the USA). Nehru realised that economic progress was vital, especially as communism seemed to be working miracles in neighbouring China. He adopted a socialist approach involving a series of Five Year Plans. The first one (1951- 6) concentrated on agriculture, introducing fertilisers, improving seed, stock and irrigation and encouraging land redistribution; it was a striking success, increasing food production by 20 per cent. The second and third plans increased industrial production. Attempts were made to provide education for all and to improve living conditions in the villages. Mrs Gandhi continued her father's work: the fourth plan aimed to provide millions of extra jobs, though it fell short of its targets. Great progress was made, but despite attempts to encourage birth control, the entire achievement was threatened by the rapidly growing population: standing at 356 million in 1951, by 1971 it had reached 550 million and threatens to be around the 1,000 million mark by the end of the century. The increases in food production could barely keep pace with the population increase and a poor harvest meant famine; there was a chronic shortage of capital for industrial expansion and the economy still remained precarious. Towards the end of 1980 inflation was rising steeply, there was industrial stagnation, acute power shortages and widespread flooding.

(v) Corruption was so widespread as to constitute a major problem; in such a poorly paid society, the acceptance of bribes, 'grease money', was common at all levels, and though Mrs Gandhi launched a determined attack, progress was slow.

(b) Foreign affairs

Nehru dominated Indian foreign policy and soon won a reputation as a statesman of international calibre. *The main issues were*:

(i) He was in favour of *non-alignment* – to avoid involvement with either of the power blocs in the Cold War and assume leadership of the world's uncommitted countries; these Third World states would be a powerful force for the maintenance of world peace. Cynics claimed that Nehru merely wanted to receive help from both sides, but in fact his motives seemed genuine. He supported the United Nations and helped to mediate in the Korean War and in Vietnam (1954). Although India became a republic in 1950, Nehru kept her in the Commonwealth because it would make for better understanding between Europe and Asia, and improve India's chances of qualifying for British aid. When the Indians expelled the Portuguese from their colony of Goa he was strongly criticised, but his action could be defended on grounds of nationalism.

(ii) *Relations with China* deteriorated in the late 1950s over a border dispute in Ladakh, a barren and sparsely populated area of Kashmir. Oddly, Nehru, probably afraid of outraging Indian nationalist feeling, refused to compromise. In 1962 fighting broke out in which Indian troops suffered humiliating defeats, but when it seemed that northern India was open to a full-scale invasion, the Chinese withdrew. Relations continued to be uneasy, however, and the dispute remained unsettled. The incident was important: fear of Chinese attack forced Nehru to accept American military aid, so that strictly speaking, India was no longer non-aligned. Nehru's reputation suffered because he was thought to have neglected India's defences.

(iii) *Relations with Pakistan* were tense over a number of issues:

- There was a dispute about which of them should own the rich province of *Kashmir*, bordering northern India and West Pakistan. Fighting twice broke out (1947 and 1965) (see Section 19.3(h)) and after the second war the Russian Prime Minister, Mr Kosygin, got Shastri and Ayub Khan of Pakistan together at Tashkent (1966) and persuaded them to withdraw their troops to the positions held before the fighting. No permanent solution was found and Kashmir remains partitioned.

- *The Indus River dispute* arose because of West Pakistan's dependence on this river and its four great tributaries for her water supply, hydro-electric plants and irrigation. Unfortunately for the Pakistanis these rivers rise in India or the Indian part of Kashmir, and the Indians planned to build a canal to carry water from the rivers to irrigate a large desert area west of Delhi. Afraid of being left without water, the Pakistanis protested strongly; after long negotiations (1951-60), an amicable solution was found (the Indus Waters Treaty) for a sharing of the rivers. The World Bank helped by organising massive foreign loans for the building of storage dams and irrigation canals.

- India intervened in the civil war which broke out in Pakistan in March 1971 when East Pakistan declared itself the independent state of Bangladesh. West Pakistani forces fought savagely to bring Bangladesh back into the fold, but they committed the most terrible atrocities, and millions of refugees flooded over the border into India. Mrs Gandhi sent Indian troops in support of Bangladesh (December 1971) so that peace could be restored as soon as possible and the refugees, a serious drain on Indian resources, could be returned home. The Indians soon defeated the West Pakistanis and the independence of Bangladesh was assured.

- *The Simla Conference* (July 1972) seemed the beginning of a new friendship between India and Pakistan with agreement being reached about withdrawal of troops from Bangladesh and return of prisoners of war. It was also agreed to accept the 1966 cease-fire line in Kashmir as permanent. There was a temporary hitch when President Bhutto of Pakistan refused to recognise Bangladesh, though it gradually

Fig 23.2 *the Kashmir and Indus River disputes between India and Pakistan*

——— The 1949 cease-fire line, still being observed

dawned on both governments that they could ill afford to waste their meagre resources fighting each other when both still had appalling poverty to overcome. An important step in developing co-operation was a trade treaty signed in 1975, though neither her improving relations with Pakistan nor her continuing poverty dissuaded India from becoming a nuclear power – her first nuclear weapon was exploded in 1974.

23.3 PAKISTAN

Pakistan had a much less successful history than India; democratic governments repeatedly found themselves in difficulties and were removed by military coups.

(a) The first 10 years of independence were chaotic; everything seemed to go wrong for the Pakistanis. They soon lost their two most capable leaders: Jinnah died in 1948 and Liaquat Ali Khan was assassinated in 1951. There was no obvious successor and politics deteriorated into a sordid squabble, riddled with corruption from top to bottom. Governments seemed incapable of solving any of the problems facing them; they failed to cope with the 8 million Muslim refugees who flocked in from India; the country was backward industrially and agriculturally and 85 per cent of the 76 million population were illiterate; although they attempted a Five Year Plan like the Indians, little progress was made because of corrupt politicians. There were the disputes with India over Kashmir and the Indus (see Section 23.2(b)), neither of which could be solved. Most serious of all was the difficulty of holding together the two sections of the country which were a thousand miles apart and had little in common except the Muslim religion: the west spoke Urdu or Punjabi and relied on wheat production, the east spoke Bengali, grew rice and produced jute, its main export. People in the east felt they were not given equal treatment with people in the west, who dominated the army, the civil service and most other spheres of activity: discontent simmered.

(b) Ayub Khan in power (1958–69)

By 1958 parliamentary democracy had become so discredited that the army seized power and General Ayub Khan headed a new military government. His period in power was the most successful in Pakistan's history; trained at Sandhurst, Ayub turned out to be a first-rate administrator.

(i) His achievements were impressive: he removed corrupt politicians and civil servants; he introduced land reform, restricting the size of estates and taking away surplus land from wealthy landowners for redistribution among the peasants; within six months the refugees had been housed and a successful Five Year Plan for the economy was under way. Dams and hydro-electric schemes were built; production of jute, carpets and leather goods expanded, and great emphasis was laid on education. A new constitution was drawn up which would gradually return the country to full democracy, beginning with elections for local councils (1959) whose members were later allowed to elect a central parliament (1962) with limited powers. A successful solution was found to the Indus water problems, though a settlement to the Kashmir dispute eluded even Ayub after the second outbreak of war with India (1965). Apart from that Pakistan maintained good relations with both sides in the Cold War and particularly with China, India's other enemy.

(ii) *Ayub Khan's fall from power* (March 1969) came quite suddenly. In spite of his many achievements criticism mounted: the landlords had not forgiven him for land redistribution; there were still food shortages in the east; the leaders of the Muslim religion (mullahs) claimed he was not religious enough, while the politicians, especially Zulfikar Ali Bhutto, accused him of corruption and a refusal to return to genuine democracy. As disorders broke out particularly in the east, Ayub resigned and the army took power again with General Yahya Khan as President.

(c) Civil war and the loss of Bangladesh (1971)

The well-meaning Yahya Khan was unfortunate enough to preside over the dissolution of Pakistan. He promised that as soon as law and order had been restored, democratic elections would be held. He kept his word and elections went ahead with remarkable smoothness (December 1970). The results, however, precipitated a crisis: in the west Bhutto's People's Party won a large majority while in the east Sheikh Mujibur Rahman's Awami League did even better, winning all but two of the seats. This meant that when the national parliament met the Awami League would have an overall majority, and for the first time the Bengalis would be able to dominate the west. This Bhutto refused to accept even though the election had been perfectly fair and legal, and he announced that his party would boycott the new parliament. After negotiations had failed to find any compromise, Sheikh Mujib declared East Pakistan the independent republic of Bangladesh (March 1971). Yahya tried vainly to preserve the union, arresting Sheikh Mujib and sending troops to the east where the Bengalis resisted desperately. Ten million refugees crossed into India to escape the violence, starvation and disease; with help from India, Bangladesh managed to maintain its independence. Yahya Khan had to admit defeat and when the civil war ended he resigned (December 1971). Bhutto became President of Pakistan while Sheikh Mujib took over Bangladesh.

(d) Bhutto faced dreadful problems: his country was humiliated by defeat and could ill afford to lose East Pakistan's valuable trade; the economy was still precarious. Having precipitated the crisis that led to civil war, Bhutto now rashly took Pakistan out of the commonwealth (1972) in protest against the admittance of Bangladesh, just when she needed all the help available. He remained in power and won an election in 1977. However, there were accusations of corruption during the election and when violence broke out the army stepped in again and arrested Bhutto (1977). General Zia ul Haq became President heading a military government and, in spite of world-wide protests, Bhutto was executed. Once again the Pakistanis had been unable to work a democratic system.

23.4 MALAYSIA

Since independence in 1957 (see Section 22.2(a)) Malaya has been the most successful of all the former British possessions, though it too had its problems. The main issues were:

(a) The founding of the Federation of Malaysia (1963)

Malaya seemed stable under the Prime Minister Tunku Abdul Rahman. Educated at Cambridge, he retained a high regard for Britain and chose to remain in the Commonwealth. By 1960 the communist threat seemed to have been overcome and the economy, based on exports of rubber and tin, was the most prosperous in South East Asia. Thus in 1961 when Abdul Rahman proposed that Singapore and the three British colonies of North Borneo (Sabah), Brunei and Sarawak should join Malaya to form the Federation of Malaysia, Britain agreed. Abdul Rahman had something of an ulterior motive: the island of Singapore with its prosperous port would be a valuable acquisition, but since three-quarters of its population were Chinese, the Malays would be outnumbered if union took place just between Malaya and Singapore; if the other three colonies with their predominantly Malay population also joined the federation, the Malay majority would be preserved. Singapore, Sabah and Sarawak were in favour but objections came from two quarters:

(i) In Brunei groups of people opposed to joining the federation started a revolt (December 1962). Although this was quickly suppressed by British troops flown in from Singapore, the Sultan decided not to join. This was a disappointment for Abdul Rahman since Brunei had rich oil resources.

(ii) President Sukarno of Indonesia protested because he hoped that Sabah and Sarawak would become part of Indonesia once the British left.

After a United Nations investigation team reported that a large majority of the populations concerned was in favour of the union, the Federation of Malaysia was officially proclaimed (September 1963).

(b) Confrontation with Indonesia (1963–6)

Immediately the new state had to face a challenge from Sukarno who had announced a policy of 'confrontation' with Malaysia. His motives were not clear: he may have intended to seize Sabah and Sarawak; perhaps he hoped to manoeuvre the entire federation into becoming part of Indonesia as he had with West Irian in 1962 (see Section 19.3(a)); or the campaign may have been a ploy to divert attention away from Indonesia's domestic troubles. 'Confrontation' consisted of propaganda, attempts to stir up racial troubles between Malays and Chinese in Singapore, a boycott of trade with Malaysia, guerrilla attacks on Sabah and Sarawak and an airdrop of paratroops at Labis in Malaya itself. Well before the end of 1965 it was clear that Sukarno's efforts were not going to cause Malaysia to disintegrate:

(i) The Commonwealth, particularly Britain, Australia and New Zealand, sent troops and their extensive use of helicopters helped them to control the situation.

(ii) The United Nations condemned Indonesia for aggression and the International Monetary Fund stopped giving aid, while the trade boycott disrupted Indonesia's economy more than Malaysia's.

(iii) Domestic squabbles between communists and the army drew Indonesian attention away from Malaysia and Sukarno called off 'confrontation' in June 1966.

Fig 23.3 *Malaysia and Indonesia*

▤ The Federation of Malaysia

▨ Indonesia (formerly Dutch East Indies)

(c) Dispute with Singapore

Singapore's membership of the federation was uneasy from the beginning, and the feeling rapidly grew that she would be better off going it alone. She had already enjoyed independence from 1959 until 1963 under her energetic Prime Minister, the Cambridge-educated Lee Kuan Yew. The mainly Chinese population, though they had voted to join the federation, now felt that their interests were not sufficiently looked after by the Malay-dominated government at Kuala Lumpur (the federal capital); they were annoyed at the tariffs introduced to protect Malaysian industries whereas they, depending for much of their income on the port, wanted free trade to encourage business. Serious race riots broke out in Singapore between Chinese and Malays (September 1964) though these were aggravated by Indonesian agents. Tension remained high until in August 1965 Singapore left the federation and became an independent republic again.

(d) Problems of racial harmony still remained.

The Malays resented the Chinese minority either because, being involved in business, they became wealthy, or because they were suspected of being communist agents. Serious anti-Chinese rioting erupted in 1969 which was controlled only with difficulty.

(e) Communist terrorism

broke out again in 1974. Operating from the mountainous jungle near the frontier with Thailand they launched a campaign which culminated in the assassination of Perak state's police chief. Malaysian and Thai troops co-operated in a flushing-out operation, but the guerrillas had still not been entirely suppressed at the end of

1980; alarm increased after the communist victory in Vietnam (1975) and even more so when communist incursions began to take place into Thailand from Kampuchea (formerly Cambodia).

Abdul Rahman (until his retirement in 1970) and his successor, Abdul Razak, at first worked on the theory that prosperity was the best way to keep communism out. Reliance on rubber and tin was reduced by promoting pineapple and rice growing, fishing and livestock farming; Malaysia processed more of its own rubber in the manufacture of tyres; new markets were found in America and Japan, while education and health services were extended. In 1980 a large development programme was started for the neglected north and a new 72-mile east-west highway was due to be opened in 1981 linking Penang to the east coast. In the late 1970s the government also began to build up its military strength, buying 88 Skyhawk planes, 60 tanks and other assorted equipment. By 1984 the army expected to be able to mobilise half a million troops, if the need arose.

23.5 THE AFRICAN NATIONS

(a) Common problems
All the new African nations, not just the former British possessions, faced similar problems.

(i) They each contained a number of different tribes which had only been held together by the foreign colonial rulers and had united in the nationalist struggle for freedom from the foreigners. As soon as the Europeans withdrew there was little incentive to stay together and they tended to regard loyalty to the tribe as more important than loyalty to their new nation. In Nigeria and the Congo (now Zaire) tribal differences became so intense that civil war developed.

(ii) Like many other Third World states, they were economically underdeveloped, often relying on one or two commodities for export, so that a fall in the world price of their products was a major disaster. There was a shortage of capital and of skills of all kinds, and the population was growing at a rate of over 2 per cent a year. Loans from abroad left them heavily in debt, and as they concentrated on increasing exports to pay for the loans, food for home consumption became scarcer.

(iii) Faced with such difficulties the politicians, lacking experience of how to work the systems of parliamentary democracy left behind by the Europeans, failed to cope and governments became corrupt. This led to the creation of one-party states as the only way to achieve progress. In many states such as Kenya and Tanzania, this worked well providing stable and effective government; on the other hand since it was impossible to oppose such governments by legal means, violence was often the only answer and the military coup to remove unpopular politicians became common. President Nkrumah of Ghana for example was removed by the army in 1966 after two assassination attempts had failed.

(b) Ghana

Kwame Nkrumah ruled Ghana from independence in 1957 until his removal by the army in 1966.

(i) *His achievements* were impressive to begin with. He was a socialist in outlook and wanted his people to enjoy a higher standard of living that would come from efficient organisation and industrialisation. Production of cocoa (Ghana's main export) doubled, forestry, fishing and cattle-breeding expanded and the country's modest deposits of gold and bauxite were more effectively exploited. The building of a dam on the Volta River (begun 1961) provided water for irrigation and hydro-electric power, producing enough electricity for the towns as well as for a new aluminium smelting plant. Government money was provided for village projects in which local people built roads and schools. Nkrumah also gained prestige internationally: he strongly supported the pan-African movement, believing that only through a federation of the whole continent could African power make itself felt. As a start an economic union was formed with Guinea and Mali, though nothing much came of it. He supported the Organisation of African Unity (set up 1963) and usually played a responsible role in world affairs, remaining in the commonwealth while at the same time forging links with the USSR and China.

(ii) *Why was Nkrumah overthrown?* He had tried to introduce industrialisation too quickly and had borrowed vast amounts of capital from abroad, hoping to balance the budget from increased exports. Unfortunately Ghana was still uncomfortably dependent on cocoa exports and a steep fall in the world price of cocoa left her with a huge balance of payments deficit. There was criticism that too much money was being wasted on unnecessary projects like the 10-mile stretch of motorway from Accra (the capital) to Tema. Probably the most important reason was that Nkrumah gradually began to abandon parliamentary government in favour of a one-party state and personal dictatorship. He justified this on the grounds that the opposition parties, which were based on tribal differences, were not constructive and merely wanted more power in their own areas; they had no experience of working a parliamentary system and as Nkrumah himself wrote: 'Even a system based on a democratic constitution may need backing up in the period following independence by emergency measures of a totalitarian kind.' From 1959 opponents could be deported or imprisoned for up to five years without trial. Even the respected opposition leader, J. B. Danqua, was arrested in 1961 and died in prison. In 1964 all parties except his own were banned, and even within his own party no criticism was allowed. He began to build up the image of himself as the 'father of the nation'. Slogans such as 'Nkrumah is our Messiah, Nkrumah never dies' were circulated and numerous statues of the saviour were erected. This struck many people as absurd but again Nkrumah justified it, claiming that the population could identify itself better with a single personality as leader than with vague notions of the state. All this, plus the fact that he was believed to have amassed a personal fortune through corruption, was too much for the army who seized control when Nkrumah was on a visit to China.

The military government promised a return to democracy as soon as a new constitution could be drawn up, complete with safeguards against a return to dictatorship. The constitution was ready in 1969 and the elections returned Dr Kofi Busia, leader of the Progressive Party, as the new Prime Minister (October 1969).

(iii)   *Kofi Busia* lasted only until January 1972 when he too was overthrown by the army. An academic who had studied economics at Oxford, Busia illustrates perfectly the difficulties of democratically elected politicians in the African situation. In power in the first place only by permission of the army, he had to produce quick results. Yet the problems were enormous – rising unemployment, rising prices and massive debts to be repaid. Canada and the USA were prepared to wait for repayment but other countries, including Britain, were not so sympathetic. Busia, who had a reputation for honesty, tried genuinely to keep up payments, but these were using up about 40 per cent of Ghana's export profits. In 1971 imports were limited and the currency devalued by nearly 50 per cent. Busia was hampered by the tribal squabbles which re-emerged under the free democracy and the economic situation deteriorated so rapidly that in January 1972 he was evicted, without resistance, by Colonel Ignatius Acheampong who headed a military government until July 1978. As Ghana continued to flounder amid her economic problems, Acheampong was himself removed from power by General Fred Akuffo, for alleged corruption. In June 1979 a group of junior officers led by J. J. Rawlings (of mixed Ghanaian–Scottish parentage) seized power on the grounds that corrupt soliders and politicians needed to be weeded out before a return to democracy. They launched what was described as a 'house-cleaning' exercise in which Acheampong and Akuffo were executed after secret trials. In July elections were held as a result of which Rawlings returned Ghana to civilian rule with Dr Limann as President (September 1979). However, it is impossible to feel optimistic about Ghana's future: President Limann described the plight of his country as one of 'virtual bankruptcy', and in February 1980 there was serious labour unrest and strikes in protest at low wages and soaring food prices.

(c) Nigeria

Superficially Nigeria, which gained independence in 1960, seemed to have advantages over Ghana; it was potentially a wealthy state, extensive oil resources having been discovered in the eastern coastal area. The Prime Minister was the capable and moderate Sir Abubakar Tafawa Balewa assisted by the veteran nationalist leader Azikiwe, who was made President when Nigeria became a republic in 1963. However, in 1966 the government was overthrown by a military coup and the following year civil war broke out which lasted until 1970.

(i) *What caused the civil war*? A combination of problems of the type mentioned in Section 23.5(a) led to the outbreak. Nigeria's tribal differences were more serious than Ghana's, and although the constitution was a federal one in which each of the three regions (north, east and west) had its own local government, the regions felt that the central government in Lagos did not safeguard their interests sufficiently. Balewa came from the north where the Hausa and Fulani tribes were powerful, and the Yorubas of the west and Ibos of the east were constantly complaining about northern domination, even though Azikiwe was an Ibo. To make matters worse there was an economic recession. By 1964 prices had risen 15 per cent, unemployment was rising and wages were, on average, well below what had been calculated as the minimum living wage. Criticism of the government mounted and Balewa replied by arresting Chief Awolowo, Prime Minister of the western region, which for a time seemed likely to break away from the federation. The central government was also accused of corruption after blatantly trying to 'fix' the election results of 1964. In January 1966 there as a military coup carried out by mainly Ibo officers, in which Balewa and other politicians were killed. After this the situation deteriorated steadily: in the north there were savage massacres of Ibos who had moved into the region for better jobs and the new leader, General Ironsi, himself an Ibo, was murdered by northern soldiers. When a northerner, Colonel Yakubu Gowon, emerged supreme, almost all the Ibos fled from other parts of Nigeria back to the east whose leader Colonel Ojukwu announced that the eastern region had seceded from Nigeria to become the independent state of Biafra (May 1967). Gowon launched what he described as a 'short surgical police action' to bring the east back to Nigeria.

(ii) *The civil war*. It took more than a short police action as the Biafrans fought back vigorously. It was a bitter and terrible war in which Biafra lost more civilians from disease and starvation than troops killed in the fighting. Neither the United Nations nor the Commonwealth was able to mediate, and the Biafrans hung on to the bitter end as Nigerian troops closed in on all sides; the final surrender came in January 1970. Nigerian unity had been preserved.

(iii) *Recovery after the war* was remarkably swift. There were pressing problems: famine in Biafra, inter-tribal bitterness, unemployment and economic resources strained by the war. Gowon showed considerable statesmanship in this difficut situation: he made every effort to reconcile the Ibos and persuaded them to return to their jobs in other parts of the country; he introduced a new federal system of 12 states, later increased to 19, to give more recognition of local tribal differences. Nigeria was able to take advantage of rising illus 23.1 *Biafra – a fifteen-year-old victim of war and famine*

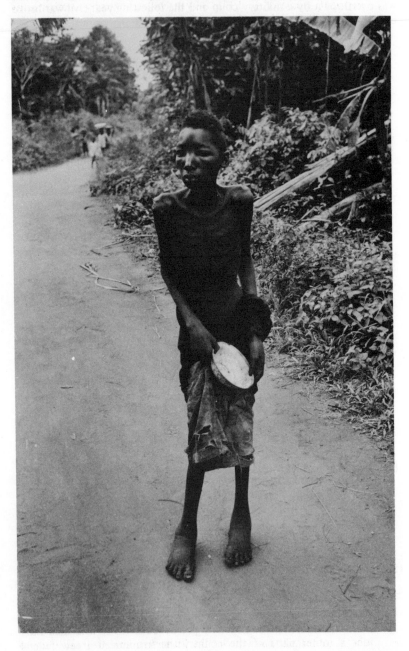

oil prices in the mid-1970s which gave her a healthy balance of payments position. In 1975 Gowan was removed by another army group, which probably he intended to return the country to civilian rule too early. Nigeria continued to prosper and the army kept its promise of a return to democratic government in 1979. Elections were held as a result of which President Shagari became head of a civilian government. With Nigeria's oil much in demand abroad, prosperity seemed assured and prospects for a stable government bright. She is by far the strongest of the Commonwealth African states both militarily and in size of population.

Of the new states of East and Central Africa, Uganda followed the pattern of Ghana and Nigeria: President Milton Obote was overthrown by General Idi Amin (1971) who was himself removed after a brutal dictatorship (1979). In 1980 the country was still in a state of chaos, no stable system having emerged. However, the other states managed to avoid such upheavals, mainly because of the skill of their respective leaders.

(d) Kenya

Jomo Kenyatta ruled undisturbed from 1963 until his death in 1978 when his Vice-President, Daniel arap Moi, took over smoothly.

(i) *Problems*. There were the usual tribal rivalries: Kenyatta himself came from the largest tribe, the Kikuyus, while other influential ones were Luos, Massais and Hamitics. There were also racial difficulties: out of a population of 10 million, 200,000 were Asians, about 50,000 British and 30,000 Arabs, and non-Africans held most of the dominant positions in the professions and commerce: Kenyatta wanted Africans to fill these jobs. The economy was too dependent on exports of tea and coffee and there was hardly any industry and very few resources.

(ii) *Kenyatta's achievements* were considerable in spite of such an unpromising situation. In the first decade of independence he ruled firmly and decisively while managing to avoid the sort of semi-dictatorship adopted by Nkrumah in Ghana. He handled the tribal rivalries skilfully, although there was a crisis in 1969 when his Vice-President Tom Mboya, a Luo, was assassinated in Nairobi by a Kikuyu. Luo tribesmen rampaged through the city smashing up cars and shops in revenge, but violence subsided after the assassin was arrested and hanged. He worked towards *Africanisation* (allowing Africans equal opportunities with other races to achieve top positions) but at the same time aimed for a multi-racial society in which Asians and other non-Africans were welcome provided they took Kenyan citizenship. Pressure was brought to bear on those, particularly Asians, who refused and in 1968 over 60,000 of them fled from Kenya to Britain, causing the British government to limit entry to about 5,000 Asians a year. After that Kenyatta relaxed the pressure and allowed Asians to leave gradually under a quota system; over 100,000 Asians remained after taking Kenyan citizenship.

Economic problems were tackled by carefully worked out Five Year Plans, the first three of which (1964–79) showed promising results. Tea and coffee output increased and industries such as paper manufacturing and soda production for making glass expanded rapidly. Cotton production increased from 30,000 bales in 1977 to 70,000 in 1979. Foreign investment by governments and firms helped: British Leyland, for example, became a partner in a vehicle assembly plant at Thika. As a result the economy was generally healthy with especially good years in 1976 and 1977 when tea and coffee prices reached record heights.

(iii) *Criticisms can be made of Kenyatta*, however. In the mid-seventies there was a distinct drift towards a one-party state, Kenyatta's party, the Kenya African National Union (KANU). There was less tolerance of criticism: in 1975 a prominent Kikuyu politician, Josiah Kariuki, was found dead in the bush shortly after condemning corrupt 'get-rich-quick' politicians (in which he included Kenyatta). In spite of the economic boom, too much of the profits went to foreign share-holders; and though many African politicians and businessmen made ample profits, the mass of the population felt no benefit whatsoever; it made little difference to them whether Kenya was a British colony or an independent state run by Africans.

(iv) *Daniel arap Moi* was unfortunate in that he became President (August 1978) just as the economic boom ended, and there was a sharp fall in the world prices of coffee and tea, which still accounted for 60 per cent of Kenya's exports. The value of exports fell by 25 per cent causing an unfavourable balance of payments, and there was a serious food shortage and rocketing prices after a poor harvest. This brought to light a glaring example of inefficiency and corruption among government officials: it was discovered in March 1980 that the maize reserve of two million bags had vanished and it emerged that certain officials had declared the reserves unfit for human consumption and allowed them to be bought at bargain prices by merchants who resold them abroad at a handsome profit. President Moi, a former headmaster with a reputation for honesty, came to power on a wave of goodwill as he freed many political prisoners and promised reform, especially a war on corruption. The fourth Five Year Plan was launched in 1979 with the aim of alleviating poverty; in the early 1980s the goodwill still seemed to be there, but so too were the problems.

(e) Tanzania

Tanganyika became independent in 1961 and was joined in 1964 by the island of Zanzibar to form Tanzania. It was ruled continuously by *Dr Julius Nyerere*, leader of the Tanzanian African Nationalist Union (TANU), who had to deal with formidable problems: Tanzania was arguably the poorest state in the whole of Africa, with very little industry, few mineral resources and a heavy dependence on coffee production; in addition there were the usual tribal and racial problems plus, later, Tanzania's expensive involvement in military operations to oust President Amin of Uganda.

(i) *Nyerere's approach and achievements.* His approach was different from that of any other African ruler. He began conventionally enough by expanding the economy: during the first ten years of independence, production of coffee and cotton doubled and sugar production trebled, while health services and education expanded. But Nyerere was not happy that Tanzania seemed to be developing along the same lines as Kenya, with an ever-widening gulf between the wealthy élite and the resentful masses. His proposed solution to the problem was set out in a remarkable document known as *the Arusha Declaration* published in 1967: the country must be run on socialist lines. All human beings should be treated as equal; the state must have effective control over the means of production and must intervene in economic life to make sure that people were not exploited by other groups, and that poverty, ignorance and disease were eliminated; there must be no great accumulations of wealth or society would no longer be classless; bribery and corruption must be eliminated. According to Nyerere, Tanzania was at war and the enemy was poverty and oppression; the way to victory was not through money and foreign aid but through hard work and self-reliance; the first priority was to improve agriculture so that the country could be self-sufficient in food production.

Nyerere strove hard to put these aims into practice: all important enterprises, including those owned by foreigners, were nationalised; five-year development plans were introduced. Village projects were encouraged and given aid by the government; these involved *ujamaa* ('familyhood' or self-help): families in each village pooled resources and farmed collectively using more modern techniques. Foreign loans and investments as well as imports were reduced to a minimum to avoid running into debt. Politically Nyerere's brand of socialism meant a one-party state run by TANU, but elections were still held. It seemed that some elements of genuine democracy existed since voters in each constituency had a choice of two TANU candidates and every election resulted in a large proportion of MPs losing their seats. Nyerere himself provided dignified leadership and with his simple life style and complete indifference to wealth he set the perfect example for the party and the country to follow. The enterprise was a fascinating experiment which tried to combine socialist direction from the centre with the African traditions of local decision making; it tried to provide an alternative to western capitalist society with its pursuit of profit, which most other African states seemed to be copying.

(ii) *Success or failure?* Despite Nyerere's achievements, it was still not clear, as Tanzania moved into the 1980s, whether the experiment would be a lasting success. Many western observers were quick to point out the system's failings: it was difficult to prevent TANU from developing into a privileged élite; corruption crept in because many officials were not as high-minded as Nyerere himself; only a very small percentage of the villages became genuinely collective; factory workers went on strike, claiming that the spirit of the Arusha declaration was being ignored, since they were not treated equally with the management. 'Will he ever admit', asked Xan Smiley (*Observer* article, 10 August 1980), 'that his plans, worth a noble attempt at implementing 15 years ago, have proven fundamentally impractical?' On the other hand it has to be remembered that Nyerere's relations with Britain were often strained: he supported Biafra while Britain sided with Nigeria in the civil war, and relations were actually broken off when Nyerere took a firm stand against the continuation of white rule in Rhodesia (see Section 24.2); consequently many Europeans who pronounced on Tanzanian affairs were less than sympathetic. What is certain, however, is that from the end of 1978 Tanzania was in economic difficulties because of the fall in world prices of coffee and tea (her main exports), rising oil prices (which used up almost half of her earnings from exports), poor harvests and the expenses of the war against Amin (at least £1,000 million). In August 1980 the International Monetary Fund (IMF) agreed to a loan of £100 million, though only on its own terms; the following October Nyerere was re-elected unopposed for a further five-year term as President. Time will tell whether his new sort of society is impractical or whether its full realisation has merely been delayed by a set of unfortunate circumstances.

(f) Zambia

Formerly Northern Rhodesia, Zambia, like Tanzania, was fortunate in having an outstanding and dedicated President, Dr Kenneth Kaunda. The son of a Methodist minister, he cared deeply about his people, was aware of their problems and genuinely tried to build a successful multi-racial society in Zambia. Amid a mass of complex problems he was a major force for good. *What were the problems and how successfully did Kaunda deal with them?*

(i) *Tribal rivalry* was more serious than in Tanzania; there were over 70 different tribes and Kaunda, himself a Nyanja, tried to include a wide tribal representation in his government. However the Bembas of the north and the Lozis of the north-west wanted to break away, even though Kaunda appointed Simon Kapwepwe, a Bemba, as his Vice-President. In the late 1960s it became increasingly difficult for Kaunda to get his policies accepted, and when a disagreement arose between Kaunda and Kapwepwe, who wanted a harder line towards South Africa (see Section 24.3), the President felt compelled to make a stand, if any progress at all was to be achieved. By 1973 he had turned Zambia into a one-party state (the United National Independence Party), and although he was criticised for this outside Zambia, it seemed the only way to prevent the country disintegrating into tribal groups.

(ii) *There were serious racial problems* as thousands of whites stayed on after independence; there were extreme racialists of all colours. Kaunda managed to overcome the extremists with his humane and sensible approach and to make a multi-racial society work. So great was his prestige that even white South Africans working in the copper mines were prepared to risk staying on, provided Kaunda remained in power.

(iii) *Zambia had the misfortune to border onto Southern Rhodesia* which illegally declared itself independent of Britain in 1965 (see Section 24.2). Zambia found herself caught up in the front line of the struggle to bring down the Smith regime, and suffered serious inconvenience as a result. When Britain helped by the United Nations imposed economic sanctions on Rhodesia, Zambia, which depended on Rhodesian railways for carrying her oil supplies and her copper exports, was probably worse hit than Rhodesia. The irony of it was that while Zambia genuinely tried to maintain sanctions, to her own detriment, British and French companies as well as those of many other nationalities, which considered profit more important, ignored them and Rhodesia continued to obtain oil supplies and to sell her products abroad. In desperation Zambia and Tanzania turned to China who agreed to build the ZamTan Railway; started in 1971 this provided a vital new trade link to the coast through Tanzania.

When it became clear that sanctions were ineffective, black African nationalists, determined to free Zimbabwe (the African name for Rhodesia) from white control, began a guerrilla campaign operating from bases in Zambia and Mozambique (after 1975 when Mozambique became independent from Portugal). The Smith government retaliated by bombing guerrilla bases in Zambia. A further complication was that other black African states expected Zambia to play a more active role against Rhodesia, but Kaunda was anxious to avoid all-out war; he knew that Zambia could not afford such extravagance, and apart from that Zambia and Rhodesia shared the Kariba Dam whose generating stations were all on the Rhodesian side; Kaunda dared not risk losing vital electricity supplies. It was the end of a major headache when the Rhodesian problem was apparently solved early in 1980.

(iv) Zambia's economy seemed reasonably healthy for the first few years after independence: she had more of an industrial base than Tanzania, having extensive copper resources which were mined and exported. Tobacco and cotton were grown and there was a small textile industry. The weakness was that copper made up 90 per cent of Zambia's exports; in 1971 a sudden fall in the world price of copper threw her economy into disarray – she had an unfavourable balance of payments for the first time since independence. Although prices fluctuated after that, they never fully recovered, and Zambia, with her weak bargaining position, tended to get lower prices from wealthy industrial nations than other copper producers did. At the same time certain foreign companies took advantage of Zambia (and of other African states as well) by charging over-inflated prices for vital goods which could not be obtained elsewhere (spares for tractors for example). For the average Zambian this situation meant a fall in real wages and growing discontent.

As Zambia celebrated the sixteenth anniversary of independence (October 1980), President Kaunda was still in power. He had steered his country skilfully through tribal, racial and foreign problems, but had still to find a solution to the economic problems: the need for self-sufficiency in food production; two poor maize harvests led to severe food shortages which had to be made good by costly imports; and the need to diversify industrial production in order to reduce Zambian dependence on copper and so earn valuable foreign exchange. Food shortages and rising prices could no longer be blamed on the Rhodesian war and growing discontent led to strikes and a resurgence of tribal rivalry; in October 1980 several hundred prominent citizens, including many Bembas, were suddenly arrested. It was not clear whether the government had forestalled a Bemba coup or was trying to divert attention away from the problems, but whichever was the case it seemed likely that President Kaunda's rule would face a growing challenge unless the economic situation improved.

QUESTIONS

1. Outline the main social, economic, political and foreign problems facing India *or* Pakistan since independence.
2. Describe the foreign policy of India since independence until 1974.
3. Explain the issues over which conflict has occurred since 1947 between India and Pakistan and show the outcome of each of these conflicts.
4. Outline the problems in the Indian subcontinent after 1947 which faced Jawaharlal Nehru and Indira Gandhi. Estimate the success which each achieved in dealing with them.
5. Outline the history of Pakistan since the death of Liaquat Ali Khan (1951). Describe and explain the emergence of an independent Bangladesh in 1971.
6. Give an account of the events which led to the establishment of the Federation of Malaysia (1963). Describe and explain (a) the confrontation with Indonesia and (b) Singapore's withdrawal from the Federation in 1965.

7. What problems have faced Malaysia since independence and how successfully have they been dealt with?

8. Outline the history of *one* of the following countries since independence: Ghana, Nigeria, Kenya, Tanzania, Zambia.

9. What were the main problems facing the emerging African nations? Choose any one African nation which has achieved independence since 1957 and show how far it has succeeded in overcoming its problems.

10. Why have so many African states adopted a one-party system of government? With reference to at least *two* states show (a) benefits and (b) the price of one-party government to Africa.

11. Describe the achievements and indicate the importance to his country of *three* of the following: Nkrumah (Ghana), Kenyatta (Kenya), Nyerere (Tanzania), Kaunda (Zambia).

CHAPTER 24

PROBLEMS IN AFRICA

SUMMARY OF EVENTS

Three special problems in Africa were those of the former Belgian Congo, Rhodesia and South Africa. *The Congo*, which became independent in 1960, was immediately ravaged by a civil war which lasted until 1963. This turned out to be a special case because the United Nations became deeply involved, mounting one of its largest and most successful operations: the unity of the new state was preserved, though affairs remained chaotic until 1968. The country changed its name to Zaire in 1971. In 1977 problems flared up again and though the government gradually restored order, unity seemed fragile in the early 1980s.

Rhodesia provided a special case in that it was the only British dependency in which the resident white settlers carried their resistance to black rule to extreme lengths. The problem became serious in 1965 when the white government, ignoring British pressure to allow black Africans more say in the running of the country, illegally declared Rhodesia independent of Britain. After economic sanctions had failed to bring down the illegal white government, pressure from black African states built up and a guerrilla campaign against Rhodesia escalated. In 1979 when it seemed that the whole country might be engulfed in bloodshed, a solution was found: the whites gave way, free elections were held, and power was handed over, relatively peacefully to the black Africans. Rhodesia became legally independent as Zimbabwe.

South Africa is very much a special case: it remains the last bastion of white rule on the continent of Africa, and the white minority is determined to hold out to the bitter end against black nationalism. In 1948 the government of South Africa, still a British dominion, alarmed at the upsurge of black nationalism, introduced the policy known as *apartheid* – separated development or segregation for the different races in South Africa. This was designed to bolster up white supremacy and was widely condemned outside the country. Opposition at the 1961 Commonwealth Conference was so bitter that South Africa left the commonwealth, became an independent republic, and has since gone its own way, taking little notice of world opinion.

24.1 THE CONGO

(a) Why and how did civil war develop?

(i) The Belgian government made little attempt to prepare the Africans for independence. African nationalism seemed much less advanced in the Congo than elsewhere and the Belgians were taken by surprise when there was widespread rioting in the capital, Leopoldville, in January 1959. In fact the rioting was as much in protest against unemployment caused by a recent recession as it was against Belgian rule, but the Belgians agreed to allow independence in June 1960. This was, to say the least, ill advised. Unlike most other African states, there was no experienced group of Africans to which power could be handed over. The Congolese had not been educated for professional jobs, very few had received any higher education and no political parties had been allowed. There was just over a year to make up the deficiencies, but this was not enough.

(ii) There were about 150 different tribes which would have made the Congo difficult to hold together even with experienced administrators. Violent and chaotic elections were held in which the Congolese National Movement (MNC) led by a former post office clerk, Patrice Lumumba, emerged as the dominant party, but there were over 50 different groups. Agreement of any sort was going to be difficult; nevertheless the Belgians handed power over to a coalition government with Lumumba as Prime Minister, and Joseph Kasavubu, the leader of another group, as President.

(iii) A mutiny broke out in the Congolese army (July 1960) only a few days after independence. This was in protest against the fact that all officers were Belgians whereas the Africans expected instant promotion. Lumumba was deprived of the means of keeping law and order and tribal violence began to spread.

(iv) The south-eastern province of Katanga which had rich copper deposits, was encouraged by the Belgian company (Union Minière) which still controlled the copper-mining industry, to declare itself independent under Moise Tshombe. This was the wealthiest part of the Congo which the new state could not afford to lose; Lumumba, unable to rely on his mutinous army, appealed to the United Nations to help him preserve Congolese unity and a 3,000 strong peace-keeping force soon arrived.

(b) The civil war and UN involvement

Lumumba wanted to use UN troops to force Katanga back into the Congo, but the situation was complex: many Belgians preferred an independent Katanga which would be easier for them to influence; with this in mind the UN Secretary-General, Dag Hammarskjöld, refused to allow a UN attack on Katanga, though at the same time he refused to recognise Katangese independence. In disgust Lumumba appealed for help to the Russians, but this horrified Kasavubu who, encouraged by the

Americans and Belgians, had Lumumba arrested (he was later murdered). As the chaos continued, Hammarskjöld realised that more decisive UN action was needed and, although he was killed in an air crash while flying to Katanga to see Tshombe, his successor U Thant followed the same line. By mid-1961 there were 20,000 UN troops in the Congo; in September they invaded Katanga and in December 1962 the province admitted failure and ended its secession, while Tshombe went into exile. Though successful, UN operations had been expensive and within a few months all their troops were withdrawn. Tribal rivalries aggravated by unemployment caused disorders to break out again almost immediately and calm was not restored until 1965 when General Joseph Mobutu of the Congolese army, using white mercenaries and backed by the USA and Belgium, crushed all resistance and took over the government himself.

(c) Mobutu in power

It was probably inevitable that if the country were to stay united, a strong authoritarian government was required; this Mobutu provided. There was a gradual improvement in conditions as the Congolese gained experience of administration, and the economy began to look healthier after most of the European-owned mines were nationalised. However, in the late 1970s there were more troubles. In 1977 Katanga (now known as Shaba) was invaded by troops from Angola apparently encouraged by the Angolan government which resented Mobutu's earlier intervention in her affairs (see Section 22.4), and by the USSR which resented American support for Mobutu. Having survived that problem, Zaire found herself in economic difficulties mainly because of declining world copper prices and drought which made expensive food imports necessary. Mobutu came under increasing criticism outside Zaire for his authoritarian style of government and his huge personal fortune; in May 1980 Amnesty International claimed that at least a thousand political prisoners were being held without trial and that several hundred had died from torture or starvation during 1978-9.

24.2 RHODESIA

(a) Why did the whites make a unilateral declaration of independence?

(i) The problem sprang from the determination of the white Rhodesians never to surrender control of the country to black African rule. There were 4 million Africans, just over 200,000 whites and about 20,000 Asians, yet even under the relatively progressive constitution introduced by Sir Edgar Whitehead's government in 1961, Black voters were allowed to chose only 15 out of the 65 members of parliament. When the Africans protested that the new constitution was unfairly weighted, Whitehead banned the African National Democratic Party; when one of the main African leaders, Joshua Nkomo, began another party, the Zimbabwe African People's Union (ZAPU), that too was banned.

(ii) The right-wing Rhodesian Front Party won the elections of December 1962 and Winston Field, a tobacco farmer, became Prime Minister. The Front was strongly racialist and felt that Whitehead had been too sympathetic towards the blacks. When the Central African Federation broke up in December 1963 (see Section 22.3(c)) and it became clear that Zambia and Malawi would soon be granted independence, Field assumed that Rhodesia would receive the same treatment and put in a formal request for independence. This was refused by the British Conservative government: independence would be granted only if the constitution were changed to allow Africans at least a third of the seats, which would enable them to prevent changes in the constitution after independence which might exclude them from government altogether. Field was prepared to go on negotiating, but many whites were beginning to want something more.

(iii) The more aggressive Ian Smith took over as Prime Minister from Field (April 1964). At first he continued to negotiate but made it plain that the Rhodesian Front would offer no concessions. He argued that continued white rule was essential in view of the problems being faced by the new black governments in other African states, particularly the Congo, and because the Zimbabwe nationalists were divided: a new party had been formed, the Reverend Ndabaningi Sithole's Zimbabwe African National Union (ZANU), which seemed to be involved in constant gang warfare with the rival ZAPU.

(iv) Harold Wilson, the new British Labour Prime Minister, continued to refuse independence. The British attitude was: no independence without a change in the constitution to prepare the way for rule by the black majority. Smith's attitude was: no change in the constitution; white rule must continue. Since no compromise seemed possible, Smith unilaterally declared Rhodesia independent (meaning without approval from Britain, the other party to the dispute). UDI, as it became known, took place on 11 November 1965.

(b) Outside reaction to UDI

(i) *Britain* immediately condemned UDI as an act of rebellion, but, much to the disappointment of the black African states, decided not to use force against the illegal Smith government. It was hoped to bring the country to its knees by economic sanctions and Britain stopped buying tobacco and sugar from Rhodesia.

(ii) *The United Nations* also condemned the Rhodesian action and called on all member states to place a complete trade embargo on the country.

(iii) *South Africa*, also ruled by a white minority government, and *Portugal,* which still owned neighbouring Mozambique, were sympathetic to Rhodesia's plight and refused to obey the Security Council resolution so that Rhodesian trade was able to continue through these territories. Many other countries, while publicly condemning UDI, privately evaded the embargo: the USA, for example, bought Rhodesian chrome because it was the cheapest available. Companies and business-men in many countries, including British oil companies, continued to break sanctions, and although the Rhodesian economy suffered to some extent, it was not serious enough to topple the Smith regime.

(iv) *The commonwealth* was seriously shaken: Ghana and Nigeria wanted Britain to use force and offered to supply troops. Zambia and Tanzania hoped that economic sanctions would suffice and their relations with Britain became extremely cool when it seemed that she was deliberately soft-pedalling sanctions, especially as Zambia was suffer-ing more from them than Rhodesia. When Wilson twice met Smith (aboard HMS *Tiger* in 1966 and HMS *Fearless* in 1968) to put new proposals, there was a howl of protest that he was about to betray the black Rhodesians. Perhaps fortunately for the future of the commonwealth, Smith rejected both sets of proposals, but the African commonwealth members remained deeply distrustful of Britain's intentions. When the Smith government began to discriminate against the blacks even more, especially under the new constitution of 1970, the Zambian government allowed guerrillas to make raids over the border into Rhodesia.

(c) Rhodesia under the Smith regime

African rights were gradually whittled away until the blacks were suffering similar treatment to that experienced by blacks in South Africa under the system of apartheid (see next section). There was a strict press censor-ship, people could be arrested and imprisoned without trial and almost half the land was reserved for whites, although there were about 18 times more blacks than whites. In 1970 Rhodesia declared itself a republic and introduced a new constitution under which whites and non-whites were on separate voting lists, voting only for MPs of their own colour; there was a built-in guarantee that white MPs would always be in a large majority. Extra land was allocated to the whites and any Africans who happened to be living in those areas were forcibly removed. Black schools were down-graded so that Africans would have little chance of reaching the educational level enjoyed by whites. In spite of world-wide criticism and some reduction in exports because of sanctions the whites remained unmoved until 1976, but early that year the first signs appeared that they would have to compromise.

(d) Why did the whites give way?

(i) Mozambique's independence from Portugal (June 1975) was a serious blow to Rhodesia. The new President Machel applied economic sanctions and allowed Zimbabwean guerrillas to operate from Mozam-bique. Thousands of black guerrillas were soon active in Rhodesia, straining the white security forces to their limits and forcing Smith to hire foreign mercenaries.

(ii) The South Africans became less inclined to support Rhodesia after their invasion of Angola (October 1975), in support of the FNLA which was receiving help from the USSR and Cuba (see Section 22.4), had been called off on American orders.

(iii) The USA, which had also backed the FNLA, feared that the USSR and Cuba might become involved in Rhodesia unless some compromise could be found; together with South Africa, she urged Smith to make some concessions to the blacks before it was too late.

(e) The end of white rule

Towards the end of 1976 Smith admitted that black majority rule would have to come within a few years, but he was determined to try every trick he knew to delay it as long as possible. Though a conference to consider possible solutions met at Geneva, it was impossible to pin Smith down to a definite commitment. He was able to present the divisions between the Zimbabwean nationalist leaders as his excuse for the lack of progress. This was a genuine problem: ZAPU, the party of the veteran nationalist Joshua Nkomo, and ZANU, Sithole's party, seemed to be bitter enemies; in addition there was Bishop Abel Muzorewa's United African National Council (UANC), as well as the supporters of Robert Mugabe, leader of the guerrilla wing of ZANU. However in 1978, with the guerrilla war escalating, Smith at last began concessions, which were soon to lead to the transference of power to the blacks. This happened in two stages:

(i) Smith introduced his own scheme which allowed blacks to vote on equal terms. A general election was held in April 1979 for a new parliament in which 72 of the 100 MPs were to be black. Bishop Muzorewa's party won 51 seats, and Smith stepped down for Muzorewa to become Prime Minister. However, this was not a success: ZAPU decided not to fight the election and both Britain and the USA felt that any viable settlement must include Nkomo and Mugabe; Sithole, whose party had won only 12 seats, claimed that the whites had rigged the elections so that the more amenable Muzorewa would win. Both the UN and the Organisation of African Unity (OAU) condemned the elections as invalid. The guerrilla war continued and by November 1979 the Patriotic Front (the two main guerrilla groups led by Nkomo and Mugabe) had 15,000 troops in Rhodesia fighting against the Muzorewa government. Smith was forced to concede that his scheme had failed.

(ii) *The Lancaster House Conference* (September–December 1979) convened by Britain and held in London, involved representatives from all parties including the Patriotic Front. After skilful manoeuvring by Lord Carrington, the British Foreign Secretary, the conference agreed on a constitution for the new republic of Zimbabwe, arrangements for elections and an end to the guerrilla war. Muzorewa agreed to step down as Prime Minister and Lord Soames was to be governor during the transitional period until elections were held. These were contested by all parties and Mugabe's ZANU won a sweeping victory taking 57 out of the 80 seats reserved for Africans in the 100-seat parliament. Nkomo's ZAPU won 27 while Muzorewa's UANC was reduced to 3 seats. With a comfortable overall majority Mugabe, a self-proclaimed Marxist, became Prime Minister and Zimbabwe became officially an independent republic (April 1980). The transference to black majority rule was welcomed by all African and commonwealth leaders as a triumph for common sense and moderation, though some British Conservatives accused the British government of betraying Muzorewa and allowing Zimbabwe to fall to Marxism. During the first year of independence, the main danger was that the long tribal hatred between ZANU and ZAPU, shelved temporarily during the fight against Smith, might flare up into civil war.

24.3 SOUTH AFRICA

(a) The Union of South Africa, a British dominion, dated from 1910 when the two former Boer republics, Transvaal and Orange Free State, joined Cape Colony and Natal, following the Boer War (1899–1902). Since then power has remained firmly in the hands of the whites, though they formed less than 20 per cent of the population. In 1974 there were almost 18 million black Africans, known as Bantus, 2.3 million Coloureds, 700,000 Asians and 4.2 million whites. Roughly two-thirds of the whites were of Dutch (Boer) origin and known as Afrikaaners; the rest were of British origin. With the granting of independence to India and Pakistan in 1947, white South Africans became alarmed at the growing racial equality within the commonwealth and were determined to preserve their supremacy. Most of the whites were against racial equality but the most extreme were the Afrikaaner Nationalists led by Dr Malan, who claimed that the whites were a master race and that non-whites were inferior beings. The Dutch Reformed Church (the official state church) supported this view, though the Christian Church in general believes in racial equality. The Nationalists won the 1948 elections with promises to rescue the whites from the 'black menace'; Malan's policy was apartheid.

(b) Apartheid in operation

Malan (Prime Minister 1948–54) aimed to separate or segregate the different races in order to preserve the racial purity of the whites and thus their supremacy. Later Prime Ministers, Strijdom (1954–8), Verwoerd (1958–66), and Vorster (1966–78) continued Malan's policy and developed it further. There had been some segregation before 1948; for example Africans were forbidden to buy land outside special reserve areas; but Malan's apartheid was much more systematic.

(i) There was complete separation of blacks and whites as far as possible at all levels. In country areas blacks live in special reserves; in urban areas they have separate townships at suitable distances from white residential areas. Whole communities of Africans were uprooted and 're-grouped' in the reserves to make separation as complete as possible. There are separate buses, coaches, trains, park benches, cafés, toilets, shops, hospitals, beaches, sports and even churches. Black children are educated in separate schools and receive a much inferior education. In fact complete separation was impossible because over half the non-whites work in white-owned industries and other concerns; the economy would collapse if all non-whites were moved to the reserves.

(ii) Every person was given a racial classification and an identity card; strict pass laws demand that non-whites remain in their reserves and townships except when going to work; otherwise movement is forbidden without police permission.

(iii) Marriage and sexual relations between whites and non-whites were forbidden, in order to preserve the purity of the white race; police spied shamelessly on anybody suspected of breaking the rules. Verwoerd introduced two new refinements, both in 1959:

(iv) The Bantu Self-Government Act set up seven regions called Bantustans, based on the original African reserves. It was claimed that they would eventually proceed to self-government; in 1976 it was announced that the first Bantustan, the Transkei, had become 'independent' with Chief Mantanzima as Prime Minister. However, the outside world dismissed this with contempt since Pretoria (the capital of South Africa) still controlled the Transkei's economy and foreign affairs. The whole policy was criticised because the Bantustan areas cover only about 13 per cent of the total area of the country and into these relatively small areas are crammed over 8 million blacks; vastly overcrowded and unable to support adequately the native populations, they became little more than rural slums. The government continued its policy undeterred and by 1970 two more African 'homelands', Bophuthatswana and Venda, had received 'independence'.

(v) Africans lost all political rights and their representation in parliament (by white MPs) was abolished.

(c) Opposition to apartheid

(i) *Inside South Africa* opposition was difficult. Anyone who objected, including whites, or broke the apartheid laws was accused of being a communist and was severely punished under the Suppression of Communism Act. Africans were forbidden to strike and their political party, the African National Congress, was helpless. In spite of this, *Chief Albert Luthuli*, the Congress leader, protested by stopping work on certain days and in 1952 attempted a systematic breach of the laws by entering shops and other places reserved for whites. Over 8,000 blacks were arrested and many were flogged; Luthuli was deprived of his chieftaincy and imprisoned for a time, and the campaign was called off. Later Luthuli organised other protests including the 1957 bus boycott: instead of paying a fare increase on the bus route from their township to Johannesburg ten miles away, thousands of Africans walked to work and back for three months until fares were reduced. Protests reached a climax in 1960 when a large demonstration against the pass laws took place at *Sharpeville,* an African township near Johannesburg. Police fired on the crowd, killing 67 Africans and wounding many more. After this hundreds of Africans were arrested, including Luthuli, and Congress was banned. It was much to the credit of Luthuli and his non-violent methods that the Africans behaved with surprising restraint in the face of such brutal treatment. He was awarded the Nobel Peace Prize in 1961 after publishing his moving autobiography *Let My People Go,* but was killed in 1967; the authorities claimed that he had deliberately stepped in front of a train.

Discontent swelled again in the 1970s because wages of Africans failed to keep pace with inflation. In 1976 when the Transvaal authorities announced that Afrikaans (the language spoken by the whites of Dutch descent) was to be used in black African schools, massive demonstrations which included young people of school age took place at *Soweto,* an African township near Johannesburg. Again police fired on the crowds, killing at least 200 Africans, but this time protests did not subside completely: according to Basil Davidson, 'from one month to the next, onwards from May 1976, the silenced multitudes had found their voice, and the voice proved angry and unafraid.'

(ii) Most of the *commonwealth* members were strongly opposed to apartheid; early in 1960 the British Prime Minister, Macmillan, had the courage to speak out against it in Cape Town; he spoke about the growing African nationalism: 'the wind of change is blowing through the continent . . . our national policies must take account of it.' His warning was ignored and shortly afterwards the world was horrified by the Sharpeville massacre. At the 1961 Commonwealth Conference criticism of South Africa was intense and many thought she should be expelled. In the end Verwoerd withdrew South Africa's application for continued membership (in 1960 she had decided to become a republic instead of a dominion, thereby severing the connection with the British crown; because of this she had to apply for readmission to the commonwealth) and she ceased to be a member of the commonwealth.

(iii) *The United Nations and the Organisation of African Unity* condemned apartheid and were particularly critical of continued South African occupation of South West Africa, given her as a mandated territory in 1919 (see Section 2.8(b)). The government ignored repeated UN calls to grant the territory (known as Namibia) independence and extended apartheid to its African population. The UN General Assembly voted to place an economic boycott on South Africa (1962) but this proved useless because not all states supported it. Britain, the USA, France, West Germany and Italy condemned apartheid in public, but took little positive action. Among other things they sold South Africa massive arms supplies, apparently hoping she would prove to be a bastion against the spread of communism in Africa. Consequently Verwoerd (until his assassination in 1966) and his successor Vorster (1966–78) were able to ignore the protests from the outside world until well into the 1970s.

(iv) External pressure became greater in 1975 when the white-ruled Portuguese colonies of Angola and Mozambique fell to the African nationalists, while the African takeover in Zimbabwe (1980) removed the last of South Africa's white satellites. She was now surrounded by hostile black states and many Africans have vowed never to rest until their fellow Africans in the republic have been liberated.

(d) First signs of compromise?

During 1979 appeared the first glimmer of hope that under increasing internal and external pressures the government might be prepared to relax some aspects of apartheid. In a speech in September 1979 which astonished many of his supporters, the new Nationalist Prime Minister, P. W. Botha, said: 'A revolution in South Africa is no longer just a remote possibility. Either we adapt or we perish. White domination and legally enforced apartheid are a recipe for permanent conflict.' He went on to suggest that the black homelands must be made viable and that unnecessary discrimination must be abolished. The first concrete concession was that blacks were allowed to join trade unions with full rights. It remains to be seen how far the government is prepared to concede, and whether this will be sufficient to avert a massive racial struggle.

QUESTIONS

1. Explain how and why independence led to civil war in the Congo. Trace the events of the civil war and its aftermath up to 1970.

2. Explain why there was a unilateral declaration of independence in Rhodesia in 1965, and show how each of the following reacted to UDI: Britain, the commonwealth, the United Nations.

3. Trace the course of events in the Rhodesian dispute since 1965, and show how and why white rule ended in 1979–80.

4. What do you understand by the term apartheid? Why has it been supported by South African voters? Describe the ways in which, since 1945, this policy had affected (a) the lives of the people of South Africa, (b) external relations.

5. Describe the policy of apartheid and the changes made in it since 1966 until the present day.

6. Show the importance of the following leaders in the history of their respective countries: Patrice Lumumba, Joseph Mobutu, Ian Smith, Daniel Malan, Albert Luthuli.

CHAPTER 25

THE MIDDLE EAST

SUMMARY OF EVENTS

The Arab lands stretch from North Africa through the Middle East to the shores of the Persian Gulf and northwards to the frontier with Turkey. The main Arab states are Morocco, Algeria, Tunisia, Libya, Eygpt, the Sudan (about half the population are Arabs), Syria, Lebanon, Jordan, Iraq and Saudi Arabia. The area known as the Middle East includes Egypt and all the Arab lands to the east of Egypt, as well as Turkey (non-Arab) and Iran (not, strictly speaking, an Arab state, though it contains many Arabs in the area at the northern end of the Persian Gulf). The Middle East also contains the Jewish state of Israel set up in 1948.

The main Arab concerns since 1945 included attempts to achieve some political and economic unity and problems caused by the fact that outside powers were constantly interfering in the Middle East because of its importance as a strategic crossroads and a source of oil. However, the dominating issue which united all the Arab states was the desire to destroy Israel, the alien within their midst. This desire caused four short and, from the Arab point of view, unsuccessful wars (1948-9, 1956, 1967 and 1973) which Israel survived.

25.1 ARAB UNITY AND OUTSIDE INTERFERENCE

(a) Since they all share the Arabic language and mostly the Muslim religion (though about half the Lebanon is Christian) many Arabs want some sort of union among the Arab states. As early as 1931 an Islamic conference in Jerusalem announced: 'The Arab lands are a complete and indivisible whole ... all efforts are to be directed towards their complete independence, in their entirety and unified.' Several attempts were made to promote unity. *The Arab League* founded in 1945 included Egypt, Syria, Jordan, Iraq, Lebanon, Saudi Arabia and Yemen; membership expanded later to include 20 states in 1980. However, it achieved very little politically and was constantly hampered by internal squabbles. In the mid-1950s Pan-Arabism seemed to receive a boost with the energetic leadership of Nasser

Fig 25.1 *the Middle East*

in Egypt who gained enormous prestige in the Arab world after the 1956 Suez Crisis (see below Section 25.3). In 1958 Syria joined Egypt to form *the United Arab Republic* with Nasser as President. However, this lasted only until 1961 when Syria withdrew because of resentment at Nasser's attempts to dominate the union. After Nasser's death in 1970, his successor President Sadat organised a loose union between Egypt, Libya and Syria, the *Federation of Arab Republics*, but it never amounted to much, and there seems little chance of any more progress being made towards full Arab unity. There are too many points at issue between the various states; for example Jordan and Saudi Arabia are still ruled by fairly conservative royal families who were often criticised for being too pro-British by the governments of Egypt and Syria which were pro-Arab nationalist as well as socialist. The whole Arab world was thrown into disarray in 1979 when Egypt, the leading Arab state, reached a separate peace agreement with Israel at Camp David (see below Section 25.6), whereupon Egypt was expelled from the Arab League.

(b) Outside interference in the Middle East was probably inevitable given the fact that the area produces over a third of the world's oil supplies and stands at the crossroads between the communist world and Africa. Disunity among the states invited interference which in turn often bred more disunity.

(i) *Iran* (Persia) came in for attention from the USSR which in 1945 tried to set up a communist government in northern Iran and demanded an oil concession. The western-educated Shah Reza Pahlevi resisted and signed a defence treaty by which the USA provided economic and military aid including tanks and jets (1950). Matters were complicated by anti-British feeling on account of the British controlling interest in the Anglo-Iranian Oil Company and its refinery at Abadan. It was widely felt that the British were taking too much of the profits and in 1951 premier Mussadiq nationalised the company. However, most of the world boycotted Iranian oil exports, bringing Mussadiq down, and in 1954 a compromise was reached in which British Petroleum was allowed 40 per cent of the shares. Iran now took 50 per cent of the profits which the Shah was able to use for a cautious modernisation and land reform programme. This was not enough for the left and for radical Islam supporters who resented the Shah's close ties with the USA and the large slice of the national wealth which found its way into his private fortune. In January 1979 he was forced to leave the country and an Islamic republic was set up under a religious leader, the Ayatollah Khomeini, who wanted non-alignment.

(ii) Britain and France tried to maintain their influence in the area against that of the USSR, and to this end Britain joined *the Baghdad Pact* (1955) which also included Iraq, Iran, Turkey and Pakistan. Egyptian hostility to this contributed towards the 1956 Suez Crisis and the pro-British policy of King Feisal and Premier Nuri-es-Said of Iraq caused a revolution in which they were both murdered (1958). The new government was sympathetic towards Egypt and withdrew from the Baghdad Pact which was replaced by the Central Treaty Organisation (CENTO), now defunct, sponsored by the USA as a buffer against the spread of communism.

(iii) The Russians seized the chance to intervene during the Suez Crisis with strong support for Egypt. Friendship with the Arab world would provide a useful link for the Russians with Africa and might enable them to threaten the west's oil supplies. This prompted the USA to issue *the Eisenhower Doctrine* (1957) offering aid to any Arab states which wanted to resist 'communist aggression'.

(iv) The USA was committed to support Israel against the Arab states, another reason for the Russians to work for an Arab alliance.

During the 1970s both east and west became much more cautious in their attitudes towards the Middle East; the west particularly took care not to offend the Arab states in case oil supplies were cut off.

25.2 THE CREATION OF ISRAEL AND THE ARAB/ISRAELI WAR OF 1948-9

(a) What caused the war?

(i) The trouble began soon after the First World War when large numbers of Jews began to settle in Palestine, a British mandate,

Fig 25.2 *Israel and her Arab enemies*

Territory conquered by the Israelis, June 1967

hoping to set up a Jewish 'national home' (see Section 11.4(c)). The Arabs in Palestine were implacably hostile to the idea of a separate Jewish state in what they considered to be their homeland. In order to retain Arab friendship and their own oil supplies the British limited Jewish immigration to 10,000 a year (1939).

(ii) The Second World War intensified the problem with hundreds of thousands of Jewish refugees from Hitler's Europe looking for somewhere to go. In 1945 the USA pressed Britain to admit 100,000 of them into Palestine; this demand was echoed by David Ben Gurion, one of the Jewish leaders, but the British refused, not wanting to offend the Arabs.

(iii) The Jews, after all that their race had suffered at the hands of the Nazis, were determined to fight for their 'national home'. They began a terrorist campaign against both Arabs and British, the most spectacular incident of which was the blowing up of the King David Hotel, the British headquarters in Jerusalem, with the loss of 91 lives (1946). The British responded by arresting Jewish leaders and by turning back ships such as the *Exodus* crammed with intending immigrants.

(iv) The British, weakened by the war, were unable to cope; Ernest Bevin, the Foreign Secretary, invited the United Nations to deal with the problem, and in November 1947 the UN voted to partition Palestine, setting aside roughly half of it to form an independent Jewish state.

(v) Early in 1948 the British abandoned the mandate and withdrew their troops, though fighting was already taking place between Jews and Arabs, who bitterly resented the loss of half of Palestine. In May 1948 Ben Gurion declared the new state of Israel independent. It was immediately attacked by Egypt, Syria, Jordan, Iraq and Lebanon.

(b) The war and its results

Against apparently overwhelming odds, the Israelis managed to survive and even to capture more of Palestine including the port of Eilat on the Red Sea, seized from Egypt. The UN played an important part in bringing the fighting to an end. Israeli success was due partly to their own desperate resistance and to the fact that the Arabs were divided amongst themselves and poorly equipped; King Abdullah of Jordan was less than enthusiastic about the war because the partition gave him the chance to seize the section of Palestine west of the River Jordan (known as the West Bank). The most tragic result of the war was the plight of the Palestinian Arabs who found themselves inside the new state of Israel. After Jewish terrorists had slaughtered the entire population of an Arab village, nearly a million Arabs fled into Egypt, Lebanon, Jordan and Syria where they lived in miserable refugee camps. Jerusalem was divided between Israel and Jordan, and although the USA, Britain and France guaranteed Israel's frontiers, the Arab states did not regard the cease-fire as permanent; this was only the first round in the struggle to destroy Israel and liberate Palestine.

25.3 THE SUEZ WAR 1956

(a) The causes of the war were complex: partly the Arab/Israeli conflict, partly the result of the struggle between Arab nationalism and the British and French who wanted to prolong their influence in the Middle East, and an episode in the Cold War between the USA and the USSR.

(i) Colonel Gamal Abdel Nasser, the new ruler of Egypt (who came to power in 1954 soon after the overthrow of the unpopular King Farouk), was aggressively in favour of Arab unity and independence including the liberation of Palestine from the Jews.

(ii) He organised guerrilla bands (*fedayeen*: self-sacrificers) to sabotage and murder inside Israel and blockaded the Gulf of Aqaba leading to the Israeli port of Eilat.

(iii) He insisted that Britain evacuate her base at Suez (the agreement signed in 1936 allowing her to keep the base expired in 1956), sent aid to the Algerian Arabs in their struggle against France, prodded the other Arab states into opposing the British-sponsored Baghdad Pact and forced King Hussein of Jordan to dismiss his British chief of staff.

(iv) In September 1955 Nasser signed an arms deal with Czechoslovakia for Russian fighters, bombers and tanks, and soviet experts went to train the Egyptian army.

(v) The Americans saw this as a Russian attempt to 'move into' the Middle East and cancelled a promised grant of 56 million dollars towards the building of a dam at Aswan (July 1956); the intention was to force Nasser to abandon his new links with the communists.

(vi) Nasser immediately retaliated by nationalising the Suez Canal, intending to use its revenues to finance the dam; share-owners, a majority of whom were British and French, were promised compensation. However, British Prime Minister Anthony Eden believed that Nasser was on the way to forming a united Arabia under Egyptian control and communist influence which could cut off Europe's oil supplies at will. This must be prevented at all costs.

(vii) Secret negotiations took place between Britain, France and Israel who agreed on a joint attack on Egypt. The British and French hoped to bring down Nasser while the Israelis wanted to stop *fedayeen* raids and open the Gulf of Aqaba.

(b) The war began with an Israeli invasion of Egypt (29 October) which within a week had captured the entire Sinai peninsula. Meanwhile the British and French bombed Egyptian airfields and landed troops at Port Said at the northern end of the Suez Canal. The attacks caused an outcry from the rest of the world, and the Americans, who were afraid of alienating the Arabs and forcing them into closer ties with the USSR, refused to support Britain although they had earlier hinted that support would be forthcoming. At the United Nations Americans and Russians joined in demanding a cease-fire (see Section 19.3(d)); with the pressure of world opinion against them, Britain, France and Israel agreed to withdraw, while UN troops moved in to police the frontier between Egypt and Israel.

(c) The results of the war were important. It was a complete humiliation for Britain and France who achieved none of their aims and were shown to be weak. They had failed to topple Nasser whose prestige as leader of Arab nationalism against European interference was greatly increased. The Egyptians blocked the canal, the Arabs reduced oil exports to western Europe, where petrol rationing had to be introduced for a time, and illus 25.1 *President Nasser of Egypt acclaimed by wildly cheering crowds in Cairo after proclaiming the nationalisation of the Suez Canal*

Russian aid replaced that from America. British action seriously embarrassed Premier Nuri-es-Said of Iraq who now came under increasing attack from other Arabs for his pro-British attitude; he was murdered in 1958. The Algerians were encouraged in their struggle for independence from France which they achieved in 1962. From Israel's point of view the war was something of a success: although she had been compelled to hand back all captured Egyptian territory, she had inflicted heavy losses on Egypt in men and equipment which took several years to make good. For the time being *fedayeen* raids ceased and Israel had a breathing-space in which to consolidate.

25.4 THE SIX DAY WAR 1967

(a) Background to the war

(i) Iraq, after the murder of Nuri-es-Said, had an aggressive nationalist government prepared to co-operate with Egypt. President Aref announced (1 June 1967): 'Our goal is clear – to wipe Israel off the map'.

(ii) Political upheavals in Syria brought to power the left-wing Ba'ath Party (1966) which supported El Fatah, the Palestine Liberation Movement, a more effective guerrilla force than the *fedayeen*. The Syrians also bombarded Jewish settlements from the Golan Heights overlooking the frontier.

(iii) Nasser was now immensely popular in Egypt because of his leadership of the Arab world and his attempts to improve conditions inside the country with his socialist policies, which included limiting the size of farms to 100 acres and redistributing the surplus land to peasants. Attempts were made to industrialise the country and over a thousand new factories were built, almost all under government control. The Aswan Dam project was vitally important, providing electricity, and water for irrigating an extra million acres of land. After initial delays at the time of the Suez Crisis, work on the dam eventually got under way and the project was completed in 1971. With all going well at home and the prospect of effective help from Iraq and Syria, Nasser seems to have decided that the time was ripe for another attack on Israel. He began to move troops up to the frontier in Sinai, asked the UN to remove its troops policing the narrow strip of land along the coast connecting Gaza with the rest of Egypt, and closed the Gulf of Aqaba (May).

(iv) Syria, Jordan and Lebanon also massed troops along their frontiers with Israel while contingents from Iraq, Saudi Arabia and Algeria joined them. Israel's situation seemed impossible.

(v) Moshe Dayan, the new Israeli Minister of Defence, decided that the best policy was to attack first rather than sit about waiting to be destroyed. It has been suggested that Israel wanted a war to unite the country, solve the unemployment problem and attract American dollars. Seizing the opportunity provided by the ponderous Arab troop build-up, the Israelis launched a series of devastating air strikes which destroyed most of the Egyptian air force on the ground (5 June).

Israeli troops moved with remarkable speed, capturing the Gaza strip and the whole of Sinai from Egypt, the rest of Jerusalem and the West Bank from Jordan and the Golan Heights from Syria. The Arabs had no choice but to accept a UN cease-fire order (10 June). Reasons for the brilliant Israeli success were their superiority in the air and inadequate Arab preparation and communications.

(b) Results of the war

This time the Israelis ignored a UN order to return captured territory. This meant that defence would be easier but it left them with the problem of how to deal with an extra million Arabs who now found themselves under Israeli rule; many of these were living in the refugee camps on the West Bank and in the Gaza Strip set up in 1948. The Arab states, though humiliated, were no less determined on the ultimate destruction of Israel.

25.5 THE YOM KIPPUR WAR 1973

Two elements combined to produce a joint Egyptian/Syrian attack on Israel in October 1973.

(i) Pressure was brought on the Arab states by the Palestine Liberation Organisation (PLO) under its leader Yasser Arafat for some action. The PLO tried by committing acts of terrorism, to draw world attention to what it considered to be the grave injustice done to the dispossessed Arabs: hijacking aircraft, shooting down passengers waiting in airport lounges, and killing members of the Israeli team at the 1972 Munich Olympics. However, such outrages only alienated world sympathy.

(ii) Egypt (ruled since 1970 by President Sadat) and Syria re-equipped their armies with Russian help, and felt justified in attacking Israel to regain territory lost in 1967. They were probably incited by the Russians who informed them, incorrectly, that Israel was about to attack them.

Egyptian and Syrian forces attacked early on the feast of Yom Kippur, a Jewish religious festival, hoping to catch the Israelis off guard. After initial Arab successes the Israelis, using mainly American weapons, were able to turn the tables, managing to hang on to all territory captured in 1967 and even crossing the Suez Canal into Egypt. This time the fighting was more evenly balanced and both sides were glad to accept a cease-fire organised by the USA and the USSR with UN co-operation. At the end of the war came a glimmer of hope for some sort of permanent settlement when Egyptian and Israeli leaders came together (though not in the same room) at Geneva. The Israelis agreed to move back from the Suez Canal (closed since the 1967 war) which enabled the Egyptians to clear and open the canal in 1975 (but not to Israel).

An important development during the war was that the Arab oil-producing states tried to bring pressure to bear on the USA and western European states friendly to Israel by reducing oil supplies. This caused serious oil shortages especially in Europe. At the same time producers, well aware that oil supplies were not unlimited, saw their action as a way of preserving resources. With this in mind, the illus 25.2 *The child soldiers of the Palestine refugee camps; trained from the age of seven, these boys and girls will be front-line soldiers by the time they reach fifteen*

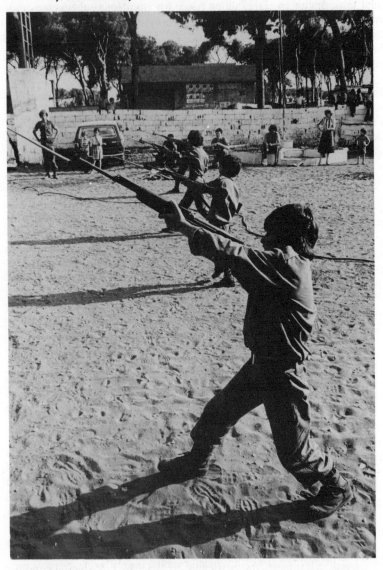

Organisation of Petroleum Exporting Countries (OPEC) began to raise oil prices substantially, contributing to inflation and causing an energy crisis in the world's industrial nations.

25.6 CAMP DAVID AND THE EGYPTIAN/ISRAELI PEACE 1978-9

Egypt and Israel showed a readiness to continue negotiations and President Sadat took the courageous step of becoming the first Arab leader to talk peace to Israel. Even to talk with Israeli leaders meant a recognition of the lawful existence of the state of Israel, and this would be resented by the PLO and the more aggressive Arab states, Iraq and Syria. However, Sadat was becoming increasingly convinced of the foolishness of squandering Egyptian resources on fruitless wars; at the same time Israel, in spite of her success in farming, industry and commerce, was facing economic problems partly caused by her enormous defence expenditure, and partly by the world recession. The USA, apparently growing impatient with the Middle East situation, pressed Israel to settle her differences with at least some of the Arabs. Sadat visited Jerusalem (November 1977) and Menahem Begin, the Israeli Prime Minister, visited Egypt the following month. President Carter of the USA played a vital role in bringing about the opening of negotiations between the two leaders at Camp David (near Washington) in September 1978. With Carter acting as intermediary, the talks resulted in a peace treaty being signed in Washington (March 1979) which ended the state of war that had existed between Egypt and Israel since 1948. Israel promised to make a phased withdrawal from Sinai, while Egypt undertook not to attack Israel again and guaranteed to supply her with oil from the recently opened wells in southern Sinai.

The treaty was condemned by the PLO and most Arab states (except Sudan and Morocco), and there was clearly a long way to go before similar treaties could be signed by Israel with Syria and Jordan. World opinion began to move against Israel and to accept that the PLO had a case, but when the USA tried to bring Israel and the PLO together in an international conference, the Israelis declined to co-operate. In November 1980 Begin announced that Israel would never return the Golan Heights to Syria even in exchange for a peace treaty, and would not allow the West Bank to become part of a Palestinian state, which would be a mortal threat to Israel's existence. At the same time resentment among West Bank Arabs mounted at the Israeli policy of establishing Jewish settlements on land owned by Arabs. Many observers feared fresh violence unless Begin's government adopted a more moderate approach.

25.7 THE IRAQI/IRANIAN WAR 1980

The Middle East and the Arab world were thrown into fresh confusion in September 1980 when war erupted between Iraq and Iran over the disputed Iranian province of Khuzestan, peopled largely by Arabs and over control of the Shatt-el-Arab waterway, which formed part of the frontier between the two states. Since Iraq was being supplied with arms by the USSR there was consternation in the west which feared the growth of Russian influence in the oil-rich Persian Gulf. The war produced a dangerous split in the Arab ranks: the more conservative states - Jordan and Saudi Arabia gave cautious support to Iraq, but Syria, Libya, Algeria, South Yemen and the PLO were critical of Iraq, believing that the Arab states should be concentrating on the destruction of Israel instead of squandering resources elsewhere. Moreover the PLO was on good terms with the Khomeini government in Iran. On the other hand the Saudis, suspicious of Khomeini's extreme brand of Islam, wanted to see Iran's ability to dominate the Persian Gulf controlled.

In the midst of the confusion, an Arab summit conference in Amman, the Jordanian capital (November 1980), to draw up new plans for dealing with Israel, never got off the ground, since the anti-Iraqi states, led by Syria, refused to attend. The Syrians were afraid that Jordan would co-operate with the new American president, Reagan, in a deal to set up a small Palestinian state based on the West Bank, thus leaving Syria alone to face Israel.

As the war dragged on through 1981, the prospects of healing the rift in the Arab ranks seemed uncertain. The problem of the continued existence of Israel too seemed likely to remain for the foreseeable future.

QUESTIONS

1. Explain the importance of the following in the history of the Near and Middle East since 1945: Iranian oil crisis 1951; the Arab League; the Baghdad Pact 1955; the Aswan Dam project 1955-71; the Eisenhower Doctrine 1977; the war between Iraq and Iran 1980.

2. Show the importance of President Nasser (a) as ruler of Egypt; (b) as leader of the Arab world. Why were his attempts to bring about Arab unity not more successful?

3. Explain why an independent state of Israel was set up in 1948 and why the Arabs objected (see also Section 11.5).

4. How do you explain the hostility between the Arabs and the Jews, 1948-9? Account for the inability of the Arab nations to crush Israel in successive compaigns since that date.

5. Write an account of the causes, events and results of two of the following wars: Arab/Israeli War 1948-9; Suez War 1956; Six Day War 1967; Yom Kippur War 1973. Why has a lasting settlement of the conflict proved so difficult to achieve?

FURTHER READING

Books marked with an asterisk * are particularly suitable for 'O' Level students. 'Purnell' refers to *Purnell's History of the 20th Century* (10 volumes), London: BPC Publishing, 1969. The place of publication is London unless otherwise stated.

CHAPTER 1

Turner, L. C. F., *Origins of the First World War* (Arnold, 1970)

CHAPTER 2

Clark, A., *Suicide of the Empires* (Macdonald, 1970)*
Horne, A., *Death of a Generation* (Macdonald, 1970)*
Horne, A., *The Price of Glory* (Macmillan, 1962)
Liddell-Hart, B., *The First World War* (Cassell, 1970)
Taylor, A. A., *The First World War* (London University Tutorial Press 1972)*
Taylor, A. J. P., *The First World War* (Harmondsworth: Penguin, 1966)

CHAPTER 3

Austin, M., *The Great Experiment: a Study of Russian Society* (English Universities Press, 1975)*
Catchpole, B., *A Map History of Russia* (Heinemann, 1974)*
Freeborn, R., *A Short History of Modern Russia* (Hodder and Stoughton, 1966)
Fry, D., *Russia: Lenin and Stalin* (Hamish Hamilton, 1966)*
Hill, C., *Lenin and the Russian Revolution* (English Universities Press, 1970)
Kochan, L., *The Making of Modern Russia* (Harmondsworth: Penguin, 1970)
Pickering, S., *20th Century Russia* (Oxford: University Press, 1970)*

Quinn, J. G., *The Russian Revolution* (London University Tutorial Press, 1972)*
Stacey, F. W., *Lenin and the Russian Revolutions* (Arnold, 1970) (documentary)*
Taylor, A. J. P., *Lenin: October and After* (Purnell, vol. 3, ch. 37)

CHAPTER 4

Lloyd, T. O., *Empire to Welfare State* (Oxford: University Press, 1970)
Marquand, D., *Ramsay MacDonald* (Jonathan Cape, 1976)
Medlicott, W. N., *Contemporary England 1914–64* (Longman, 1976)
Montgomery Hyde, H., *Stanley Baldwin* (Hart Davis, 1973)
Morris, M., *The General Strike* (Harmondsworth: Penguin, 1976)
Mowat, C. L., *Britain Between the Wars* (Methuen, 1976)
Mowat, C. L., *The General Strike 1926* (Arnold, 1969) (documentary)*
Rowland, P., *Lloyd George* (Barrie and Jenkins, 1975)
Seaman, L. C. B., *Post-Victorian Britain, 1902–1951* (Methuen 1975)
Taylor, A. J. P., *English History 1914–45* (Harmondsworth: Penguin, 1965)

CHAPTER 5

Bury, J. P. T., *France: The Insecure Peace* (Macdonald, 1972)*
Bury, J. P. T., *France 1814–1940* (Methuen University Paperback, 1976)
Cobban, A., *A History of Modern France,* vol. 3 (Harmondsworth: Penguin, 1970)
Holland, P., *20th Century France* (Oxford: University Press, 1970)*
Knapp, W., *France: Partial Eclipse* (Macdonald, 1972)*
Shirer, W. L., *The Collapse of the Third Republic* (Heinemann, Secker and Warburg, 1970)

CHAPTER 6

Gregory, D., *Mussolini and the Fascist Era* (Arnold, 1968) (documentary)*
Hibbert, C., *Benito Mussolini* (Harmondsworth: Penguin, 1965)
Rowlands, B. R., *Modern Italy* (London University Tutorial Press, 1970)*
Tannenbaum, E., *Fascism in Italy* (Allen Lane, 1973)
Wiskemann, E., *Fascism in Italy: its Development and Influence* (Macmillan, 1970)

CHAPTER 7

Bassett, M., *The American Deal* (Auckland: Heinemann, 1977)*
Catchpole, B., *A Map History of the United States* (Heinemann, 1972)*
Conkin, P. K., *The New Deal* (Routledge, 1968)*
Galbraith, J. K., *The Great Crash* (Harmondsworth: Penguin, 1969)
Hill, C. P., *A History of the United States* (Arnold, 1974)*

Hill, C. P., *The USA Since the First World War* (Allen and Unwin, 1967)*
McCoy, D. R., *Coming of Age: The United States during the 1920s and 1930s* (Harmondsworth: Penguin, 1973)

CHAPTER 8

Bullock, A., *Hitler - A Study in Tyranny* (Harmondsworth: Penguin 1969)
Bumstead, P. J., *Hitler* (London University Tutorial Press, 1977)*
Catchpole, B., *20th Century Germany* (Oxford: University Press 1970)*
Craig, G. A., *Germany, 1866-1945* (Oxford: University Press, 1978)
Delmer, S., *The Weimar Republic* (Macdonald, 1972)*
Fest, J., *Hitler* (Weidenfeld and Nicolson, 1974)
Hiden, J. W., *The Weimar Republic* (Longman, 1974)
Phillips, D. M., *Hitler and the Rise of the Nazis* (Arnold, 1968) (documentary)*
Ryder, A. J., *Twentieth Century Germany from Bismarck to Brandt* (Macmillan, 1973)

CHAPTER 9

Austin, M., *The Great Experiment: a Study of Russian Society* (English Universities Press, 1975)*
Bassett, J., *Socialism in One Country* (Auckland: Heinemann, 1978)*
Conquest, R., *The Great Terror* (Macmillan, 1968)
Freeborn, R., *A Short History of Modern Russia* (Hodder and Stoughton, 1966)
Kochan, L., *The Making of Modern Russia* (Harmondsworth: Penguin 1973)
Montgomery Hyde, H., *Stalin* (Hart-Davis, 1971)
Pickering, S., *20th Century Russia* (Oxford: University Press, 1970)*
Stacey, F. W., *Stalin and the Making of Modern Russia* (Arnold, 1970) (documentary)*

CHAPTER 10

Allen, L., *Japan: the Years of Triumph* (Macdonald, 1971)*
Kinross, Lord, *Ataturk - the Rebirth of a Nation* (Weidenfeld and Nicolson)
Snellgrove, L. E., *Franco and the Spanish Civil War* (Harlow: Longman, 1965)
Storry, R., *A History of Modern Japan* (Harmondsworth: Penguin, 1960)
Thomas, H., *The Spanish Civil War* (Harmondsworth: Penguin, 1968)

CHAPTER 11

Watson, J. B., *Empire to Commonwealth, 1919 to 1970* (Dent, 1971)*
Woodward, G. W. O., *Divided Island: Ireland, 1910-1949* (Auckland: Heinemann Educational, 1976)*

CHAPTER 12

Fitzsimmons, O., *Towards One World* (London University Tutorial Press, 1974)*
Gibbons, S. R., and Morican, P., *League of Nations and UNO* (Harlow: Longman, 1970)

CHAPTERS 13 AND 14

Allen, L., *Japan: The Years of Triumph* (Macdonald, 1971)
Bullock, A., *Hitler - A Study in Tyranny* (Penguin, 1969)
Bumstead, P. J., *Hitler* (London University Tutorial Press, 1977)*
Fest, J., *Hitler* (Weidenfeld and Nicolson, 1974)
Gilbert, M., *Appeasement in Action* (Purnell, vol. 4 ch. 57)
Gilbert, M., and Gott, R., *The Appeasers* (Weidenfeld and Nicolson, 1963; paperback ed., 1967)
Mowat, C. L., *Britain Between the Wars 1918-1940* (Methuen, 1955; paperback ed., 1968)
Rowlands, B. R., *Modern Italy* (London University Tutorial Press, 1973)*
Seaman, L. C. B., *Post Victorian Britain 1902-1951* (Methuen, 1966; paperback ed., 1970)
Stone, R., *The Drift to War* (Auckland: Heinemann, 1975)*
Storry, R., *A History of Modern Japan* (Harmondsworth: Penguin, 1960)
Tannenbaum, E., *Fascism in Italy* (Allen Lane, 1973)
Taylor, A. J. P., *English History, 1914-1945* (Harmondsworth: Penguin, 1965)
Taylor, A. J. P., *The Origins of the Second World War* (Harmondsworth: Penguin, 1964)
Thorne, C., *The Approach of War, 1938-1939* (Macmillan, 1967)

CHAPTER 15

Arnold-Forster, M., *The World at War* (Collins, 1973)*
Liddell-Hart, B. H., *History of the Second World War* (Cassell, 1970)
Mortimore, M. J. A., *The Second World War* (London University Tutorial Press, 1974)*
Taylor, A. J. P., *The Second World War* (Hamish Hamilton, 1975)

CHAPTER 16

Feis, H., *From Trust to Terror: The Onset of the Cold War 1945-1950* (Blond, 1970)
Frankland, M., *Khrushchev* (Harmondsworth: Penguin, 1966)
Heater, D., *The Cold War* (Oxford: University Press, 1970)*
Knapp, W., *A History of War and Peace 1939-1965* (Oxford: University Press, 1967)
Laqueur, W. Z., *Europe Since Hitler* (Harmondsworth: Penguin, 1972)

CHAPTER 17

Fitzgerald, C. P., *Communism Takes China* (Macdonald, 1969)*
Matthews, H. L., *Castro* (Allen Lane, 1969)
Mitchison, L., *China in the Twentieth Century* (Oxford: University Press, 1970)*
Roper, M., *China in Revolution 1911-1949* (Arnold, 1969) (documentary)*
Tarling, N., *Mao and the Transformation of China* (Auckland: Heinemann, 1977)*
Thomas, H., *Cuba or the Pursuit of Freedom* (Harper Row, 1971)

CHAPTER 18

Frankland, M., *Khrushchev* (Harmondsworth: Penguin, 1966)
Gray, J., *China under Mao* (Purnell vol. 6 ch. 89)
Harkness, D., *The Post-War World* (Basingstoke: Macmillan, 1974)
Matthews, H. L., *Castro* (Allen Lane, 1969)
Mitchison, L., *China in the 20th Century* (Oxford: University Press, 1970)*
Morgan, R., *Tension in Eastern Europe* (Purnell vol. 5, ch. 80)
Morgan, R., *Eastern Europe: Hopes and Realities* (Purnell vol. 6, ch. 83)
Morgan, R., *The Czechoslovak Spring* (Purnell vol. 6, ch. 94)
Moseley, G., *China, Empire to People's Republic* (Batsford, 1968)
Tarling, N., *Mao and the Transformation of China* (Auckland: Heinemann, 1977)*
Thomas, H., *Cuba or the Pursuit of Freedom* (Harper Row, 1971)
Westwood, J. N., *Khrushchev and After* (Purnell vol. 6, ch. 83)

CHAPTER 19

Fitzsimmons, O., *Towards One World* (London University Tutorial Press, 1974)*
Gibbons, S. R., and Morican, P., *League of Nations and UNO* (Longman, 1970)

CHAPTER 20

Cobban, A., *A History of Modern France,* vol. 3 (Harmondsworth: Penguin, 1970)
Crozier, B., *De Gaulle: the Statesman* (Methuen, 1974)
Farr, W., *Daily Telegraph Guide to the Common Market* (Collins, 1972)
Laqueur, W., *Europe since Hitler* (Harmondsworth: Penguin, 1972)
Ryder, A. J., *Twentieth Century Germany from Bismarck to Brandt* (Macmillan, 1973)
Wiskemann, E., *Italy since 1945* (Macmillan, 1971)

CHAPTER 21

Bassett, M., *The American Deal, 1932--64* (Auckland: Heinemann, 1977)*
Beals, C., *Latin America : World in Revolution* (New York: Abelard-Schuman, 1963)
Hill, C. P., *The USA Since the First World War* (Allen and Unwin, 1967)*
Snowman, D., *America Since 1920* (Heinemann, 1978)
Storry, R., *A History of Modern Japan* (Harmondsworth: Penguin, 1975)

CHAPTER 22

Courriere, Y., *The Algerian War* (Purnell vol. 6, ch. 81)
Davidson, B., *Africa in Modern History* (Allen Lane, 1978)
Hatch, J., *Africa -- the Rebirth of Self-Rule* (Oxford: University Press, 1970)*
Horne, A., *Dien Bien Phu* (Purnell vol. 6, ch. 81)
Moon, P., *India: Independence and Partition* (Purnell vol. 5, ch. 75)
Phillips D., *Cyprus: The Failure of Force* (Purnell vol. 6, ch. 91)
Rose, S., *Indonesia Gains Independence* (Purnell vol. 5, ch. 75)
Watson, J. B., *Empire to Commonwealth* (Dent, 1971)*

CHAPTER 23

Davidson, B., *Africa in Modern History* (Allen Lane, 1978)
Hoskyns, C., *Two Tragedies: Congo and Biafra* (Purnell vol. 6 ch. 85)
Mackie, J., *The Indonesian Confrontation* (Purnell vol. 6, ch. 91)
Pandey, B. N., *The Rise of Modern India* (Hamish Hamilton, 1972)
Stephens, I., *The Pakistanis* (Oxford: University Press, 1968)
Watson, J. B., *Empire to Commonwealth* (Dent, 1971)*

CHAPTER 24

Davidson, B., *Africa in Modern History* (Allen Lane, 1978)
Hoskyns, C., *Two Tragedies: Congo and Biafra* (Purnell vol. 6, ch. 85)
Le May, G. L., *Black and White in South Africa* (Macdonald, 1969)*
Luthuli, A., *Let My People Go* (Fontana, 1963)
Mason, P., *Rhodesia: Great Britain's Dilemma* (Purnell vol. 6, ch. 81)
Watson, J. B., *Empire to Commonwealth* (Dent, 1971)*

CHAPTER 25

Bullard, R., *The Persian Oil Crisis* (Purnell vol. 5, ch. 80)
Dodd, C. H., and Sales, M., *Israel and the Arab World* (Routledge, 1973)
Hunter, R. E., *The Six Day War* (Purnell vol. 6, ch. 94)
Jones, D., *The Arab World* (Hamish Hamilton, 1969)*
Nussbaum, E., *Israel* (Oxford: University Press, 1968)*
Sykes, C., *The Birth of Israel* (Purnell vol. 5, ch. 78)
Thomas, H., *The Suez Affair* (Weidenfeld and Nicolson, 1967)

INDEX